HAVING CHILDREN

HAVING CHILDREN

Philosophical and Legal Reflections on Parenthood

ESSAYS EDITED FOR THE SOCIETY
FOR PHILOSOPHY AND PUBLIC AFFAIRS

Onora O'Neill and William Ruddick

NEW YORK

OXFORD UNIVERSITY PRESS

1979

Copyright © 1979 by Oxford University Press, Inc.
Second printing, 1979
Library of Congress Cataloging in Publication Data

Main entry under title:

Having children.
An anthology from the Society for Philosophy and Public Affairs.

1. Parenthood—Moral and religious aspects—Addresses, essays, lectures.
2. Children's rights—Addresses, essays, lectures.
I. O'Neill, Onora, 1941– II. Ruddick, William, 1931–
III. Society for Philosophy and Public Affairs.
HQ755.8.H38   301.42'7   78–2951
ISBN 0–19–502412–5

Editors' note: The Library of Congress has classified this as a
work in sociology. We hope that the sociologists (as well as
philosophers and lawyers) will take interest, but not offense.

Excerpts from Jean-Jacques Rousseau, *Emile,* Everyman edition, trans.
B. Foxley. Published by J. M. Dent & Sons; in the United States
of America by E. P. Dutton & Co. Reprinted by permission.

Excerpts from John Locke, *Two Treatises of Government,* ed.
Peter Laslett (© Cambridge University Press, 1960, with
amendments, 1963). Reprinted by permission. All references
in the notes are to page and paragraph numbers in this edition.

Printed in the United States of America

CONTENTS

HAVING CHILDREN

GENERAL INTRODUCTION

Philosophical Writing on Families

Philosophers have written very little about families. This is perhaps biographically unsurprising, for many of the great philosophers since antiquity have been rather solitary and childless people. But the result is a curious hiatus: within a tradition of writing that has been critical and rigorous in its discussion of the justification of political institutions and of individual decisions, we find an often unreflective acceptance of relations between the sexes and the generations. There is a dearth of arguments which seek either to justify or to criticize institutional forms of family life, or the principles which individuals invoke and the decisions they make when forming, continuing, or leaving their families. Family arrangements are regarded as below the level of attention of political theory, familial decisions as involving no ethical problems distinct from those which may arise between any two individuals. A territorial division of normative questions into political theory and ethics has left questions about the family in no man's land, which, perhaps significantly, is often regarded as woman's sphere.

Some of the supposed exceptions to this neglect are instructive. Plato saw a restructuring of familial arrangements as required for his just society. He fantasized that a combination of organized coupling and communal child-rearing might produce new generations whose members, besides being eugenically optimal, would feel fraternally (!) toward all their fellows and would reach positions of power by merit alone. The new men and women of the Republic would be liberated from the partiality, the intimacy, the divisiveness of family life. For them, indeed, the laws would be parents and all other citizens brothers. Their very socialization would be political. Plato's alleged focus on the family in his political theory turns out to be, in large part, a rejection of everything which distinguishes familial from (other) political arrangements. This absorption of familial arrangements into the political sphere is particularly implausible in Plato's case, since he seeks to construct an ideal and therefore unhistorical polity. Family relations, in contrast, are distinguished precisely by histories of particular connections between particular persons. So, Plato's discussion of the family provides little help for those who find themselves trying to decide either about the legal or social regulation of familial arrangements or about their conduct as members of an actual family.

3

Yet Plato was perhaps right to stress the continuity between familial and political institutions. Marxist writing on the family has stressed its integration into the economic and political structures of each era, and the degree to which the distinction between public and private spheres of life is illusory. As the producers of human capital, families play an indispensable economic role. If we are convinced by such an analysis, our perception of the available possibilities for families may change. But the analysis itself is of little help when it comes to choosing between the available options. After we have unmasked the division of labor between the sexes, the nature of women's employment, or the discipline of homes or schools and seen the political and economic function of each, we have still to reflect on the social and legal decisions to be made about the regulation of family life. We have still to choose whether to form, foster, or leave our families.

Perhaps one of the main reasons why political theory which is neither utopian nor Marxist has said so little about family life lies in Locke's writings. Locke is the exception among liberal political theorists in having much to say about families. But his main point is that there is little connection or similarity between familial and political institutions. Kings are not like fathers, and governments cannot claim the unlimited authority of fathers—not only because the analogy is poor but because fathers have, in the first place, a quite limited authority over their children. So convincing was Locke's demolition of the grand and Christian tradition which linked divine with kingly with fatherly authority that later political theorists often left the entire domestic sphere untouched. However, Locke's argument neither shows, nor was intended to show, that familial arrangements raise no distinctive normative problems. On the contrary, some of his discussions—for example, of the similarity between mothers' and fathers' authority, or of the use of parental authority to form characters which will submit to no other authorities—are the background of several contributions to this book.

If a philosophical discussion of familial arrangements is to be relevant either to policy decisions affecting families or to the dilemmas which arise for people in their family lives, it must start from premises which are less utopian than Plato's and more normative than Marx's, and it must go beyond the Lockean beginnings to reclaim and explore these distinctive normative questions in the light of a sensitive awareness of the psychological, pedagogic, and legal considerations that answers to these questions require.

Aristotle remarks that we deliberate concerning the possible, but when we want or have to make decisions, we look not at the whole range of logical possibilities but at a narrower range of choices which are available from where we find ourselves. What we ought to do or may do must be not merely logically possible but something which we can do. Utopian ideals and Marxist analyses may make us aware of some possibilities that we might otherwise overlook, or that some possibilities we thought were available are in fact not so, and may suggest to us long-term, perhaps revolutionary, strategies for making presently unavailable options available. But not all decisions can be postponed until after the revolution. In the meantime, lives are led, families form, flourish and fail, and legal and social regulation of the forms of family life takes one direction or another.

This book consists of reflections on the grounds for making and justifying such pre-revolutionary decisions. The pieces in it are therefore practical in two senses, though not in a third sense which is perhaps the most common. They are practical in the sense of being normative—that is, concerned with reasoning about action or decisions. And they are practical in that they are written with some awareness of the available options for family life in our time. However, they are not practical in the sense of being concerned with the varying details of managing late twentieth century family life. This book has nothing to say about discipline of children, diet, manners, or being considerate toward spouse or parents. It has, however, a good deal to say about patterns of argument and reflection which might underlie decisions about such details.

Scope and Origin of this Anthology

These practical reasonings on family life all focus on one central familial relationship: the relationship between children and those who bring them up. We would have liked to put together a larger book, which would have included similar reflections on the institutional regulation and individual dilemmas of other familial relationships. Such a book might have included papers on the grounds for and against legal regulation of marriage; on the grounds for recognizing kinship (but not friendship) in legislation on taxation, inheritance, and medical practice; on the arguments for and against governments fostering or individuals entering into alternative forms of familial arrangements. But this particular book, like particular families, has a history. It grew in the following way.

The Society for Philosophy and Public Affairs is a loosely organized group of philosophers who are interested in bringing philosophical analysis to bear on issues of public concern. The society has previously edited books on political morality and international affairs, and has run numerous symposia over the last decade on a wide range of political and social issues. In 1975 and 1976, the Society organized symposia under the general heading of "The Family and Public Policy." It soon became clear that the majority of papers submitted for consideration at these symposia were concerned with the situation of children in families.

The prevalence of this focus reflects, in part, the same concerns which have given rise to the present children's rights movement. Paternalism is now widely questioned, not only when extended to persons no longer children but when applied to children themselves. Writers on education have questioned the rationale for compulsory schooling laws; in many jurisdictions the age of majority has been lowered, and the legal disabilities of minors, though instituted for their protection, have been questioned. Many writers see children's liberation as a natural continuation of a broad social movement which has sought the liberation of women and of many minority groups. These writers stress the *similarities* between children and others whose liberation has been sought. They point to the large overlap between children's and others' capacities for rational choice and deliberation. There is much evidence for these similarities when we consider older children, those for whom the ironic appelation "mature minor" is intended. But for infants and younger children, it seems that the preconditions of liberation are indeed absent.

A concern with liberation is in the main a concern with establishing what are often known as *liberty rights*—rights to non-interference by others— and so to self-determination in various aspects of life. Liberty rights are commonly thought to include rights to choose one's religion, abode, activities, associates, and entertainments. For children whose capacities for self-determination are still undeveloped, liberty rights are of relatively slight concern. For such children, on the other hand, the availability of caring and coping adults is crucial—indeed, needed if they are either to survive or to develop capacities for self-determination, and so an interest in liberty rights. The rights that are of most importance to younger children are *claim rights* rather than liberty rights—rights to services from particular others, not just to non-interference by all others. If we take claim rights seriously, then we must show that particular others have the corresponding obligation to meet these claims. A serious discussion of children's claim rights must be more than a listing of children's presumed needs. It must show who has the duty to supply which of these needs under what circumstances.

The United Nations Declaration of the Rights of the Child, which the U.N. General Assembly adopted in 1959, speaks of children's rights to "adequate nutrition, housing, recreation and medical services" and to "an atmosphere of affection and moral and material security." These aspirations are admirable but empty until we know who has the obligation to supply each of these needs, to what standard, at what costs to themselves, and for how long. It is because we take the rights, including the claim rights, of children seriously that this book is as much concerned with those who bring children up as it is with children.

We do not, however, believe that the deepest moral issues raised by family arrangements are issues about rights and obligations at all. This book is much concerned with rights, and for two reasons. First, discussion of rights and obligations is well-charted moral terrain. The topography here is known with relative precision—which (surprisingly) is not true of many ethical issues. Second, attempts to improve child and family welfare by legislation have produced a great deal of discussion of the *legal* rights and obligations of parents and children. This discussion sometimes illuminates, but also sometimes obscures, the corresponding ethical debate. Of far greater importance to family members, however, are those modes of action which either weave claims and obligations into the warm, solid fabric of a shared life or, on the other hand, expose the pressing of those claims and the filling of those obligations as a meager and grudging substitute for family life.

What appeals to most of us about family life is the continual rendering of services, kindnesses, attentions, and concerns beyond what is obligatory between persons whose lives are intimately and enduringly connected. Often we think of those services, kindnesses, attentions, and concerns as being in a wider sense, a matter of duty. But the sort of duties which we then have in mind are those "imperfect duties" to whose performance no other can lay rightful claim. Good parents, children, and families submerge the performance of their obligations to one another in ways of life whose continuity, familiarity, and at times power to irritate are in no way obligatory.

Since this is the core of family life, we do not see the relationship between children and those who rear them as more than partially and regrettably adversarial. The enormous increase in our knowledge about childhood which has accumulated over the last century has revealed not only burdens which families impose upon their children, but the costs which the absence of family life imposes upon children. We now know far more about different kinship structures, about the history of the family, about the psychodynamics of family life, and about the possibilities and limitations of pedagogy. This increase in knowledge has indeed shown much about the damage and the burden of history and of guilt that families lay upon their children, but it has also shown the results of seeking to rear children without intimate and sustained contact with particular others. Successful socialization requires that we risk—and benefit from—the nightmare of the past. We have few reasons to choose either undiluted paternalism or the complete liberation of young children.

However, this new knowledge has not simplified the task of choosing among intermediate options, either when selecting forms of social regulation of family life or when considering how to conduct oneself with one's own family. Such deliberations have, in fact, become harder over the last century because the range of available options is far larger. Some of these new options have a technical basis. Birth control has made it possible for people to choose childlessness without celibacy and to limit the size of their families. Medical advances have greatly lowered the risk that early death of family members will destroy chosen forms of family life. It may be that further advances in medicine will open up additional options, such as choosing the sex or even more specific characteristics of children. Secondly, new options have been made available by changes in the legal regulation of family life. In many jurisdictions divorce is now legal, and in some, abortion is legal (as well as medically safe); adoption and fostering agencies have been set up which will take over or reassign the care and control of children under certain circumstances. Here, too, further changes may add to the available options. For example, legalized euthanasia might alter certain family patterns. Finally, options are more readily available for forms of family life, which, though not absent in the past, carried heavy social stigma. Today some people choose single parenthood, which, though not absent in the past, was then more often the result of unintended illegitimate births or premature parental deaths. Some persons now openly form stable homosexual unions. More women and men find that they have some choice in the amount of time they can devote to bringing up children and the amount they can devote to earning a living.

We have tried to choose papers for this book which reflect an awareness of the increase in both our knowledge about and our options for family life. We have arranged the papers so as to take up the decisions and dilemmas of family life roughly in the order in which they occur for particular families with children. The first group of papers considers procreation decisions and the public interest in regulating both these decisions and the treatment of a fetus whose procreators are unwilling or unable to care for it. The second, and largest, group of papers in the book focuses on the earlier years of childhood, the years when a child's claims rather than his or her liberty and when the child rearers' services rather than their authority are the main issues. Within this section we have included discussions of the differences (if any) between a child's claims on his or her mother and on his or her father, and discussions of the relative weight of parental and public interest in making decisions (medical or developmental) which have fundamental effects on a child's life prospects. The last section of the book considers the problems of public regulations and parental authority which arise in the later years of childhood and thereafter, when a child has the capacity to choose his or her own life and activities and questions of self-determination become important.

I

BECOMING PARENTS

Parental decisions and choices begin before parenthood itself. Persons not yet parents may aim to bring a child (or a lot of children) into the world; may seek to bring up children others have begotten or borne; or may choose to remain childless, whether by relying on celibacy or contraception, or, if they do conceive, on abortion or adoption agencies. Such preparental choices have become more complicated in our time, both because more possibilities can be chosen and because more is known about each of these possibilities. Parenthood is no longer the standard result of a non-celibate life, to be welcomed or endured but hardly chosen or rejected. For more and more people, parenthood or nonparenthood is a chosen form of life. Contraception, safe and legal abortion, and organized adoption and fostering procedures have made it far easier for persons to choose not to become parents. The adoption and fostering agencies, coupled with A.I.D. and advances in treating infertility, make it easier for those who cannot easily beget or bear children to become parents. Genetic screening and engineering are making it possible for parents to choose some of the characteristics of the children they will have.

Preparental decisions and choices are not the only ones which affect, or even determine, the lives of future children. These decisions are made in the face of legislation which aims to regulate many characteristics of the next generation. For it is misleading to think of extreme cases, such as Nazi attempts to secure the breeding of purely Aryan children, as typical of social regulation of preparental decisions. Such regulation is generally accomplished by a wide array of legislation providing (or denying) contraceptive

9

and other medical services, and also by the whole set of legal and social provisions which affect persons' lives and so the preparental decisions they can and do make.

Since such policies may either extend or limit persons' preparental choices, the classic conflicts between liberty and coercion, between individual rights and social justice, arise repeatedly. These conflicts have become more numerous as medical advances have made more and more aspects of human reproduction matters of choice. Once it is possible to choose how many children should be born into the next generation, it can be a matter of dispute who should make this choice. Are population control policies—or some such policies—a violation of persons' autonomy, or are they necessary to the welfare (and so also to the autonomy) of future generations? Or are they both? Is genetic screening, backed by selective abortion of defective fetuses, a matter for parental choice—or for legal requirement? Or is it perhaps a technological impertinence which should be forbidden? Does pregnancy always (or usually, or sometimes, or never) oblige biological parents—or, more particularly, women—to nurture the life they have conceived? How should the answer to that question be reflected in the legal regulation of abortion, adoption, and custody determinations? May or should natural parents be obliged (as adoptive parents now are) to demonstrate some minimal competence for and commitment to being parents? Whose reproductive aims should be taken into account if genetic engineering makes it possible to choose the characteristics of future persons in some detail?

These issues are in many ways more novel and less clearly defined than those which the papers in later sections of this book confront. Parents and policymakers have always faced choices about caring for children and releasing children from their dependent status. Though there is much disagreement about parents' obligations and authority, there is also a well-established tradition of debate in these matters. But the revolutions in medical safety, in contraceptive technology, and in human genetics are recent and presumably unfinished. They are not matched by comparable revolutions in the techniques of child rearing or of pedagogy. As a result, the papers in this part of the book are probably less conclusive and more contentious than the later papers. We have chosen them because, unlike much of the discussion of moral and legal aspects of population control, abortion and genetic engineering, these papers take account of the *parental* and *familial,* as well as the *individual,* implications of decisions and policies affecting human reproduction.

The papers in this section proceed from current political concerns and measures to fanciful personal hopes and fears. The first two papers look at conflicts between the public interest and individuals whose reproductive decisions cumulatively affect the society into which they may bring children. The rights to procreate and to form a family are often taken to be as basic as any human rights could be; yet the public interest in controlling population growth and size may also be very great. Michael Bayles and

Onora O'Neill consider diferent grounds for restricting rights to procreate and give different accounts of the conflict between such rights and population policies.

The next three papers discuss parental or preparental decisions posed by unwanted pregnancy. Martha Bolton considers the abortion decision and Raymond Herbenick the decision to bear a child for adoption by others. They deal with the moral considerations that people, especially women, must weigh in deciding whether to undertake child-rearing obligations or to delegate or deny them to others. The Supreme Court's *Danforth* opinion rules on the role of a woman's (or girl's) husband, parents, and physician in her reproductive deliberation and decision.

The last three selections address the most recent, and potentially most revolutionary, changes in preparental decisions. Parents or preparents currently decide how many children to have and when to do so. Genetic discoveries are beginning to offer choices as to (some of) the genetic makeup of future children. Ruth Macklin reviews the moral issues that genetic information generates for parents and those who counsel them. Seymour Lederberg takes a sober look at the near future of genetic engineering. Russell Baker teases us with the family troubles parents may cause by their genetic choices in the more remote future.

Individual decisions to procreate can beget dramatic growth and decline in populations. These unintended results of many (mainly intended) individual acts may seriously damage the life-prospects of the next and later generations. This is one case where no benign, invisible hand guarantees that the results of isolated individual decisions are for the public good. Yet policies which interfere with these individual decisions may restrict personal freedom in very fundamental ways. If we think, as many do, that present rates of population growth may have disastrous results, then we have strong reasons for trying to identify the more acceptable ways by which population control policies may try to affect individual reproductive decisions.

Michael Bayles seeks to classify reproductive policies as more or less coercive, but then argues that even the most coercive policies may be morally permissible if other measures fail and population growth is sufficiently threatening. His argument is exemplary of much liberal thought about these problems, for he takes liberty rights seriously but thinks that really dire circumstances justify their restriction. To question his conclusion is to question his premises: Is rapid population growth always a disaster, or is it sometimes, as third world writers urge, a boon? Do population control policies work, or is the only route to a demographic transition by which birth rates would fall to match death rates in the third world through economic growth? Are incentives to encourage small families non-coercive, or are they for the very poor precisely "an offer they can't refuse"? Should we think of the poverty of the countries where population growth is fastest as itself the greatest coercion of those persons which should be first redressed?

LIMITS TO A RIGHT TO PROCREATE

MICHAEL D. BAYLES

In a statement issued through the United Nations' Secretary General thirty world leaders asserted that "the opportunity to decide the number and spac-

From *Ethics and Population,* ed. M. Bayles, © Schenkman (Cambridge, Mass.), 1976, pages 41–55. Reprinted by permission.

ing of their children is a basic human right" of all persons.[1] This principle may be called a human right to procreate. Some persons argue that policies of population control would violate this right and are, therefore, immoral. Human rights are justifiable claims of everyone against everyone or governments (usually both) to perform actions providing or promoting goods.[2] They involve correlative obligations upon everyone or governments. A human right to procreate is the opportunity or liberty to decide when and how many children one will have. This liberty may be called the liberty to procreate. A human right to procreate thus implies an obligation on everyone or governments not to limit people's liberty to procreate. Population control is the regulation of a population's size or other characteristics to achieve a desired goal. In the present world situation any reasonable population program would attempt to control procreation. Thus, governmental population policies would apparently limit the liberty to and violate the right to procreate.

This paper analyzes the extent to which a human right to procreate presents a moral objection to the legal implementation of population control. In this article it will be assumed that there is a human right to procreate. First, population policies and programs will be analyzed and classified in terms of the kind of legal effect they have on the liberty to procreate. Second, an argument will be presented to justify some policy of population control stronger than most current ones and that recommended by the U.S. Commission on Population Growth and the American Future. Third, moral reasons for and against the various types of population policy will be presented.

I

Human rights are inalienable but not absolute. They are inalienable because they belong to people by virtue of their being human. So to lose a human right one must cease to be human. But since human rights are claims, they can be outweighed by other justifiable claims. That is, sometimes there are sufficient moral reasons for not respecting, or completely respecting, human rights. As in all conflicts of moral principles, human rights and other moral reasons must be weighed against one another by an as yet poorly understood and ill-defined process.

A human right to procreate involves an obligation on others not to limit a person's liberty to decide when and how many children he will have. (For purposes of this paper, only the liberty to decide the number of one's children will be considered.) But not all attempts to influence a person's decisions limit his liberty to make them. Providing information about the consequences of possible courses of action and the possibility of alternative actions does not limit a person's liberty to make decisions, nor do raising moral objections to a course of action and appealing to a person's conscience not to choose it.

Attempting to influence a person's decision by providing an incentive to choose one alternative rather than another does not limit a person's liberty to decide, or at least does not do so in a way which is *per se* morally objectionable. Instead, it increases a person's liberty or freedom to choose a certain alternative by eliminating or compensating for a feature which might restrain him from choosing it. For example, if Jones is trying to decide whether to take a position with employer A or B and A increases the salary offered, A has not limited Jones' liberty to decide. Indeed, A has attempted to compensate for factors restraining Jones from taking the position. Even if one disagrees and claims A has limited Jones' liberty to decide, he has certainly not done so in a morally objectionable way. Moral objections arise when incentives are offered to encourage a person to neglect or violate his duties or obligations, for example, bribes to a commissioner to rezone property.

The use of coercion to discourage a person from choosing an alternative, however, does limit his liberty to decide and is *per se* morally objectionable. Some coercion threatens penalties to make an alternative choice unattractive. This type of coercion does not prevent a person from choosing an alternative, but it makes an alternative less desirable, e.g., contract penalties for late delivery. A threat to deprive a person of legitimately expected benefits is also an instance of this form of coercion. Another kind of coercion operates directly to prevent an action from occurring, i.e., eliminate it as an alternative choice. The most obvious form of this type of coercion is imprisonment. But any sort of physical compulsion is of this sort. Such coercion is the most morally objectionable form of limiting liberty for it completely eliminates a person's choice as a determinant of his behavior.[3]

Most current policies and programs to control population do not limit the liberty to procreate. By far the predominant type of program is family planning. This program merely involves the distribution of information and devices for contraception with perhaps some propaganda in favor of small families. Since it is primarily an information program, it does not limit the liberty to procreate but furthers it. Indeed, the statement of world leaders asserting a right to procreate was made to support the spread of family planning programs. However, many other population control policies and programs have been proposed. Some of these would limit the liberty to procreate, but the extent to which they would do so varies.

All of these proposed policies would use law as an instrument for achieving their purpose. Professor Homer H. Clark, Jr. has argued that law cannot be of much use in population control.[4] But he limits himself to considering penal law. Clark concludes that about the only realistic uses of penal law for population control are negative, i.e., repealing penal laws which present obstacles to limiting procreation. Clark believes the primary possibilities are repealing restrictive laws on sterilization, abortion, and supplying contraceptive information.

However, there are many ways in which law can be used as an instrument of policy. Robert S. Summers has proposed a fivefold classification of the ways law can be used as an instrument of policy which he calls the techniques of law.[5] First, there is the penal technique, but it is only one. Second, there is the grievance-remedial technique which defines remedial grievances and specifies remedies (compensation, injunction, etc.) and procedures for obtaining them. Tort law primarily involves this technique. Third, there is the administrative-regulatory technique which is designed to prevent grievances from arising. With this technique regulative standards are adopted and administrative bodies given powers to ensure compliance. Various federal commissions provide examples of the use of this technique. Fourth, there is the public benefit conferral technique whereby laws order the distribution of benefits and burdens as well as many other elements of the operation of a program. Social security laws are an example of this technique. Finally, there is the private arranging technique in which laws grant citizens legal powers to make private arrangements, specify procedures to be followed to invoke these powers, and indicate the legal significance to be accorded such arrangements, e.g., resulting legal duties, remedies, statuses, etc. Laws of contract and marriage are examples of this technique.

Most proposed policies and programs of population control use more than one of these techniques. But different proposals emphasize different techniques. Most of them emphasize either the public benefit conferral or the administrative-regulatory technique. The type of technique used correlates roughly with the degree to which the policies would limit the liberty to procreate. For example, the public benefit conferral technique usually involves less of a limit on liberty than the administrative-regulatory one.

Proposed policies and programs for population control may be divided into at least four broad classes based on the legal effect they would have on the liberty to procreate.[6] First, some socioeconomic policies would provide incentives to have fewer children. These proposals primarily rely upon the public benefit conferral technique. Proposals to enhance the social role of women and provide them more job opportunities only indirectly reduce procreation. Indeed, they do more to promote equality between the sexes than to limit procreation. But since working women have fewer children than non-working women, such policies would indirectly lower birth rates. More direct effects are involved in proposals to pay benefits to people who do not have children for a period of time or, as is currently practiced in India, to those who are voluntarily sterilized. Since providing incentives for choosing a course of action is not morally objectionable *per se* and

such policies do not encourage people to violate any obligation, they do not impose a morally objectionable limit on the liberty to procreate.[7] Indeed, if incentives do not limit one's liberty to decide, they do not limit the liberty to procreate at all.

Second, other socioeconomic policies would operate by removing current incentives for having children. These policies also primarily rely on the public benefit conferral technique, but they remove benefits currently provided. For example, family allowances and maternity benefits might be limited to a specific number of children. Alternatively, free schooling and other governmental benefits might be limited to a specific number of children per family. Tax laws could be changed to omit exemptions for children. Such policies would not involve coercion. It might be thought that they involve coercion by threatening to eliminate legitimately expected benefits. But once the laws are enacted, people cannot legitimately expect such benefits. A coercive element appears to be present if one compares current legitimately expected benefits with future ones. But threats to deny people legitimately expected benefits can only be coercive if made at the time of decision. Thus, such policies would not involve a coercive limit to the liberty to procreate because (1) threats to deny such benefits cannot affect the decisions of couples concerning children they already have, and (2) in the future such benefits could no longer be legitimately expected when deciding whether to have children. But since there are features of these policies which involve different moral considerations from those in the first group, it is best to keep them in a distinct class.

Third, other socioeconomic policies

would operate by imposing penalties for having children. These policies also use the public benefit conferral technique, but they are concerned with the imposition of burdens. The most obvious policy of this sort would be to add taxes for having children or for all children beyond a specific number. Since these policies impose a penalty for choosing an alternative, they involve coercion. Thus, they involve a morally objectionable limit to the liberty to procreate. Nonetheless, this limit is much less than that involved in the next class of policies.

The last proposals involve establishing compulsory limitations on procreation. Such proposals include placing sterilants in the water supply, requiring the use of birth control devices, and compulsory abortion or sterilization after a certain number of children. These proposals involve a greater limitation on the liberty to procreate than any other proposed policies. Nonetheless, they do not primarily rely on the penal technique of law but the administrative-regulatory one. The administrative-regulatory technique may well involve the imposition of penalties, but it does not ordinarily use criminal sanctions or resort to them in the first instance. None of these proposals would use fines or imprisonment for procreation.[8]

II

The basic argument for a population policy or program stronger than family planning is as follows: A limited population size or growth rate is a public good. But it is in the interest of an individual couple taken in isolation to have more children than will lead to a limited population size or growth rate. Thus, a public decision on family size is needed. Yet it is not in an individual couple's interest to comply with that decision unless they have assurance others will do so. Thus, a public policy on family size must assure general compliance.[9]

The first premise is that a limited population size or growth rate is a public good. A good is a public good in the requisite sense if it is public and indivisible.[10] So it must be shown that a limited population size or growth rate is a good, public and indivisible. A limited population size or rate of growth is an instrumental good in that it avoids harm. The reasons for its being good depend upon the sorts of considerations which many ecologists, demographers, and some economists have been publicizing in recent years. For example, a high rate of population growth hinders economic development.[11] More obvious effects of an unlimited population size or rate of growth are unemployment, hunger, inadequate housing, pollution, overcrowded schools, and lack of recreational facilities.

Most people will agree that a limited population size or growth rate is good. But they are less apt to distinguish two levels at which it may be good. These levels depend upon the harm to be avoided. First, an unlimited population size or rate of growth may make it impossible for everyone to have a minimum standard of living. Such a minimum standard involves adequate sanitation, health facilities, etc., to prevent epidemics of communicable diseases and to provide normally good health. The failure to provide such a minimum standard of living for all is contrary to human rights specified by the United Nations' Universal Declaration of Human Rights, especially Article 25, and to social justice.[12] Many underdeveloped countries are not and will not be able to achieve such a minimum standard of living unless their population size or growth rate is limited.

For most developed countries an unlimited population size or growth rate is not an immediate threat to the ability to provide a minimum standard of living. Instead, it threatens a decrease in the quality of life. Such a decrease does not involve harm as serious as the failure to provide a minimum standard of living. Nonetheless, a decrease in the quality of life is harmful and contrary to leading conceptions of social justice. For it lessens the reasonable expectations for goods of both the average citizen and a representative member of the lowest class in society. Consequently, in most developed countries a limited population size or growth rate is a good but not as great a good as it is in most underdeveloped countries.

A limited population size or growth rate is a good of the public. It pertains to all or most of the inhabitants of a country. Of course, the concept of "the public" is relative. A storeowner is not a member of the public in his own store, but he is in another one. But this relativity does not apply here since all inhabitants are part of the relevant public. So no one is apt to deny that a limited population size or growth rate is as public as national defense, the usual paradigm of a public good.

A limited population size or growth rate is also an indivisible good. One might claim that being an instrumental good, it need not be indivisible. Its value lies in the effects it avoids, and these effects might be avoided for some but not all members of the population. And even if it does benefit all persons, it may benefit some persons more than others. But this factor is not what makes a good divisible or indivisible. National defense, it is sometimes claimed, benefits the rich more than the poor. Rather, a good is indivisible if it cannot feasibly be provided for one person without providing it for some others. Thus, one cannot defend one inhabitant of a country from foreign aggression without defending all. And one cannot avoid the effects of an unlimited population size or growth rate for one person without doing so for others. Clean air and water, recreational facilities, etc., cannot be provided for one person without providing them for at least some others. And since in practice these benefits must be provided all persons, a limited population size or growth rate is a public good.

The second premise is that under current conditions it is not in the interest of individual couples to limit the number of children they have to that compatible with the public good of a limited population size or rate of growth. The reasons why this premise is true vary between countries and cultures. For the most part these variances are ignored in the following discussion. First, most people value having children. The reasons and causes for this evaluation are complex. There are historical factors in the sexual ethic which suggest that the purpose of marriage is to have children. Many couples want a child of each sex, and it may take three or four children for them to realize this goal. Children provide companionship, love, and a purpose to life. Further, psychologists have suggested that single children are not as well adjusted as those in larger families. But it all boils down to the fact that people desire children and derive great satisfaction from having them.

The second and perhaps most important factor making it in the interest of individual couples to have more children than are compatible with the public good is that the costs are partially externalized. People do not bear the full financial burden of their children. Single persons and couples without children pay taxes for public schools, sewage plants, police protection, garbage collection, highways, and other public services at the same or sometimes higher rates than couples with children. But couples with children derive more benefits from these services than do single people or couples without children. For example, 67 per cent of the 1972–74 Kentucky state budget goes for education. Kentucky citizens without children will not derive as much benefit from their tax dollar as those with children. Of course, they will derive some benefit, but it is not proportional to that which persons with children will derive. Even so, children are still expensive. In the United States they may cost more than $25,000 each, not counting the loss of the wife's income while the children are small or the cost of college education. Nonetheless, people find this expense less important than the satisfaction derived from having children.

The result is that when each couple makes an intelligent decision about the number of children they should have in isolation from the decisions of others, they will normally decide to have more children than is compatible with the public good of a limited population size or rate of growth. If this situation pertains long enough, the result will be disastrous for the public good. But even in disastrous social conditions, it may still be in the interest of couples to have more children than are desirable in terms of the public good. Even if conditions are bad, the reasons for having children may favor having more, not

fewer, children. For example, if the death rate of children increases, couples will want more children to ensure that some survive. Hence, even disastrous consequences may not change an individual couple's interest in having more children than are compatible with a limited population size or growth rate.

The conclusion is obviously that a public decision is needed to determine a family size compatible with the public good. Only a collective decision about family size can adequately take into account the public good. Family planning programs, since they do not affect the reasons for having children, do not result in the public good of a limited population size or growth rate. They leave the decision of the number of children they will have to couples in isolation. Since couples want more children than are compatible with the public good, the public good is not achieved.[13]

At this point, the problem of assurance arises. Even granted that a good collective decision on family size has been made, people need assurance that it will be carried out. The individual couple is faced with two general possibilities although there are borderline situations. On the one hand, if most people voluntarily limit the size of their families, then it will be in the interest of a particular couple to have more than the set number of children. For they will reap the benefits of an extra child and not significantly lose any of the benefits from a limited population. On the other hand, if others do not limit the size of their families, then it is still in the interest of a couple to have more than the set number of children. For if they did limit the size of their family, they would suffer all the disadvantages of an unlimited population and sacrifice the benefits of additional children. Hence, even if there is a collective decision as to how many children couples should have, it is still in a couple's interest to have more children than that.

III

The proposed population policies which go beyond family planning may be construed as attacking, in one way or another, the problem as it was just set out. Individual couples must be assured that a sufficiently large number of other couples will limit the size of their families so that they will not suffer comparative losses by limiting theirs. Further, social factors must be changed so that it is much less in their interest to have more children when others limit their family size. These problems are solved by using a legal technique to prevent it being in the interest of couples to have more children than are compatible with the public good.

At first glance, it would seem that only three moral considerations are relevant to choosing between feasible policies, namely, the importance of the good to be achieved (ensuring a minimum standard of living or a quality of life), effectiveness of these policies, and the extent to which they limit the liberty to procreate. However, even assuming the same good to be achieved and equal effectiveness of policies, there are other moral considerations involved in choosing between policies. The following discussion indicates some of these considerations.

First, consider the socioeconomic policies which provide incentives for couples to have fewer children. While they do not involve any objectionable limitation of the liberty to procreate, there is another moral objection to them. Since they rely on economic incentives,

they would primarily decrease birth rates in the lower economic classes. Rich couples would not be as attracted by the incentives as poor ones. But it is unfair that the poor should have to make greater sacrifices than others for the public good from which all benefit. All of these policies would decrease the opportunities of the lower classes to have children, in comparison with those of the upper classes. Thus, they deny equality of opportunity for parenthood by taking into account characteristics irrelevant to the ability to be a good parent.[14]

Second, consider socioeconomic policies which remove current incentives for having children. Like the previous policies, they do not involve any coercion. But unless carefully designed, they may be subject to various objections. Like the previous policies, they may affect the poor more than the rich. For example, if all families receive the same family allowance per child, removal of that incentive would affect the poor more than the rich. Indeed, whenever the same size monetary incentive is offered or removed from both rich and poor, the poor are disproportionately affected. But if the monetary value of benefits or burdens is provided at rates proportional to couples' income and wealth, this objection will not hold. For example, if one assumes that progressive income taxes impose the same burden on rich and poor, then removal of income tax exemptions for children will not burden the poor more than the rich. For since the poor pay taxes at a lower rate, the actual taxes paid when the exemption is removed will be less than for the rich.[15]

Moreover, unless the benefit is only removed for children born after some future date, such policies impose a harm on couples with children. For example, suppose income tax exemptions for children are removed as of this date. Then all couples with children will have to pay more taxes. As previously stated, this increased tax burden does not constitute coercion because it cannot affect the couples' decision to have the children. But it is a harm in that it is a denial of a benefit they could legitimately expect when they decided to have their children.

Finally, the loss of benefits may fall upon the children more than their parents. In practice, such a loss might result in poorer education, clothing, housing, and diet for children. These sorts of conditions ought not be imposed on children for being born through no fault of their own. But this aspect of policies can be avoided by other policies providing goods directly to children, e.g., free education, medical care, meals, etc.[16] Nonetheless, to avoid this objection, such population policies must be adopted in the context of a welfare state ensuring equality of opportunity. Hence, this objection has considerable force in underdeveloped countries.

Third, proposals which would impose penalties for having children or having more than a specific number of them face all the previous objections. Limits will fall more heavily upon the poor unless made proportionate to income and wealth. The burdens may be passed on to the children. In addition, they involve the harm of a penalty, which in this context constitutes a form of coercion limiting the liberty to procreate. So besides the difficulties with the other policies, these policies would also infringe the right to procreate.

Finally, proposals for compulsory limitation of procreation, while involving more coercion than those just considered, avoid many of the other problems. They would not fall upon children or unequally upon the various economic classes in society. In these respects, they may well be preferable to many proposals of the previous sorts. However, there are other moral objections to them which do not apply to any of the previous types of policy. Under the previous policies, a couple can decide that the satisfaction of another child is worth the cost. If so, they can satisfy their stronger desire for more children. But under the compulsory policies, no matter how strong a couple's desire for another child may be, that desire cannot be satisfied. Hence, these policies would involve a greater decrease in the total want satisfaction when intensity of desire is considered than the other kinds of policy.

Further, they limit the liberty to choose the means of birth control. For example, a recent proposal would require everyone in society to be injected with a long-term reversible sterilant.[17] This method of birth control would be contrary to the moral beliefs of Roman Catholics. A policy requiring such a sterilant or regular sterilization after a person had a specified number of children would leave people greater liberty to choose a method of birth control. But it too would eliminate that liberty in some circumstances.

To sum up, a human right to procreate, assuming there is one, does not constitute an insuperable moral objection to population control. Human rights are not absolute. Current policies of family planning further this right and do not infringe it. But they will not limit population to a point compatible with the public good. Socioeconomic policies providing incentives not to have children or removing current incentives for having children would not impose any morally objectionable limit to the liberty

to procreate. Thus, they would not infringe a right to procreate. The moral
objections to such policies arise from
other considerations, but many of them
can be avoided by careful selection of a
policy. Only policies involving penalties
for having children or compulsory limitation on family size involve a morally
objectionable limit to the liberty to procreate. But even with them, the infringement of a right to procreate may not be
the major objection.

Socioeconomic policies providing or
eliminating incentives appear justified if
they will at least prevent a decrease in
the quality of life. Of course, they should
be chosen to minimize the other objections to them. But, even if they fall more
heavily upon the lowest economic class,
overall the lowest class will probably be
better off sacrificing some opportunity
for having children in order to obtain
clean air, water, recreational opportunities, etc. The only other alternative policies for limiting population to gain or
maintain these benefits involve coercion
and are less desirable from the point of
view of the lowest class.

Policies limiting the liberty to procreate are justified to avoid the inability
to provide a minimum standard of living. The liberty to procreate is partially
sacrificed, but the gains are more significant. For liberty is of little value if one
is incapable of taking advantage of it.
The point is not that hungry or ill people cannot also have the liberty to procreate, but that its comparative value to
them is less than it is for healthy, well-
fed people.

Finally, it must be noted that none
of the proposed policies completely denies the liberty to procreate. None denies people the choice whether or not to
have children; only the number of chil-

dren couples may have is limited. The
minimal right to have some children is
not abrogated.

Appendix

Several issues were glossed over in
the body of this paper. At least two of
them deserve brief comment. First, many
people argue that voluntary programs of
population control should be tried before others. It is not always clear what is
meant by a voluntary program. Frequently, family planning is meant. One
of the main points of this paper, however, is that incentive policies do not
limit couples' liberty to decide the number of children they have; hence, such
policies may be viewed as voluntary.
Moreover, the point of the argument in
section two is that family planning will
not in fact work if it is in the interest of
couples to have more children than desirable for a limited population size or
growth rate. It has been suggested that
it may not be in the interest of couples
to have so many children.[18] This claim
is more likely true for developed countries than for underdeveloped ones; indeed, because industrialization changes
couples' interest in having large numbers of children, it results in the demographic transition.

There is also a practical problem
with the suggestion that voluntary family planning be thoroughly tried before
any other policies are adopted. It requires a number of years before one can
determine the effectiveness of a policy.
Furthermore, it takes about twenty-five
years before lower fertility rates have
much effect upon the size of the labor
force, and almost twice that long before
they have a substantial effect upon pop-

ulation size. Thus, no policy adopted now can have a very significant effect until the end of the century. If family planning alone is tried for five or ten years and fails, then it will be well into the next century before major benefits from reduced fertility rates can occur.

Second, a few comments should be made about technological issues. There is considerable disagreement about the relation between population size and environmental pollution, food supplies, etc. Population size and growth are probably not the major cause of environmental pollution in developed countries; production technology and life styles are more important. However, population size and growth are contributing factors; at some point they must also be limited. Since population size and growth must be limited sooner or later, it seems unwise to wait until a crisis is reached to do something effective.

With respect to underdeveloped countries, it is sometimes suggested that industrialization should be emphasized, for it will improve the standard of living of those persons currently alive and bring about the demographic transition to lower population growth rates. Unfortunately, the economic improvement of underdeveloped countries is much more difficult with rapid population growth. Lower growth rates would make it easier for such countries to develop economically.

Another alleged technical problem is the absence of reliable, safe, and easy-to-use contraceptives. However, the importance of such contraceptives has probably been overstated. European countries and the United States underwent the demographic transition, significantly lowering birth rates, without the availability of birth control pills, IUDs,

etc. Hence, the difficulty does not appear to be lack of means of preventing conception but lack of will to do so.

Finally, there is a technological "bind" with respect to the population policies that may be justifiable. Policies limiting the liberty to procreate are justifiable in order to avoid the inability to provide a minimum standard of living. In essence, that means they are justifiable in underdeveloped countries but not developed ones. However, underdeveloped countries generally do not have the administrative, economic, and medical capability to implement such policies, whereas developed countries do. Hence, those countries which can implement such policies are not justified in doing so, while those countries which are justified in adopting such policies cannot implement them.

Notes

1. Quoted by John D. Rockefeller, III, in the Introduction to *Family Planning Programs*, ed. Bernard Berelson (New York: Basic Books, 1969), p. 7.
2. For a detailed analysis of human rights see my "The Human Right to Population Control," in *Human Rights: Amintaphil I*, ed. Ervin H. Pollack (Buffalo, N.Y.: Jay Stewart, 1971), pp. 396–402.
3. For a more detailed discussion of types of coercion see my "A Concept of Coercion," in *Coercion: Nomos XIV*, ed. J. Roland Pennock and John W. Chapman (Chicago: Aldine-Atherton, 1972), pp. 17–24.
4. "Law as an Instrument of Population Control," *University of Colorado Law Review* 40 (1967–68), 179–98.
5. "The Technique Element in Law," *California Law Review* 59 (1971), 733–51.
6. See Bernard Berelson, "Beyond Family

Planning," *Science* 163 (1969), 533–43, for a listing of about thirty different proposed population policies and a discussion of criteria for choosing between them.

7. The natural law obligation to procreate is, at least as presented by Thomas Aquinas, only an obligation on the human species to preserve itself, not an obligation on individuals to breed limitlessly. See F. C. Copleston, *Aquinas* (Harmondsworth, Middlesex: Penguin Books, 1955), p. 215.

8. There is one proposal which does not quite fit any of these categories. Kenneth E. Boulding has suggested that each girl be given licenses for 2.2 children and permitted to sell them to others. This proposal involves a combination of the administrative-regulatory and private arranging techniques. See his "Marketable Licenses for Babies," in *Population, Evolution and Birth Control*, ed. Garrett Hardin, 2nd ed. (San Francisco: W. H. Freeman, 1969), pp. 340–41.

9. This argument is similar to that of Garrett Hardin, "The Tragedy of the Commons," reprinted in this volume, pp. 3–18. I shall not compare my argument with his. My argument is based on an anaylsis of public good problems in John Rawls, *A Theory of Justice* (Cambridge, Massachusetts: Belknap Press of Harvard University Press, 1971), pp. 266–70. The problem is essentially a variant of the prisoner dilemma in game theory.

10. See Rawls, p. 266; and Mancur Olson, Jr., *The Logic of Collective Action*, Harvard Economic Studies, Vol. 124 (Cambridge, Massachusetts: Harvard University Press, 1965), p. 14; cf. Norman E. Bowie, *Towards a New Theory of Distributive Justice* (Amherst: University of Massachusetts Press, 1971), p. 45.

11. Ansley J. Coale, "Population and Economic Development," in *The Population Dilemma*, ed. Philip M. Hauser, 2nd ed. (Englewood Cliffs, N.J.: Prentice-Hall, 1969), pp. 59–84.

12. Bowie, pp. 114, 122–23.

13. See Kingsley Davis, "Population Policy: Will Current Programs Succeed?" in *Population, Evolution and Birth Control*, pp. 341–55, esp. p. 362.

14. For statements and defenses of the conception of equality of opportunity, see Rawls, p. 73 and *passim;* and Bernard Williams, "The Idea of Equality," in *Philosophy, Politics and Society*, ed. Peter Laslett and W. G. Runciman, 2nd series (Oxford: Basil Blackwell, 1962), pp. 124–27.

15. Brian Barry, *Political Argument* (London: Routledge and Kegan Paul, 1965), p. 165, n. 2.

16. See Gunnar Myrdal, *Asian Drama*, 3 vols. (New York: Twentieth Century Fund, 1968), II, 1503.

17. Edgar R. Chasteen, *The Case for Compulsory Birth Control* (Englewood Cliffs, N.J.: Prentice-Hall, 1971), pp. 202–10.

18. Arthur J. Dyck, "Population Policies and Ethical Acceptability," in *Rapid Population Growth*, National Academy of Sciences (Baltimore: Johns Hopkins Press, 1971), pp. 632–33.

Generally parents both bring children into the world and bring them up in it. They give the children both biological and biographical life. But there is no essential connection between these roles. Some persons bring up children they have neither begotten nor borne; some procreators do not bring up their children. It seems, then, that the grounds for child-rearing obligations cannot be biological, yet unclear what other grounds can be given for holding particular persons bound to bring up particular children.

Onora O'Neill argues that preparental decisions are usually the grounds for parental obligations, and hence, that such decisions are unjustifiable if they do not reflect a plan to bring the child up at least to some minimal level of independence. Persons have no unrestricted right to procreate, but a right (at most) to have children whose upbringing they can either undertake or effectively delegate. It follows that conflicts between population control policies and rights to procreate arise only for persons whose children have reasonable prospects; yet population control policies are justifiable precisely when most children lack reasonable prospects. If this connection between parental obligation and children's prospects is established, then population policies may not generally coerce.

BEGETTING, BEARING, AND REARING

ONORA O'NEILL

1. Rights to Procreate and Parental Obligations

Jean-Jacques Rousseau and his mistress had five children, whom they took as infants to the foundling hospital and abandoned there. If we believe that persons have an unrestricted right to procreate, then Jean-Jacques and Thérèse acted within their rights. But plainly, most people, when they speak of a right to procreate, don't have in mind a right to do as they did, but rather a right to become a parent, where being a parent includes rearing as well as begetting or bearing children, and is sometimes confined to rearing without biological reproduction. I shall argue that the right to beget or bear is not unrestricted, but contingent upon begetters and bearers having or making some feasible plan for their child to be adequately reared by themselves or by willing others. Persons who beget or bear without making any such plans cannot claim that they are exercising a right. A corollary of this claim is that some coercive population control policies do not usually violate persons' rights to procreate, though they may commonly violate some other liberty rights.

This restricted view of rights to procreate is endorsed by the International Bill of Human Rights.[1] Article 16 of this charter states that "men and women of full age . . . have the right to marry and found a family." The view that parents are primarily the *rearers* of children is confirmed by the systematic delineation of the parental duties of rearers who are not begetters or bearers in diverse legal codes. There are even societies in which child-rearing duties are usually delegated to someone other than the natural parents; and there are many circumstances in all societies in which one or both natural parents do not rear their child. Begetters and bearers, then, may sometimes not become or not remain parents in the wider sense of the term. Conversely, many persons are parents to children whom they neither begot nor bore. Adoptive parents, foster parents, some stepparents and guardians, as well as other relatives and officials of social agencies, may come to have some or all of the rights and responsibilities of parents. Hence, the basis of parents' obligations and rights cannot lie solely or necessarily in a biological relationship between child and parents.

However, biology is not irrelevant to parental obligations, for a standard way of acquiring obligations is to undertake them, and a standard way of undertaking parental obligations is to decide to procreate. Natural parents misinterpret such decisions if they think of them just as decisions to "have a baby." Wherever natural parents are the normal child rearers, decisions to pro-

create are (and are known to be) decisions to undertake the far longer and more demanding task of bringing up a child or arranging for its upbringing, to at least that level which will minimally fit the child for independent adult life in its society. Just how demanding such an undertaking will prove can vary greatly. Different societies demand very different minimal levels of competence of their adult members; individual children may be healthy, cooperative, and quick to learn—or none of these; individual parents may be competent and resilient—or neither. I shall, therefore, not try to give any detailed account of the *content* of parental obligations. I shall assume that these obligations do not go beyond doing whatever is minimally needed for the child when grown to lead an independent life, whatever that may involve in particular circumstances. Good parents will, of course, do more for their children. They provide cheerful homes and varied activities, chatter and games, as well as bread and shelter. Of course, for some children the goal of independent adult life is unattainable. I shall also not try to work out the limits of parental obligations in such cases. To discuss the right to procreate, I must first try to determine *who* has parental obligations, rather than more detail about *what* the discharge of these obligations requires in particular circumstances.

I shall not claim that obligations arise *only* when undertaken. But this is at least one standard way in which they arise. By exploring how parental obligations are undertaken, it should be possible to identify some persons who have those obligations. By contrast, an attempt to ground obligations only in needs or interests will not, by itself, tell us who has an obligation to meet those needs and interests. By considering children's needs and interests, we might reach a more detailed understanding of the content and limits of parental obligations; but it would remain unclear, in most cases, on whom particular children have legitimate claims for satisfying which of their needs or interests. Insofar as children's needs and interests can be met only by assigning them liberty rights, this raises no problems, for liberty rights impose a duty of non-interference uniformly on all others. But the needs and interests which are most important for children, especially for younger children, cannot be met by others' non-interference, but only by the services of particular others. Children don't survive if they are merely accorded liberties; they need to be able to claim others' services. Except in those rare cases where there are particular others who uniquely have the capacity to meet some child's needs and interests, a consideration of needs and interests cannot show who (if anyone) has the obligation to meet the claims of a particular child. If we are to take the claim rights of children seriously, we must look for arguments which will show which persons owe which services to particular children.[2]

Normally, when we undertake obligations, we have a fairly clear idea of what we are letting ourselves in for and whether we can fulfill the obligation. Normally, also, we will do nothing wrong if we either discharge or transfer or gain release from the obligation. Parental obligations are atypical for a number of reasons. Frequently prospective and new parents have only the haziest ideas of what and how much they are letting themselves in for. They cannot foresee in any detail what will be needed if they are to give their child

even a minimally adequate upbringing. And frequently both new and seasoned parents find that they have misjudged their own inclinations or capacities, or that their inclinations and capacities diminish or change. Childhood is so long that parents cannot foresee with any assurance what they or their lives will be like by the time their children are grown. Yet parental obligations are unlike others in that there is no way in which a young child can waive his claims on those who bring him up and release them from their obligations. These are perhaps some of the reasons why parental obligations are so often transferred wholly or partly to others.

Begetters and bearers who find that they cannot or do not want to become parents may take various courses. If they think abortion is permissible and medical services are available, they may ensure that no child is born to them. If abortion is unavailable, or they feel it impermissible, but they think exposure permissible, they may, where not prevented by law or deterred by others, discharge their parental obligations quite quickly. Exposure is no longer widely practiced, but there is a good deal of evidence (mainly in the form of a suspiciously high proportion of male children) that some societies tolerate or demand malign neglect of some (mainly female) infants, who, unsurprisingly, die.[3] These drastic methods of avoiding parental obligations raise peculiar ethical problems. I mention them only for completeness, since I do not plan to discuss the morality of abortion, exposure, or malign neglect here.

When such methods are rejected, begetters and bearers who cannot or will not take on parental obligations may decide to release their child for rearing by willing and competent others, provided such arrangements can be made. (To release a child for rearing by others who are incompetent or unwilling amounts to exposing the child; after all, even exposed children have *some* chance of surviving—for example, if picked up by honest shepherds.) In Rousseau's day, releasing a child for others to rear might mean taking it to a foundling hospital; today, it would more likely mean releasing the child for adoption.[4] Such arrangements may also be temporary or partial. Begetters and bearers have at various times delegated or transferred some or all of their tasks to wet nurses, relations, tutors, servants, foster homes, and schools, including boarding schools. Provided they take reasonable steps to ensure that their children will be adequately reared, they do not breach but transfer their parental obligations, or some part of those obligations. If we suspect that Jean-Jacques and Thérèse breached rather than transferred their parental obligations, this is probably because we suspect that foundling homes do not rear children at even a minimally adequate standard. And we also have good reason to think that Rousseau knew this, for no one protested louder than he that paternal and maternal duties should not be delegated or divided among many persons.[5]

We can transfer only the obligations that we have incurred. If the ground of parental obligations is that they are undertaken, then it seems that at least some begetters and bearers have no parental obligations, for they have never undertaken to have and care for a (further) child. This is evidently the case for most bearers who have been raped (or conceived as a result of forced intercourse with their husbands) and for most begetters or bearers whose partner deceives them in order to con-

ceive. However, even in these two cases, some begetters and bearers may accept, and even welcome, the resulting pregnancy and child; and in such cases, it is reasonable to think that they too have undertaken parental obligations, and so must either discharge or transfer them.

Quite often, it is harder to tell whether begetters and bearers have undertaken parental obligations. If intercourse is voluntary, neither partner deceives the other, and reasonable care is taken to avoid conception but conception occurs, have the begetters and the bearer any parental obligations? A child born under such circumstances is in one way an accident in the lives of the begetters and bearers; but the birth was not an unforseeable risk in the way a birth which results from rape is an unforseeable risk in the mother's life. On the contrary, it is well known that most contraceptive methods fail at times.

One model for thinking about the obligation of unintending begetters and bearers might be by analogy with the strict liability often imputed to persons who have unintentionally caused harm by forseeably risky actions. A motor accident is generally unintended and undesired; but it is a forseeable risk of driving, and one which motorists are obliged to take pains to avoid and to insure against. When they inflict harm by their driving, they (or their insurance companies) are obliged to compensate the victims. A similar principle covers some other actions whose results, though unintended and undesired, are forseeable risks. Companies must compensate those harmed by dangerous or defective products they have sold; neighbors must make amends when their ball games break windows. In some cases, persons might analogously be held strictly liable for harm to the unconceived. For example, the manufacturers of Thalidomide could not claim that they harmed no one because the victims were (in most cases) unconceived when the drug was manufactured and distributed.

But unintending parents may reasonably point to a significant difference between themselves and the manufacturers of Thalidomide. The manufacturers harmed persons whose lives would otherwise have been much better. Unintending parents may point out that, however neglectful or rejecting they are, they do not *worsen* their children's lives. But for the unintentional conception, the children would have had no life at all. The only case in which it might be plausible to say that unintending parents harm their children would be if they make the children's lives worse than non-existence. But the comparison between the merits of not existing and of particular lives seems thoroughly obscure.[6]

I shall, therefore, leave unresolved the question of whether unintending parents who at no time take on parental obligations to their child have any obligations to that child. In practice, this omission is not very important to the argument of this paper for two reasons.

First, begetters and bearers who neither intended to conceive nor later undertook to rear are in practice faced by the same dilemmas as those who at some time undertook parental obligations and later found themselves either unwilling or unable to discharge these obligations. They may seek abortion (if acceptable to them and available) or kill the child by exposure or malign neglect (if acceptable to them and not prohibited); or they may arrange to transfer the rearing of the child to willing and competent others. If no such others can be found, and if they cannot countenance abortion, exposure, or malign neglect, the only remaining option is for one or both of them to be minimal parents, however reluctantly. Secondly, my interest is mainly with the obligations and rights of persons who *decide* to procreate. If persons making such decisions are also undertaking to discharge, or failing that, to transfer parental obligations, then begetters and bearers cannot base decisions to procreate just on their *desires* to beget or bear, nor even on their desires to rear. Their decisions must also reflect some judgment about the feasibility of their project. Those who have good reason to believe themselves unable or unwilling to rear or arrange for the rearing of a child cannot reasonably choose to procreate. It is, of course, hard to know exactly what the minimal requirements for child rearing in a given society are; hard to foresee one's own capacities and situation over a long stretch of life; and impossible to foretell what difficulties a particular child may bring. Even so, it is not difficult to identify some situations, such as serious ill health or abysmal poverty or distaste for children, which, if there were no available alternative arrangements for the child's rearing, would make a decision to procreate unreasonable. A person who faces such disabilities might reasonably be held to have no right to procreate under those conditions. If decisions to procreate create parental obligations, then those who realize (or who should realize, given the information available to them) that they can neither discharge nor transfer such obligations have no right to procreate at that time.

Some persons may say that the above argument shows only that begetters and bearers who can neither discharge nor transfer parental obligations *should not procreate,* but not that they have *no right to procreate.* However, I do not believe that this is correct. We sometimes say of liberty rights—e.g., of the right of free speech—that the right was intact although a person should not exercise it with regard to a particular subject. This would leave open the presumption that the person had a right to speak freely on other matters. But there is only one way to exercise the right to procreate. Hence, there is little point (and some chance of misleading) in saying that a person who should not procreate at some time still has a right to procreate at that time.

There is another reason why one might feel that persons who cannot discharge or transfer parental obligations still have a right to procreate, though they should not do so. One may believe that liberty rights ought to be respected even when they are misused. For example, we would not want the right of free speech to be overridden just because someone uses it to tell (not very harmful) lies, which he ought not to do. However, some restrictions are presumed to be built into rights. The right of free speech is commonly supposed to be justifiably restricted both to preserve others' right of free speech and to prevent (at least) grave harms. It is not part of anyone's right of free speech to shout down others or to slander maliciously. It is not part of anyone's right to procreate either to prevent others from procreating or to cause grave harm by their procreation. I have not considered cases where A's procreation prevents B from doing so, though such situations are imaginable (consider two brothers who farm jointly, of whom one has as many children as both can support; or the more widespread parallel situation

which some neo-Malthusians predict for whole populations). But I have argued that decisions to procreate generally create parental obligations, and so create claims which cannot be overridden or discarded just by citing a right to procreate. What would we think of a person who discarded her intentionally conceived child at birth, claiming that the only part of parenthood she enjoys is pregnancy? We would hardly believe that she is exercising a right to procreate. It is only of situations where less grave harm is done—for example, when people have more children than they can bring up *well*—that we would say that they had a right to procreate but, all things considered, should not have done so. Where persons can foresee that they cannot or will not be minimally adequate parents, they should not merely avoid procreating, but have no right to do so.

2. Parental Obligations and State Obligations to Children

If this account of a standard basis of parental obligations is right, then we should have no difficulty in understanding how persons who are not natural parents acquire such obligations. Like natural parents, adoptive and foster parents, as well as some guardians and stepparents, can acquire partial or complete, long-term or temporary, parental obligations by undertaking to fulfill such obligations for particular children.

But the obligations of the state and of state agencies toward children cannot have the same basis, for there is usually no occasion on which the state or state institutions make such undertakings to particular children. Only if the state controls and mandates procreation—as in Plato's *Republic*—could one hold that the state acquires the same sort of obligations as persons do by deciding to procreate, so undertaking to rear. Only in this case would the state, or certain state agencies, have chosen to bring dependent human beings into existence and so be committed to care for them and to train them until they can live independent lives.

Where those decisions are made by individuals, or where children are conceived unintentionally, state obligations to children must rest on different foundations. One plausible basis for such obligations is the public interest in ensuring that the next generation is reared in ways that will make its members at least adequate citizens. We all have good reasons to set up social arrangements which will care for children who, for whatever reason, find themselves without willing and competent caretakers. If this is the basis of state obligations to children, then these are essentially "backup" obligations. They are meant to ensure, first, that basic parental tasks are carried out for each child by some person or persons, and second, that any further steps that are necessary, but beyond the competence of most parents, are taken. State obligations of the first sort include protecting children who are abused or neglected, settling disputes of custody, and assigning custody of children whose parents are dead, incapable, or unwilling. State obligations of the second sort may include supplementing the child-rearing of otherwise adequate and willing persons by providing services, such as formal education or medical care, which are beyond the capacity of some or all parents but needed if children are to become adequate citizens.

These "backup" obligations may be seen as extensive if one makes strong assumptions about the incompetence of parents or about the expertise of child care professionals. Those who believe that the relative competence of experts is great may think it necessary to assign many aspects of child rearing to state agencies. Those who are more confident about parents may think state activities should be quite restricted. The relative capacities of the experts and parents of a given society to rear children who will make good or at least adequate citizens, are much disputed. The battle lies between the champions of the "helping" professionals, employed by state agencies, who trust in the advance of expertise, and those skeptics and libertarians who suspect that the choices and decisions of ordinary parents may offset ignorance of theory with involvement, commitment, and knowledge of the particular case.

3. Justifying Procreation Decisions and Population Policies

If this sketch of the differing bases of state and parental obligations to children is right, there are strong differences between the two. Parental obligations are incurred by persons who undertake to rear a child in whole or in major part. These obligations are often difficult and sometimes impossible to meet; yet there is a deep public interest in their being met, and indeed, in better than minimal upbringing of children. Consequently, state obligations to children include facilitating and backing up the child-rearing efforts of parents. This might suggest that there will be no conflicts between parents and state over child rearing except when parents fail (or are believed to fail) in discharging their obligations to their children. However, if the state has an obligation to ensure and facilitate adequate child rearing, and so to maintain social conditions required for such child rearing, it may in some situations need to try to raise or to reduce the birth rate in order to make it more likely that those born will be adequately brought up. There are presumably additional public interests which can be threatened by some sorts of population increase and decrease. In such cases also, the state might have an obligation to seek to raise or to lower the number of births. If there is sufficient public interest in some population control policies, then there may be considerable conflicts between state obligations based on these interests and parents' decisions to procreate.

I now want to consider how extensive this conflict is, and in particular, to what extent justifiable population control policies conflict with rights to procreate, if such rights are restricted (as I have argued that they are) by procreators' having or making feasible plans for their child's upbringing.

Most contemporary discussion of population policies assumes that state interests lie in reducing (or reversing) the rate of population growth. But there have been other, even recent, periods in which many states have pursued pronatalist policies by encouraging large families and removing financial burdens from parents; and there are still some areas where economic problems appear to arise from under- rather than overpopulation.[7] There are also state interests in population trends which are independent of concern about over- or underpopulation. For example, rapid fluctuations in birth rates lead to demographic imbalances between age groups and difficulties in planning for educational and welfare systems. They can

also produce situations in which the proportion of a population which is economically active varies widely over quite short periods, with consequent economic dislocations.

So that the possible conflicts between population policies and procreation decisions can be as clear as possible, I shall assume that the problem population policies have to confront, and which may also affect the justification of procreation decisions, is the problem of overpopulation.

In order to know whether justifiable population policies conflict with rights to procreate, we need to have some idea of the grounds which might justify such policies. Two aspects of population policies can be distinguished whose justification is rather separate. On the one hand, one can consider the justification of the *goal* of some policy—for example, zero population growth, or some target rate of population growth or decline. On the other hand, one can consider the *methods* by which a policy proposes to implement these goals—for example, family planning services, tax incentives to have small families, postponement of marriage, or sterilization of those who have already had a certain number of children.

Discussions of justifiable goals of population policies which do not consider methods amount to discussions of the optimal size or rate of increase of a population. One such recent discussion[8] focuses on the differences between population policies which aim to maximize the *total* utility of a population and those which aim to maximize the *average* utility of a population. Is it better to aim for a large population, even though persons may not on the average be very happy, or to aim for a smaller population whose total happiness is less but whose members are generally happier than the members of the larger population? For populations of fixed size, anything which raises total utility will raise average utility. But when population size is changing, a policy which would produce the greatest average happiness might not produce the greatest total happiness. To maximize total happiness, it might be necessary to have a population policy which permitted, indeed fostered, population growth until any further new persons could be expected to be generally unhappy and so would reduce total utility. But to maximize average happiness, it might be necessary to have a population policy which restricted population growth if further new persons could be expected to have lives which were on average less happy than the further lives of existing persons. (Such calculations are complicated, for the happiness of existing persons will be affected in various ways by the population policy chosen. Some persons might be made unhappy by not being able to have families as large as they would like; others might be made unhappy by the pressures on them and their families resulting from runaway population growth.) By and large, the goal of maximizing total utility suggests that population growth should be sought in spite of lowered life prospects, so long as this lowering is offset by the existence of additional persons whose life prospects are good enough to outweigh the loss. On balance, the goal of maximizing average utility suggests that population growth should be avoided if it threatens to reduce (or to prevent the increase of) average life prospects.

Even if one is inclined to accept the (loosely) utilitarian framework of this discussion, it has a particular narrowness. For the goals of many possible population policies might be thought desirable on broadly utilitarian grounds, even though they aimed to maximize neither the total nor the average utility of a population. One might, for example, favor a policy which sought to maximize total utility subject to some constraint about average utility, encouraging population growth unless it threatened to push average happiness below some level. Alternatively, one might seek to maintain (though perhaps not to maximize) average happiness, but not at the cost of a really steep population decline in future generations.

Beyond the utilitarian framework, many additional possible goals for population policies can be envisioned. A society might prefer a population policy which maximizes something other than utility or happiness, such as resources available to future persons, or life expectation. Or it might prefer a population policy which fostered a particular goal, such as maintaining or enhancing some way or quality of life, rather than seeking to maximize any specific dimension of life.

Perhaps one reason why this discussion of justifying the goals of population policies is often very partial is that the methods of such policies seem to present deeper and more immediate problems of justification. For the methods on which some antinatalist policies rely (whatever their specific goals and the justification of these goals) are often thought to be unjustifiable, in part because they infringe on the right to procreate.

Michael Bayles has recently argued, in "Limits to a Right to Procreate,"[9] that sometimes the goal of a population policy can justify overriding the right to procreate. He divides population policies into three groups, according to the methods they propose. There are *family planning* policies, which disseminate information and devices for contraception; *incentive* policies, which may institute incentives for small families; and *coercive* policies, which penalize (perhaps even sterilize) those who fail to limit their families. (Analogous types of policies might be used to increase population size or achieve some other demographic ends, such as avoiding rapid, short-term fluctuations in the birth rate.)

Bayles argues that information and incentive policies are morally unobjectionable but unfortunately likely to be ineffective. This position is quite controversial. Perhaps the wrong incentives have been tried. Some economists and population experts argue that only economic growth can motivate people to have smaller families. And perhaps some incentives are coercive. For the desperately poor, a cash bonus for sterilization may be precisely "an offer they can't refuse." But I shall accept Bayles' distinctions for the present purposes. He argues that since an effective population control policy is essential, "policies . . . limiting the liberty to procreate are justified," at least when this is necessary to avoid a plunge in living standards. In reaching this conclusion, he relies on a broadly utilitarian argument that liberty rights may be overridden if this is required for the general welfare.

Bayles construes the right to procreate as a liberty right forbidding others to "limit a person's liberty to decide when and how many children he will have."[10] Let us suppose that we indeed have *some* right to procreate. Even so, it is not plausible, if the argument of the first section of this paper is convincing, that this right to procreate is an entirely unrestricted right. At the very least, it is

hedged by the requirement that procreators not have children whom they cannot or will not rear or arrange to have reared. (There may, of course, be further, but from the viewpoint of our present concerns extraneous, limits on the rights to procreate; perhaps we have no right to procreate if it would destroy our own health.) If the right to procreate is a narrower right than Bayles suggests, then the area of conflict between that right and coercive population policies will be smaller and more specific than he suggests.

Let us assume that we can agree on what would constitute a minimally adequate quality or standard of life. This minimally adequate standard might be characterized in terms of utility level, or resources (physical or economic), or some account of the quality of life. This account of a minimally adequate standard can then be used both in arguments which justify the goals of population policies and in arguments which justify particular procreation decisions. A justifiable population policy must be one which seeks to achieve or to maintain some adequate or better quality or standard of life, however this is specified. A justifiable procreation decision must be one which is based on a feasible plan for any child which is born to have at least a minimally adequate standard of upbringing, however this is specified. Even when they appeal to the same account of minimally adequate standards or quality of life, procreation decisions may reasonably take a narrower focus than population policies. Begetters and bearers need only be sure that they have *some* feasible plan for their child to have a minimally adequate standard or quality of life during the years when they or willing others will be bringing the child up.

If persons procreate without having or making any feasible plan for their child to be adequately reared, then a policy which prevented those persons from procreating would not infringe on their right to procreate—for their proposed procreation would have gone beyond that right. There is no *general* clash between coercive population policies and the right to procreate, but rather a variety of circumstances in which particular coercive population policies conflict in specific ways with certain rights. I shall discuss a few of these conflicts.

4. Conflicts Between Justifiable Population Policies and Liberty Rights

In this section, I shall continue to assume that whatever account of a minimally adequate standard or quality of life might be used to justify a population policy should also be appealed to by persons making decisions to procreate.

Given this assumption, one conflict that might arise is between persons' rights to procreate when they have good reason to believe that they can rear any child they might have to at least a minimally adequate level, and a population policy which seeks to prevent such births on the grounds that the child's long-term prospects are less than adequate. This is a straightforward clash between population policies and procreation decisions which appeal to the same standard of minimal adequacy. One way of resolving it might be to argue for a stronger restriction on the right to procreate than I have adopted here. One might argue that decisions to procreate can be justified only if begetters and bearers have (or make) not only a feasible plan for the rearing of their child but some plan for the longer-term life of that child.[11] Such a restriction might plausibly forbid those whose children would have no adequate long-term prospects to procreate. Such an extension of the restrictions which parental obligations place on procreation rights would eliminate this straightforward conflict between population policies and the rights of procreators who appeal to the same standard of minimal adequacy. In practice, the importance of this extension is hard to estimate. Childhood is so long, and the evidence that might be reasonably cited in predicting the entire life prospects of persons born as a result of present procreation decisions is meager. There are few cases in which persons could be reasonably sure that they could adequately rear the child they propose to have, but that the life prospects of that child would be inadequate.

In fact, the only cases where this seems likely are ones in which parents believe that they could shield or protect their child while young from the impact of some handicap, or where they believe that they can isolate their child from some sort of persecution he would suffer while adult. Parents may sometimes reasonably think that they could give a retarded or genetically abnormal child a minimally adequate or better childhood but no adult life. Persons who are persecuted—for example, Jews in hiding in the Nazi years—may believe that they can bring up a child without his being exposed to conditions that would make life less than adequate, but that this protection could not be extended indefinitely. But these are not the most usual sorts of situations when circumstances are hard enough to warrant a coercive population control policy, for the reasons which might usually be given to justify such policies are things such as great poverty or epidemic disease, intense pollution or overcrowding, and the threat of violence or famine. On the whole, parents cannot shield their children from these threats. On the contrary, children are one of the most vulnerable groups in any population suffering conditions of this sort. If a coercive population policy is justified by threats of war, famine, disease, poverty, pollution or overcrowding, then most persons considering procreation will conclude, even if they consider only the years of their children's dependence, that they have no right to procreate, because they can make no adequate plan for a child's upbringing in the face of those threats.

Whenever a coercive population policy can be justified, *most* would-be parents will find that, since their right to procreate is restricted by an obligation to have feasible rearing plans, they have no right to have children that the policy then forbids them, provided they appeal to standards of minimal adequacy which the policy invokes. But there will often be some parents who can argue that though conditions are generally so bad that a population control policy can be justified, still they, through good fortune or good management, are so placed that their children will both grow up in and live a life which is (more than) minimally adequate. They can justify having (further) children, though others cannot. Hence, any population policy which forbade them (further) children would violate *their* rights to procreate.

Such claims have two important features. First, they will always and at best be claims which a minority of persons can make, for only a minority can be unusually fortunate. If circumstances are dire enough to warrant a population control policy, then for most persons circumstances will be dire enough for their rights to procreate to be correspondingly restricted. Second, these claims of fortunate persons rest on the assumption that the right to procreate should be overridden by other rights, for example, rights to property, on which their usual good fortune depends. If the right to procreate is overridden by property rights, there is nothing wrong when some persons' property rights are so restricted that they may have no children, or fewer children than others of larger property have. If, on the other hand, property rights are overridden by the right to procreate, then persons whose holdings of resources so restrict others' lives that those others have no (or lesser) rights to procreate have, if liberties are to be equal, no right to all of those resources. (Which is not to say that they may not have rights to larger than average resources, but only that some of their excess over others' resources violates more basic rights of those others.) On this supposition, a respect for persons' rights would commit us to achieving a sufficient redistribution of resources to ensure that no persons found themselves with less than standard rights to procreate because they lacked the resources to meet minimal parental obligations. I do not propose to investigate the relative standing of property rights and rights to procreate, nor to provide any general account of the foundation of liberty rights or the methods for resolving conflicts between such rights. I omit this with regret because it seems to me that any serious appeal to rights, and in particular to liberty rights (of which the rights to procreate and to seek property are two), must try to provide some way of showing that the different rights involved are mutually consistent; and this demonstration would require a method for settling conflicting rights claims. However, this task is too demanding and intricate to be handled here. I think it is at least useful to see that the dilemma—in cases where there is a *prima facie* conflict between rights to procreate and some justifiable population policy—is a conflict between the right to procreate and those other rights which place some persons in a favored position with respect to the rights to procreate.

Justifiable coercive population policies will not, if the above arguments are sound, always conflict with persons' present rights to procreate. But these policies may, if they rely on certain methods, conflict with persons' future rights to procreate as well as with certain other liberty rights which persons presumably have if they have any liberty rights at all. These conflicts arise not from the goal of certain population policies but from the particular methods some policies rely on to achieve those goals.

Today, the most effective birth control techniques are certain forms of sterilization which are not, or not reliably, reversible. Since some persons may have no right to procreate at a given time because they cannot fulfill or arrange for others to fulfill even minimal parental tasks, but may later be in a position to fulfill them, so have rights to procreate at that later time, forcible sterilization does violate the right to procreate even when applied to persons who at a given time have no right to procreate. Alternative methods of preventing conception are, of course, available, but are less reliable, more expensive, and harder for persons in poverty-stricken circumstances to use. But were there a method of birth control as safe and effective as sterilization, and reliably reversible, its imposition by a justifiable antinatalist population policy would not violate the right to procreate of persons who at that time had no right to procreate. It is the *irreversibility* rather than the *imposition* of sterilization which violates the right to procreate.

Other methods of birth control, and sterilization as well, may violate rights other than the right to procreate, if imposed on persons without their consent. Both sterilization and the insertion of IUDs may violate persons' bodily integrity; chemical contraceptives may impose risks on some persons (though perhaps not risks as great as the risk of a further pregnancy). If we think that the liberty of the person includes rights to bodily integrity and freedom from forced chemical treatment, then we must conclude that population policies which impose these methods of contraception violate those rights. These violations are not different in principle from those which we may decide are acceptable—or intolerable—in considering matters such as compulsory immunization campaigns or the addition of chemicals which inflict risk as well as benefit to water or food which persons cannot easily avoid consuming. Here again, it is the *method* and not the imposition of a population policy whose goal is justified which violates rights. If a justifiable population policy could be imposed by methods which were reversible, nonintrusive, and not endangering, then it would not violate rights other than in a *minority of cases* the right to procreate.

5. Conclusions

I have argued in this paper that debates about population control are misconceived if we forget that people bring children up as well as bring them into the world. If we have a right to procreate, this is no unrestricted right to populate the world, but a right which is hedged by the parental obligations which procreators usually acquire.

Coercive population policies can be justified only by the threat of major harm, the threat of the destruction of people and of standards of life, and not by lesser inconveniences and impoverishments. But such major harm would also threaten most individuals and their standards of life, and leave them with reduced prospects of bringing up children adequately, and so with restricted rights to procreate. Coercive population policies may violate many rights; but when justifiable they will not, in most cases, violate the right to procreate.[12]

Notes

1. *International Bill of Human Rights.*
2. Compare the discussion in Jeffrey Blustein, "Child Rearing and Family Interests," below, especially pages 115–22.
3. See Susan C. M. Scrimshaw, "Cultural Values and Behaviors Related to Population Change," Institute of Society, Ethics and Life Sciences, Hastings on Hudson, N.Y., 1977, for a summary of the evidence and a more general account of pre-modern approaches to limiting family size.
4. Cf. Raymond M. Herbenick, "Remarks on Abortion, Abandonment and Adoption Opportunities," below, pp. 52–57.
5. Cf. Jean-Jacques Rousseau, *Emile,* excerpted below, pp. 221–26.
6. The whole question of obligations and harms to unconceived, and therefore unindividuable, persons is only now being explored. See, for example, Derek Parfit, "On Doing the Best for Our Children," in *Ethics and Population,* ed. Michael D. Bayles, Cambridge, Mass., 1975, or Michael D. Bayles, "Harm to the Unconceived," in *Philosophy and Public Affairs,* Vol. 5, No. 3, Spring 1976.
7. For a lucid survey of population trends and policies past and present, see "The Human Population," *Scientific American,* September 1974. For a consideration of contemporary population problems which may not be overpopulation problems, see Michael E. Conroy, Kathleen Kelleher, and Rodrigo I. Villamizar, "The Role of Population Growth in Third World Theories of Development," Institute of Society, Ethics and the Life Sciences, Hastings on Hudson, N.Y., 1977.
8. Cf. Jan Narveson, "Utilitarianism and New Generations," *Mind,* 76, 1967, and "Moral Problems of Population," in Michael D. Bayles (ed.), op. cit. The second article contains references to a number of other contributions to this debate.
9. Michael D. Bayles, "Limits to a Right to Procreate," above, pp. 13–24.
10. Ibid., p. 14.
11. See William Ruddick, "Parents and Life Prospects," below, pp. 123–37.
12. Special thanks to Jerry Katz, William Ruddick, and Robert Shultz for their comments on earlier versions of this paper.

The best way of avoiding parental obligations is to avoid undertaking them. But often persons find themselves faced with a pregnancy when they are unable or unwilling to rear a child. Their options currently are abortion or child bearing for adoption by other individuals or institutions. These alternatives are take up in the next two papers. The distinct question, Who is entitled to decide? is addressed in the Supreme Court's *Danforth* opinions reprinted in part, below, pp. 58–79.

No issue of family policy has stirred more public outcry or philosophical discussion in the last decade than the question of abortion. Most of the debate has focused on the moral status of the fetus. Anti-abortionists have portrayed (often with photographs) the fetus as a person with a right not to be killed, except by the pregnant woman in defense of her own life. Pro-abortionists have denied that the fetus is a person until after birth, or if a person, it has no claim on the woman's physical support, especially if she has become pregnant against her will, as a result of rape, defective contraception, or miscalculation.

This debate cannot be settled merely by determining whether a fetus is a person. On the one hand, persons may sometimes be justifiably killed; on the other hand, the killing of non-persons is sometimes not justifiable. This is perhaps fortunate, since attempts to demarcate the class of persons, and so to discover whether (some) fetuses fall within it, have not inspired conviction. Philosophers are now free to attend to the moral considerations that often play a part in women's actual abortion decisions.

Martha Brandt Bolton draws attention to the moral context of a woman's abortion decision. Typically women have commitments to people who depend on their assistance or talents. Does a pregnant woman have an obligation to nurture and develop her fetus and potential child, and if so, how is that obligation to be weighed against prior obligations? Anti-abortionists claim that in general there is such an obligation and it should take priority over other obligations.

Bolton argues that anti-abortionists thereby treat the fetus as *more* than a person and the woman as *less* than a responsible moral agent. Our obligation to help persons is limited by our resources, and someone whose need overtaxes them is done no wrong if we return him to his own (inadequate) resources, in order to honor our commitments to others who depend on us. If we may not do this in the case of a fetus, then the fetus has the status of a super-person. If the fetus does have that status, then women typically cannot have a coherent or full moral life. If a pregnant woman has to undertake this special obligation, then she may be in the anomalous position of being urged, as a morally responsible person, to do something morally irresponsible—namely, to undertake an obligation she cannot fulfill, either because of other commitments or personal disabilities (drug addiction, emotional ambivalence) or lack of social support (pre- and post-natal assistance, adoption possibilities). And if, to avoid this morally incoherent situation, a woman must avoid competing moral commitments to others during the years in which she might have to take on this special responsibility to a fetus and child, she is denied the life of a full moral agent.

RESPONSIBLE WOMEN AND ABORTION DECISIONS

MARTHA BRANDT BOLTON

I

When a pregnant woman considers whether or not to seek an abortion, is she facing a choice between doing what is morally wrong and doing what is morally right, or is her choice without moral significance? There are two answers to this question which have become familiar to all of us, and I want to argue that both of them are wrong.

One answer comes from those who hold that the fetus is already a living human being and a person; they hold that a fetus, like every other person, has a right not to be deliberately killed. Some who hold this view allow that circumstances may permit the killing of the fetus—for example, when it is necessary to save the life of the pregnant woman. Generally speaking, however, according to those who advocate the fetus' "right to life," the decision to have an abortion is comparable to the decision to murder. Thus, they hold that in general, abortions are morally wrong.

The second familiar answer to our question is that, in general, an abortion has no moral significance; it is not morally wrong, but neither is it morally permissible or right. It is a personal and private decision comparable to the decision to have an abscessed tooth pulled or a bothersome tumor removed. According to this view, neither the fetus nor anyone else has rights which are violated by abortion. A woman is free to have, or not to have, an abortion as she chooses. I should clarify at once a point about this position that abortion is morally insignificant. It must be distinguished from that taken by a majority of the Supreme Court in the 1973 decision that laws prohibiting abortion during the first three months of pregnancy are unconstitutional. The Court found that abortion does not violate anyone's *constitutional* rights, and it is not the sort of action which the *state* has an interest in prohibiting. The position with which I am concerned has it that abortion violates no one's *moral* rights and cannot be prohibited, or required, on *moral* grounds.

As I have said, I think that both of these familiar views about the morality of abortion are wrong. Let me begin with the anti-abortionists, who claim that a fetus has a right not to be killed comparable to that of any person. Anti-abortionists make this claim, in part, because they hold that a fetus is already a person.[1] The thought that a newly conceived fetus is a person seems absurd to some, but it seems credible to others. The reason is that there is no readily available or widely accepted view about exactly what a person is.

One distinctive characteristic of persons is that they are entitled to special consideration. We are obligated to treat the lives, needs, and desires of other *persons* with consideration equal to that we think should be given to our own. For instance, conflicts between my needs and wants and those of other persons cannot automatically be decided in favor of me; the others have rights against my actions, and I am morally obligated to respect them. It is true that I may have moral obligations to animals, which are clearly not persons. But the point about persons is that I have *special* obligations to them, and they have *particular* rights that limit what it is morally permissible for me to do. The category of persons is in part a moral one; having certain rights and participating in a certain network of obligations is at least part of what it is to be a person.

The problem is that we do not know how to describe, in a general way, what creatures entitled to this special consideration must be like. We all agree about most cases we confront (although historically there has been debate about black people and women, in general). But even the most sensitive and honest of us can conceive of cases in which we would not know what to think.

One sort of puzzling case concerns creatures that are clearly not biological humans or *homo sapiens*. Imagine the moral questions that might arise if we encountered highly developed forms of life on other planets, or if we discovered creatures who are the "missing link" in the evolution of humans from apes. Should we force such creatures to work for us? Should we eat them? What about cross-breeding? Non-fictional cases may actually be at hand. Does the gorilla from the San Francisco Zoo, who is able to use language, have any of the rights of a person? The biological facts do not provide answers to these questions. Creatures that are indisputably not *homo sapiens* may nevertheless be entitled to the special consideration we owe to *persons*. By the same token, the fact that a creature *is* a biological human being does not settle such questions either. Consider cases of extreme criminal insanity or humans deep in coma with no hope of regaining consciousness. No doubt, we do have certain obligations to these humans, but we probably do not have the full range of obligations that we have to others in our community. If so, then a human being may be a person at one stage of his/her biological life and a non-person at other stages. Whether or not this is the case, and which stages of development are person-stages, will not be settled by biological facts about us.

II

Anti-abortionists begin the discussion of the morality of abortion with the claim that a fetus is a person. Most base this claim on biological facts, but as I have said, such facts do not settle the question. Others, recognizing that there is legitimate doubt that a fetus is a person, reason that the fetus should be given the benefit of the doubt. From there, anti-abortionists argue that it is a fundamental right of a person not to be deliberately killed.[2] This right is forfeited in certain circumstances where killing is justified, most notably in self-defense.[3] But the fact is that these circumstances rarely arise in pregnancy; they are confined to cases in which the life or health of the pregnant woman is seriously threatened by the presence of the fetus. Thus, a fetus cannot be killed (or can only very rarely be killed) if the fetus has the rights of a person.

I have already said that the assumption that a fetus is a person is unfounded, but I think that the anti-abortionist has a more serious problem. I think the claim that the fetus has the *same* rights as an undisputed person does can be shown to be clearly wrong.[4] If I am correct in thinking that a fetus cannot have the same right not to be killed as an undisputed person has, then the anti-abortionists are wrong when they prohibit abortion on grounds that persons as such have a right not to be killed.

To see the incoherence in the anti-abortionists' argument, we need to look at the gaps in their account of what is at stake in an abortion. They emphasize the fetus' alleged "right to life." They do not emphasize a matter which is equally important. This is that if a pregnant woman is obligated not to kill a fetus, then she is obligated to do a great deal more than that. She can meet the alleged obligation not to kill only if she takes on the various obligations involved in bearing and having a child. At the least, she must nurture the fetus, carry it to term, and give it birth; she must then care for the infant or make alternative arrangements for its care. Of course, there may be others willing to adopt the infant and raise the child; but we should not loose sight of the fact that for some babies there are not likely to be adoptive parents. For pregnant women whose potential babies will not be accepted for adoption, the responsibilities involved in caring for the fetus loom very large. For any pregnant woman, the only way to avoid killing a fetus is to take responsibility for nurturing and giving birth to it; for some, the alternative is undertaking to care for and raise a child. Anti-abortionists insist on the fetus' right not to be killed; they discount the fact that a fetus has that right *only if* it also has a right to be nurtured by the pregnant woman and raised by her or someone else.

It is important to describe the fetus' alleged right in this way, rather than in the way in which anti-abortionists typically do. Respecting the right of another person not to be killed is relatively simple. It is a matter of refraining from doing something. But respecting a fetus' right to be nurtured and developed involves a complex pattern of activities which form a prominent, demanding, and (in some cases) permanent part of one's life. It is relatively easy to live without deliberately killing someone; but it may require an indefinitely large commitment of time, energy, emotion, and physical resources to nurture and care for a child. Furthermore, the obligation not to kill is conceptually simple; it extends to *all* other persons, and the situations in which it is forfeited are familiar (for instance, self-defense). In contrast, the obligation to nurture and develop others is conceptually complex. It is not entirely clear how much of one's resources such obligations demand, nor is it clear how far they extend. Surely they do not extend to *all* other persons, for anyone's personal resources are too slight to meet such massive demands. By the same token, the limitations on any one person's resources make it inevitable that obligations to help different persons will conflict; some will have to be chosen over others. When anti-abortionists emphasize the obligation not to kill a fetus, they make it seem as if our obligations to fetuses were as simple as our obligations not to kill other persons. But this is seriously misleading. Fetuses differ from persons in that a pregnant woman cannot avoid killing a fetus unless she undertakes to nurture and develop it. Her obligations to a fetus cannot be any more simple than her obligations to help in the growth and development of others who may need it; and I have suggested that these obligations are complex and limited.

Let me illustrate what I mean when I say that obligations to aid the development and growth of others are limited and complex. Consider a mother with several children, one of whom has a disability which retards normal development. Suppose that with expensive treatment and patient training, the retarded child will slowly develop many capacities that other children acquire rapidly and without special help. The woman's resources are limited; her money, time, physical strength, and emotional capacity are not inexhaustible. Developing a certain capacity in the retarded child—say, the ability to make short unaccompanied trips outside the house—may put a severe strain on her resources. Her time and energy are needed to support the family, and she hasn't the money to engage someone else to work with the special child. There is a point beyond which she is not morally required to devote resources to the growth and development of the special child. Because her resources are limited, she must choose how they will be used. Her obligations to aid the special child are limited not

only by her own strength and resources but also by her obligations to the other children. The mere fact that a child needs help in order to develop does not always establish an overriding obligation for the mother to meet the need.

So far, I have been considering limitations on the mother's obligation to supply what is needed for the child to develop a specific skill. This affects the child's prospects for a satisfying life, but not the child's life itself. But clearly, similar considerations bear on the resources required to sustain the child's basic care. If resources are severely strained, the mother may have to relinquish all care of the child. Usually, she can make satisfactory alternative arrangements, and there is surely nothing morally wrong about her doing so. Even if alternative arrangements are not available, she may be forced to stop caring for the child if her resources are sufficiently strained. The point is that her obligations to support the development of a particular child are limited by her situation, and they are complex. Both her resources and her other obligations determine their extent.

I have been saying that a mother does not have *limitless* obligations to aid in the development of a child, or even to sustain a child's life. The same holds for any one person's obligations to support the growth, or even the life, of any other person. The basic fact that any one person's time, energy, and other resources have limits makes it absurd to suggest otherwise.

There are, then, *two* features of a person's rights and obligations which are relevant to the issue of abortion, and the anti-abortionists' insistence on one of them obscures the other. The features are: first, that a person has a right not to be killed which extends to virtu- ally all circumstances except those of self-defense; and second, that any one person's obligations to aid another's growth or sustain another's life must, in the nature of the case, have limits.

Where the rights and obligations of undisputed persons are concerned, these fundamental features are fully compati- ble. One person's obligation to sustain the life of another stops at a certain point; at that point, the other's require- ments may not be fully met and he/she may die. In refusing further aid, a per- son does not violate the other's right not to be killed; he/she may only be acting responsibly given his/her other commit- ments and in any case, there are limits to the extent to which anyone is obli- gated to sustain the life of another. Let us see how this works in a couple of cases. Consider a family supporting an elderly member who needs expensive medical care; suppose the medical situ- ation worsens, and care becomes pro- hibitively expensive for the family. To reserve enough money to supply other basic needs, they must withdraw finan- cial support for the medical care and, as a result, the elderly person dies. The withdrawal of support is regrettable, but not morally wrong; surely the el- derly person's right not to be killed has not been violated. The elderly person is simply left to his/her own resources; when they do not suffice, the person is allowed to die. Or, consider a situation in which one person rescues another from nearly drowning and administers artificial respiration. For a while, the ar- tificially provided oxygen sustains the victim's life, but the life-sustaining ac- tivity of the rescuer cannot be continued indefinitely. At some point, the person must be returned to his/her own means of sustaining life and, if they are inade-

quate, the person must be allowed to die. The death is by drowning; no one would suggest that the person was killed by the one who attempted to save his/ her life. No one would think that the victim's right not to be killed had been violated. In cases like these, where one person's life is sustained by the activities or resources of another, we can distin- guish between two sorts of actions: (i) the one person's ceasing the activity which sustains the other's life and (ii) the one person's deliberately killing the other. Actions of the first sort do not vio- late a person's right not to be the victim of actions of the second sort.

I suggest that what enables us to make this important distinction is that persons typically have resources of *their own* for sustaining their lives. At some time in their lives, undisputed persons have carried on their own life functions without direct dependence upon others. When such a person's life functions are later sustained by someone else, we sup- pose the person has (currently inade- quate) resources to which he/she can be returned.

However, a fetus is importantly dif- ferent from an undisputed person. We cannot distinguish between the pregnant woman's withdrawing her support for its life functions and her killing it.[5] I sug- gest that the reason is that a fetus, or at least one not yet viable, has no resources of its *own* for carrying on life functions.[6] A fetus cannot be returned to its own re- sources and allowed to die. If the woman ceases her support for its life, we seem forced to say that the fetus has been killed. So, whereas we can reconcile the limits on our obligations to sustain life of an undisputed person with our obligation not to kill such a person, we *cannot* do so in the case of a (previable) fetus. It is this that convinces me that a fetus cannot have the *same* right not to be killed that an undisputed person has.

Let me summarize. An undisputed person has a right not to be deliberately killed and (at best) a right to limited aid in growth and sustaining his/her life from a particular other person. Now consider a fetus. If a fetus has a right not to be deliberately killed (except in self-defense), then it has a right to be nurtured by the pregnant woman, and this is *not* a limited claim on her resources. Thus, a fetus has a right to demand more than an undisputed person does, and so its rights are not *the same* as such a person's are. On the other hand, if a fetus has only the same right to help from the pregnant woman that an undisputed person has, then there are limits to her obligations to it. Then, there will be a point at which the woman's obligations cease and the fetus can be killed, even though the killing is not done in self-defense. It follows, again, that a fetus does not have *the same* rights that an undisputed person does. A fetus cannot be accorded one of the relevant rights which undisputed persons have without also being given either a stronger right to help or a weaker right not to be killed than we accord to such persons.[7] Thus, a fetus cannot have the same right not to be killed that undisputed persons have.

III

If my view so far is correct, anti-abortionists cannot coherently support a general prohibition against abortion by appeal to the claim that a fetus has the rights of a person. Their response may be that, in fact, a pregnant woman's obligations to a fetus are *stronger* than her obligations to a person.[8] Anti-abortionists may claim she has a special duty to care for the fetus, so that her obligations to it are not limited in the ways obligations to other persons are. Accordingly, an anti-abortionist might persist in maintaining that aborting a fetus is generally morally wrong.

I think that this anti-abortionist position also is untenable. In particular, it distorts the situation of a woman as a morally responsible agent. It appeals, on the one hand, to the pregnant woman's ability to choose to do what is morally right (concerning abortion); on the other, it implies that she cannot be a responsible participant in a full moral life. Let me explain why I think that this is so.

The important fact about a pregnant woman's moral situation is the one I have been emphasizing: if she does not have an abortion, she must shoulder the more or less extensive and demanding responsibility of caring for the fetus. Now, many women have the various resources required to nurture the fetus and care for the potential child, or at least to make arrangements for its care. But many other women *do not*, and we need to be particularly concerned about their situation. Suppose that a pregnant woman knows that she cannot properly care for the fetus, or that the needs of the potential child will not be met. To undertake to nurture the fetus and give birth to a child, given her situation, would be morally irresponsible; it would be to accept obligations which she *knows* she cannot meet. No coherent moral rule requires a person to accept obligations which he/she knows cannot be fulfilled. Yet this is precisely what the anti-abortionists' moral stance requires of a pregnant woman in this situation. It requires that she refrain from abortion, and she cannot do so without incurring obligations to care for the fetus; in the sorts of circumstances with which I am concerned, she knows she must fail to meet them.[9]

Situations of the sort in question are, unfortunately, not merely hypothetical. Consider a case in which there is extreme emotional trauma connected with the woman's pregnancy, so that she is deeply ambivalent about the fetus. Such emotional ambivalence could be the result of her having been the victim of rape, or it could result from the unexpected death of the father of the fetus, or from the extreme youth and immaturity of the mother. The woman may recognize that her emotional ambivalence will keep her from providing adequate care for the fetus. It is important to realize that her inability to care for the fetus may be a genuine one which would be impossible to overcome. In another sort of case, she may know that she will be unable to provide adequate care for the fetus, either because she is addicted to alcohol or other harmful drugs or because she does not have access to the proper food or medical care. Or, she may know that she will be unable to care for the potential child and, further, that no one else in her community will be willing or able to do so.[10] Of course, pregnant women who face grave difficulties of these sorts are sometimes able to overcome them, especially if help from others in the community is available. But there will inevitably be cases in which it would be unreasonable, even irresponsible, to think that the difficulties could be overcome. Sometimes the resources required to nurture a fetus and care for a child are simply not available to a particular pregnant woman. For a woman in such a situation, the anti-abortionists' position has absurd implications. It implies that she is morally obligated to undertake responsibilities which she knows she must fail to meet. In brief, it places on her a moral responsibility to do what is morally irresponsible.

In less dire circumstances, a pregnant woman is still placed in an anomalous moral situation by the anti-abortionists' position. That position gives her an overriding obligation to care for the fetus. Now, what if the woman has already made important commitments which conflict with her developing the fetus? What if others are depending upon her? She has a responsibility to take reasonable precautions against conception, but responsible action of this sort is not a guarantee against pregnancy. If her obligation to the fetus takes precedence, she must fail to follow through on her commitments. But then, she should never have taken them on. Knowing that she might become pregnant, she should have recognized that she might be unable to fulfill her commitments. Accepting them was irresponsible. She should have avoided projects of helping others in which they could come to depend upon her, because she was liable to incur overriding obligations to a fetus. Thus, throughout child-bearing years, a woman can act responsibly only by truncating her participation in activities in which others come to depend upon her. But I think this is untenable, for it is central to the life of a morally responsible person to aspire to projects of this sort.

I think it is also central to the life of a morally responsible person that he/she develop abilities which make him/her a useful, productive, contributing member of the community.[11] Doing so often requires large commitments of a person's time, thought, and other personal resources; such commitments are liable to conflict with the activity of nurturing a fetus and raising a child. So, while moral responsibility generally involves a more or less demanding program of developing one's contribution to the community, the anti-abortionists' view requires that a woman refrain from that sort of program. I think that this account of the moral situation of a woman is untenable.

IV

I have argued that the anti-abortionist position that abortion is virtually always wrong is untenable, but I think the other extreme position—that abortion is morally neutral—is equally mistaken. As I have said, I do not think that a fetus can usefully be regarded as a person in discussions of abortion. But it seems to me that the mere fact that it will become a human being, if properly nurtured, indicates that it is entitled to some sort of consideration.[12] I am inclined to think that a pregnant woman has some obligation to nurture a fetus although her obligation is far from absolute.

Further, it is clear that the decision to have, or *not* to have, an abortion does not affect the pregnant woman, alone. It determines whether or not a new member will be brought into the woman's family, her living situation, and her community. Its outcome stands to affect a wide range of others, favorably or unfavorably; their welfare and interests are at stake. Moreover, decisions concerning abortions often occur in situations where there are conflicting commitments and obligations. So, the decision to have an abortion, or not to have one, is not a purely personal matter without moral significance.[13]

I now want to say something about what sorts of considerations generally seem to bear upon the problem of the moral value of a particular abortion.[14]

There seem to me to be (at least) three sorts of considerations relevant to the decision. The first is that as a potential human being, a fetus has some claim to be nurtured; like other claims on her aid, this one can be overridden by other factors in a particular woman's situation. The second relevant consideration is the way in which bearing a child, and possibly raising it, fits into the life of the pregnant woman; she must be able to plan a morally coherent life. Will nurturing the fetus prevent her from fulfilling important obligations to others? Will it prevent her from pursuing her plans for becoming a productive and useful member of her community? Is she in a situation in which she can successfully meet her responsibility to the fetus, if she undertakes to nurture it? It seems to me that the answers to these questions are critical. They may indicate that abortion is morally permissible, and they may even indicate that it is morally required. The third relevant consideration is the way in which having a child will affect others in the woman's family, living situation, and the larger community with which she identifies. If their welfare would be severely diminished by her child-raising activity, then I think she ought not to engage in it. On the other hand, if the welfare of others in her community would be enhanced by her having the child, then I think this is relevant. She then has some obligation to have the child, just as she has some obligation to undertake other projects which contribute to the well-being of others. As a morally sensitive person, she ought to pursue some projects of this sort, but there are limits to her obligations to pursue any one in particular. Let me fill in some of the details.

I believe the most important consideration is how bearing and raising a child would fit into the pregnant woman's life. As I have said, nurturing and developing a child requires a major commitment of one's mental and physical resources. A fetus has some claim on these resources, but it does not take precedence over the claims of others to whom the woman has conflicting obligations. She must choose those projects for helping others and strengthening her productive capability which she will pursue. Projects which interest her, engage her particular skills and talents, and those she will find especially rewarding may be given preference over others. If these factors suggest that she is better suited to other projects, then I think she is not morally obligated to nurture the fetus instead; in such cases, abortion is permissible. I am not suggesting that it is morally permissible to ignore all projects of helping others or contributing to their welfare. It is just that it must be permissible to exercise some control over the projects one undertakes; otherwise, it would be impossible to lead a coherent, morally responsible life.[15]

Consider a couple of examples. Take a young woman in college studying to go to medical school and looking forward to the practice of medicine. If she decides to give birth to a child, and especially if she decides to raise it, she is unlikely to complete her studies.[16] She must choose between nurturing the fetus and preparing herself to help her community in other ways. I see no reason why she should be obligated to choose one project rather than the other. It is a question of which she is more interested in, which she considers more important, which she finds herself better suited to pursue. What about a teen-aged woman who is emotionally immature and, in addition, has no

means of supporting herself? If she cannot successfully meet the obligations involved in nurturing the fetus—say, because of her immaturity or the ridicule to which she is subject in her community—then I think it is absurd to suggest that she is morally required to do so. In another sort of case, a pregnant woman may already have begun projects which make large demands on her resources. They may be projects of raising other children, working with the elderly in her community, or employment in which others are counting on her continued participation. She may face a choice between failing to meet her obligations to others (in case she bears the child) and seeking an abortion. I think she is permitted to choose abortion. In extreme cases of dependence of others on her, she may even be required to seek abortion.

The final consideration relevant to the decision to have an abortion is the welfare of the pregnant woman's family, living companions, and the members of the larger community with which she identifies. Situations in which the welfare of these persons is endangered by her having a child are rare; but suppose, for example, that the family or community does not have resources to feed or care for an additional member, or that the fetus will have a tendency to infection or to socially destructive acts which the community is unable to control. In such cases, the interest of others in preserving their lives or health is violated by admitting the child into their community, and it seems to me that the woman ought not to bear the child (at least in that community). In most such cases, I think the woman would not want to bear the child, since she identifies with the community. Even if she does want to bear the child, I think she ought not to endanger others by doing so.

There are also cases in which others stand to benefit from the pregnant woman's bearing a child. Suppose, for example, that her family needs additional members to help with the production of food, to protect itself, or to carry on some other activity of value to them. Or, there may be those in the woman's community anxious to adopt the child. Another case is found among certain American Indian tribes; they have so few members that there is danger that the gene pool will become too small to sustain a healthy population. Now, the pregnant woman is in a position to benefit these others by having the child, and I think she ought to choose some projects which benefit others. The relevant factors are by now familiar: does she have conflicting prior obligations? Is the strain on her resources excessive? Does she strongly prefer alternative projects for contributing to the welfare of others?[17] If so, her obligation to have the child is overridden. If not, then she ought to have it. The (possible) benefit to others functions like the background claim of the fetus to be nurtured. Both provide reasons why a pregnant woman should decide against abortion and choose to nurture the fetus. But other facts about her situation are also relevant, and the reasons against nurturing the child may outweigh these reasons for it. In a wide variety of situations, abortion may be morally permitted, and in some it is morally required.[18]

Notes

1. For an account of the anti-abortionist position, see Roger Wertheimer, "Understanding the Abortion Argument," *Philosophy and Public Affairs*, 1, 1971. The official Roman Catholic stance on abortion is more complex, and elusive, than the ones discussed here; see Susan T. Nicholson, "The Roman Catholic Doctrine of Therapeutic Abortion," in *Feminism and Philosophy*, ed. by Mary Vetterling-Braggin, Frederick A. Elliston, and Jane English (Totowa, N.J.: Littlefield, Adams, 1977).

2. This argument has most fully and forcefully been made by Baruch Brody in *Abortion and the Sanctity of Human Life* (Cambridge, Mass.: M.I.T. Press, 1975); also see John Finnis, "The Rights and Wrongs of Abortion," *Philosophy and Public Affairs*, 2, 1973.

3. It is difficult to say whether there are other circumstances in which killing is justified—e.g., in cases of capital punishment, or where many lives may be saved by killing a few. It is also difficult to say precisely what sorts of self-defense justify killing—e.g., how immediate and violent the threat must be, how severe the threatened bodily harm must be. Some of these issues are discussed in Brody, op. cit.

4. Of course, no one claims that a fetus has all the rights of a mature person. The fetus is claimed to have the same right as an undisputed person not to be killed, and it is this claim that I want to dispute.

5. Some defenses of the morality of abortion in a fairly wide range of cases depend upon a distinction between removing the fetus and killing it. The general argument is that the pregnant woman may have a right to have the fetus removed, even though she has no right to have it killed. See Judith Jarvis Thomson, "A Defense of Abortion," *Philosophy and Public Affairs*, 1, 1971, and Nicholson, op. cit. My view is that where a pre-viable fetus is concerned, the distinction will not bear this weight.

6. Strictly speaking, this is true only of a fetus prior to the time at which it becomes viable (sometime after the

twenty-fourth week, as things now stand). My claim is that as long as no distinction can be made between withdrawing support of the fetus and killing it, the fetus cannot have the same rights that undisputed persons do. In cases where this distinction can be made, I offer no reason to think that fetuses cannot be treated as undisputed persons.

7. In some of the most interesting discussions of abortion, this point is ignored. Having decided to treat a fetus as a person, the discussants must proceed to make dubious claims about the rights undisputed persons would have in situations comparable to those of fetuses. Thus, Thomson, op. cit., maintains that you are not morally obligated to refrain from killing another person by refusing him/her "the use of your body" when granting it is excessively burdensome. But Brody, op. cit., counters that a person has a right not to be killed, no matter what burdens this restraint places on others (including use of their bodies). Thomson begins with (something like) the point that a person's obligations to aid another are limited and ends by distorting the other's right not to be killed. Brody begins with a person's right not to be killed and ends by distorting another's obligations to aid the person. There appears to be no way to resolve this dispute. The problem, I think, is that the conflict concerns the rights persons are supposed to have in a sort of situation in which undisputed persons are *never found;* and the fact that they are never found in such situations is an indispensable condition of their having the rights they do. In the crucial case, undisputed persons are simply *dis*analogous to fetuses.

8. This would seem to be a better strategy, in any case. For our paradigms of persons are mature, capable, and relatively autonomous adults. Fetuses are much more like very young children than paradigmatic persons. Moreover, it would generally be conceded that a parent's obligations to care for his/her children are much stronger than his/her obligations to help other persons in general.

9. At the same time, a woman who recognizes that she would be unable to fulfill obligations to a fetus or child should take reasonable measures to prevent conception. A pregnant woman in this situation may, or may not, have accepted the responsibility to use whatever safe, effective, and humane means of contraception are available to her. However, in either case, I think that she cannot be morally required to bear responsibilities she knows she cannot meet.

10. The extent to which a woman's activities must be curtailed to meet the obligations involved in nurturing a fetus obviously depends upon the degree to which her community supports her activity. Thus, the absurdity of the anti-abortionists' position, whether it makes reasonable development of a full moral life more or less compatible with meeting one's obligations to fetuses, depends upon the arrangements in any particular community. This, in itself, is reason to be suspicious of the view that abortion, in itself and regardless of the circumstances of the pregnant woman, is morally wrong.

11. There is not space here to argue for the connection between development of one's capacities and a fully moral life; for one interesting treatment, see Larry Blum et al., "Altruism and Women's Oppression," *Philosophical Forum,* 5, 1973–74.

12. This consideration does not seem to me to extend to human eggs or sperms, or other substances which could be developed into human beings. The ovum and sperm are "ingredients" that yield a human being, whereas it is the fetus that becomes a human being. Further, the fact that the genetic makeup of the

fetus is determined, whereas that of an egg or sperm is not, seems to be relevant.

13. Different arguments for a similar view are given by Jane English, "Abortion and the Concept of a Person," *Canadian Journal of Philosophy*, 5, 1975.

14. I will consider only women who did not choose to become pregnant. It is important to remember that a woman may well have accepted the responsibility to use reasonable contraception techniques and still have become pregnant.

15. For a discussion of the role of abortion in exercising responsible control over one's life, see Howard Cohen, "Abortion and the Quality of Life," in *Philosophy and Feminism*, op. cit.

16. If her community provides far-reaching support for child-bearing and rearing-activity, the conflict between having a child and other sorts of useful activity can be greatly diminished. The support provided by public institutions, or other agencies, bears on the decision to have an abortion in almost every case. It is an unfortunate consequence that those who receive least support from their society (the poor and disadvantaged) will be morally required to seek abortion more frequently than those who receive more support. This injustice results from injustice elsewhere in the society.

17. For discussion of the obligations a black woman has to contribute to her community by bearing children, see Toni Cade, "On the Issue of Roles," in *The Black Woman*, ed. by Toni Cade (New York: New American Library, 1970).

18. Thanks are due to Amèlie Rorty, Martin Bunzl, and Onora O'Neill for useful comments on various versions of this paper which began as a talk to undergraduates.

A pregnant woman who is unable or reluctant to bring up the child she bears is often urged to bring the fetus to term and delegate parental duties to others, by offering the child for adoption. She is not faced with the often hard choice: abort or bring up the child.

Raymond Herbenick proposes legal and other measures to enable adoption to occur before birth. The state, he thinks, currently has legal resources in the law of child abandonment, and the duty to employ them to this end. A woman's intention to seek the abortion of a viable fetus is, he urges, tantamount to the "total withdrawal of care and support" that justifies the state in declaring a child abandoned by its parents and making it available for adoption. In applying this law to fetuses, it would be serving the just claims of a minority who currently lack "equal opportunities for parenthood." By increasing the number of completed pregnancies, the state would not only be protecting fetal lives but also redistributing benefits under the "principles of institutional justice." And a woman who bore a child for adoption could count herself as "meeting a social responsibility to those disadvantaged in regard to an equality of opportunity" a just society legally protects for all citizens.

This proposal may be viewed in the light of previous discussions of a woman's right to procreate and her obligations to others, as well as the *Danforth* decision below regarding freedom from interference in reproductive decisions.

REMARKS ON ABORTION, ABANDONMENT, AND ADOPTION OPPORTUNITIES

RAYMOND M. HERBENICK

Some arguments on the legality and morality of elective abortions center on the description of abortion as taking the life of a human fetus. Such arguments often

From *Philosophy and Public Affairs,* © Princeton University Press, 5:1 (Fall 1975), pages 98–104. Reprinted by permission.

assume two things: (1) elective abortions conceptually and practically entail the loss of human fetal life; and (2) elective abortions may justifiably deny the equality of opportunity for parenthood.

The technological prospects of fetal transplantation to natural or artificial wombs suggest that the first assumption need not hold, since technology could make it possible to terminate a human pregnancy in an elective abortion without the loss of fetal life. And Rawlsian principles of institutional justice suggest that the second assumption should not hold since a minority, disadvantaged by nature or social arrangement in its abilities to bear or rear children, would be denied opportunities that normally hold for all under principles of equal citizenship. Such minorities would include the father of a human fetus; the one in ten couples whose marriage is naturally childless; a woman or man not desirous of marriage but desirous of, and qualified for, child rearing; a couple who wish to adopt a child rather than naturally bear children because they are concerned about overpopulation.

If the first assumption does not hold and the second should not hold, views of abortion based on those assumptions require revision.

Sissela Bok has discussed the view that elective abortion is not just taking the life of the human fetus but is also "cessation of bodily life support" or "cessation of continued support."[1] However, neither she nor anyone else has related such redescriptions to the concept of abandonment as it occurs in adoption law. This possibility merits exploration, for it would have important consequences.

The redescription of elective abortion of a human fetus as voluntary abandonment of a child does not, to be sure, conform strictly to the legal concept of the abandonment of a person. Under current judicial usage, abandonment applies to someone already born. But the proposed redescription does seem to respect the following uses of the term "child": (a) the ordinary view that when the fetus is in utero the woman is "with child"; (b) the civil law's view of the unconceived and unborn child as one's next kinship generation, whether natural or adopted; (c) the probate court practice that permits initiation of private adoption proceedings of an unwanted human fetus anytime during pregnancy; (d) the United States Supreme Court's ruling of 18 March 1975 in *Burns* v. *Alcala* that the child in utero may but need not be counted for added welfare benefits to meet the growing nutritional and health care needs of both mother and fetus;[2] and (e) a United States District Court ruling in 1964 permitting a needed fetal blood transfusion contrary to the religious wishes of the parents on the grounds that "the State as *parens patriae* will not allow a parent to abandon a child and so it should not allow this most ultimate of voluntary abandonments."[3] (I shall not examine the possibility that elective fetal abortions could be redescribed as voluntary abandonments of children viewed as property or could conform to the legal concept of the abandonment of property.)

In the general legal theory of adoption in this country, adoption exists only by virtue of statute and not as a matter of natural right. A state thus has the right and power to determine the recipient of the privilege of adoption of one of its wards. It may extend this right to couples or individuals meeting certain qualifications who want the opportunity to adopt and rear a child for their own enhancement and that of the child. Likewise, a state may declare who is a candidate for adoption. Adoption need not even be restricted to minor children. Also, some states permit initiation of adoption proceedings (in the case of a private adoption) through probate court in early pregnancy, although adoption does not take hold until a final decree that is contingent upon live birth, subsequent investigations by a friend of the court, and final consent of the mother. In short, given a state's interest in promoting adoption opportunities for childless and thereby disadvantaged citizens, it may legislate with regard to adoptee, adopter, and adoption procedures.

In the general theory of adoption law, establishment of the legal relationship of adopter and adoptee has the following consequences, at least: (a) entitlement of the adoptee to the name of the adopter, (b) entitlement of the adoptee as an heir of the adopter, (c) entitlement of the adopter to treat the adoptee as his own child so long as the statutory laws are satisfied, and (d) the cessation with the final decree of all legal relationships between natural parent(s) and the adoptee.

A further feature of general adoption law is provision for the case of abandonment. Such abandonments include any conduct on the part of the parent which indicates a firm resolution to forego all parental duties, to relinquish all parental claims to the child, and to renounce and forsake the child entirely. A state is said to be justified in asserting its interest in the child's welfare if one or both parents neglect or refuse to perform both natural and legal obligations of care and support. Thus, even without parental consent and even against parental opposition, a state may assert custody of the child and thereby provide for its placement with, surrender to, and adoption by, qualified persons who will take an interest in the promotion of the child's own interests.

These features are worth noting, for if the elective abortion decision can be redescribed at all as a case of voluntary abandonment of a child on the part of the parent(s), then it follows that a state could assert custody of the child *in utero* and compel surrender upon birth even against the opposition of the parents. But can a plausible case be made for considering an abortion decision on the part of the parent(s) an abandonment? I think a case might be made for this view in at least the matter of elective abortions. The problem of abortions indicated strictly on medical grounds will not be discussed, although such cases could be construed as involuntary or nonvoluntary abandonments.

Two reasons can be produced, the first by examining the point of the two types of decision and the second by comparing the key legal properties of each.

The point of an affirmative elective decision to abort one's fetus for whatever reason, given today's technology, is to terminate the life of a human fetus or to cause it to be delivered dead. Total care and support can thus be said to be withdrawn. Indications of such intent and consent occur in the case of a "botched" elective abortion after which the living but delivered abortus is permitted to die, or positive steps to terminate its life are taken by the physician. In the standard case of a successful abortion, such intent is also present when the abortus is delivered dead. In either case, the point of an affirmative elective abortion decision seems to be to say "no" to pregnancy and childbirth as well as to the future care and support of one's natural child while in utero and at birth. Such voluntary refusal to perform natural and legal obligations of care and support in the present and in the future is tantamount, on this view, to voluntary abandonment in the strong sense, whereas the normal sense of abandonment requires only insufficient care and support through omission, voluntary or involuntary, of natural and legal obligations.

By saying "no" with settled purpose to sufficient, let alone complete, care and support in the abortion decision, the parent(s) seem voluntarily to: relinquish all present and future parental claims to the child in utero and upon live birth; forego all present and future parental duties to the child in utero and upon live birth; and, with the refusal to care for and support the child in utero and in the future, renounce and forsake the child entirely, despite any past due care and support given.

I dare say that the decisions voluntarily to abort and voluntarily to abandon are very similar if not structurally the same except for the time frames. One need only imagine advertisements in a newspaper indicating a one-year-old child for sale and a three-month-old human fetus for sale to perceive the structural similarities. A public agency might very well enter either of these cases on grounds of possible abandonment.

The similarity between elective abortion and voluntary abandonment can be seen by reference to the features of adoption law theory already noted. In an elective abortion it is clear that the parent(s): (a) no longer wish to bestow their legal name on the child in utero and once born; (b) no longer wish to retain the child in utero and, once born, as a legal heir to property; (c) no longer wish to provide support for the child in utero and, once born, as their own; and (d) no longer wish to retain any legal relationship to the child.

Under these conditions, the child in utero might easily be regarded as le-

gally liable for adoption by a suitable adopter who under state law can satisfy these conditions since for all practical purposes the parent(s) refuse total care and support. In principle then and in practice, there seems to be no reason why the elective abortion decision cannot be redescribed as an abandonment decision on the part of the parent(s). Their voluntary consent to a medical abortion is sufficient for the state to intervene by regulatory laws to provide opportunities prior to an abortion for adoption by interested citizens, or for the state itself to place the child in custody in utero as a ward of the state. And if the settled elective abortion judgment occurs at any point in the pregnancy, a state, under this theory, could define procedures for asserting its legitimate redistributive interests on behalf of minorities denied the equal opportunity of parenthood.

Having examined the analogy between elective abortion and voluntary abandonment, a few brief remarks are in order on some of the new policies and practices that would probably have to be considered out of fairness to the parties concerned.

First, it would be necessary to shorten the period before which a state could assert custody of a human fetus. In Ohio, for example, there is a two-year period covering the abandonment of a child, and this might in any case be shortened to reduce the abuse possible through such a lengthy period of time before assertion of custody. Perhaps upon a final decision to have an elective abortion and upon consent to the operation after due professional counseling, a state could treat this consent as evidence of a decision to abandon and thus as a declaration with settled purpose to abandon the fetus forever—no matter when in pregnancy the decision was made.

In the second place, it would be necessary to offer some form of financial assistance, pre-natal medical care and other help needed to protect the health and life of both mother and fetus. This could be justified on the ground that when the state asserts its interest in abandonment it should compensate a woman for any inconvenience she undergoes by carrying a child to term. Such compensation might be funded either directly by the potential adopter or by the state. But protections would be needed to avert "fetal cartels" and "black markets."

Third, it would be necessary to set up an early education program so that adoption could be looked upon as favorably as bearing one's own natural children. Such an early education program could include the establishment of a state or national registry of voluntary adopters of children who wish to adopt an older child, a younger child, or even a human fetus in utero upon the settled consent of the parent(s) to abandon it. Such a registry system could serve to make more consistent the residency requirements for adoptive parents but would require nondiscriminatory protective devices.

In the fourth place, some change in taxation systems would be needed to encourage adoption as an alternative to elective abortions. Adoptive procedures are quite expensive when compared with the cost of an elective abortion. Perhaps an attractive incentive would be to permit a parent in an elective abortion and abandonment decision to receive federal and state tax credit for carrying the human fetus to term. While the human fetus is still a ward of the state, the adoptive parents or parent might also be allowed a federal and state tax credit for a dependent they have agreed to adopt and whose costs they will incur. This double tax credit could provide, in effect, some form of financial relief for the natural parent(s) as well as for the adoptive parent(s). The economic implications doubtless deserve more scrutiny, but such a policy merits review since the costs of abortion should be balanced against the costs of the alternatives to permit a moral choice not unduly constrained by economics.

Fifth, if an elective abortion were viewed as an abandonment, the potential adoptive parent(s) could be more confident of obtaining a child than under present circumstances. While there may be good reasons for a waiting period of six months or longer in other cases, in the case of an elective abortion decision viewed as abandonment the reasons seem much weaker.

In the sixth place, an adoptive insurance system for potential adoptive parents might be set up to insure parents against the trauma of a defective child requiring extraordinary care or of a change of mind by the natural mother after birth.

Seventh, revision of the penalties for abandonment (which presently include imprisonment) would be in order with a view towards rehabilitation.

Finally, under such a system persons who genuinely did not want another child could—in all honesty—say to themselves that the child was abandoned but its life not taken, thus meeting a social responsibility to those disadvantaged in regard to the equality of opportunity for parenthood.

If the preceding redescription of elective abortion as voluntary abandonment is plausible, then any justification for elective abortions requires not merely a defense of taking fetal life but also a defense of totally withdrawing care and support in violation of one's natural or legal obligations. And if a justification for total withdrawal of care and support is forthcoming, this view still seems to require the promotion and satisfaction of equal opportunities for parenthood rather than their denial to minorities disadvantaged in this respect in a society committed to equality of opportunity under law for all citizens.

Notes

1. Sissela Bok, "Ethical Problems of Abortion," *Hastings Center Studies* 2, no. 1, January 1974, 34.
2. Burns v. Alcala, 420 U.S. 575 (1975).
3. Application of President of Georgetown University Hospital, 331 F. 2d 1000 at 10009 D.C. Cir. (1964), cert. denied 337 U.S. 985 (1964). Cited in John T. Noonan, Jr., *The Morality of Abortion* (Cambridge, Mass.: Harvard University Press, 1970), pp. 244–245.

Much philosophical debate ignores the parental and familial aspects of an abortion decision. A pregnant woman does not ask, Is the fetus a person? and wait for a reasoned philosophical answer. She faces the urgent question, Shall I become a parent (again)? Her answer has serious consequences not only for her fetus, whatever its metaphysical status, but also for her husband and/or lover, her other actual and possible children, and her own parents. What part should they or their interests play in her decision?

Traditionally, these family voices have allowed her little say in the matter. But new techniques of contraception and abortion have given women new power that is reflected somewhat in recent Supreme Court rulings. In *Roe* v. *Wade*, the Court excluded the State from first-trimester abortion decisions. But the Missouri legislature, among others, tried to preserve the traditional authority of husband and parents, by requiring spousal consent or, if the woman were unmarried and under age, parental consent to a first-trimester abortion.

In the opinions reprinted here, the Court majority ruled that such power of consent would give husband or parents "absolute, and possibly arbitrary veto" over a decision that a woman and her physician were granted in *Roe*. Only a minority endorsed the judgment by the State that "the mother's interest in avoiding the burdens of child rearing do [*sic*] not outweigh or snuff out the father's interest in participating in bringing up his own child." This same minority held parental consent necessary if a minor is to make "this important and irreparable" decision in the light of her own best interests. (They did not, however, ask whether required parental *consultation,* rather than consent, would be equally effective in this regard.) The majority found this inconsistent with *Roe*.

It also rejected Missouri's attempt to prohibit second-trimester abortions by saline amniocentesis, on grounds of the technique's threat to "maternal health." (We do not reprint the detailed opinions on this matter, even though they show how professed concern for "maternal health" may be a devious way of prohibiting second-trimester abortions.) And, although the majority of justices question the legislature's motives (see notes 5 and 6, pp. 70–1), they endorse written consent required from the woman herself in order to "insure that the pregnant woman retains control over the discretions of her consulting physician."

Thereby the Court has limited, not only parents, but physicians and legislators who would act *in loco parentis*. Nevertheless, *Roe* v. *Wade* and this decision allow State paternalistic supervision in the second trimester and the State's interference, as *parens patriae* (of the fetus) in the third. In some respects, women are still treated as minors by the law in reproductive matters.

PLANNED PARENTHOOD OF CENTRAL MISSOURI V. DANFORTH, ATTORNEY GENERAL OF MISSOURI

PLANNED PARENTHOOD OF CEN-
TRAL MISSOURI et al., Appellants, v.
JOHN C. DANFORTH, Attorney General of the State of Missouri, et al. (No.
74-1151). JOHN C. DANFORTH, Attorney General of the State of Missouri,
Appellant, v. PLANNED PARENT-
HOOD OF CENTRAL MISSOURI et
al. 428 U.S. 52 (1976). Argued before the
United States Supreme Court March 23,
1976. Decided July 1, 1976.

Summary

In litigation instituted in the United
States District Court for the Eastern District of Missouri, a challenge was made
to the validity, under the United States
Constitution, of a Missouri statute setting forth conditions and limitations on
abortions and establishing criminal offenses for noncompliance with the various conditions and limitations. The specific provisions of the statute attacked
were (1) a viability definition provision
defining "viability," for purposes of a
provision that no abortion not necessary
to preserve the life or health of the
mother should be performed unless the
attending physician would certify with
reasonable medical certainty that the
fetus is not viable, as that stage of fetal
development when the life of the unborn
child may be continued indefinitely outside the womb by natural or artificial
life-supportive systems, (2) a pregnant
woman's consent provision, requiring
that a woman, prior to submitting to an
abortion during the first 12 weeks of
pregnancy, must certify in writing her
consent to the procedure and that her
consent is informed, freely given, and not
the result of coercion, (3) a spousal consent provision, requiring the prior written consent of the spouse of a woman
seeking an abortion during the first 12
weeks of pregnancy, unless the abortion
were certified by a physician to be necessary for preservation of the mother's
life, (4) a parental consent provision, requiring, with respect to the first 12 weeks
of pregnancy where the pregnant woman
is unmarried and under 18 years of age,
the written consent of a parent or person
in loco parentis unless the abortion were
certified by a physician as necessary for
preservation of the mother's life, (5) a
saline amniocentesis prohibition provision, describing the saline amniocentesis
technique of abortion as one whereby

the amniotic fluid is withdrawn and a saline or other fluid is inserted into the amniotic sac, and prohibiting such method of abortion after the first 12 weeks of pregnancy, (6) recordkeeping and reporting provisions, imposing requirements upon health facilities and physicians concerned with abortions irrespective of the pregnancy stage, and (7) a standard of care provision, declaring, in its first sentence, that no person who performs or induces an abortion shall fail to exercise that degree of professional skill, care, and diligence to preserve the life and health of the fetus which such person would be required to exercise in order to preserve the life and health of any fetus intended to be born and not aborted, and providing, in its second sentence, that any physician or person assisting in an abortion who failed to take such measures to encourage or sustain the life of. the child would be deemed guilty of manslaughter if the child's death resulted. The District Court upheld the constitutionality of the several challenged provisions of the statute with the exception of the first sentence of the standard of care provision (392 F Supp 1362).

On direct appeals from the decision of the three-judge District Court, the United States Supreme Court affirmed in part, reversed in part, and remanded. In an opinion by BLACKMUN, J., it was held: expressing the unanimous view of the court, that (1) the viability definition provision, which reflected the fact that the determination of viability, varying with each pregnancy, was a matter for the judgment of the responsible attending physician, was not unconstitutional, since it did not circumvent the permissible limitations on state regulation of abortions, (2) the pregnant woman's consent provision was not un-

constitutional since the state could validly require a pregnant woman's prior written consent for an abortion to assure awareness of the abortion decision and its significance, and (3) the record-keeping and reporting provisions were not constitutionally offensive in themselves and imposed no legally significant impact or consequence on the abortion decision or on the physician-patient relationship; expressing the view of six members of the court, that (4) the spousal consent provision was unconstitutional, since the state, being unable to regulate or proscribe abortions during the first stage of pregnancy when a physician and patient make such decision, could not delegate authority to any particular person, even a pregnant woman's spouse, to prevent abortion during the first stage of pregnancy, (5) the first sentence of the standard of care provision was unconstitutional, since it impermissibly required a physician to preserve the life and health of a fetus, whatever the stage of the pregnancy, such unconstitutional first sentence not being severable from the second sentence establishing manslaughter for violation of the standard of care, notwithstanding that the Missouri statute contained a severability provision; and, expressing the view of five members of the court, that (6) the parental consent provision was unconstitutional, since the state did not have the constitutional authority to give a third party an absolute, and possibly arbitrary, veto over the decision of a physician and his patient to terminate the patient's pregnancy, regardless of the reason for withholding the consent, and (7) the saline amniocentesis prohibition provision was unconstitutional since it failed as a reasonable regulation for the protection of maternal health, being instead an unreasonable or arbitrary regulation designed to inhibit the vast majority of abortions after the first 12 weeks of pregnancy.

STEWART, J., joined by POWELL, J., concurring, expressed the view that (1) the critical factor upholding the constitutionality of the viability definition provision was that there was little chance that a physician's professional decision to perform an abortion would be chilled since under the Missouri statute a physician could not be punished for erroneously concluding that a fetus was not viable, (2) with respect to the constitutionality of the pregnant woman's consent provision, the state was not precluded from enacting a law aimed at insuring that the abortion decision was made in a knowing, intelligent, voluntary fashion, (3) as to the unconstitutionality of the spousal consent provision, a woman's constitutionally protected right to decide whether to terminate her pregnancy outweighed the constitutionally protected right of a man to father children and enjoy the association of his offspring, (4) the parental consent provision was unconstitutional since it imposed an absolute limitation on a minor's right to obtain an abortion, and (5) the saline amniocentesis prohibition provision was unconstitutional since, at the time the provision was enacted, the prohibition of the technique was almost tantamount to a prohibition of any abortion in the state after the first 12 weeks of pregnancy.

WHITE, J., joined by BURGER, Ch. J., and REHNQUIST, J., concurred in part, but dissented on the ground that (1) the spousal consent provision was valid as representing the state's permissible judgment that a mother's interest in avoiding the burdens of child rearing did not outweigh a father's interest in participating in bringing up his own child, (2) the parental consent provision was valid since

Missouri was entitled to protect a minor unmarried woman from making the important and irreparable abortion decision by requiring parental consultation and consent, (3) the saline amniocentesis prohibition provision could not be struck down, since there was no evidence that a safer method of abortion was unavailable at any time relevant to the case, and (4) the standard of care provision was constitutional, being plainly intended to require, as the state might permissibly require, that where a fetus had the capability of meaningful life outside the mother's womb, an abortion had to be handled in a way that would preserve that life, notwithstanding the mother's desire to terminate it.

STEVENS, J., concurring in part and dissenting in part, expressed the view that (1) the Missouri legislature could, consistent with the Constitution, outlaw one of two abortion procedures equally available to Missouri women which the legislature found to be the less safe, but that the legislature's prohibition of the saline amniocentesis technique was unconstitutional since at the time the provision was enacted the prohibition of such technique was almost tantamount to a prohibition of any abortion in the state after the first 12 weeks of pregnancy, and (2) the parental consent provision was valid, since the state had a sufficient interest in the welfare of its young citizens to support such a requirement.

Opinion of the Court

Mr. Justice Blackmun delivered the opinion of the Court.

This case is a logical and anticipated corollary to Roe v. Wade, 410 US 113, 35 L Ed 2d 147, 93 S Ct 705 (1973), and Doe v. Bolton, 410 US 179, 35 L Ed 2d 201, 93 S Ct 739 (1973), for it raises issues secondary to those that were then before the Court. Indeed, some of the questions now presented were forecast and reserved in Roe and Doe. 410 US, at 165 n 67, 35 L Ed 2d 147, 93 S Ct 705.

I

. . . In June 1974, somewhat more than a year after Roe and Doe had been decided, Missouri's 77th General Assembly, in its Second Regular Session, enacted House Committee Substitute for House Bill No. 1211 (hereinafter referred to as the "Act"). The legislation was approved by the Governor on June 14, 1974, and became effective immediately by reason of an emergency clause contained in § A of the statute. The Act is set forth in full as the Appendix to this opinion. It imposes a structure for the control and regulation of abortions in Missouri during all stages of pregnancy.

II

Three days after the Act became effective, the present litigation was instituted in the United States District Court for the Eastern District of Missouri. The plaintiffs are Planned Parenthood of Central Missouri, a not-for-profit Missouri corporation which maintains facilities in Columbia, Mo., for the performance of abortions; David Hall, M.D.; and Michael Freiman, M.D. Doctor Hall is a resident of Columbia, is licensed as a physician in Missouri, is chairman of the Department and Professor of Obstetrics and Gynecology at the University of Missouri Medical School at Columbia, and supervises abortions at the Planned Parenthood facility. He was described by the three-judge court in the 1973 case as one of four plaintiffs who were "eminent,

Missouri-licensed obstetricians and gynecologists." No. 73–426, Danforth v. Rodgers, Juris. Statement A7. Doctor Freiman is a resident of St. Louis, is licensed as a physician in Missouri, is an instructor of Clinical Obstetrics and Gynecology at Washington University Medical School, and performs abortions at two St. Louis hospitals and at a clinic in that city.

The named defendants are the Attorney General of Missouri and the Circuit Attorney of the city of St. Louis "in his representative capacity" and "as the representative of the class of all similar Prosecuting Attorneys of the various counties of the State of Missouri." Complaint 10.

The plaintiffs brought the action on their own behalf and, purportedly, "on behalf of the entire class consisting of duly licensed physicians and surgeons presently performing or desiring to perform the termination of pregnancies and on behalf of the entire class consisting of their patients desiring the termination of pregnancy, all within the State of Missouri." Id., at 9. Plaintiffs sought declaratory relief and also sought to enjoin enforcement of the Act on the ground, among others, that certain of its provisions deprived them and their patients of various constitutional rights: "the right to privacy in the physician-patient relationship"; the physicians' "right to practice medicine according to the highest standards of medical practice"; the female patients' right to determine whether to bear children; the patients' "right to life due to the inherent risk involved in childbirth" or in medical procedures alternative to abortion; the physicians' "right to give and plaintiffs' patients' right to receive safe and adequate medical advice and treatment, pertaining to the decision of whether to carry a given pregnancy to term and method of termination"; the patients' right under the Eighth Amendment to be free from cruel and unusual punishment "by forcing and coercing them to bear each pregnancy they conceive"; and, by being placed "in the position of decision making beset with . . . inherent possibilities of bias and conflict of interest," the physician's right to due process of law guaranteed by the Fourteenth Amendment. Id., at 10–11.

The particular provisions of the Act that remained under specific challenge at the end of trial were § 2(2), defining the term "viability"; § 3(2), requiring from the woman, prior to submitting to abortion during the first 12 weeks of pregnancy, a certification in writing that she consents to the procedure and "that her consent is informed and freely given and is not the result of coercion"; § 3(3), requiring, for the same period, "the written consent of the woman's spouse, unless the abortion is certified by a licensed physician to be necessary in order to preserve the life of the mother"; § 3(4), requiring, for the same period, "the written consent of one parent or person in loco parentis of the woman if the woman is unmarried and under the age of eighteen years, unless the abortion is certified by a licensed physician as necessary in order to preserve the life of the mother"; § 6(1), requiring the physician to exercise professional care "to preserve the life and health of the fetus" and, failing such, deeming him guilty of manslaughter and making him liable in an action for damages; § 7, declaring an infant, who survives "an attempted abortion which was not performed to save the life or health of the mother," to be "an abandoned ward of the state under the juris-

diction of the juvenile court," and depriving the mother, and also the father if he consented to the abortion, of parental rights; § 9, the legislative finding that method of abortion known as saline amniocentesis "is deleterious to maternal health," and prohibiting that method after the first 12 weeks of pregnancy; and §§ 10 and 11, imposing reporting and maintenance of record requirements for health facilities and for physicians who perform abortions. . . .

For convenience, we shall usually refer to the plaintiffs as "appellants" and to both named defendants as "appellees."

III

In Roe v. Wade the Court concluded that the "right of privacy, whether it be founded in the Fourteenth Amendment's concept of personal liberty and restrictions upon state action, as we feel it is, or, as the District Court determined, in the Ninth Amendment's reservation of rights to the people, is broad enough to encompass a woman's decision whether or not to terminate her pregnancy." 410 US, at 153, 35 L Ed 2d 147, 93 S Ct 705. It emphatically rejected, however, the proffered argument "that the woman's right is absolute and that she is entitled to terminate her pregnancy at whatever time, in whatever way, and for whatever reason she alone chooses." Ibid. Instead, this right "must be considered against important state interests in regulation." Id., at 154, 35 L Ed 2d 147, 93 S Ct 705.

The Court went on to say that the "pregnant woman cannot be isolated in her privacy," for she "carries an embryo and, later, a fetus." Id., at 159, 35 L Ed 2d 147, 93 S Ct 705. It was therefore "reasonable and appropriate for a State to decide that at some point in time another interest, that of health of the mother or that of potential human life, becomes significantly involved. The woman's privacy is no longer sole and any right of privacy she possesses must be measured accordingly." Ibid. The Court stressed the measure of the State's interest in "the light of present medical knowledge." Id., at 163, 35 L Ed 2d 147, 93 S Ct 705. It concluded that the permissibility of state regulation was to be viewed in three stages: "For the stage prior to approximately the end of the first trimester, the abortion decision and its effectuation must be left to the medical judgment of the pregnant woman's attending physician," without interference from the State. Id., at 164, 35 L Ed 2d 147, 93 S Ct 705. The participation by the attending physician in the abortion decision, and his responsibility in that decision, thus, were emphasized. After the first stage, as so described, the State may, if it chooses, reasonably regulate the abortion procedure to preserve and protect maternal health. Ibid. Finally, for the stage subsequent to viability, a point purposefully left flexible for professional determination, and dependent upon developing medical skills and technical ability,[1] the State may regulate an abortion to protect the life of the fetus and even may proscribe abortion except where it is necessary, in appropriate medical judgment, for the preservation of the life or health of the mother. Id., at 163–165, 35 L Ed 2d 147, 93 S Ct 705.

IV

. . . Our primary task, then, is to consider each of the challenged provisions of the new Missouri abortion statute in the particular light of the opinions and decisions in Roe and in Doe. To this we now turn, with the assistance of helpful briefs from both sides and from some of the amici.

A

[4] *The definition of viability.* Section 2(2) of the Act defines "viability" as "that stage of fetal development when the life of the unborn child may be continued indefinitely outside the womb by natural or artificial life-supportive systems." Appellants claim that this definition violates and conflicts with the discussion of viability in our opinion in Roe. 410 US, at 160, 163, 35 L Ed 2d 147, 93 S Ct 705. In particular, appellants object to the failure of the definition to contain any reference to a gestational time period, to its failure to incorporate and reflect the three stages of pregnancy, to the presence of the word "indefinitely," and to the extra burden of regulation imposed. It is suggested that the definition expands the Court's definition of viability, as expressed in Roe, and amounts to a legislative determination of what is properly a matter for medical judgment. It is said that the "mere possibility of momentary survival is not the medical standard of viability." Brief for Appellants 67.

In Roe, we used the term "viable," properly we thought, to signify the point at which the fetus is "potentially able to live outside the mother's womb, albeit with artificial aid," and presumably capable of "meaningful life outside the mother's womb," 410 US, at 160, 163, 35 L Ed 2d 147, 93 S Ct 705. We noted that this point "is usually placed" at about seven months or 28 weeks, but may occur earlier. Id., at 160, 35 L Ed 2d 147, 93 S Ct 705.

We agree with the District Court and conclude that the definition of viability in the Act does not conflict with what was said and held in Roe. In fact, we believe that § 2(c), even when read in conjunction with § 5 (proscribing an abortion "not necessary to preserve the life or health of the mother . . . unless the attending physician first certifies with reasonable medical certainty that the fetus is not viable"), the constitutionality of which is not explicitly challenged here, reflects an attempt on the part of the Missouri General Assembly to comply with our observations and discussion in Roe relating to viability. Appellant Hall, in his deposition, had no particular difficulty with the statutory definition.[2] As noted above, we recognized in Roe that viability was a matter of medical judgment, skill, and technical ability, and we preserved the flexibility of the term. Section 2(2) does the same. Indeed, one might argue, as the appellees do, that the presence of the statute's words "continued indefinitely" favor, rather than disfavor, the appellants, for, arguably, the point when life can be "continued indefinitely outside the womb" may well occur later in pregnancy than the point where the fetus is "potentially able to live outside the mother's womb." Roe v. Wade, 410 US, at 160, 35 L Ed 2d 147, 93 S Ct 705.

In any event, we agree with the District Court that it is not the proper function of the legislature or the courts to place viability, which essentially is a medical concept, at a specific point in the gestation period. The time when viability is achieved may vary with each pregnancy, and the determination of whether a particular fetus is viable is, and must be, a matter for the judgment of the responsible attending physician. The definition of viability in § 2(2) merely reflects this fact. The appellees do not contend otherwise, for they insist

that the determination of viability rests with the physician in the exercise of his professional judgment.[3]

We thus do not accept appellants' contention that a specified number of weeks in pregnancy must be fixed by statute as the point of viability. See Wolfe v. Schroering, 388 F Supp 631, 637 (WD Ky 1974); Hodgson v. Anderson, 378 F Supp 1008, 1016 (Minn 1974), dismd for want of jurisdiction sub nom Spannaus v. Hodgson, 420 US 903, 42 L Ed 2d 832, 95 S Ct 819 (1975).[4]

We conclude that the definition in § 2(2) of the Act does not circumvent the limitations on state regulation outlined in Roe. We therefore hold that the Act's definition of "viability," comports with Roe and withstands the constitutional attack made upon it in this litigation.

B

[5] *The woman's consent.* Under § 3(2) of the Act, a woman, prior to submitting to an abortion during the first 12 weeks of pregnancy, must certify in writing her consent to the procedure and "that her consent is informed and freely given and is not the result of coercion." Appellants argue that this requirement is violative of Roe v. Wade, 410 US, at 164–165, 35 L Ed 2d 147, 93 S Ct 705, by imposing an extra layer and burden of regulation on the abortion decision. See Doe v. Bolton, 410 US, at 195–200, 35 L Ed 2d 201, 93 S Ct 739. Appellants also claim that the provision is overbroad and vague.

The District Court's majority relied on the propositions that the decision to terminate a pregnancy, of course, "is often a stressful one," and that the consent requirement of § 3(2) "insures that the pregnant woman retains control over the discretions of her consulting physician." 392 F Supp, at 1368, 1369. The majority also felt that the consent requirement "does not single out the abortion procedure, but merely includes it within the category of medical operations for which consent is required."⁵ Id., at 1369. The third judge joined the majority in upholding § 3(2), but added that the written consent requirement was "not burdensome or chilling" and manifested "a legitimate interest of the state that this important decision has in fact been made by the person constitutionally empowered to do so." 392 F Supp, at 1374. He went on to observe that the requirement "in no way interposes the state or third parties in the decision-making process." Id., at 1375.

[6] We do not disagree with the result reached by the District Court as to § 3(2). It is true that Doe and Roe clearly establish that the State may not restrict the decision of the patient and her physician regarding abortion during the first stage of pregnancy. Despite the fact that apparently no other Missouri statute, with the exceptions referred to in n 5, supra, requires a patient's prior written consent to a surgical procedure,⁶ the imposition by § 3(2) of such a requirement for termination of pregnancy even during the first stage, in our view, is not in itself an unconstitutional requirement. The decision to abort, indeed, is an important, and often a stressful one, and it is desirable and imperative that it be made with full knowledge of its nature and consequences. The woman is the one primarily concerned, and her awareness of the decision and its significance may be assured, constitutionally, by the State to the extent of requiring her prior written consent.

[7] We could not say that a requirement imposed by the State that a prior

written consent for any surgery would be unconstitutional. As a consequence, we see no constitutional defect in requiring it only for some types of surgery as, for example, an intracardiac procedure, or where the surgical risk is elevated above a specified mortality level, or, for that matter, for abortions.⁷

C

[8] *The spouse's consent.* Section 3(3) requires the prior written consent of the spouse of the woman seeking an abortion during the first 12 weeks of pregnancy, unless "the abortion is certified by a licensed physician to be necessary in order to preserve the life of the mother."⁸

The appellees defend § 3(3) on the ground that it was enacted in the light of the General Assembly's "perception of marriage as an institution," Brief for Appellees 34, and that any major change in family status is a decision to be made jointly by the marriage partners. Reference is made to an abortion's possible effect on the woman's child-bearing potential. It is said that marriage always has entailed some legislatively imposed limitations: reference is made to adultery and bigamy as criminal offenses; to Missouri's general requirement, Mo Rev Stat § 453.030.3 (1969), that for an adoption of a child born in wedlock the consent of both parents is necessary; to similar joint consent requirements imposed by a number of States with respect to artificial insemination and the legitimacy of children so conceived; to the laws of two States requiring spousal consent for voluntary sterilization; and to the long-established requirement of spousal consent for the effective disposition of an interest in real property. It is argued that "[r]ecognizing that the consent of both parties is generally necessary . . . to begin a family, the legislature has determined that a change in the family structure set in motion by mutual consent should be terminated only by mutual consent," Brief for Appellees 38, and that what the legislature did was to exercise its inherent policymaking power "for what was believed to be in the best interests of all people of Missouri." Id., at 40.

The appellants, on the other hand, contend that § 3(3) obviously is designed to afford the husband the right unilaterally to prevent or veto an abortion, whether or not he is the father of the fetus, and that this not only violates Roe and Doe but is also in conflict with other decided cases. See, e.g., Poe v. Gerstein, 517 F2d 787, 794–796 (CA5 1975), Juris Statement pending, No. 75–713; Wolfe v. Schroering, 388 F Supp, at 636–637; Doe v. Rampton, 366 F Supp 189, 193 (Utah 1973). They also refer to the situation where the husband's consent cannot be obtained because he cannot be located. And they assert that § 3(3) is vague and overbroad.

In Roe and Doe we specifically reserved decision on the question whether a requirement for consent by the father of the fetus, by the spouse, or by the parents, or a parent, of an unmarried minor, may be constitutionally imposed. 410 US, at 165 n 67, 35 L Ed 2d 147, 93 S Ct 705. We now hold that the State may not constitutionally require the consent of the spouse, as is specified under § 3(3) of the Missouri Act, as a condition for abortion during the first 12 weeks of pregnancy. We thus agree with the dissenting judge in the present case, and with the courts whose decisions are cited above, that the State cannot "delegate to a spouse a veto power which the state itself is absolutely and totally prohibited from exercising during the first trimester of pregnancy." 392 F Supp, at 1375. Clearly, since the State cannot regulate or proscribe abortion during the first stage, when the physician and his patient make that decision, the State cannot delegate authority to any particular person, even the spouse, to prevent abortion during that same period.

[9a] We are not unaware of the deep and proper concern and interest that a devoted and protective husband has in his wife's pregnancy and in the growth and development of the fetus she is carrying. Neither has this Court failed to appreciate the importance of the marital relationship in our society. See, e.g., Griswold v. Connecticut, 381 US 479, 486, 14 L Ed 2d 510, 85 S Ct 1678 (1965); Maynard v. Hill, 125 US 190, 211, 31 L Ed 654, 8 S Ct 723 (1888).[9] Moreover, we recognize that the decision whether to undergo or to forgo an abortion may have profound effects on the future of any marriage, effects that are both physical and mental, and possibly deleterious. Notwithstanding these factors, we cannot hold that the State has the constitutional authority to give the spouse unilaterally the ability to prohibit the wife from terminating her pregnancy, when the State itself lacks that right. See Eisenstadt v. Baird, 405 US 438, 453, 31 L Ed 2d 349, 92 S Ct 1029 (1972).[10]

It seems manifest that, ideally, the decision to terminate a pregnancy should be one concurred in by both the wife and her husband. No marriage may be viewed as harmonious or successful if the marriage partners are fundamentally divided on so important and vital an issue. But it is difficult to believe that the goal of fostering mutuality and trust in a marriage, and of strengthening the marital relationship and the marriage institution, will be achieved by giving the husband a veto power exercisable for any reason whatsoever or for no reason at all. Even if the State had the ability to delegate to the husband a power it itself could not exercise, it is not at all likely that such action would further, as the District Court majority phrased it, the "interest of the state in protecting the mutuality of decisions vital to the marriage relationship." 392 F Supp, at 1370.

We recognize, of course, that when a woman, with the approval of her physician but without the approval of her husband, decides to terminate her pregnancy, it could be said that she is acting unilaterally. The obvious fact is that when the wife and the husband disagree on this decision, the view of only one of the two marriage partners can prevail. Since it is the woman who physically bears the child and who is the more directly and immediately affected by the pregnancy, as between the two, the balance weighs in her favor. Cf. Roe v. Wade, 410 US, at 153, 35 L Ed 2d 147, 93 S Ct 705.

We conclude that § 3(3) of the Missouri Act is inconsistent with the standards enunciated in Roe v. Wade, 410 US, at 164–165, 35 L Ed 2d 147, 93 S Ct 705, and is unconstitutional. It is therefore unnecessary for us to consider the appellant's additional challenges to § 3(3) based on vagueness and overbreadth.

D

[10] *Parental consent.* Section 3(4) requires, with respect to the first 12 weeks of pregnancy, where the woman is unmarried and under the age of 18 years, the written consent of a parent or person in loco parentis unless, again, "the abortion is certified by a licensed physician as necessary in order to preserve the life of the mother." It is to be observed that only one parent need consent.

The appellees defend the statute in several ways. They point out that the law properly may subject minors to more stringent limitations than are permissible with respect to adults, and they cite, among other cases, Prince v. Massachusetts, 321 US 158, 88 L Ed 645, 64 S Ct 438 (1944), and McKeiver v. Pennsylvania, 403 US 528, 29 L Ed 2d 647, 91 S Ct 1976 (1971). Missouri law, it is said, "is replete with provisions reflecting the interest of the state in assuring the welfare of minors," citing statutes relating to a guardian ad litem for a court proceeding, to the care of delinquent and neglected children, to child labor, and to compulsory education. Brief for Appellees 42. Certain decisions are considered by the State to be outside the scope of a minor's ability to act in his own best interest or in the interest of the public, citing statutes proscribing the sale of firearms and deadly weapons to minors without parental consent, and other statutes relating to minors' exposure to certain types of literature, the purchase by pawnbrokers of property from minors, and the sale of cigarettes and alcoholic beverages to minors. It is pointed out that the record contains testimony to the effect that children of tender years (even ages 10 and 11) have sought abortions. Thus, a State's permitting a child to obtain an abortion without the counsel of an adult "who has responsibility or concern for the child would constitute an irresponsible abdication of the State's duty to protect the welfare of minors." Id., at 44. Parental discretion, too, has been protected from unwarranted or unreasonable interference from the State, citing Meyer v. Nebraska, 262 US 390, 67 L Ed 1042, 43 S Ct 625, 29 ALR 1446 (1923); Pierce v. Society of Sisters, 268 US 510, 69 L Ed 1070, 45 S Ct 571, 39 ALR 468 (1925); Wisconsin v. Yoder, 406 US 205, 32 L Ed 2d 15, 92 S Ct 1526 (1972). Finally, it is said that § 3(4) imposes no additional burden on the physician because even prior to the passage of the Act the physician would require parental consent before performing an abortion on a minor.

The appellants, in their turn, emphasize that no other Missouri statute specifically requires the additional consent of a minor's parent for medical or surgical treatment, and that in Missouri a minor legally may consent to medical services for pregnancy (excluding abortion), venereal disease, and drug abuse. Mo Laws 1971, p 425–426, HB No. 73, §§ 1–3. The result of § 3(4), it is said, "is the ultimate supremacy of the parents' desires over those of the minor child, the pregnant patient." Brief for Appellants 93. It is noted that in Missouri a woman who marries with parental consent under the age of 18 does not require parental consent to abort, and yet her contemporary who has chosen not to marry must obtain parental approval.

The District Court majority recognized that, in contrast to § 3(3), the State's interest in protecting the mutuality of a marriage relationship is not present with respect to § 3(4). It found "a compelling basis," however, in the State's interest "in safeguarding the authority of the family relationship." 392 F Supp, at 1370. The dissenting judge observed that one could not seriously argue that a minor must submit to an abortion if her parents insist, and he could not see "why she would not be entitled to the same right of self-determination now explicitly accorded to adult women, provided she is sufficiently mature to understand the procedure and to make an intelligent assessment of her circumstances with the advice of her physician." Id., at 1376.

Of course, much of what has been said above, with respect to § 3(3), applies with equal force to § 3(4). Other courts, that have considered the parental consent issue in the light of Roe and Doe, have concluded that a statute like § 3(4) does not withstand constitutional scrutiny. See, e. g., Poe v. Gerstein, 517 F2d, at 792; Wolfe v. Schroering, 388 F Supp, at 636–637; Doe v. Rampton, 366 F Supp, at 193, 199; State v. Koome, 84 Wash 2d 901, 530 P2d 260 (1975).

We agree with appellants and with the courts whose decisions have just been cited that the State may not impose a blanket provision, such as § 3(4) requiring the consent of a parent or person in loco parentis as a condition for abortion of an unmarried minor during the first 12 weeks of her pregnancy. Just as with the requirement of consent from the spouse, so here, the State does not have the constitutional authority to give a third party an absolute, and possibly arbitrary, veto over the decision of the physician and his patient to terminate the patient's pregnancy, regardless of the reason for withholding the consent.

[11] Constitutional rights do not mature and come into being magically only when one attains the state-defined age of majority. Minors, as well as adults, are protected by the Constitution and possess constitutional rights. See, e. g., Breed v. Jones, 421 US 519, 44 L Ed 2d 346, 95 S Ct 1779 (1975); Goss v. Lopez, 419 US 565, 42 L Ed 2d 725, 95 S Ct 729 (1975); Tinker v. Des Moines School District, 393 US 503, 21 L Ed 2d 731, 89 S Ct 733, 49 Ohio Ops 2d 222 (1969); In re Gault, 387 US 1, 18 L Ed 2d 527, 87 S Ct 1428, 40 Ohio Ops 2d 378 (1967). The Court indeed, however, long has recognized that the State has somewhat broader authority to regulate the activities of children than of adults. Prince v. Massachusetts, 321 US, at 170, 88 L Ed 645, 64 S Ct 438; Ginsberg v. New York, 390 US 629, 20 L Ed 2d 195,

88 S Ct 1274, 44 Ohio Ops 2d 339 (1968). It remains, then, to examine whether there is any significant state interest in conditioning an abortion on the consent of a parent or person in loco parentis that is not present in the case of an adult.

One suggested interest is the safeguarding of the family unit and of parental authority. 392 F Supp, at 1370. It is difficult, however, to conclude that providing a parent with absolute power to overrule a determination, made by the physician and his minor patient, to terminate the patient's pregnancy will serve to strengthen the family unit. Neither is it likely that such veto power will enhance parental authority or control where the minor and the nonconsenting parent are so fundamentally in conflict and the very existence of the pregnancy already has fractured the family structure. Any independent interest the parent may have in the termination of the minor daughter's pregnancy is no more weighty than the right of privacy of the competent minor mature enough to have become pregnant.

We emphasize that our holding that § 3(4) is invalid does not suggest that every minor, regardless of age or maturity, may give effective consent for termination of her pregnancy. See Bellotti v. Baird, —— US ——, 49 L Ed 2d 844, 96 S Ct ——. The fault with § 3(4) is that it imposes a special consent provision, exercisable by a person other than the woman and her physician, as a prerequisite to a minor's termination of her pregnancy and does so without a sufficient justification for the restriction. It violates the strictures of Roe and Doe. . . .

The judgment of the District Court is affirmed in part and reversed in part and the case is remanded for further proceedings consistent with this opinion.

It is so ordered.

Notes

1. "Viability is usually placed at about seven months (28 weeks) but may occur earlier, even at 24 weeks." Roe v. Wade, 410 US 113, 160, 35 L Ed 2d 147, 93 S Ct 705 (1973).
2. "[A]lthough I agree with the definition of 'viability,' I think it must be understood that viability is a very difficult state to assess." Transcript 369.
3. "The determination of when the fetus is viable rests, as it should, with the physician, in the exercise of his medical judgment, on a case-by-case basis." Brief for Appellees 26. "Because viability may vary from patient to patient and with advancements in medical technology, it is essential that physicians make the determination in the exercise of their medical judgment." Id., at 28. "Defendant agrees that 'viability' will vary, that it is a difficult state to assess . . . and that it must be left to the physician's judgment." Id., at 29.
4. The Minnesota statute under attack in Hodgson provided that a fetus "shall be considered potentially 'viable'" during the second half of its gestation period. Noting that the defendants had presented no evidence of viability at 20 weeks, the three-judge district court held that that definition of viability was "unreasonable and cannot stand." 378 F Supp, at 1016.
5. Apparently, however, the only other Missouri statutes concerned with consent for general medical or surgical care relate to persons committed to the Missouri state chest hospital, Mo Rev Stat § 199.240 (1969), or to mental or correctional institutions, id., § 105.700.
6. There is some testimony in the record to the effect that taking from the pa-

tient a prior written consent to surgery is the custom. That may be so in some areas of Missouri, but we definitely refrain from characterizing it extremely as "the universal practice of the medical profession," as the appellees do. Brief for Appellees 32.

7. The appellants' vagueness arguement centers on the word "informed." One might well wonder, offhand, just what "informed consent" of a patient is. The three Missouri federal judges who comprised the three-judge District Court, however, were not concerned, and we are content to accept, as the meaning, the giving of information to the patient as to just what would be done and as to its consequences. To ascribe more meaning than this might well confine the attending physician in an undesired and uncomfortable straitjacket in the practice of his profession.

8. It is of some interest to note that the condition does not relate, as most statutory conditions in this area do, to the preservation of the life or *health* of the mother.

9. "We deal with a right of privacy older than the Bill of Rights—older than our political parties, older than our school system. Marriage is a coming together for better or for worse, hopefully enduring, and intimate to the degree of being sacred. It is an association that promotes a way of life, not causes; a harmony in living, not political faiths; a bilateral loyalty, not commercial or social projects. Yet it is an association for as noble a purpose as any involved in our prior decisions." Griswold v. Connecticut. 381 US 479, 486, 14 L Ed 2d 510, 85 S Ct 1678 (1965).

10. [9b] As the Court recognized in Eisenstadt v. Baird, "the marital couple is not an independent entity with a mind and heart of its own, but an association of two individuals each with a separate intellectual and emotional makeup. If the right of privacy means anything, it

is the right of the *individual,* married or single, to be free from unwarranted governmental intrusion into matters so fundamentally affecting a person as the decision whether to bear or beget a child." 405 US, at 453, 31 L Ed 2d 349, 92 S Ct 1029 (emphasis in original).

The dissenting opinion of our Brother White appears to overlook the implications of this statement upon the issue whether § 3(3) is constitutional. This section does much more than insure that the husband participate in the decision whether his wife should have an abortion. The State, instead, has determined that the husband's interest in continuing the pregnancy of his wife always outweighs any interest on her part in terminating it irrespective of the condition of their marriage. The State, accordingly, has granted him the right to prevent unilaterally, and for whatever reason, the effectuation of his wife's and her physician's decision to terminate her pregnancy. This state determination not only may discourage the consultation that might normally be expected to precede a major decision affecting the marital couple but also, and more importantly, the State has interposed an absolute obstacle to a woman's decision that Roe held to be constitutionally protected from such interference.

APPENDIX. HCS HOUSE BILL NO. 1211. An ACT relating to abortion with penalty provisions and emergency clause.

Be it enacted by the General Assembly of the State of Missouri, as follows:

Section 1. It is the intention of the general assembly of the state of Missouri to reasonably regulate abortion in conformance with the decisions of the supreme court of the United States.

Section 2. Unless the language or context clearly indicates a different meaning is intended, the following words or phrases for the purpose of this act shall be given the meaning ascribed to them:

(1) "Abortion," the intentional destruction of the life of an embryo or fetus in his or her mother's womb or the intentional termination of the pregnancy of a mother with an intention other than to increase the probability of a live birth or to remove a dead or dying unborn child;

(2) "Viability," that stage of fetal development when the life of the unborn child may be continued indefinitely outside the womb by natural or artificial life-supportive systems;

(3) "Physician," any person licensed to practice medicine in this state by the state board of registration of the healing arts.

Section 3. No abortion shall be performed prior to the end of the first twelve weeks of pregnancy except:

(1) By a duly licensed, consenting physician in the exercise of his best clinical judgment.

(2) After the woman, prior to submitting to the abortion, certifies in writing her consent to the abortion and that her consent is informed and freely given and is not the result of coercion.

(3) With the written consent of the woman's spouse, unless the abortion is certified by a licensed physician to be necessary in order to preserve the life of the mother.

(4) With the written consent of one parent or person in loco parentis of the woman if the woman is unmarried and under age of eighteen years, unless the abortion is certified by a licensed physician as necessary in order to preserve the life of the mother.

Section 4. No abortion performed subsequent to the first twelve weeks of pregnancy shall be performed except where the provisions of section 3 of this act are satisfied and in a hospital.

Section 5. No abortion not necessary to preserve the life or health of the mother shall be performed unless the attending physician first certifies with reasonable medical certainty that the fetus is not viable.

Section 6. (1) No person who performs or induces an abortion shall fail to exercise that degree of professional skill, care and diligence to preserve the life and health of the fetus which such person would be required to exercise in order to preserve the life and health of any fetus intended to be born and not aborted. Any physician or person assisting in the abortion who shall fail to take such measures to encourage or to sustain the life of the child, and the death of the child results, shall be deemed guilty of manslaughter and upon conviction shall be punished as provided in Section 559.140, RSMo. Further, such physician or other person shall be liable in an action for damages as provided in Section 537.080, RSMo.

(2) Whoever, with intent to do so, shall take the life of a premature infant aborted alive, shall be guilty of murder of the second degree.

(3) No person shall use any fetus or premature infant aborted alive for any type of scientific, research, laboratory or other kind of experimentation either prior to or subsequent to any abortion procedure except as necessary to protect or preserve the life and health of such premature infant aborted alive.

Section 7. In every case where a

live born infant results from an attempted abortion which was not performed to save the life or health of the mother, such infant shall be an abandoned ward of the state under the jurisdiction of the juvenile court wherein the abortion occurred, and the mother and father, if he consented to the abortion, of such infant shall have no parental rights or obligations whatsoever relating to such infant, as if the parental rights had been terminated pursuant to section 211.411, RSMo. The attending physician shall forthwith notify said juvenile court of the existence of such live born infant.

Section 8. Any woman seeking an abortion in the state of Missouri shall be verbally informed of the provisions of section 7 of this act by the attending physician and the woman shall certify in writing that she has been so informed.

Section 9. The general assembly finds that the method or technique of abortion known as saline amniocentesis whereby the amniotic fluid is withdrawn and a saline or other fluid is inserted into the amniotic sac for the purpose of killing the fetus and artificially inducing labor is deleterious to maternal health and is hereby prohibited after the first twelve weeks of pregnancy.

Section 10. (1) Every health facility and physician shall be supplied with forms promulgated by the division of health, the purpose and function of which shall be the preservation of maternal health and life by adding to the sum of medical knowledge through the compilation of relevant maternal health and life data and to monitor all abortions performed to assure that they are done only under and in accordance with the provisions of the law.

(2) The forms shall be provided by the state division of health.

(3) All information obtained by physician, hospital, clinic or other health facility from a patient for the purpose of preparing reports to the division of health under this section or reports received by the division of health shall be confidential and shall be used only for statistical purposes. Such records, however, may be inspected and health data acquired by local, state, or national public health officers.

Section 11. All medical records and other documents required to be kept shall be maintained in the permanent files of the health facility in which the abortion was performed for a period of seven years.

Section 12. Any practitioner of medicine, surgery, or nursing, or other health personnel who shall willfully and knowingly do or assist any actions made unlawful by this act shall be subject to having his license, application for license, or authority to practice his profession as a physician, surgeon, or nurse in the state of Missouri rejected or revoked by the appropriate state licensing board.

Section 13. Any physician or other person who fails to maintain the confidentiality of any records or reports required under this act is guilty of a misdemeanor and, upon conviction, shall be punished as provided by law.

Section 14. Any person who contrary to the provisions of this act knowingly performs or aids in the performance of any abortion or knowingly fails to perform any action required by this act shall be guilty of a misdemeanor and, upon conviction, shall be punished as provided by law.

Section 15. Any person who is not a licensed physician as defined in section 2 of this act who performs or attempts to perform an abortion on another as defined in subdivision (1) of section 2 of this act, is guilty of a felony, and upon conviction, shall be imprisoned by the department of corrections for a term of not less than two years nor more than seventeen years.

Section 16. Nothing in this act shall be construed to exempt any person, firm, or corporation from civil liability for medical malpractice for negligent acts or certification under this act.

Section A. Because of the necessity for immediate state action to regulate abortions to protect the lives and health of citizens of this state, this act is deemed necessary for the immediate preservation of the public health, welfare, peace and safety, and is hereby declared to be an emergency act within the meaning of the constitution, and this act shall be in full force and effect upon its passage and approval.

Section B. If any provision of this Act or the application thereof to any person or circumstance shall be held invalid, such invalidity does not affect the provisions or application of this Act which can be given effect without the invalid provision or application, and to this end the provisions of this Act are declared to be severable.

Approved June 14, 1974.
Effective June 14, 1974.

Separate Opinions

Mr. Justice Stewart, with whom Mr. Justice Powell joins, concurring.

While joining the Court's opinion, I write separately to indicate my understanding of some of the constitutional issues raised by this case.

With respect to the definition of viability in § 2(2) of the Act, it seems to me that the critical consideration is that the statutory definition has almost no operative significance. The State has merely required physicians performing abortions to *certify* that the fetus to be aborted is not viable. While the physician may be punished for failing to issue a certification, he may not be punished for erroneously concluding that the fetus is not viable. There is thus little chance that a physician's professional decision to perform an abortion will be "chilled."

I agree with the Court that the patient consent provision in § 3(2) is constitutional. While § 3(2) obviously regulates the abortion decision during all stages of pregnancy, including the first trimester, I do not believe it conflicts with the statement in Roe v. Wade, 410 US, at 163, 35 L Ed 2d 147, 93 S Ct 705, that "for the period of pregnancy prior to [approximately the end of the first trimester] the attending physician, in consultation with his patient, is free to determine, without regulation by the State, that, in his medical judgment, the patient's pregnancy should be terminated. If that decision is reached, the judgment may be effectuated by an abortion free of interference by the State." 410 US, at 163, 35 L Ed 2d 147, 93 S Ct 705. That statement was made in the context of invalidating a state law aimed at thwarting a woman's decision to have an abortion. It was not intended to preclude the State from enacting a provision aimed at ensuring that the abortion decision is made in a knowing, intelligent, and voluntary fashion.

As to the provision of the law that requires a husband's consent to an abortion, § 3(3), the primary issue that it raises is whether the State may constitutionally recognize and give effect to a right on his part to participate in the decision to abort a jointly conceived child. This seems to me a rather more difficult problem than the Court acknowledges. Previous decisions have recognized that a man's right to father children and enjoy the association of his offspring is a constitutionally protected freedom. See Stanley v Illinois, 405 US 645, 31 L Ed 2d 551, 92 S Ct 1208; Skinner v. Oklahoma, 316 US 535, 86 L Ed 1655, 62 S Ct 1110. But the Court has recognized as well that the Constitution protects "a *woman's* decision whether or not to terminate her pregnancy." 410 US, at 153, 35 L Ed 2d 147, 93 S Ct 705 (emphasis added). In assessing the constitutional validity of § 3(3) we are called upon to choose between these competing rights. I agree with the Court that since "it is the woman who physically bears the child and who is the more directly and immediately affected by the pregnancy . . . the balance weighs in her favor." Ante, at ——, 49 L Ed 2d 806.

With respect to the state law's requirement of parental consent, § 3(4), I think it clear that its primary constitutional deficiency lies in its imposition of an absolute limitation on the minor's right to obtain an abortion. The Court's opinion today in Bellotti v. Baird, —— US ——, ——, 49 L Ed 2d 844, 96 S Ct ——, suggests that a materially different constitutional issue would be presented under a provision requiring parental consent or consultation in most cases but providing for prompt (i) judi-

cial resolution of any disagreement between the parent and the minor, or (ii) judicial determination that the minor is mature enough to give an informed consent without parental concurrence or that abortion in any event is in the minor's best interest. Such a provision would not impose parental approval as an absolute condition upon the minor's right but would assure in most instances consultation between the parent and child.[1]

There can be little doubt that the State furthers a constitutionally permissible end by encouraging an unmarried pregnant minor to seek the help and advice of her parents in making the very important decision whether or not to bear a child. That is a grave decision, and a girl of tender years, under emotional stress, may be ill-equipped to make it without mature advice and emotional support. It seems unlikely that she will obtain adequate counsel and support from the attending physician at an abortion clinic, where abortions for pregnant minors frequently take place.[2]

As to the constitutional validity of § 9 of the Act, prohibiting the use of the saline amniocentesis procedure, I agree fully with the views expressed by Mr. Justice Stevens.

Mr. Justice White, with whom The Chief Justice and Mr. Justice Rehnquist join, concurring in part and dissenting in part.

In Roe v. Wade, 410 US 113, 35 L Ed 2d 147, 93 S Ct 705, this Court recognized a right to an abortion free from state prohibition. The task of policing this limitation on state police power is and will be a difficult and continuing venture in substantive due process. However, even accepting Roe v. Wade, there is nothing in the opinion in that case and nothing articulated in the Court's opinion in this case which justifies the invalidation of five provisions of House Committee Substitute for House Bill No. 1211 enacted by the Missouri Seventy-Seventh General Assembly in 1974 in response to Roe v. Wade (hereafter referred to as "the Act"). Accordingly, I dissent, in part.

Notes

1. For some of the considerations that support the State's interest in encouraging parental consent, see the opinion of Mr. Justice Stevens, concurring in part and dissenting in part. Post, at ——, ——, 49 L Ed 2d 823–825.
2. The mode of operation of one such clinic is revealed by the record in Bellotti v. Baird, supra, and accurately described in the Brief for the Appellants in that case.

   "The counseling . . . occurs entirely on the day the abortion is to be performed. . . . It lasts for two hours and takes place in groups that include both minors and adults who are strangers to one another. . . . The physician takes no part in this counseling process. . . . Counseling is typically limited to a description of abortion procedures, possible complications, and birth control techniques. . . .

   "The abortion itself takes five to seven minutes. . . . The physician has no prior contact with the minor, and on the days that abortions are being performed at the [clinic], the physician, . . . may be performing abortions on many other adults and minors. . . . On busy days patients are scheduled in separate groups, consisting usually of five patients. . . . After the abortion [the physician] spends a brief period with the minor and others in the group in the recovery room. . . ." Id., at 43–44.

I

Roe v. Wade, 410 US 113, 163, 35 L Ed 2d 147, 93 S Ct 705, holds that until a fetus becomes viable, the interest of the State in the life or potential life it represents is outweighed by the interest of the mother in choosing "whether or not to terminate her pregnancy." Id., at 153, 35 L Ed 2d 147, 93 S Ct 705. Section 3(3) of the Act provides that a married woman may not obtain an abortion without her husband's consent. The Court strikes down this statute in one sentence. It says that "since the State cannot . . . proscribe abortion . . . the State cannot delegate authority to any particular person, even the spouse, to prevent abortion. . . ." Ante, at ——, 49 L Ed 2d 805. But the State is not—under § 3(3)—delegating to the husband the power to vindicate the *State's* interest in the future life of the fetus. It is instead recognizing that the husband has an interest of his own in the life of the fetus which should not be extinguished by the unilateral decision of the wife.[1] It by no means follows, from the fact that the mother's interest in deciding "whether or not to terminate her pregnancy" outweighs the *State's* interest in the potential life of the fetus, that the husband's interest is also outweighed and may not be protected by the State. A father's interest in having a child—perhaps his only child—may be unmatched by any other interest in his life. See Stanley v. Illinois, 405 US 645, 651, 31 L Ed 2d 551, 92 S Ct 1208, and cases there cited. It is truly surprising that the majority finds in the United States Constitution, as it must in order to justify the result it reaches, a rule that the State must assign a greater value to a mother's decision to cut off a potential human life by abortion than to a father's decision to let it mature into a live child. Such a rule cannot be found there, nor can it be found in Roe v. Wade, supra. These are matters which a State should be able to decide free from the suffocating power of the federal judge, purporting to act in the name of the Constitution.

In describing the nature of a mother's interest in terminating a pregnancy, the Court in Roe v. Wade mentioned only the post-birth burdens of rearing a child, id., at p 153, 35 L Ed 2d 147, 93 S Ct 705, and rejected a rule based on her interest in controlling her own body during pregnancy. Id., at 154, 35 L Ed 2d 147, 93 S Ct 705. Missouri has a law which prevents a woman from putting a child up for adoption over her husband's objection, § 453.030 RS Mo 1969. This law represents a judgment by the State that the mother's interest in avoiding the burdens of child rearing do not outweigh or snuff out the father's interest in participating in bringing up his own child. That law is plainly valid, but no more so than § 3(3) of the Act now before us, resting as it does on precisely the same judgment.

II

Section 3(4) requires that an unmarried woman under 18 years of age obtain the consent of a parent or a person in loco parentis as a condition to an abortion. Once again the Court strikes the provision down in a sentence. It states: "Just as with the requirement of consent from the spouse, so here, the State does not have the constitutional authority to give a third party an absolute, and possibly arbitrary, veto over the decision of the physician and his patient to terminate the patient's pregnancy. . . ." Id., at ———, 49 L Ed 2d 808, 96 S Ct ———. The Court rejects the notions that the *State* has an interest in strengthening the family unit, or that the *parent* has an "independent interest" in the abortion decision, sufficient to justify the statute, and apparently concludes that the statute is therefore unconstitutional. But the purpose of the parental consent requirement is not merely to vindicate any interest of the parent or of the State. The pur-

pose of the requirement is to vindicate the very right created in Roe v. Wade, supra—the right of the pregnant woman to decide "whether *or not* to terminate her pregnancy." Id., at 153, 35 L Ed 2d 147, 93 S Ct 705 (emphasis added). The abortion decision is unquestionably important and has irrevocable consequences whichever way it is made. Missouri is entitled to protect the minor unmarried woman from making the decision in a way which is not in her own best interests, and it seeks to achieve this goal by requiring parental consultation and consent. This is the traditional way by which States have sought to protect children from their own immature and improvident decisions,[2] and there is absolutely no reason expressed by the majority why the State may not utilize that method here. . . .

Mr. Justice Stevens, concurring in part and dissenting in part.

With the exception of Parts IV-D and IV-E, I join the Court's opinion.

In Roe v. Wade, 410 US 113, 35 L Ed 2d 147, 93 S Ct 705, the Court held that a woman's right to decide whether to abort a pregnancy is entitled to constitutional protection. That decision, which is now part of our law, answers the question discussed in Part IV-E of the Court's opinion, but merely poses the question decided in Part IV-D.

If two abortion procedures had been equally accessible to Missouri women, in my judgment the United States Constitution would not prevent the state legislature from outlawing the one it found to be the less safe even though its conclusion might not reflect a unanimous consensus of informed medical opinion. However, the record indicates that when the Missouri statute was enacted, a prohibition of the saline amniocentesis procedure was almost tantamount to a prohibition of any abortion in the State after the first 12 weeks of pregnancy. Such a prohibition is inconsistent with the essential holding of Roe v. Wade and therefore cannot stand.

In my opinion, however, the parental consent requirement is consistent with the holding in Roe. The State's interest in the welfare of its young citizens justifies a variety of protective measures. Because he may not foresee the consequences of his decision, a minor may not make an enforceable bargain. He may not lawfully work or travel where he pleases, or even attend exhibitions of constitutionally protected adult motion pictures. Persons below a certain age may not marry without parental consent. Indeed, such consent is essential even when the young woman is already pregnant. The State's interest in protecting a young person from harm justifies the imposition of restraints on his or her freedom even though comparable restraints on adults would be constitutionally impermissible. Therefore, the holding in Roe v. Wade that the abortion decision is entitled to constitutional protection merely emphasizes the importance of the decision; it does not lead to the conclusion that the state legislature has no power to enact legislation for the purpose of protecting a young pregnant woman from the consequences of an incorrect decision.

The abortion decision is, of course, more important than the decision to attend or to avoid an adult motion picture, or the decision to work long hours in a factory. It is not necessarily any more important than the decision to run away from home or the decision to marry. But even if it is the most important kind of a decision a young person may ever make, that assumption merely enhances the quality of the State's interest in maximizing the probability that the decision

be made correctly and with full understanding of the consequences of either alternative.

The Court recognizes that the State may insist that the decision not be made without the benefit of medical advice. But since the most significant consequences of the decision are not medical in character, it would seem to me that the State may, with equal legitimacy, insist that the decision be made only after other appropriate counsel has been had as well. Whatever choice a pregnant young woman makes—to marry, to abort, to bear her child out of wedlock—the consequences of her decision may have a profound impact on her entire future life. A legislative determination that such a choice will be made more wisely in most cases if the advice and moral support of a parent play a part in the decisionmaking process is surely not irrational. Moreover, it is perfectly clear that the parental consent requirement will necessarily involve a parent in the decisional process.

If there is no parental consent requirement, many minors will submit to the abortion procedure without ever informing their parents. An assumption that the parental reaction will be hostile, disparaging or violent no doubt persuades many children simply to bypass parental counsel which would in fact be loving, supportive and, indeed, for some indispensable. It is unrealistic, in my judgment, to assume that every parent-child relationship is either (a) so perfect that communication and accord will take place routinely or (b) so imperfect that the absence of communication reflects the child's correct prediction that the parent will exericse his or her veto arbitrarily to further a selfish interest rather than the child's interest. A state legislature may conclude that most parents will be primarily interested in the welfare of their children, and further, that the imposition of a parental consent requirement is an appropriate method of giving the parents an opportunity to foster that welfare by helping a pregnant distressed child to make and to implement a correct decision.

The State's interest is not dependent on an estimate of the impact the parental consent requirement may have on the total number of abortions that may take place. I assume that parents will sometimes prevent abortions which might better be performed; other parents may advise abortions that should not be performed. Similarly, even doctors are not omniscient; specialists in performing abortions may incorrectly conclude that the immediate advantages of the procedure outweigh the disadvantages which a parent could evaluate in better perspective. In each individual case factors much more profound than a mere medical judgment may weigh heavily in the scales. The overriding consideration is that the right to make the choice be exercised as wisely as possible.

The Court assumes that parental consent is an appropriate requirement if the minor is not capable of understanding the procedure and of appreciating its consequences and those of available alternatives. This assumption is, of course, correct and consistent with the predicate which underlies all State legislation seeking to protect minors from the consequences of decisions they are not yet prepared to make. In all such situations chronological age has been the basis for imposition of a restraint on the minor's freedom of choice even though it is perfectly obvious that such a yardstick is imprecise and perhaps even unjust in particular cases. The Court seems to assume that the capacity to conceive a child and the judgment of the physician are the only constitutionally permissible yardsticks for determining whether a young woman can independently make the abortion decision. I doubt the accuracy of the Court's empirical judgment. Even if it were correct, however, as a matter of constitutional law I think a State has power to conclude otherwise and to select a chronological age as its standard.

In short, the State's interest in the welfare of its young citizens is sufficient, in my judgment, to support the parental consent requirement.

Notes

1. There are countless situations in which the State prohibits conduct only when it is objected to by a private person most closely affected by it. Thus a State cannot forbid anyone to enter on private property with the owner's consent, but it may enact and enforce trespass laws against unauthorized entrances. It cannot forbid transfer of property held in tenancy by the entireties but it may require consent by both husband and wife to such a transfer. These situations plainly do not involve delegations of legislative power to private parties; and neither does the requirement in § 3(3) that a woman not deprive her husband of his future child without his consent.

2. As Mr. Justice Stevens states in his dissenting opinion:
   "The State's interest in the welfare of its young citizens justifies a variety of protective measures. Because he may not foresee the consequences of his decision, a minor may not make an enforceable bargain. He may not lawfully work or travel where he pleases, or even attend exhibitions of constitutionally protected adult motion pictures. Persons below a certain age may not marry without parental consent. Indeed, such consent is essential even when the young woman is already pregnant."

We are hardly used to a world in which parenthood can be chosen or rejected; we are only beginning to look ahead to the possibility of persons choosing not just when or whether to have a child or children but what sort of children to have and which to reject. At present, these problems arise mainly for genetic counselors and for prospective parents to whom they give news of defects risked by future children or incurred by children already conceived. Knowledge of such risks, or even of actual defects, entails no action, but it poses hard choices. Where therapy can overcome the defect, parents and doctors may see clearly what to do. In other cases, it may be extraordinarily hard to choose among options such as sterilization or therapeutic abortion or living with and caring for a defective child.

Ruth Macklin sets out to identify and explore some of these dilemmas. Using a consequentialist framework, and assuming that individual rights will be strongly supported by that framework, she argues that parents—the prospective rearers of a defective child—should make reproductive decisions based on genetic information, and that genetic counselors should see themselves as responsible only to families and not to wider social groups which may be adversely affected by the birth of defective children. Eugenic aims, such as eliminating "bad" genes from a population, are for the most part either not feasible or likely to have damaging side effects. The bad effects of policies which permit procreators to risk—or even knowingly to seek—the birth of a defective child are outweighed by the bad (though often less evident) effects of eugenic policies which would deny that liberty to prospective parents.

PARENTS AND GENETIC COUNSELORS: MORAL ISSUES

RUTH MACKLIN

. . . [T]he question "valuable to what end?" is one of extraordinary complexity. For example, something obviously valuable in terms of the longest possible survival of a race (or of its best adaptation to a given climate, or of the preservation of its greatest numbers) would by no means have the same value if it were a question of developing a more powerful type. The welfare of the many and the welfare of the few are radically opposite ends.

Friedrich Nietzsche
The Genealogy of Morals

From "Moral Issues in Human Genetics: Counseling or Control?" *Dialogue* © Canadian Philosophical Association, Vol. XIV, No. 3 (1977), pp. 375–396. Reprinted by permission.

There is no question that genetic engineering in many forms . . . will come about. It is a general rule that whatever is scientifically feasible will be attempted. The application of these techniques must, however, be examined from the point of view of ethics, individual freedom and coercion. Both the scientists directly involved and, perhaps more important, the political and social leaders of our civilization must exercise utmost caution in order to prevent genetic, evolutionary and social tragedies.

> Kurt Hirschhorn, M.D.
> "Practical and Ethical Problems
> in Human Genetics," *Birth Defects,*
> vol. VIII, no. 4 (July 1972),
> pp. 29–30.

I

In the field of human genetics, the last several decades have witnessed a great increase in both theoretical knowledge and technological power. Like so many other areas in biomedical ethics, the attainment of new knowledge and the development of new technology have given rise to moral problems that never had to be faced before. But while the biomedical contexts are new, the moral problems are ancient. Such problems arise at the level both of the individual and of society, where decisions must be made about such matters as whether compulsory genetic screening programs constitute a violation of individual privacy; whether enforced sterilization of genetically unhealthy individuals is ever justifiable in the interest of socially desirable outcomes; whether genetic counselors are obligated to tell the truth, the whole truth, and nothing but the truth to their clients even in cases where learning the truth is likely to be harmful. Ethical dilemmas about such matters as the rights of individuals when these con-

flict with anticipated social benefits, the morality of withholding the truth, the acceptability of paternalistic coercion of persons "for their own good"—these age-old moral problems are found in new settings created by advances in human genetics, as is the case in other biomedical areas.

A catalogue of representative moral issues in this domain would include at least the following concerns.

1. *The ethics of screening for incurable heritable disease.*   Should tests such as the L-dopa test for pre-symptomatic Huntington's Chorea—a fatal, degenerative neurological disease—be made available to patients even in the absence of any treatment or cure? Should persons known to be at risk for such incurable hereditary conditions be informed of such tests? Urged to undergo them? Or should testing be withheld until there is something tangible to offer those who show a positive result? Ought information gained through genetic screening be made available to others besides the patient, when such knowledge may affect the decision of other family members to bear children or undergo screening themselves?

2. *Responsibilities of genetic counselors.*   To whom is the genetic counselor responsible? The patient or married couple alone? Their unborn child? Other family members? Future generations who may suffer increasing numbers of persons with genetic defects? Should genetic counselors merely present the "facts" to those who come for counseling? Or does the greater theoretical knowledge and practical experience of the genetic counselor warrant his giving advice or urging a specific course of action? It is often noted that even in

cases where a counselor believes himself to be simply imparting information, he nonetheless betrays his attitude in a way that is likely to influence a patient's decision. If this is so, does it suggest a reason for the counselor to render his own view explicit instead of trying (unsuccessfully) to remain neutral?

3. *Moral limits in the use of amniocentesis and abortion.* Are there good reasons for remaining selective in the use of amniocentesis—the technique by which a small amount of amniotic fluid is taken from a woman early in pregnancy and fetal cells are cultured to ascertain the presence of genetic disorders? Do risks to the fetus—however slight—indicate that the procedure should be used selectively? Is the use of amniocentesis and subsequent abortion justifiable for reasons such as sex determination of the fetus? Should amniocentesis be ruled out in cases where the parents indicate that they are opposed to abortion in all circumstances?

4. *The morality of positive and negative eugenics.* Do we have a moral obligation to refrain from "polluting" the human gene pool? How far into the future does our obligation to future generations lie? If there is such an obligation, ought it be mandated by government legislation and enforcement? What are the moral limits of developing and using radically new techniques such as high-precision surgery on genetic material, when there are significant risks in the form of accidental creation of hapless monsters, or abuse on the part of unethical investigators? Is some form of eugenics justifiable on the grounds that presently existing society must bear the enormous costs of maintaining defective infants and even adults who survive

because of the capabilities of modern medicine?

In all of these questions and others we shall explore shortly, the moral categories include a number of alleged rights of the individual: the "right to know" (or *not* to know); the right to make autonomous decisions; the "right to bear children," even when a high probability exists that these children will either suffer from or be carriers of genetic disease. These moral issues need not be couched in the language of rights, but may instead (perhaps more profitably) be viewed as ethical dilemmas where cogent reasons can be offered for two or more alternative courses of action. It is the existence of just such alternatives that gives rise to the need for moral decision-making on the part of individual physicians, their patients, and the larger society.

Before we can begin to answer the question "who shall make the decisions?" We must first be clear about what decisions there are to be made. Since the issues in human genetics are so complex and multilayered, I shall spend a bit of time sorting them out and try to show how the practices of genetic screening, genetic counseling, and genetic engineering pose interconnected moral problems. In the course of this paper, I shall argue for two separate but related theses. The first is that the individual (meaning also the individual couple, where appropriate) should have final decision-making authority in matters of his or her own reproductive acts and capacities, as well as continuation or termination of pregnancy, where the reasons for these decisions refer to genetic factors. The second thesis is that attempts at government-based or scientist-directed eugenic programs—whether aimed at positive or negative eugenics—

are bound to be misguided or dangerous or both. Having asserted these theses, let me now go back and lay the groundwork. I shall try, first, to identify the chief moral issues in human genetics, showing just where and in what ways the need for decision-making arises. Then I shall have the way paved for arguing the two theses just stated.

II

As the terms imply, "genetic screening" denotes a process of detection and diagnosis of heritable conditions; "genetic counseling" refers to the activity of informing or advising those who are afflicted with such conditions or are carriers; and "genetic engineering" involves manipulation of either genetic material itself or else the reproductive acts or capacities of persons. About each of these activities, the following questions must be posed: What purpose is the practice designed to serve? Who stands to benefit from the practice? What individual rights or liberties stand to be abridged? What other values are involved in decision-making in these areas?

Beginning with genetic screening, let's look briefly at each of these activities to see where the need for decision-making arises and what sorts of decisions are involved. The range of diagnostic procedures known as genetic screening can be grouped roughly into the following five categories, of which I shall discuss the first four: (1) newborn metabolic screening; (2) chromosome screening; (3) carrier screening; (4) pre-natal diagnosis; and (5) susceptibility screening.[1]

1. The most prevalent example of newborn metabolic screening is that of the relatively simple and inexpensive test for phenylketonuria (PKU), a rare autosomal recessive in which the afflicted infant has inherited one defective gene from each parent. Those suffering from phenylketonuria lack a critical enzyme for metabolizing phenylalanine, an essential amino acid. If left untreated, PKU leads to irreversible mental retardation; when treated by introducing a synthetic diet virtually free of phenylalanine and begun shortly after birth, children with PKU do not suffer the consequence of severe retardation; but there is now some evidence that the special diet does not restore intelligence totally.[2] While PKU screening is an example of genetic screening where some treatment or cure exists for afflicted individuals, its use is not free of difficulties. For one thing, there have been significant instances of false positives—a source of difficulty because the synthetic diet can be harmful to a normal child. Moreover, a serious reproduction problem has arisen, since PKU women give birth to children who are retarded, no matter what their genotype, because of a toxic uterine environment. A different sort of problem stems from the fact that most states in the United States have adopted a program of mandatory PKU screening—a practice that some believe will serve as a model for increasing numbers of medical procedures compelled by law.[3] So while PKU screening has the virtue of being a diagnostic procedure for a condition having a treatment or cure that now exists, it may, for that very reason, be an unwelcome paradigm of legally compelled medical procedures, which will make inroads into the privacy of individuals in our society.

2. The most notorious example of chromosome screening of newborns is that of the XYY chromosomal anomaly. The extra Y chromosome is thought by some to result in an unusual degree of antisocial, aggressive behavior on the

part of the so-called "super-males" who possess this abnormality. Unlike the case of PKU, there is no known "cure" or even a scientifically well-confirmed treatment program for males who have this chromosomal abnormality, nor has it been fully ascertained that this special population is significantly different in behavior patterns from "normal" XY male who come from similar backgrounds. But XYY screening has drawn sharp criticism for reasons other than those pertaining to theoretical and diagnostic uncertainties of this sort. Severe criticism has been leveled at a study in Boston, which has offered therapy to young boys found through screening to have the extra Y chromosome. One argument runs as follows:

> Either the researcher must withhold from the parents the information that the child being studied is XYY (which is probably immoral and perhaps also illegal), or that information must be disclosed, which will alter the way the parents feel about the child (probably for the worse). It will also render the study scientifically worthless, since for the study to demonstrate whether there are behavioral problems with the XYY male it is necessary that his upbringing be as "normal" as possible, so he can be compared with an XY boy.[4]

This argument is persuasive, especially given the circumstance that the therapy for aggressive or antisocial behavior is, at best, uncertain, and at worst, coercive. But even if it is morally permissible or even desirable to seek to alter the deviant behavior of XYY male children, the other points in the argument remain. The moral conflict surrounding how much and what specific information should be transmitted to whom arises directly in many cases of genetic counseling, as we shall see shortly. The problem of inform-

ing parents that they have an XYY child is wider than that raised by the Boston study. Even if no therapy were offered, there would remain the problem of adverse effects on the parents' expectations about and treatment of their sons whom they knew to possess an extra Y chromosome. While many screening programs for XYY seem to have been dropped, controversy still rages over whether it is morally permissible to employ screening techniques of this kind at all.

3. Carrier screening is different from the two varieties just discussed in that it is aimed not at those afflicted with a genetic disease but rather at a carrier— one

> who is clinically well himself, but risks having a child with a disease. These programs do not involve case-finding and treatment in the conventional sense, but rather represent an attempt to identify the person at risk and to intervene in his or her reproductive life, an approach not taken by any previous screening program.[5]

The two diseases for which carriers have been screened are Tay-Sachs disease—a rare metabolic disorder that leads to blindness, paralysis and death, usually before the age of four—and sickle-cell anemia, a painful and often life-shortening disease found largely among blacks. Tay-Sachs disease, found mostly among Jews of Eastern European descent, can be diagnosed in utero by means of amniocentesis, so afflicted fetuses can be aborted. While the condition itself has no cure, the purpose served by screening programs is to supply information for those parents who would choose abortion rather than bear an afflicted child who will certainly suffer and die within a very few years after birth. The purpose served by screening for sickle-cell carriers is not so clear, however. The disease cannot be detected in utero, so screening for carriers does not present many options. Sickle-cell anemia is autosomal recessive, which means that both parents must be carriers before it is possible to give birth to a child with the disease, and there is a one-in-four chance with each pregnancy of having an afflicted child. So parents found to be carriers can either take their chances of bearing a child who will have the disease, or choose artificial insemination with a non-carrier donor, or else seek to adopt a child. Screening programs for sickle-cell have come under fire on the grounds that they are potentially dangerous as weapons that might be used for racist purposes by whites against blacks. It is difficult to see what sorts of persuasive arguments could be offered for compulsory sickle-cell screening programs, in the absence of intrauterine detection of diseased fetuses or else a cure for the disease. Optional screening programs can be justified on the grounds that they enable couples to make a more informed choice about whether or not to have children; while some couples may well choose to take the one-in-four chance with each pregnancy, others will not. There seem to be no clear social benefits that accrue to mandatory programs, and their drawbacks lie largely in raising fear and suspicion about the possible repressive uses such programs might serve.

4. Pre-natal diagnosis as a form of genetic screening overlaps with the category of chromosomal screening discussed earlier. In one form of pre-natal diagnosis, fetal cells from the amniotic fluid are cultured and subjected to chromosomal analysis. In this way, XYY males can be detected in utero and aborted; the moral permissibility of abortion on these grounds is another issue currently under debate. A more significant use of pre-natal diagnosis is found in the case of Down's syndrome. Women over 40—or even over 35—are known to be at greatly elevated risk for having a child with Down's syndrome—the type of retardation formerly known as mongolism. Again, controversy exists over whether pre-natal diagnosis ought to be routinely offered to women of any age, or particularly to those over 35. While there seem to be sound reasons for having such programs available on a voluntary basis, there appear to be no good grounds for imposing pre-natal diagnosis on women unwilling to undergo the slight physical risk or to receive genetic information about their child. There is, further, the consideration that a chromosomal analysis will turn up other genetic information, which even parents who are eager to learn about Down's syndrome may not wish to know. Here is where the moral dilemmas raised by genetic screening intersect with those of genetic counseling.

It is evident that the primary purpose for which genetic screening is now employed is for transmitting such information to prospective parents through genetic counseling, so that they can make as informed a choice as the circumstances allow. The primary and intended impact of transmitting the information obtained by screening is to reduce suffering of presently existing persons or their children. Thus, the aim is to lessen the suffering of people in the present or next generation by preventing the birth of defective children, as in the case of Tay-Sachs disease and Down's syndrome, or by treating them at birth, like PKU children. But where there is no cure and no intrauterine detection program, as in the case of sickle-cell anemia and Huntington's Chorea, there is some question about the purposes to which the information gained through screening may be put. We shall return to this issue later in connection with genetic engineering. But first, let us look at the overlapping yet distinct set of problems that arise in the area of genetic counseling.

III

The moral issues that arise in the practice of genetic counseling are primarily those surrounding truth and information in medicine. As noted earlier, there is the overarching issue of whether the genetic counselor's role should be as neutral and objective as possible, or whether it is sometimes permissible or even desirable to offer advice or guide the patient or couple to a decision. This issue appears to be no different, in principle, in the area of genetic counseling from that of a wide range of therapeutic situations in medicine, such as elective surgery or treatment regimens for severely defective newborns. As usual in ethical contexts, it is probably unwise to adhere dogmatically to a rigid principle like "physicians or genetic counselors should never advise, but should always and only inform." While a general presumption in favor of fully autonomous decision-making by the patient or client is appropriate, sometimes that presumption may justifiably be overriden. There are cases in which a patient or couple asks directly for advice from the counselor, cases where it is evident to the counselor that the prospective parents fail to comprehend the enormity of caring for and raising a severely defective child, and still other instances where some measure of denial on the part of the parents stands in the way of their facing reality and making a rational decision. As with

any other intermediate moral principle, the precept that genetic counselors should remain neutral and objective may justifiably be breached. Although some may argue that the genetic counselor's role includes some eugenic obligations, the purpose of counseling is to help the pregnant woman or prospective parents as much as possible in making an informed choice that is in accord with their own preferred values.[6] It has often been noted that many people suffer guilt, and react unpredictably and often irrationally in the face of information about their role in transmitting defective genes to their offspring. A sensitive and compassionate genetic counselor, observing such situations, would be acting in accordance with a sound and widely held ethical precept in helping such parents come to a decision that is in accordance with their basic value scheme and that they can live with comfortably.

There are special circumstances, in addition to the more common problematic situations in counseling just noted, where the decisions to be made are straightforward medical decisions requiring significant medical expertise. An example is the sex assignment for an intersex child, where the decision depends on knowledge and experience that the parents most likely do not have. As one physician argues:

> Sex assignment is basically a therapeutic problem because it requires surgery to correct the anatomical anomalies of intersex. Once you remove a phallus there's really not much choice any more—you have to raise that child as a female. And the basis for such a decision is medical experience regarding prospective adequacy of sexual performance. There are phalluses that will never be functional no matter how much surgery you do. Therefore, in such

a situation it would be advisable to strongly suggest conversion to female gender. . . . We still see many tragedies where the physician makes the wrong decision because of a lack of experience, or because the parents have their minds set on the sex of their child, and the physician allows his decision to be swayed by their attitude.[7]

These observations serve to remind us that although recent work in the field of medical ethics has uncovered a variety of contexts in which decisions formerly considered purely medical ones have been shown not to require special medical expertise, we must nevertheless be careful not to err in the opposite direction by relegating to patients decisions that properly require a knowledgeable medical judgment.

There are still other situations in genetic counseling which pose different sorts of moral dilemmas from those just described. One such problem is whether or not it is ever permissible for a genetic counselor to withhold information from patients. In our discussion of the XYY chromosomal anomaly, we noted some difficulties that might arise if parents are apprised of the fact that their son's genetic endowment is one that has been found to correlate highly with overly aggressive behavior and even with criminal tendencies. Other sorts of cases usually revolve around potential psychological harm to an individual or damage to a marriage likely to result from disclosure of genetic information. One physician cites the following two instances in which he believes that withholding information is justifiable.

One example is where the genetic disorder of the child opens the possibility of non-paternity—where the husband's genotype indicates he may not be the child's father. Disclosure of full information in this case could lead the father to question his acceptance of the child, as well as of his marital relationship.

Another example would be the case of testicular feminization in which a genotypic 46,XY male develops as a female because of the failure of tissues to respond to testosterone stimulation. One might withhold this information from some parents because they would have difficulty relating to the child or would withhold it from the child herself when she is old enough to be counseled. . . . In cases in which the information can do serious psychological damage, I feel withholding it is justified.[8]

In these sorts of cases, it would seem that a rigid adherence to a moral principle that enjoins persons always to tell the truth, the whole truth, and nothing but the truth is an instance of dogmatism in ethics. Other moral principles sometimes override the precept that mandates truth-telling; or, to put it another way, the duty to tell the truth is sometimes superseded by another moral duty, when the two come into conflict. The dilemma here seems to be more of an epistemological one than an ethical one: how can we know in advance when telling the truth or disclosing full information will yield greater harm than good? How can we judge whether it is better, on the whole, for one member of a couple to be told about the infidelity of the other? Do we have an adequate basis for knowing how much and what sorts of psychological harm will be done by informing parents about their child's sexual anomaly, as in the example cited earlier? The ethical principle here seems rather clear: perform that act likely to produce least harm to everyone who stands to be affected. But one can accept this consequentialist moral position and yet still not know how to act because of the epistemological difficulties just noted. This should serve to remind us that not all the problems in moral contexts arise out of uncertainty about which ethical principle to adopt or what to do when two basic moral precepts come into conflict. In the cases just noted, it is likely that general agreement can be secured about the appropriateness of a utilitarian or consequentialist approach. Disagreement is more likely to arise over just which course of action is, in fact, likely to produce more harm, on balance. Aside from other kinds of disputes concerning what properly constitutes harm in such cases, the difficulty does seem to be more of an epistemological one than an ethical one.

The foregoing treatment of moral issues in genetic counseling has rested on the presupposition that the genetic counselor's responsibility is to the patient or client. Based on this presupposition, I have supported the general presumption that favors decision-making autonomy on the part of those being counseled. If, however, the genetic counselor were properly viewed as having an obligation to society at large or to future generations, then the presumption about autonomy might have to be overridden in some cases. In answer to the question, "To whom is the genetic counselor responsible?" one geneticist replies:

> Basically, I think that genetic counselors may be misguided if they feel that their ethical obligation is in *any way* to future generations. . . . [A]ll too often, I get the feeling that some genetic counselors are acting on the hidden assumption that they are somehow participating in that particularly Western predilection for attempting to create "ideal situations," in this instance, that of building a better gene

pool through "negative eugenics." . . . The genetic counselor's obligation, I will maintain, never should extend beyond the family within his purview. . . . Properly, a genetic counselor's job should not, in any way, be construed as eugenic in practice.[9]

Now, if we accept this view—that the genetic counselor has a responsibility to the family he is counseling and not to society at large or to future generations—then it is but a few small steps to the conclusion that individuals or couples should have final decision-making authority in matters of their own reproductive acts and capacities. But before such a conclusion can be reached, we must first explore the question of the feasibility or desirability of genetic engineering. Even if it is not the business of the genetic counselor to make recommendations to families on the basis of what is best for the human gene pool, it might still turn out that government-based or scientist-directed eugenic programs could override personal decisions in these matters. So before concluding that ultimate decision-making authority ought to rest with individual persons or couples, we must first reject any presumptions to the contrary that stem from eugenic considerations. In the remaining time, I shall explore some issues in genetic engineering, with the aim of showing that government-based or scientist-directed eugenic programs are misguided or dangerous or both.

IV

The notion of genetic engineering appears to have both a narrower and a broader definition. The narrow conception refers to approaches involving laboratory manipulation of genes or cells: somatic cell alteration and germ cell alteration.[10] When this meaning is assigned to genetic engineering, the term "eugenics" is used to refer to selection of parents or of their germ cells.[11] But sometimes the term "genetic engineering" is used in a fully general sense, to refer to any manipulation of the reproductive acts or capacities of persons or their parts. It is this latter sense that will be used in the remainder of this account.

At least the idea behind eugenics—if not the practice itself in some form—is ancient. Positive eugenics was promoted in Plato's *Republic* long before the science of genetics provided the theoretical basis and systematic data that today's proponents of genetic engineering have to work with. The lack of personal freedoms allowed the citizens in the *Republic* is well known to those familiar with Plato's work, and is evident in the following passage discussing regulation of unions between the sexes:

> It is for you, then, as their lawgiver, who have already selected the men, to select for association with them women who are so far as possible of the same natural capacity. . . . [A]nything like unregulated unions would be a profanation in a state whose citizens lead the good life. The Rulers will not allow such a thing. . . . [I]f we are to keep our flock at the highest pitch of excellence, there should be as many unions of the best of both sexes, and as few of the inferior, as possible, and . . . only the offspring of the better unions should be kept. . . . Moreover, young men who acquit themselves well in war and other duties, should be given, among other rewards and privileges, more liberal opportunities to sleep with a wife, for the further purpose that, with good excuse, as many as possible of the children may be begotten of such fathers.[12]

But lest we conclude that a eugenics movement can only be promoted or gain

adherents in a rigidly controlled society like Plato's *Republic* or a totalitarian regime such as Nazi Germany, let us consider the view of a twentieth century Nobel Prize-winning geneticist. The late Hermann Müller was an arch proponent of positive eugenics, based on his belief that the human gene pool is deteriorating. Müller argued for voluntary programs of positive eugenics, rejecting any form of state-imposed regulations. He claimed that "democratic control . . . implies an upgrading of the people in general in both their intellectual and social faculties, together with a maintenance or, preferably, an improvement in their bodily condition."[13] Müller was one of a number of contemporary geneticists who have made gloomy prophecies about the increasing load of mutations in the human gene pool. The particular brand of positive eugenics that he advocated was a voluntary artificial insemination program using donor semen (AID). He envisaged preserving the semen of outstanding men for future use in artificial insemination, choosing such greats as Einstein, Pasteur, Descartes, Leonardo, and Lincoln as men whose child no woman would refuse to bear.[14]

Müller's method of freezing the semen of intellectual and creative men is only one of several proposals favoring some form of *positive* eugenics—a program for improving the species, breeding a better race, or trying to prevent further deterioration by taking active countermeasures. Greater attention has been directed to the question of whether *negative* eugenics should be practiced on carriers or those afflicted with heritable diseases, in the form of enforced or encouraged abortions, sterilization, or less repressive but nonetheless coercive measures. The dilemma of choosing between preserving the individual freedom to marry and procreate as one chooses, and preventing further pollution of the gene pool would, indeed, pose an agonizing moral choice if the facts were as clear-cut as the eugenicists take them to be. There seems, however, to be enough uncertainty about the possible and probable outcomes of any attempts at eugenics to warrant extreme caution in mounting such grandiose schemes for genetic improvement. Many scientists agree that trying to reduce the load of mutations in the human gene pool through negative eugenics would be ineffective, at best. And the arguments against positive eugenics point to a number of potentially infelicitous outcomes. There are at least five separate arguments against the feasibility or desirability of any large-scale attempt at genetic engineering for eugenic purposes —arguments which, if taken together, give strong support to my conclusion that genetic engineering with this aim is misguided or dangerous or both. A sixth argument is the religious one that creating or modifying the human species is a task not for man, but for God.[15] For those to whom this sort of argument is compelling, it may lend added strength to the other five. I shall confine my discussion to four of the five considerations that do not require belief in a supernatural deity. Each of the following arguments against a systematic effort to mount any sort of eugenics program will be discussed in turn below:

1. We're too ignorant to do it right;
2. In any case, we are likely to alter the gene pool for ill;
3. Negative eugenics can't possibly work unless carriers are eliminated, but this would soon eliminate the entire species;
4. Some methods of genetic engineer-

ing carry grave moral risks of mishap.

The fifth argument is essentially that most—if not all—methods of genetic engineering are dehumanizing in basic ways.[16] While I think this attack contains some interesting points and raises questions of value that generally deserve important consideration, it is a gratuitous argument in this context. If the first four arguments are sound, they obviate the necessity for the fifth, since the scientific and practical objections to eugenic programs would rule them out before the value issues need be brought into consideration. So I shall treat only the first four arguments in what follows.

1. The claim that we are too ignorant to do the job right has several variants, each with significant implications. The first consideration points to our general ignorance about the value of a gene to a given race or to the species. As one prominent geneticist notes:

> We know only about its value to the individual carrying it and then only in instances where the effect is severe. In the light of such ignorance, it seems to me that the best procedure is to avoid all changes in the environment which are likely to change the mutation rate. . . . The quality of a gene or genotype may be determined only by the reaction of the associated phenotype in the environment in which it exists. A phenotype may be disadvantageous in some environments, essentially neutral in others, and advantageous in others. In the face of a rapidly changing and entirely new environment (new in an evolutionary sense), I do not believe that we can determine the value of specific genotypes to the species.[17]

This brand of ignorance constitutes our lack of knowledge of what to select for— a form of ignorance that some may argue is confined to the present state of development of the science of genetics. But a second variant of the "we're too ignorant" argument notes that "if we alter the gene pool, independent of environment, we are acting on the basis of present environmental criteria to select a gene pool for the future. Since the environment is changing a thousandfold times faster than our gene pool, it would be a disastrous approach."[18] But the difficulty here is not simply one of our inability to predict accurately what the future will be like. Questions of value enter in—questions that invariably resurrect the memory of attempts at positive eugenics among the Nazis. One writer asks:

> Who will be the judges and where will be the separation between good and bad? The most difficult decisions will come in defining the borderline cases. Will we breed against tallness because space requirements become more critical? Will we breed against nearsightedness because people with glasses may not make good astronauts? Will we forbid intellectually inferior individuals from procreating despite their proved ability to produce a number of superior individuals?[19]

The last variant on the "we're too ignorant" theme that we shall consider here requires us to recall Hermann Müller's proposal for positive eugenics. Müller would not be alone in including Abraham Lincoln on a list of men whose child no woman would refuse to bear. Yet there is now considerable evidence that Lincoln was afflicted with Marfan's syndrome, a heritable disease of the connective tissue that is transmitted by a dominant gene. The evidence is based on a number of factors. Lincoln's bodily characteristics and facial features—the very qualities we term "Lincolnesque"—

are typical features of bone deformities common to Marfan's syndrome. The disease was first named in 1896, some thirty years after Lincoln's death. It was believed for some time that Lincoln had Marfan's disease, on the basis of physical defects he was known to have had, as well as the early death of one of his children. One sign of the disease was Lincoln's abnormally long limbs. Also, casts made of Lincoln's body in the year of his inauguration reveal that his left hand was much longer than his right hand, and his left middle finger was elongated. He is also known to have suffered from severe farsightedness, in addition to having difficulty with his eyesight that stemmed from distortions in his facial bone structure. These bodily asymmetries are common to Marfan's syndrome, as is cardiac disease. It is believed that Lincoln inherited the disease from his father's side. His father was blind in one eye, his son Robert had difficulties with his eyes, and his son Tad had a speech defect and died at the age of eighteen, probably from cardiac trouble. The likelihood that Lincoln himself suffered from Marfan's syndrome was further confirmed in 1959, when a California physician named Harold Schwartz recognized the disease in a boy of seven who was known to share an ancestor with Lincoln.[20] Since the gene for Marfan's disease is dominant, those who have it and reach childbearing age stand a 50 percent chance of having an afflicted child.

Now consider the consequences for the gene pool if Lincoln's frozen sperm were to be disseminated widely in the population. At least until the facts became evident, the result would be exactly the opposite of what Müller intended by his proposal. And if the mistake went beyond the case of Lincoln and Marfan's syndrome, including other individuals who, despite their outstanding achievements, might be afflicted with or be carriers of other little known or as yet undiagnosed genetic diseases, the results would be dysgenic in the extreme. This last consideration leads directly to the second argument against eugenics programs, to which we turn next.

2. This argument holds that in any event, we are likely to alter the gene pool for ill. Leaving aside the less likely incidence of this occurrence as exemplified just now in the Abraham Lincoln story, we may look at another prominent consideration noted by some geneticists.

This consideration is often referred to as "heterozygote advantage." One geneticist explains the situation as follows:

> There is . . . good evidence that individuals who carry two different forms of the same gene, that is, are heterozygous, appear to have an advantage. This is true even if that gene in double dose, that is, in the homozygous state, produces a severe disease. For example, individuals homozygous for the gene coding for sickle-cell hemoglobin invariably develop sickle-cell anemia, which is generally fatal before the reproductive years. Heterozygotes for the gene are, however, protected more than normals from the effects of the most malignant form of malaria. It has been shown that women who carry the gene in single dose have a higher fertility in malarial areas than do normals.[21]

Here again, it is not only in the cases where there is known heterozygote advantage that the likelihood exists of altering the gene pool for ill by trying to eliminate genes for heritable diseases. There are, in addition, all of the cases where heterozygote advantage may exist but is at present unknown. If one uses risk-benefit ratios or something like a utilitarian schema for deciding moral issues in biomedical contexts, the evidence seems clearly to indicate a greater risk of dysgenic consequences than a possibility of beneficial results from attempts to alter the human gene pool by means of negative eugenics. A successful effort to eliminate carriers for heritable diseases would result at the same time in eliminating heterozygote advantage, which is believed to be beneficial to the species or to subpopulations within the species. While little is known at the present stage of inquiry in genetics about all of the particular advantages that exist, it is an inference made by many experts in the field on the basis of present data and well-confirmed genetic theory. One biologist asks us to

> Consider the gene leading to cystic fibrosis (C.F.). Until quite recently homozygotes for this gene died in infancy. Yet the gene causing C.F. is very common among all Caucasoid populations thus far studied. . . . It is too widespread in the race to be accounted for by genetic drift. The gene is also too frequent for it to be likely to be maintained by mutation pressure. Hence, we are driven to assume heterozygote advantage.[22]

It would seem, then, that what is gained by the elimination of homozygotes may well be lost by the elimination of heterozygotes, resulting in no clear benefits and possibly some significant disadvantages in populations that suffer from genetic diseases. But the argument just given assumes that it would in fact be possible to eliminate genes for heritable diseases by preventing carriers from reproducing and thereby passing on such genes to future generations. The next argument against genetic engineering questions such a possibility.

3. This argument maintains, in sum, that negative eugenics can't possibly work unless carriers are eliminated as well as diseased individuals; but a successful attempt to prevent all carriers of potentially lethal genes from reproducing would effectively eliminate the entire species. The effects of negative eugenics on the general population are assessed by one geneticist as follows:

> With a few exceptions, dominant diseases are rare and interfere severely with reproductive ability. They are generally maintained in the population by new mutations. Therefore, there is either no need or essentially no need for discouraging these individuals from reproduction. . . . The story is quite different for recessive conditions. . . . [A]ny attempt to decrease the gene frequency of these common genetic disorders in the population by prevention of fertility of all carriers would be doomed to failure. First, we all carry between three and eight of these genes in a single dose. Secondly, for many of these conditions, the frequency of carriers in the population is about 1 in 50 or even greater. Prevention of fertility for even one of these disorders would stop a sizable proportion of the population from reproducing. . . .[23]

If this assessment is sound, it has significant implications for the prospects of favorably altering the human gene pool by negative eugenics. Such an argument is persuasive if the purpose of negative eugenics is viewed as that of improving the human gene pool for the sake of future generations. But if the purpose of negative eugenics is seen as improving the quality of life for those in the present and next generation, then the argument just given is beside the point. We should recall the dual purpose for which proposals for genetic engineering are put forth. The one we have been discussing here is the proposed improvement or prevention of deterioration of the gene pool for the sake of future generations of humans. The other purpose, tied to voluntary genetic screening programs and the activity of genetic counseling, is to present options to individuals or couples that will help them avoid the birth of a defective child whose quality of life will be poor and who will most likely be a burden on both parents and society. For this latter purpose, the practice of negative eugenics through voluntary screening and sensitive genetic counseling can serve to improve the quality of life of persons in this and the next generation. But when transformed into a program designed to control the reproductive acts or capacities of people for the sake of future generations, then the practice of negative eugenics seems to be scientifically and practically misguided. Indeed, taking this argument and the previous one together, the conclusion may be put succinctly in the words of one writer:

> Neither positive nor negative eugenics can ever significantly improve the gene pool of the population and simultaneously allow for adequate evolutionary improvement of the human race. The only useful aspect of negative eugenics is in individual counseling of specific families in order to prevent some of the births of abnormal individuals.[24]

4. The fourth argument against genetic engineering focuses specifically on those practices involving manipulation of genetic material itself. This argument raises questions about the grave risks involved in any such manipulation, especially since mishaps that may arise are

likely to be far worse than what happens when nature takes its course. One geneticist sees the prospects as follows:

> The problem of altering an individual's genes by direct chemical change of his DNA presents technically an enormously difficult task. Even if it became possible to do this, the chance of error would be high. Such an error, of course, would have the diametrically opposite effect to that desired and would be irreversible; in other words, the individual would become even more abnormal.[25]

Some observers fear the creation of hapless monsters as a result of various manipulations on genetic material. Whether or not the laboratory techniques are sufficiently refined at present to enable researchers to develop procedures for widespread use, it is likely that these techniques will be available soon enough to deserve careful reflection now. We need to ask, once again, whether the purpose served by laboratory methods of genetic engineering is helping those who are at risk for bearing defective children to prevent such occurrences, or instead, breeding a genetically improved species for the future. If such techniques are perfected and become available for use in spite of the attendant risks of mishap, they would then be offered to couples on a voluntary basis in the same way that current methods of genetic intervention are employed. Where a practice is aimed at the genetic impovement of a couple's own progeny, there are no grounds for methods that involve coercion. What is needed in such cases is counseling and education, not coercion and control.

At the outset, I said I would argue for two separate but related theses. First, the individual or couple should have final decision-making authority in matters of his or her own reproductive acts and capacities, as well as in continuation or termination of pregnancy where the reasons for these decisions refer to genetic factors. Second, attempts at government-based or scientist-directed eugenics programs are bound to be misguided or dangerous or both. The four arguments at the end were offered in support of the second thesis. If those arguments are sound, they demonstrate that there is no warrant for those in power to take final decision-making authority away from the individual where the reasons for such actions refer to eugenic considerations. Recall also our earlier conclusion that final decision-making should be left to the individual or couple in the context of genetic counseling, except in cases where the decision requires medical expertise that a patient is unlikely to have. Now if genetic screening should be practiced on a voluntary basis; and if decisions arising out of counseling should be left to the individual; and if, in addition, positive and negative eugenics aimed at future generations is basically misguided; then there seems to be only one consideration remaining that might argue in favor of limiting individual rights for the sake of social benefits. That consideration points to the burden placed on society for treating and maintaining defective infants and others who might have been aborted or never even conceived by dint of state policy.

Time does not permit an examination of this last issue, but it is worth making a final observation in closing. If the notion of social benefit is understood largely in terms of increased financial resources that would otherwise be allocated to caring for those afflicted with heritable diseases, then something crucial is being left out of the balance between individual rights and social benefits. What is socially beneficial must be viewed not only in terms of increases in financial and other tangible resources but also in terms of a range of freedom and autonomy that members of a society can reasonably expect to enjoy. It is important to preserve that freedom and autonomy through ensuring the individual's right to decide about his or her own reproductive acts and capacities. With increased availability of voluntary genetic screening programs and widespread education of the public, it is hard to imagine that most people will choose to burden themselves and society with defective children when other options are open to them. Even if there are some who refuse screening or abortion, society as a whole would be better off to accommodate their freely chosen reproductive acts than to impose compulsory genetic screening, abortion, or sterilization on its members.

Notes

1. Tabitha Powledge, "Genetic Screening," *Encyclopedia of Bioethics* (in press).
2. Ibid.
3. Ibid.
4. Tabitha Powledge, "The XYY Man; Do Criminals Really Have Abnormal Genes?" *Science Digest*, January, 1976, p. 37.
5. Powledge, "Genetic Screening," op. cit.
6. A view similar to this is argued by Marc Lappé, "The Genetic Counselor: Responsible to Whom?" *The Hastings Center Report*, No. 2, September, 1971.
7. Kurt Hirschhorn, "Symposium: Ethics of Genetics Counseling," *Contemporary OB/GYN*, vol. 2, no. 4, 117.
8. Robert F. Murray, Jr., ibid., 120.
9. Marc Lappé, op. cit., 6.
10. Bernard D. Davis, "Threat and Promise in Genetic Engineering," in Preston Williams (ed.), *Ethical Issues in Biology and Medicine* (Cambridge, Mass.: Schenkman Publishing Company, 1973), pp. 17–24.
11. Ibid.
12. Francis MacDonald Cornford (tr.), *The Republic of Plato* (New York: Oxford University Press, 1945), pp. 157–160.
13. Hermann J. Müller, "Genetic Progress by Voluntarily Conducted Germinal Choice," in Gordon Wolstenholme (ed.), *Man and His Future* (Boston: Little, Brown and Co., 1963), p. 256.
14. Theodosius Dobzhansky, *Mankind Evolving* (New Haven: Yale University Press, 1962), p. 328.
15. Such arguments are offered by Paul Ramsey in *Fabricated Man* (New Haven: Yale University Press, 1970).
16. This argument is given by Ramsey, op. cit., and also by Leon R. Kass, "Making Babies—The New Biology and the 'Old' Morality," *The Public Interest*, vol. 26, Winter 1972, pp. 18–56.
17. Arthur Steinberg, "The Genetic Pool. Its Evolution and Significance—'Desirable' and 'Undesirable' Genetic Traits," in Simon Btesh (ed.), *Recent Progress in Biology and Medicine: Its Social and Ethical Implications* (Geneva: Council for International Organizations of Medical Sciences, 1972), pp. 83–93.
18. Kurt Hirschhorn, op. cit., p. 128.
19. Kurt Hirschhorn, "Practical and Ethical Problems in Human Genetics," *Birth Defects*, vol. VIII, July, 1972, 28.
20. Ibid., 23.
21. Arthur Steinberg, op. cit.
22. René Dubos and Maya Pines, *Health and Disease* (New York: Time, Inc., 1965), pp. 123–24.
23. Kurt Hirschhorn, "Practical and Ethical Problems in Human Genetics," 22–23.
24. Ibid., 25.
25. Ibid., 27.

Making reproductive decisions in the light of genetic information permits prospective parents only a limited range of choices over their future children. Other techniques offer more reproductive choice. Artificial insemination has vastly altered animal populations, and could similarly affect human populations. Cloning offers still further possibilities of standardization. This is the asexual reproduction of an organism from a single cell of one parent, to whom the new organism is genetically identical. If cloning can be extended to humans (and there are claims that it has been), it would be possible to create whole classes of genetically homogeneous persons.

Many see these techniques as threatening a reproductive revolution which would dwarf the contraceptive revolution, end family life, and herald a Brave New World of cohorts of genetically identical pseudo-siblings. Seymour Lederberg argues that cloning (like artificial insemination) can be seen as extending rather than limiting reproductive choices, since it can offer the possibility of reproduction to couples who are otherwise infertile or unwilling to procreate by the usual means. Indeed, if we count *self-reproduction* as a primary reproductive goal of individuals, then cloning seems to offer the most desirable of genetic possibilities. Lederberg finds the fears expressed unrealistic. Human cloning, he argues, poses far less threat of socioeconomic castes than do other social practices. Rather than trying to forestall misuse of cloning by regulating current research, a government would do better to foster diversity of education and employment for people, however similar or dissimilar in genotype. As for family life, cloning might lead to recrimination and even lawsuits by children critical of their parents' reproductive choices. But this trouble would be offset by the benefits cloning would confer on otherwise infertile couples.

LAW AND CLONING— THE STATE AS REGULATOR OF GENE FUNCTION

SEYMOUR LEDERBERG

The Biology of Cloning

Cloning is the asexual reproduction of cells from a single parent so that the genetic constitution of the progeny cells is the same as that of the parent cell. The process is widespread throughout the microbial and plant world, lower animals, and in the natural growth and regeneration of the tissues of adult higher animals. We, ourselves, are the clones derived from a parental zygote, the formation of the latter being the only sexual step in going from two germ cells to the one zygote cell to the 10^{14} cells that we are.

For some microbes and for all higher forms of life, cloned cells, although genetically like the parent cell and each other, take on separate specialized activities. They make different biological products, they associate with other cells selectively, and they share different roles in organizing a multicellular stage of life. This remarkable differentiation of cloned cells to make biological man is followed by cultural development to form the social person. In this sense, cloned man has been fabricated since his genesis. The processes of biological differentiation which lead to our adult selves have been at the core of

From *Genetics and the Law,* A. Milunsky and George J. Annas, eds., © Plenum Publishing Corp., 1976, pp. 377–385. Reprinted by permission.

scientific inquiry for millennia and are still not understood.

One of the forms taken by such inquiry was to question whether differentiation of the clone from a zygote involved the irreversible loss of genetic potentialities at some early embryonic stage to form separate lines of progeny cells increasingly committed to specific functions. This would explain the unilateral direction of differentiation, despite the appearance of continuity of the same genotype. Germ cell lines, of course, would be spared this irreversible loss.

The question was approached experimentally by injecting the nucleus from a cell from the embryonic stage of the leopard frog, *Rana pipiens,* into a frog egg whose own nucleus had been removed. Some of the eggs treated in this manner went on to develop into normal post-neurula embryos.[1] Improved versions of the nuclear transplant technique promoted unrestricted normal development to the adult stage in several species of *Amphibia* and *Insecta.*[2-4] Overall, the basic conclusion to emerge is that the genetic totipotency of a differentiated cell can be conserved, since nuclei of adult differentiated tissues remain competent to direct complete development of an enucleated egg into a normal, fertile adult. Irreversible changes or losses of genes are not the cause of differentiation and need not arise from it.

The transplanted nucleus has an informational function. Its genes provide the coded directions for making nucleic acid messages which are translated into proteins. In the differentiated somatic cell only selected genetic regions were functioning; the remainder either were repressed by complexing with a controlling molecule, or were inactive because of the absence of a molecular signal. Enucleation of the egg destroys its resident genetic information but leaves the cell's biosynthetic capacity to work with the chromosomes and genes of a nucleus, should these be reintroduced.

Somatic cells in culture can fuse and coordinate the biosynthetic programs directed by the two coexisting sets of genes. Therefore, in principle, any biological obstacle to using enucleated eggs of one species as the incubator for the nucleus of another would depend primarily on whether cytoplasmic signals left in the heterologous egg were adequate to initiate use of the new nucleus. As activation of the transplanted nucleus proceeded, the egg's newly made biosynthetic apparatus would be increasingly derived from the transplant. The same cell fusion technique may provide a means for transferring somatic nuclei to mammalian eggs whose small size makes them technically difficult to manipulate.[5]

The genetic totipotency of somatic plant nuclei has been demonstrated directly, using single dissociated plant cells from carrots and tobacco.[6] Normal somatic animal cells have not yet been shown to be capable of the same dedifferentiation and activation without transfer to an egg cell. However, transfer studies with animal cell nuclei may be expected to lead to our ability to promote directly such regulation changes involving gene function.

Issues Arising when Cloning is Applied to Gene Regulation during Development

Even as the original observations on nuclear transfer grew out of interest in fundamental questions of biology, the same motivations relate to the ongoing development of this work on the factors which regulate the expression of different components of our genome. Inasmuch as the principles at work pervade the phenomena of cancer, human embryological development and genetic disorders, nuclear transplant techniques will be increasingly employed in basic research concerning such health problems.

One particular medical application relates to the host acceptability of tissue and organ transplants. There is a greater medical need of human transplantable organs than can be supplied from donors of any source. The search for the technology to create synthetic replacement parts can be complemented by a search for the biological regulatory controls which can be manipulated to allow organ regeneration in vitro from organ samples, or if dedifferentiation is needed, to allow embryonic organs to develop in vitro. If these are derived from the person in whom they are ultimately reintroduced, the antigenic identity of host and organ would be expected to prevent immune rejections of the implant.

A major ethical issue that arises here stems from the extent of embryonic development that is needed prior to isolating an embryonic organ or tissue. Current federal guidelines[7] for the protection of human subjects, pursuant to the National Research Act,[8] regulate experimentation on the human conceptus when it has been implanted in the donor of the ovum. At root are concerns for the sanctity that human fetal life shares with human persons, the impossibility for obtaining consent from a human fetus for experimentation, and pressures for minimizing incentives for abortion and for maximizing the ability of a woman to reverse a decision to schedule an abortion.

Present guidelines which refer to a human ovum fertilized by a human sperm do not apply to a human somatic cell activated without involvement of a human ovum; nor do they apply to any use of ova other than human fertilized by any sperm. To expedite discussion of the applicability of research guidelines, the term "clonus" is proposed for the early division products of the activation of a somatic nucleus irrespective of the cell which is its host. Clonus is the asexual homolog of conceptus.

The versions of the clonus described here are studied in vitro and so have no substantial relevance to a woman's decision on abortion even as the donor of an enucleated egg. Therefore, this leaves to an Ethical Advisory Board and human experimentation consent committee[9] the issue of the disposition of the clonus and cell lines derived from it. Since the focus of the studies would be on embryonic differentiation, the Board will presumably also review any attempts to develop for the human clonus and in vitro conceptus an in vitro attachment and metabolic exchange surface comparable to the collagen layer successfully used for substantial development of the mouse embryo.[10] The first question facing the Board will be whether the clonus is classed as a tissue or organ culture or as a conceptus. If classed as the latter, is the study of the factors which promote its attachment and development on surfaces in vitro the same as a study of im-

plantation? If so, is such a study therapeutic because it is constructive to the development of that clonus, or non-therapeutic because for any variable under study some subjects may receive non-optimal treatment?

The present guidelines apply restrictive protections to the conceptus, whatever the nature of the conception process, upon implantation into "the donor of the ovum."[11] Presumably, protection upon implantation in the uterus of any woman will be a preferred future reading of the rules. With anticipated advances in mammalian organ and embryo culture, cultivation of the clonus or conceptus in vitro may be able to be sustained longer. If the stage of development achievable in vitro is comparable to a post-implantation stage in vivo, then a difficult question arises: Is it the continuous in vitro history or the developmental maturity which will determine if the embryo warrants the protection of due process? Compounding this is our ignorance of whether prolonged cultivation in vitro increases the probability of subsequent successful transfer to a uterus, or whether the probability of such integration diminishes as the embryo's complexity progresses.

Issues Arising when Cloning is Applied as an Alternative to Artificial Insemination, Adoption, and Conception

At present, the socially acceptable alternatives for a male-sterile infertile couple to develop a family are by adoption or artificial insemination. Adoption poses the disadvantage of absence of the pre-natal and neonatal emotional experiences for the couple, the concern for psychological trauma should the natural parents attempt to reassert their relationship, the absence of a genetic contribution to the next generation, and the limited availability of children from backgrounds acceptable to the couple. Artificial insemination by donor sperm (A.I.D.) has none of these disadvantages, but can have serious legal consequences.

Although some jurisdictions have statutes establishing the legitimacy of a child conceived by A.I.D.,[12] case law differs widely in court holdings. A child conceived by A.I.D. consented to by the husband was considered illegitimate by New York trial courts,[13,14] although other jurisdictions held such a child to be "lawfully begotten."[15] An extreme position taken earlier by Canadian[16] and British[17] courts was that A.I.D. was adultery. It would appear that for an infertile couple, implanting a clonus drawn from the enucleated egg of the woman and a somatic nucleus of either parent would avoid the possible stigma of adultery for them and illegitimacy for their children. They would acquire none of the disadvantages of adoption or A.I.D., and each parent's genes would have an opportunity to be transmitted to their offspring. Parenthetically, we note that any desired sex ratio among their children could be obtained.

Without yielding my own preferences for a less complicated mode of procreation, I cannot fault this option. The couple will be 25 to 35 years older than the children, so resemblances will appear strong but not identical. If the family elects to have one boy and one girl, the two will be dissimilar; if not, the family presumably risks psychological trauma of unknown severity.

An action by a child for "wrongful life"[18] might arise as a result of the mental distress and emotional suffering encountered as a cloned person, but the holding in *Williams* v. *State* denied recovery for being born under one set of circumstances or parents rather than to another.[19]

Now, until we learn how to coordinate the pace of the divisions of the transplanted somatic nucleus with the biosynthetic abilities of the enucleated host ovum, the clonus risks chromosomal aneuploidy. Implantation itself represents an enormous technological barrier whose overcoming has yet to be reliably documented.[20] Presumably, an abnormal clonus or embryo has a high probability of spontaneous abortion, since this is the customary fate of a chromosomally abnormal conceptus.[21] We can assist this natural screening by amniocentesis in the 14th-16th week of gestation on the assumption that the couple is at higher than average risk for chromosomal errors.

Should a defective child be brought to term, there is the possibility of tort liability by the investigator for prenatal injury[22,23] if it could be shown that the trauma was initiated after the clonus was formed and was caused by negligence of a duty owed by the investigator. This possibility makes an amniocentesis diagnosis by the investigator virtually mandatory.

A state may choose to regulate and prohibit development of a cloned cell to a human. The Massachusetts statute[24] on fetal research might not apply if the procedures used to learn the optimum conditions for development were accepted as diagnostic or remedial procedures to determine or preserve the life or health of *that* fetus.

Counter to this type of statute would be the due process appeal that the state was invading the couple's right to privacy and to procreate,[25] that the state was in effect affecting involuntary birth control on the male partner by prohibiting his only way to transmit his genes to children, and that the interest of the state to interfere with experimental procedures in development of the clonus was irrational rather than compelling, since absent optimum experimental conditions the clonus would not develop normally.

If cloning is allowable for the infertile family, the application of the equal protection of law suggests that it could not be denied per se to the fertile family, and it makes no sense for public policy to encourage a vasectomy in order to qualify for access to cloning technology. Any family which desired to continue the genotype of one of the parents, or of another person, might elect to clone offspring. A "socially desirable" genotype which would otherwise be reassorted on subsequent sexual reproduction could be thereby protected. Genetic variability in our population would be maintained through ongoing mutation and parallel sexual reproduction, with selected genotypes conserved for the next generations to obtain the "tempered clonality" proposed by Joshua Lederberg.[26] The choice of mode of procreation could still be a personal decision influenced as always by the social pressures which modify autonomous perception of desirability and rationality. Overall, however, the motivation for this pathway for a fertile family is dubious because of the alternate modes of procreation available.

Issues Arising when Cloning is Applied to Create Homogeneous Channeled Social Groups

The gravest concern over cloning comes from its possible use to create large classes of identical people selected for some genetically determined set of characteristics.[27-34] Presumably, excellence in specialized talents and occupations would be the phenotypic criteria used for the classification, and therefore, socioeconomic castes would emerge, as in Huxley's *Brave New World*. [*Eds.* Compare Russell Baker's vision below, pp. 104–5.]

It has been suggested that the nobility clauses[35] of the Constitution may be construed to bar the granting of special privilege to socially prestigious cloned classes.[36] The Thirteenth Amendment,[37] prohibiting slavery and involuntary servitude, has been proposed to cover cloning, since a "genetic bondage" which diminishes autonomy is deliberately designed to reduce the option of choices which create individuality.[38] The constraints on nobility would deny a governmentally imposed differential on the access to the technology of cloning, and that on servitude would bar a public policy which coerced cloning of an individual.

However, there is a stage in the formation of socioeconomic strata which is more benignly amenable to governmental regulation. Up to now, a cloned person has been considered as operatively identical to the parent and to similarly derived sibs. Attention has focused on the replication of like behavioral and intellectual traits. Yet, this decade has seen profound doubts arise over the extent to which genetic endowments and environmental experience create differentials in these attributes. An alphabet caste system requires a structured cultural cloning to convert genetic opportunity into people behaving in a replicate manner. *Without such an imposition of identical nurture, the rigid definition of an individual fails, and he*

*remains free to choose his own develop-
ment.*

The real danger of stratification of our society then comes from the unequal access to cultural experiences which now quite effectively channel us independently of our genetic makeup. To escape this danger, we need to affirm the position espoused by the Supreme Court in *Meyer* v. *Nebraska* that the Spartan model of education and training does "violence to both letter and spirit of the Constitution."[39] The governmental policy most likely to prevent cloning technology from being misused to create castes can do this with least risk to our welfare, not by limiting research or procreative instruments but by truly providing people with opportunities for diversity in education, professional training, employment, and cultural experience.

Notes

1. R. Briggs and T. J. King, "Transplantation of Living Nuclei from Blastula Cells into Enucleated Frog's Eggs," *Proceedings of the National Academy of Science*, vol. 38, 1953, 445.
2. J. G. Gurdon, "Adult Frogs Derived from the Nuclei of Single Somatic Cells," *Developmental Biology*, vol. 4, 1962, 256.
3. T. J. King, "Nuclear Transplantation in Amphibia," in D. M. Prescott (ed.), *Methods in Cell Physiology*, Vol. II, (New York, Academic Press, 1966), pp. 1–34.
4. J. B. Gurdon, *The Control of Gene Expression in Animal Development* (Cambridge, Harvard University Press, 1974).
5. C. F. Graham, "Virus Assisted Fusion of Embryonic Cells," E. Diczfaulzy (ed.), *Karolinska Symposia on Research Methods in Reproductive Endocrinology,*

Symposium 3 (Stockholm, 1971), p. 154.
6. F. C. Steward, From cultured cells to whole plants: The induction and control of their growth and differentiation, *Proceedings of the Royal Society* B 175:1 (1970).
7. Federal Register 38:27382, October 9, 1973; 38:31738, November 16, 1973; 39:18,914, May 30, 1974; 39:30648, August 23, 1974.
8. PL:93-348 National Research Service Award Act of 1974, Title II—Protection of Human Subjects of Biomedical and Behavioural Research.
9. See, *supra* 7.
10. Y.-C. Hsu, "Differentiation *in Vitro* of Mouse Embryos to the Stage of Early Somite," *Developmental Biology*, vol. 33, 1973, 403.
11. See, *supra* 7.
12. E. Sagall, "Artificial Insemination," *Trial*, January/February, 1973, 59.
13. *Gursky* v. *Gursky*, 242 N.Y.S. 2d 406 (Superior Court 1963).
14. *Anonymous* v. *Anonymous,* 246 N.Y.S. 2d 886 (Superior Court 1964).
15. *People* v. *Sorenson*, 66 Cal. Reporter 7, 437 P.2d 499 (1968).
16. *Oxford* v. *Oxford,* 58 Dom. Law Reports 251 (Ontario Superior Court 1921).
17. *Russel* v. *Russel,* A.C. 687 at p. 148 (1924).
18. *Zepeda* v. *Zepeda,* 41 Ill. App. 2d 240, 190 N.E. 2d 890 (Appellate Court, First District, 1963).
19. *Williams* v. *State*, 18 N.Y. 2d 481, 276 N.Y.S. 2d 885 (Court of Appeals, 1966).
20. D. DeKretzer, P. Dennis, B. Hudson et al., "Transfer of a Human Zygote," *Lancet*, vol. 2, 1973, 720.
21. J. L. Hamerton, *Human Cytogenetics* (New York, Academic Press, 1971), vol. II, pp. 388–389.
22. *Smith* v. *Brennan,* 31 N.J. 353, 157 A. 2d 497 (Supreme Court 1960).
23. *Sylvia* v. *Gobeille*, 101 RI 76, 222 A. 2d 222 (Supreme Court 1966).

24. Mass. Gen. Laws, Chapter 112, Section 12J.
25. See S. Lederberg, "State Channeling of Gene Flow by Regulation of Marriage and Procreation," in A. Milunsky and G. J. Annas (eds.), op. cit., pp. 247–266. (Case history on privacy and procreation is developed in this companion paper.)
26. J. Lederberg, "Experimental Genetics and Human Evolution," *American Naturalist*, vol. 100, 1966, 519.
27. *Idem.*
28. J. Fletcher, "Ethical Aspects of Genetic Controls," *New England Journal of Medicine,* vol. 285, 1971, 776.
29. J. Fletcher, *The Ethics of Genetic Control* (Garden City, N.Y., Anchor Press/Doubleday, 1974).
30. L. Kass, "New Beginnings in Life," in M. Hamilton (ed.), *The New Genetics and the Future of Man* (Grand Rapids, Mich., Eerdmans Publishing Company, 1972).
31. C. P. Kindegran, "State Power Over Human Fertility and Individual Liberty," *Hastings Law Journal,* vol. 23, 1972, 1401.
32. F. C. Pizzulli, "Asexual Reproduction and Genetic Engineering: A Constitutional Assessment of the Technology of Cloning," *Southern California Law Review,* vol. 47, 1974, 476.
33. P. Ramsey, *Fabricated Man* (New Haven, Conn., Yale University Press, 1970).
34. L. H. Tribe, *Channeling Technology Through Law* (Chicago: The Brockton Press, 1973).
35. U.S. Constitution, Article I, Section 9, Clause 8. No Title of Nobility shall be granted by the United States: And no Person holding any Office of Profit or Trust under them, shall, without the Consent of the Congress, accept of any present, Emolument, Office, or Title, of any Rival whatever, from any King, Prince or Foreign State.
Article I, Section 10, Clause 1. No State Shall enter into any Treaty, Alliance, or Confederation; grant Letters of Marque and Reprisal; coin Money; emit Bills of Credit; make any Thing but gold and silver Coin a Tender in Payment of Debts; pass any Bill of Attainder, ex post facto Law, a Law impairing the Obligation of Contracts, or grant any Title of Nobility.
36. See, *supra* 32, at p. 579.
37. U.S. Constitution—Amendment 13, Section 1. Neither slavery nor involuntary servitude, except as a punishment for crime whereof the party shall have been duly convicted, shall exist within the United States, or any place subject to their jurisdiction.
U.S. Constitution—Amendment 13, Section 2. Congress shall have power to enforce this article by appropriate legislation.
38. See, *supra* 32, at p. 517.
39. *Meyer* v. *Nebraska,* 262 U.S. 390, at p. 402 (1923).

Parents take care!

TINKER PEOPLE

RUSSELL BAKER

Until a few years ago, people just happened. As a result, most of them were hodgepodges, like London and Rome, which also just happened.

Occasionally you might run into somebody who had been planned, like Washington, D.C. These planned people were the produce of Planned Parenthood. Their parents had sat down with architects. The architects had shown them blueprints of beautiful families in which all the siblings would be as neatly spaced as the oaks on a Washington boulevard.

Later, when the siblings were all precisely spaced in their assigned spots on the calendar, they were very much like people who had just happened, except for a tendency to think of themselves as siblings. Where the old kinds had hated their brothers and sisters as rivals for the throne and hired thugs to dispose of them, these people hired psychologists to dispel their sibling rivalries.

As a result, Erica Jong replaced William Shakespeare as the chronicler of humanity's foibles. Otherwise, the emergence of planned people had little effect. Now, however, family architecture has become fancier. For $40, a cou-

ple planning a person can buy a Gender Selection Kit which—its marketers assert—makes it possible for parents to assign the sex of their choice to their little production. It is hard to guess what the upshot of this will be. Historically, men have decided what kind of car the family would have and women have had the last word on sofas and refrigerators. How will it go when they sit down to decide whether the person on the drawing board will be male or female?

A feminist tells me that male ego will prevail, that the country will end up with a vast surplus of men, and women will be in huge demand. I don't know. My guess is that a lot of productions will never get off the drawing board on account of the planners deciding to get divorced rather than go on fighting about whether they ought to create a man or a woman.

In view of children's natural disposition to frustrate parents, we can also look for a big boom in sex-change surgery, particularly during the adolescent years of the planned generation. Nowadays a young man who hates his family's insistence that he go to college and become a lawyer has to drop out of school and become a tanner. In the future he will be able to send the old folks up the wall by going to Johns Hopkins and becoming a woman.

It would be interesting to know what it feels like to be a fully planned person. Having your sex determined by your parents, of course, is surely only a primitive beginning on the intricate architecture which biology will make possible in another generation or so. Before the century is out, science will probably enable parents to decide not only what size and shape their productions will take, but also how bright they will be and what careers they will pursue.

Most people will probably go for very smart, mildly acquisitive doctors and lawyers. Economically, this could lead to a well-balanced nation, with the lawyers suing the doctors for outrageous sums and the doctors recovering their losses by charging the lawyers fees which, they know all too well, the traffic can bear.

If we could anticipate a perfectly closed economy, with the money circling from doctors to lawyers and back again, the country would be too occupied with suing and suturing to be subject to the fits of unhappiness it now suffers. Unfortunately, there is always somebody who rocks the boat to Paradise.

Imagine, for example, a man who has been totally planned by a pair of parents who think they have a great sense of humor. He has come off the blueprint to their exact specifications and is the complete fulfillment of their dream to play a good joke on the world. As a result, he is not very bright, has no talent for either courtroom or hospital, and not much interest in anything else.

If you are in this pickle nowadays— as most people are—there's not much to do about it but blame God or fate. In the new dispensation, parents will have replaced these invulnerable objects of man's disenchantment.

I think the person in this example is going to make a very loud fuss about parents being to blame for the mess the world is in. And I think a lot of lawyers who are suing doctors eight hours a day, and a lot of doctors who are extracting lawyers' gall bladders until midnight, are going to start listening to him, and that the lawyers are going to start asking why they have to stand around in musty old courtrooms all their lives and the doctors are going to start asking why they have to spend their lives up to the elbows in iodine, and that everybody is going to say, "It's parents who made this mess."

Many persons say this now, of course, but without real conviction, knowing the joker is really God or fate or something equally impervious to a kick in the pants. When parents become God or fate, they will get to know what angry is.

II

CARING
FOR CHILDREN

Men and women who choose to be parents have also to choose what sort of parents they will be. Legislators and lawyers, educators and doctors have to choose what sorts of child care and education they will seek or foster when their work affects children. These choices cannot be made by referring to some single, hallowed set of child-rearing practices. In heterogeneous and open societies, parents and professionals alike are besieged by conflicting advice and confronted with diverse practices. The essays in this section discuss some of the principles which might help one to choose among available practices and policies for dealing with children. They do not describe the findings of psychology, pedagogy, and medicine relevant to such choices. The principles with which we are here concerned are normative principles. Using them, parents and professionals who are reasonably informed about these "factual" matters may be able to distinguish what *must* be done from what is optional (even if beneficial) and what must *not* be done from what is permissible (even if not beneficial).

Such normative concerns have been brought to public attention by the many writers and protagonists of the "children's rights movement." We begin this section with one of the fundamental documents of that movement, the U.N. Declaration of the Rights of the Child. In this declaration, children are said to have a right to many good things, including material and physical security, education, and health care. Little is said, however, about the corresponding duties to provide these benefits.

There are, it is true, some sorts of rights for which we need not specify on whom the corresponding duty falls. For example, the liberty rights of children (or others) impose a uniform duty of non-interference on all others. But most of the benefits and services required for the care of children can be provided only by the action of particular other persons. Only a particular person, or a very small group of persons, can give a child meals or consolation, bandage a knee, or read a bedtime story. It is idle to talk about the claim rights of children to specific services or benefits without specifying on whom the corresponding duty falls.

The U.N. Declaration, though it uses the vocabulary of rights, is best construed as a statement of children's interests, whose fulfillment might be and should be taken as a social and legislative goal. But this goal could not be achieved by setting up some duty roster specifying who should meet which interests of which children, for young children especially have a strong interest in having their various needs met mainly by the same person or persons. Parents, natural or substitute, are indispensable if children's interests are to be met.

If the main burden of meeting a child's interests falls on parents, then plainly, children cannot have a right to have all their interests met. Parents have finite capacities, other obligations, and interests of their own. Children's claim rights must then be less extensive than their interests, and parents' obligations less demanding than their ideals. Parents need to know which of their children's interests they must try to meet, and which are optional. This topic is approached in different ways in the essays by Jeffrey Blustein and William Ruddick. Both investigate the interdependence of children's and parents' interests, and use these considerations to state which claim rights of children can be taken seriously because grounded on corresponding parental obligations. The case of *Seiferth* shows the difficulty of legally separating interests of parent and child, even when those interests are conceptually distinguishable.

Both Blustein and Ruddick emphasize that parental duties require some parental control and authority. If we take seriously children's claim rights to specific services and benefits, then we must accept that children have less than standard liberty rights. Parents have legitimate standing in making some, even (as in the Seiferth case) life-affecting decisions, for their children. This conclusion is broadly similar to that reached by Lawrence Crocker in his discussion of parents' position in making decisions about children's future sexual orientation. This conclusion might be extended to decisions which parents of the future may have to make about even more fundamental, genetically determined characteristics of their children.

However, for the most part, we have postponed discussion of parents' authority and children's liberty rights until Part III. The reason for this untidy arrangement is that liberty rights are mostly of concern and in dispute when children are older. Though the limits of parental authority may be questioned when parents make life-affecting decisions for the future of young children, they are often in daily and mundane dispute as children grow older. The essays in Part III consider the bases for restricting children's liberties in matters where (legal) adults are permitted to choose for themselves.

A further reason for postponing consideration of children's liberty rights until Part III is that the entire framework of rights and obligations, with its adversarial implications, applies less clearly to the problems and possibilities of earlier childhood. A discussion limited to children's rights would focus entirely on claims and liberties. Thus, it would miss much of what is most distinctive about family life, especially about the lives of families with young children, where the identification of parents and children, and the interlocking of their interests, is often greatest.

The claim rights of younger children are, nevertheless, the central topic of this section. Meeting these is the core of parental activity, and at least some of these rights are legally enforceable via abuse and neglect statutes. Such statutes determine a minimal level of care to which children are entitled and which the state will secure for them.

Four selections in Part II probe this area. Natalie Abrams examines the various standards used in defining child abuse and parental negligence. She then proposes a link between a revised definition and an explicit theory of parental obligation. In *Roe* v. *Conn* the judges discuss adequate and inadequate grounds for removing children from their parental home, as well as various remedies to use in place of removal. Robert Mnookin criticizes judicial use of a "best interests of the child" test in removing children from their natural parents and assigning them to state-controlled "temporary" foster care, and proposes a new test. Rena Uviller sets out the dilemmas which confront child advocates when interests of parents and children conflict.

Ideally, abuse and neglect statutes should hold parents to a standard of care compatible with the claims their children have on them. However, some abuse and neglect statutes have required of parents actions incompatible with their obligations. For example, parents who keep a child from a school they judge to be unsafe or corrupting are seeking to meet their parental obligations conscientiously, as are many parents who apply eccentric standards in matters of dress, diet, or medical treatment. The legal resolution of such conscientious resistance by parents is a recurrent theme of litigation over children.

It would perhaps be possible to ensure that abuse and neglect statutes were so framed and applied that they did not require parents to fail in any parental obligations. But it does not follow that these statutes can or should be formulated so as to provide legal remedies for every deficiency of parental care. The very poverty and clumsiness of the remedies such legislation can offer restrict its use to protecting children from major failure on the part of their parents. For lesser infractions of parental obligations, social intervention is often a more harmful "cure" than the ill it seeks to remedy. Not all parental obligations are legal obligations, and parents need principles of obligation as well as a knowledge of their statutory duties if they are to meet their children's claims.

Beyond the area of obligation, parents must also resolve moral dilemmas which have nothing to do with their children's claims or their own obligations. Reflection on their obligations cannot, for example, help parents to choose how much to involve their children in their own lives and concerns, or how overt an influence they should exercise on their children's activities and career plans, or which mistakes it is wise to let children make for themselves. Regretfully, we have included few pieces dealing with the requirements of good—as opposed to merely adequate—parents. In part, the omission reflects the priority of obligations over supererogation; in part, it reflects the fact that parental policies in such matters are often so much dependent on the personality and history of parents that they are not matters for conscious choice and reflection. A complete theory of parenthood would, however, have to include principles and reflections on the non-obligatory activities of parents which contribute so much of the tone and texture, and of the happiness or misery, of family life.

In a third subsection we do, however, go beyond the issue of children's claims and parents' obligations. How are parental activities to be divided between mothers and fathers who live together? Between mothers and fathers who live apart? Parents, judges, and others are often unsure whether there are two (or more?) distinct parental roles, called "mothering" and "fathering," or whether there is just an indeterminate list of parental activities, customarily, and perhaps unfortunately, allocated in gender-stereotyped ways.

We have included a strong statement of the traditional sex-linked division. Rousseau in *Emile*, his long treatise on education and childhood, confidently claims that there are precisely two parental roles, and they cannot be exchanged between mothers and fathers or delegated to others without bad results. By contrast, Virginia Held explores what an *equal* division of parental responsibilities would amount to.

Confidence here calls for knowledge of psychological and sociological study of alternative styles of child rearing and of effects of various divisions of child care among several people. Much has changed in a world where families frequently move, where the working lives of men and women have become more similar than they were in the recent past, and where there are many distinct possibilities for the social provision of specific sorts of child care, both inside and outside the child's home.

We have given the last word in this section to John Locke, who among political theorists takes more account than any other of the distinctive features of parental activity and authority. Since much of what he has to say concerns the limits of parental authority, this selection might also have found a place in Part III. However, since Locke links the limitation of parental authority to the peculiar quality of parental duties, whose performance requires parents of younger children to exercise an authority which they simultaneously aim to end, Locke's views also form a fitting end to these discussions of child care.

1. Children's Interests, Parents' Obligations

The U.N. Declaration of the Rights of the Child was adopted by the U.N. General Assembly in 1959. It supplements the 1948 Universal Declaration of Human Rights (which did not specifically mention children) and expands the older Geneva Declaration of the Rights of the Child, which the League of Nations had adopted in 1924.

"Mankind," asserts the Preamble, "owes to the child the best it has to give." This assumption about obligations explains much of the content of the Declaration.

First, it explains the Declaration's lack of concern with children's liberties. Though the Preamble speaks of children's "rights and freedoms," the ten principles presented say more about restricting than about respecting children's liberties (see especially Principles 7 and 9). Once we have thought of rights as something which humanity, or legislators, give or withhold, this focus is not surprising. Liberty rights have traditionally been seen as something which legislators may respect (or violate) but do not confer. However, liberty rights too are vulnerable if not guaranteed by legislation; so their omission from the Declaration is not trivial.

Second, the emphasis on "the best mankind has to give" explains the Declaration's focus on children's maximal claims. Children are here said to be entitled to legislation which secures their best interests, and no distinction is drawn between those interests and a lesser core of benefits to which children are entitled. However, we know, merely from the fact that interests conflict, that we cannot enact any set of rights which respects the best interests of all parties, or even of all children. If we want to secure certain rights for children (or others), we need to look for an enforceable set of claims, even though it may not include everything which would be in the best interest of each child. For example, legislators setting up school systems cannot possibly guarantee each child the education which would be optimal, for the interests of some children would conflict with the interests of other persons, including those of other children.

Third, the view that children's rights are owed them "by mankind" explains the Declaration's vagueness about the assignments of obligations to persons or agencies. But claim rights are not taken seriously unless they are claims against specifiable others and can, if needed, be pressed and enforced. Mankind, after all, is ill equipped to bathe a particular baby or to teach a particular group of children to read. Legislators have to try to create a framework of institutions which assigns enforceable obligations. They are likely, therefore, to guarantee children rights to minimal rather than optimal benefits, so that these can be grounded in the corresponding obligations and accountability of specifiable others. The U.N. Declaration leaves it open which set of less than optimal benefits legislators should seek to guarantee for children.

UNITED NATIONS DECLARATION OF THE RIGHTS OF THE CHILD

A five-point Declaration of the Rights of the Child was stated in 1923 by the International Union for Child Welfare, with 1948 revisions in a seven-point document. The League of Nations adopted the IUCW declaration in 1924. The following Declaration of the Rights of the Child was adopted by the United Nations General Assembly in 1959.

Declaration of the Rights of the Child
Preamble

Whereas the peoples of the United Nations have, in the Charter, reaffirmed their faith in fundamental human rights and in the dignity and worth of the human person and have determined to promote social progress and better standards of life in larger freedom,

Whereas the United Nations has, in the Universal Declaration of Human Rights, proclaimed that everyone is entitled to all the rights and freedoms set forth therein, without distinction of any kind, such as race, color, sex, language, religion, political or other opinion, national or social origin, property, birth, or other status,

Whereas the child, by reason of his physical and mental immaturity, needs special safeguards and care, including appropriate legal protection, before as well as after birth,

Whereas the need for such special

United Nations, General Assembly Resolution 1386(XIV), November 20, 1959, published in the *Official Records of the General Assembly, Fourteenth Session, Supplement No. 16,* 1960, p. 19.

safeguards has been stated in the Geneva Declaration of the Rights of the Child of 1924, and recognized in the Universal Declaration of Human Rights and in the statutes of specialized agencies and international organizations concerned with the welfare of children,

Whereas mankind owes to the child the best it has to give,

Now therefore,

The General Assembly

Proclaims this Declaration of the Rights of the Child to the end that he may have a happy childhood and enjoy for his own good and for the good of society the rights and freedoms herein set forth, and calls upon parents, upon men and women as individuals, and upon voluntary organizations, local authorities, and national governments to recognize these rights and strive for their observance by legislative and other measures progressively taken in accordance with the following principles:

Principle 1

The child shall enjoy all the rights set forth in this declaration. All children, without any exception whatsoever, shall be entitled to these rights, without distinction or discrimination on account of race, color, sex, language, religion, political or other opinion, national or social origin, property, birth, or other status, whether of himself or of his family.

Principle 2

The child shall enjoy special protection, and shall be given opportunities and facilities, by law and by other means, to enable him to develop physically, mentally, morally, spiritually, and socially in a healthy and normal manner and in conditions of freedom and dignity. In the enactment of laws for this purpose the best interests of the child shall be the paramount consideration.

Principle 3

The child shall be entitled from his birth to a name and a nationality.

Principle 4

The child shall enjoy the benefits of social security. He shall be entitled to grow and develop in health; to this end special care and protection shall be provided both to him and to his mother, including adequate prenatal and postnatal care. The child shall have the right to adequate nutrition, housing, recreation, and medical services.

Principle 5

The child who is physically, mentally, or socially handicapped shall be given the special treatment, education, and care required by his particular condition.

Principle 6

The child, for the full and harmonious development of his personality, needs love and understanding. He shall, wherever possible, grow up in the care and under the responsibility of his parents, and in any case in an atmosphere of affection and of moral and material security; a child of tender years shall not, save in exceptional circumstances, be separated from his mother. Society and the public authorities shall have the duty to extend particular care to children without a family and to those without adequate means of support. Payment of state and other assistance toward the maintenance of children of large families is desirable.

Principle 7

The child is entitled to receive education, which shall be free and compulsory, at least in the elementary stages. He shall be given an education which will promote his general culture, and enable him on a basis of equal opportunity to develop his abilities, his individual judgment, and his sense of moral and social responsibility, and to become a useful member of society.

The best interests of the child shall be the guiding principle of those responsible for his education and guidance; that responsibility lies in the first place with his parents.

The child shall have full opportunity for play and recreation, which should be directed to the same purposes as education; society and the public authorities shall endeavor to promote the enjoyment of this right.

Principle 8

The child shall in all circumstances be among the first to receive protection and relief.

Principle 9

The child shall be protected against all forms of neglect, cruelty, and exploitation. He shall not be the subject of traffic, in any form.

The child shall not be admitted to employment before an appropriate minimum age; he shall in no case be caused or permitted to engage in any occupation or employment which would prejudice his health or education, or interfere with his physical, mental, or moral development.

Principle 10

The child shall be protected from practices which may foster racial, religious, and any other form of discrimination. He shall be brought up in a spirit of understanding, tolerance, friendship among peoples, peace and universal brotherhood, and in full consciousness that his energy and talents should be devoted to the service of his fellow men.

As family patterns and other social arrangements change, different practices and institutions often become badly coordinated. Parents may desire and produce more children than they can care for long after changed mortality and economic patterns have undercut older reasons for having many children. Women's employment has greatly increased in many developed countries. However, there has been no corresponding change either in family structure or in the child care socially provided to carry out all the parental tasks for which the mothers of the recent past had (at whatever costs to their independence and self-respect) more time. Over the last century, young people have found their entry into the adult world delayed later and later, even though they have been reaching physical and sexual maturity at earlier and earlier ages. It is reasonable to think that any optimal or even desirable set of familial arrangements would not be badly coordinated in ways like these. Here as elsewhere, coherence is a necessary (and presumably insufficient) condition of merit.

In "Child Rearing and Family Interests," Jeffrey Blustein assumes that we can base claim rights on interests. But it does not, in his view, follow from this assumption that children have a right to whatever it would be in their interests to have. For others too have interests (including interests in children being adequately reared), which cannot be met without limiting children's claims; and children themselves have interests in others' interests, especially those of their parents, being met. Parents whose own interests are always sacrificed to those of their children are likely to end up not exemplary but resentful. The problem of working out the reciprocal duties of parents, children, and social agencies is therefore a coordination problem which requires us to find a coherent set of social practices conferring corollary rights and duties which satisfy the interlocking interests of all parties. This line of argument does not show that there is a unique, coherent, hence optimal set of child-rearing practices; but it shows that at least some possibilities can be rejected because their different elements are not well coordinated.

CHILD REARING AND FAMILY INTERESTS

JEFFREY BLUSTEIN

Why do parents have duties to their children? I shall begin by arguing that parents' duties are not procreators' duties. Biology alone cannot be a sufficient explanation of the basis of parental duties, because normally procreation is relevant to parental duty only insofar as social practices and customs make it relevant. Our attention is therefore directed to the social practices and their justification, not to the fact of causation. In order to justify any set of child-rearing practices—and there is a wide variety of ways in which such practices can and do assign duties to care for children—we need to know how it accommodates three distinct but closely interwoven interests: the interests of the child, those of the parents (or child rearers), and those of society.

The justification of child-rearing practices is important not only because it validates parental duties but also because without it, no conclusive justification of children's duties to their parents is possible. The filial duties I discuss are ones children have to their parents only during the child-rearing years, and they have them in order to help parents discharge their child-rearing duties. If a particular distribution of parental duties by a social practice were not a justifiable distribution, then children would be required to help parents discharge duties they should not have been assigned.

1. Are Parents' Duties Procreators' Duties?

I shall consider the suggestion that the ground of parental duties is procreation, and shall try to show that this explanation is insufficient. This will pave the way for a constructive account of the source of parental duties.

According to this suggestion, parents have duties to care for their child, because they have brought this needy being into existence. This is not to deny that adoptive parents, for example, may have all the duties that biological parents have, though the source of adoptive parents' duties cannot lie in their causal

agency. It is only to claim that causal agency is *an* explanation of the source of parental duties, and indeed perhaps the most common explanation.

Yet the biological fact that parents have caused their child to exist is not in itself morally decisive. The moral issue is not who caused the child to exist but who is to bear primary responsibility for preventing harm or suffering that might come to this needy being. For it is these persons who have special duties to the child. The fact that parents have caused a needy being to exist does not in itself imply that they have any more of a duty to prevent harm and suffering coming to that child than anyone else. Some additional premise is needed to reach this conclusion.

One can cause harm to another either positively, by doing something to him, or negatively, by failing to do something for him. Sidgwick considers negatively caused harm to be one of the bases of parental duties:

> For the parent, being the cause of the child's existing in a helpless condition, would be indirectly the cause of the suffering and death that would result to it if neglected.[1]

Sidgwick does not make clear here what the relationship is between causing the child to exist in a helpless condition and being morally blameworthy for harming the child through neglect. Perhaps the explanation is that biological parents are somehow in a *better position* than most other people to care for their child and therefore to harm him by failing to do certain things for him. The injunction not to harm the child negatively is not addressed exclusively to the biological parents, but has special force in their case. Parents' causing their child to exist would be a source of parental duties if there is a connection between causing the helpless child to exist and being in a better position to harm it through failing to do certain things. A description of this connection would then be our missing premise.

This argument fails to show that causation *by itself* can be a source of parental duties. For why is it that biological parents *are* ordinarily in a better position to care for and to harm their child? Isn't it because we customarily allow the biological parents to have almost exclusive care and control of their child? And we cannot justify this custom by repeating that biological parents have a special duty to care for their child. Normally parents are in a better position to harm their child, not because they have caused the child to exist but because of a set of practices which assign them a special duty to care for their needy child. It is the social practices that are crucial, and need to be justified. We could have practices, as other societies have and have had, in which the fact of causation was less relevant to parental duty than it is now, and it is not obvious that these practices are unjust. Children might be brought up not by biological parents, but by specially selected nurses. As it is, even in our society, the task of child rearing is split between parents and schools. If it is only the social practice of assigning care and control to biological parents that gives those who cause children to exist parental duties, the source of parental duties cannot be the fact of causation itself.

If what I have been saying up to now is correct, it would be preferable to speak of the duties of child rearers rather than of parents, so avoiding the suggestion that biology is the basis of parents' duties.

2. Child-rearing Duties and Social Practices

I shall now argue that the source of child-rearing duties lies not in procreation but in social practices and in the legitimate interests of various parties in these practices.

There is an enormous variation among social practices of child rearing. During Hitler's *Lebensborn* program, for example, the duty of Aryan parents was thought to be not to their children but to the Third Reich. Aryan mothers were required to have their children in specially selected clinics, and to leave them in the care of nurses appointed by officials of the program. In many cases, the biological parents were not permitted to visit their children, and they never heard from them again. Similar practices existed in the militant societies of Sparta and early Rome. Less extreme is the Israeli practice of communal child rearing on certain kibbutzim, where physical care and social rearing are not the responsibilities of biological parents. Primary responsibility for a kibbutz child's care, education, and socialization is assigned to his nurses and teachers, not to his biological parents. Biological parents are required to contribute to the physical care of their children. However, the fruits of their labor are given not directly to their children but to the community, which provides for all children. A childless person must contribute as much to the children's care as a biological parent.[2] Finally, there is a variety of state statutes in the United States which permit a child to be taken from the custody of his biological parents, though usually only in cases of gross neglect or abuse.

I shall not discuss in detail the practices on this partial list, for my intention in mentioning them is only to confirm that our focus should be upon social practices and their assessment. I shall now indicate what general considerations are relevant to selecting one practice over another.

In assessing any social practice of child rearing, we have to consult three separate, legitimate, and interrelated types of interests: those of the child, those of the child rearers, and those of society. The legitimate interests of the child include an interest in physical care, in education and socialization, and in the warmth, consistency, and continuity of the relationship he has with the person who takes care of him.

The legitimate interests of child rearers are more difficult to ascertain, but it is fairly clear that the benefits should not *all* fall on the side of the child. First, children may represent, as it were, a kind of investment or insurance policy. The returns, though deferred for a few years, will eventually be paid to the child rearers in the form of economic aid, of support in old age, and even, sometimes, of cash returns, as when a bride-price is received for a daughter when she marries. But as the tasks of providing economic security and protection for the aged are taken over more and more by the state, this interest of child rearers becomes less important.

There is, however, another interest, by no means universally shared, that cannot be supplanted in this way. Hegel speaks of this interest as follows:

In substance marriage is a unity, though only a unity of inwardness or disposition; in outward existence, however, the unity is sundered in the two parties. It is only in the children that the unity itself exists externally, objectively, and explicitly as a unity, because the par-

ents love the children as their love, as the embodiment of their own substance.[3]

This passage depicts the family as a community characterized by mutual love and the harmonious development of personalities. Within this community, a man and a woman love their children not only for themselves but also as outward signs of the love they have for one another. Here children are valued not because they will continue the family, or are potential sources of relief and aid, but because they are new bonds of love. Their lives become part of the personal lives of both child rearers, to be harmoniously shared like other personal values, and mutual love of child rearers becomes inextricably bound up with a common love for their children. This may happen whether or not the child rearers are their children's biological parents.

If child rearers have this interest in raising children, they also have an interest in a certain degree of privacy and non-interference in their child rearing. Interference in child rearing and even uncertainty about the extent of familial privacy would undermine the intimacy of the relationship between child rearers and children.

The interests child rearers have in raising children are limited not only by social interests and children's interests but by child rearers' interests in being free to engage in other, unrelated activities. Child rearers cannot be completely defined by their role as child rearers. Usually they wish to pursue other desires and interests that are quite independent of child rearing. But if child rearers perceive the raising of their children as an overwhelming burden which makes it impossible to pursue these other desires and interests, child rearing becomes intolerable, and they are likely to become resentful of their children. Hence, children too have an interest in their rearers being free to pursue other desires and interests.

Legitimate social interests in child-rearing practices include the following: first, an interest in the maintenance of a certain level of procreation, and in the physical care, education, and socialization of children; second, an interest in seeing that the institutions responsible for carrying out these tasks mesh with other social institutions. A complete discussion of social interests in the family would require an assessment of various population policies and of the importance of the institution of marriage to procreation of the species, but these are subjects which fall outside the concerns of this paper. Therefore, I shall focus instead on social interests in the allocation of responsibility for the care, education, and socialization of children once they are born.

That child rearing is not, nor should be, the exclusive concern of individual child rearers is not a novel claim. Legislation in many countries today recognizes that child rearers may injure (or fail to benefit) their children, so that children sometimes need the protection of the state against those who rear them. More generally, the public has a legitimate concern with the selection of child rearers and with the way in which children are reared, because a society's children are its future citizens and the future contributors to its material, cultural, and moral advancement. Collectively, children are a social asset.

Society also has a legitimate interest in ensuring the coordination of child-rearing practices with other social practices, and in seeing that different so-cial practices do not place incompatible demands upon individuals. There is, of course, no general and informative answer to the question, "What way of allocating responsibility for raising children fits in best with other social practices?" The answer depends on what those other social practices are. On the Israeli kibbutz, where economic growth is a primary goal, most of the responsibility for raising children is allocated to specially selected nurses and teachers, partly because this frees the biological parents for economic production. Under different social conditions—for example, where isolated peasant households predominate—the best way to allocate responsibilities may be to assign most child-rearing duties to biological parents. Under still other conditions, like those of modern urban society, institutional coordination may dictate the transfer of many child-rearing responsibilities to nonfamilial structures of the society, and the retention of the family as a more specialized institution.

The justification of a particular set of child-rearing practices, and its assignment of duties to care for, educate, and socialize children, depends on how the practices accommodate the various legitimate interests of the child, the child rearers, and the society. There is no reason to expect that only one set of child-rearing practices is justified, since both social structures and the interests of child rearers vary. But whatever the social practice that is justified in a particular context, one thing is clear. It is impossible to justify a set of child-rearing practices by assigning weights to, ranking, or aggregating the various sets of interests. The interests are too interdependent for this approach. Often it is in A's interest that B's interest be regarded. For example, it is in the child's interest that his rearers' interests be considered; it is in society's interest that children's interests be considered. Mutual adjustment of interests, not their ranking or aggregation, is required.

3. Child-rearing Duties and Children's Duties to Their Rearers

Sections 1 and 2 focused on the duties of parents—or, better, child rearers, to children. I shall now turn to the duties dependent children have to their rearers. These discussions of child rearers' duties and filial duties are interdependent, for at least two reasons. First, an account of filial duties cannot be complete without an account of how we decide to *whom* the duties are owed. The duties of children to child rearers are duties owed to specific individuals, and we cannot just assume that these individuals will normally be the child's biological parents. Second, and closely related to the first reason, no conclusive justification of filial duties can be given without knowing whether the particular distribution of child-rearers' duties by a social practice is a justifiable distribution. The word "conclusive" must be emphasized here, for children may have duties to their rearers even when the social practices that allocate child-rearing duties are *not* justifiable.

The justification of child-rearing duties is a higher-order account that takes into consideration three separate, though interrelated, sets of interests. Filial duties, too, can be grounded on such a higher-level account. For example, one might show that a certain pattern of filial duties stabilizes a just social scheme of distributing child-rearing duties. But filial duties can also arise directly out of the relations between individuals. It is

this second suggestion that I wish to explore.

I shall consider here those filial duties the child is called upon to fulfill while still dependent on his rearers. These include what I shall call duties of *facilitation and non-interference.* Their source can be explained schematically, in the following way. We start with the assumption that child rearers have certain duties to care for, educate, and socialize their children. The successful discharge of these duties requires the child's active cooperation, or at least non-interference with the rearers' endeavors. Therefore, the child has duties to facilitate and not to interfere with the rearers' reasonable efforts to discharge their duties. This class of filial duties is a corollary of the rearers' duties to the child, and aids in the fulfillment of the latter. In a sense, facilitation and non-interference are duties which children have to themselves, rather than to their rearers. The liberty of the child, as well as that of rearers, is restricted in various ways in order to secure the well-being of the child. Duties of facilitation and non-interference include duties of obedience, but are not confined to cases in which rearers have issued commands. Further, children may have duties of obedience (e.g., the parent says, "Leave me alone, I'm tired") which have nothing to do with facilitation and non-interference.

This explanation of filial duties of facilitation and non-interference is contingent upon rearers' duties to their children; they are not unconditional duties. But it is not easy to state under what conditions filial duties of facilitation and non-interference cease. They surely cease when rearers have shown gross moral or psychological unfitness to raise their children, or willful failure to give them a decent upbringing. It is also clear, I think, that past a certain stage of the child's development, these duties cease. Duties of facilitation and non-interference are contingent upon rearers' duties to care for, educate, and socialize (or see to the education and socialization of) their child, so that once the child is able to take care of himself, child rearers' duties end.

Since duties of facilitation and non-interference are contingent on rearers' discharging (or making reasonable efforts to discharge) their *duties,* these duties of children are not correlated with rearers' *rights.* Rearers cannot properly claim acts of facilitation and non-interference as *their due.* It is the *child* to whom care, education, and socialization are due, and the duties of facilitation and non-interference are grounded on the social interests, child rearers' interests, and child's interests in decent child rearing. The child rearers are to be temporary trustees of the child's welfare. They may command performance of acts of facilitation and non-interference if they are called for but not forthcoming, and apply sanctions to the child if he does not heed their commands. But as the child gradually comes to take more and more responsibility for his own life, and the duties of child rearers become fewer and fewer, so do the concomitant filial duties of facilitation and non-interference.

Children's duties of facilitation and non-interference are based on a more general moral principle, which states the following: If A has a duty to B to do x for B, then either (i) B has a duty to A to facilitate or at least not prevent A's discharging his duty to do x, or (ii) B has a duty to release A from his duty to B. So long as child rearers are making reasonable efforts to discharge their du-

ties to their child, the child (if he is below a certain age) is bound by the first option (i). Since the child lacks the cognitive and emotional capacities for making fully rational decisions, and is therefore likely to harm himself or to fail to advance his own good, he is incapable of releasing his rearers from their duties to him. By the time the child is capable of releasing his rearers, many or all of their duties will have ceased.

I have been concerned only with those duties children have to their rearers while still dependent on them, and have said nothing specifically about the duties of grown children. Though I cannot pursue this matter to any great extent here, I shall conclude with a few suggestions for further reflection.[4]

Perhaps two of the most promising explanations of why grown children do have duties to their rearers are compensation and gratitude. Children, it is often said, have duties to compensate and show gratitude to their rearers for all the years they spent feeding, clothing, nurturing, educating, and loving them. But this claim raises a number of difficult questions. Is gratitude suitable as a subject for duty? If in some sense it is, how do we identify appropriate acts of gratitude? Can children have duties to compensate their rearers or show gratitude to them for benefits they (the children) did not voluntarily accept? Do children have such duties with respect to benefits their rearers had a duty to provide? [See pp. 351–56 below.]

These are some of the problems that an account of the duties of adult children must deal with. But however they are resolved, it is clear that if adult children do have duties to their rearers, it is not for the same reason that children have duties of facilitation and non-interference. Children have these duties only while they are still dependent on their rearers, and they have them in order to ensure their own well-being.

Notes

1. *The Methods of Ethics* (University of Chicago Press, 1962), p. 249.
2. On child rearing in Israeli kibbutzim, see Melford E. Spiro, "Is the Family Universal—The Israeli Case," in *The Family*, Norman Bell and Ezra Vogel, eds. (New York, Free Press, 1960), pp. 64–75.
3. *Philosophy of Right*, T. M. Knox, trans. (Oxford University Press, 1967), p. 117.
4. For a further discussion of compensation and gratitude, see my article "On The Duties of Parents and Children," *The Southern Journal of Philosophy*, XV (Winter 1977), pp. 427–441.

Two metaphors underlie much of our thought about parents and children. Parents may be seen as *creators*, or *producers*, entitled like other producers to the fruits of their labors. Guided by this metaphor, we readily understand the special status of parents in making decisions—including those which drastically affect life prospects—on behalf of their children; and we do not doubt that parents, like other producers, may sometimes put their own interests ahead of those of their product. But we cannot so readily understand that their product should have autonomous interests at all. Alternatively, parents may be seen as *guardians*, or *trustees*, whose special status in deciding and acting for their child is limited, revocable, and appropriately governed by a concern for the best interests of the child. Trustees have typically limited obligations to their charges, but in discharging them, they may not take their own interests into account. If parents are trustees, then they are charged with uniquely onerous and lasting duties in which they may take no account of their own interests.

William Ruddick argues that the metaphors of both trustee and producer distort our picture of parents' obligations, activities, and authority. Children, uniquely, are products who become persons. But they do so gradually. Just as the child's body and capacity for life gradually become distinct from the mother's, so do the child's interests and capacity to lead his or her own life gradually become distinct from the interests and life of the family. Parents may not (though other producers may) disregard the independent interests of what they have produced. On the contrary, much parental work consists of equipping the child to know and assert those interests in varied circumstances. On the other hand, parents may (as trustees may not) take their own interests into account when they decide and act on behalf of their child.

Parents are not committed to relentless self-sacrifice; but their conduct is limited by the aim of enabling their child to pursue interests and ultimately some life plan of his or her own. The principle of parenthood (the "Prospect Provision Principle") which Ruddick extracts from these considerations requires parents to seek for their children life possibilities which the children could accept and which are not dependent on unending parental assistance, and some of which could be realized in each likely future state of the world. But it permits parents who foster such life possibilities to consider their own preferences in choosing among them. Parents, then, are neither the owners nor the trustees of their children.

PARENTS AND LIFE PROSPECTS

WILLIAM RUDDICK

We do not think clearly about parents and children. Our personal experiences as children and as parents may be too fraught with emotion and detail for general reflection. And the current feminist attack on patriarchy is unsettling old assumptions. There is also a metaphysical cause of confusion: children become distinct beings only gradually. They do not spring into the world like Athena from the head of Zeus. They develop slowly within and from the bodies and lives of their parents. We have no criteria, apart from legal convention, for deciding when in pregnancy there are two human bodies rather than just one, or when in adolescence there are two distinct lives, that of the "child" and that of the parent(s), independently pursuable.

In short, there are no criteria for individuating child from parent, or for defining the beginning or end of parenthood and childhood. In various respects at various times, parent and child are not distinct individuals.

This "bio-metaphysical" fact should discourage facile application of familiar moral principles and categories, derived as they are from adult dealings with one another. The Principle of Utility, for example, requires us to count "each as one and no more than one," but when are a child's interests sufficiently distinct from those of its parents to warrant separate entry in our calculations? If we count the child "as one" before it has distinct interests or desires, we thereby give the parents' interests double weight, thus violating the "no more than one" clause. If we ignore the child's emerging interests, we violate the "each as one" clause.

Likewise, the parent-child relationship does not comfortably fit a theory of moral rights. When do the rights and duties of parenthood begin? Before the fetus is viable? Before it is born? At what stage or age of a child's development do parental duties or rights end? And when do children become bearers of rights that can conflict with or override those of their parents? How early may parents become guilty of paternalism? Here again, the metaphysical complexity of a child's gradual development produces moral indeterminacy and confusion, even worse than for Utilitarians. The "rights" model requires counting parent and child not only as separated but also as adversarial.

Where can we look for help? We have two resources: folk wisdom and family law. Admittedly, both arise in dubious quarters. Folk wisdom derives from an age in which women and children were beatified or ignored. And family law derives from parental failures and attempts to remedy them. To draw a general moral sketch of parent-child relationships from family law is somewhat like abstracting human physiology from a pathology manual. But in the absence of familiar moral principles and categories, we have no better starting points.

I shall examine first the folkloric analogy of parents to *gardeners* and then the legal conception of parents as *guardians*. Each is faulty, but their combined virtues help define a notion of parenthood that does justice to parents, children, and their bizarre metaphysical and moral bonds. By way of preview: the gardening analogy reflects the fact that a child is a parent's *product,* the result of intentional effort, but a product with the unique capacity to become the equal of its producers. Hence, child-producers may not treat children as if they were and would remain artifacts or property. Children have the capacity for becoming members of a Kingdom of Ends, and a presumed interest in so becoming that imposes restraints on their producers and requires protection. Hence, the virtue of the legal metaphor of parents as guardians. A parent is, as it were, a Guardian-Gardener. Less metaphorically, a parent is (as I explain in section 3) a provider of life prospects.

For a philosophy of parenthood, we must then find principles that reflect a child's product-origin *and* its autonomous future, while respecting parental productive hopes. Parents beget, bear, and raise children to fulfill certain aims, sometimes eccentric or personal. Their productive aims may be *re*productive, in the service of continuing some aspect of their own lives through their children.

To exclude such reproductive aims would make parenthood more of a burden than it is. Children are not their parents' chattels, but they should not be allowed to become their parents' crosses, too heavy for all but self-sacrificial saints to bear. We must find principles that make parenthood a reasonable, rewarding undertaking. Now that parenthood is a matter of choice, rather than a biological or cultural fate for women, we must coordinate parents' desires and children's needs under principles that will guide parental actions with a minimum of regret, resentment, or legal enforcement.

In the last section, I propose such a principle. It requires a parent to foster a variety of life prospects, wide enough to encompass various future desires and opportunities yet all within the scope of a parent's (re)productive hopes. By way of illustrating and testing this "Prospect Provision Principle" (PPP), I use it to classify and consider some medico-legal cases. In these cases, actual and contrived, parents refuse medical or surgical remedies for their children's ailments.

1. Parents and Gardeners

Parenting is often compared to various adult occupations: sculpting, teaching, governing, animal training, financial investing. But the oldest and perhaps closest analogy is to gardening. Urged to "be fruitful," a man plants his seed. Initially, it grows out of public view and without need for public support or protection. Only gradually does it emerge and call for protection, direction, and support. ("As the twig is bent, so grows the tree.")

The analogy so sketched casts the father as gardener, the mother as nurturing, passive Mother Earth. But, if the analogy is to be of use, the gardener must be female, even during pregnancy. A woman not only lends her body to the growth of the fetus; she must actively maintain her body, often in novel and onerous ways. Although the fetus may take from her body what it needs, she must replenish it and protect herself (and the fetus) from dietary poisons. She is advised to "eat for one, not for two," but she cannot continue to eat just what she likes. In this and other ways, pregnancy is no passive, mindless, carefree, blessed condition; it must count as work long before labor or labor pains begin. She is not "with child," but "making a baby." She is not just "in the family way"; she is already mothering. Pregnancy, especially for women, is not a condition but an activity. (Hence, grammatical scruples should not lead us to reject the term "parenting." Nor should we take too seriously philosophers' comparison of a woman reluctantly pregnant to a passive captive of kidnappers or house-breakers.)

If pregnancy is a state of work, and if a fetus is the product of a woman's labors, what are the moral consequences? May a woman abort if the work begins to go badly or to interfere with more pressing demands on her time and talents? That, of course, depends on her productive relationships with others. Few workers are autonomous, free agents—least of all women in our society.

Traditionally, conception has been counted as *pro*creation. Procreators, like proconsuls, are deputies for a higher authority and therefore do not enjoy a creator's control. It has been God the Father who has been the creator, or His surrogate the human patriarch. It has been God or men who have decided whether the work (construed as a passive condition) must continue. Recent legal decisions (see *Planned Parenthood* v. *Danforth* and *Roe* v. *Conn,* reprinted here on pp. 58–79 and pp. 165–78) have denied fathers superior standing, but the State, as *parens patriae,* still claims the right to continue the woman's work, at least after the fetus is viable. (See the Supreme Court abortion decision in *Roe* v. *Wade.*)

But even if a woman's work is freed from these claimants, there is still a bar to her total control over her own product after birth—if perhaps not before—namely, the peculiar character of the product itself. Trees and plants have no interests or desires of their own, present or future, even if *we* would benefit from a legal fiction to that effect. Whether, for example, a plant is to grow to maturity depends entirely on the appetite or

color schemes of a gardener (or her employer).

But, in making a baby, a woman is also beginning to make a man or woman; in time, her product can become her moral and metaphysical equal. Gardeners cull, graft, crossbreed, and pick at will, but their product is flowers or vegetables or trees, *not* potential or apprentice gardeners. Even after we reject the notion of procreation and the claims of creators other than the woman herself, her productive work is human reproduction nonetheless.

The law insists that parents, as reproducers, are guardians of future members of (adult) society. How fitting is this legal model of parenthood?

2. Parents as Guardians or Trustees

The law defines various guardians for a child: guardians of property, guardians *ad litem* (for representation in court cases), and guardians of a child's person, or personal guardians. Personal guardians have many of a parent's rights to decide matters of conduct, domicile, and medical care. But, unlike natural parents, they cannot consent to adoption or nominate guardians for the child in their wills. Nor do they have a parent's duty to support a child.[1]

Parents, as "natural guardians" in the eyes of the law, are more than personal guardians. Conversely, they may be less than guardians of a child's property; for example, a trust may be settled on children with trustees other than the parents. It seems, then, that parents are guardians in some comprehensive sense which the law makes precise in special circumstances for special interests. Nonparents are usually assigned powers otherwise enjoyed without legal confirmation by the parents during their child's minority.

This undefined sense of guardianship fits well with the traditional notion of procreation: parents are entrusted by God with the general well-being of the child. Some Christians may define well-being in terms of salvation and require parents to protect those prospects, at whatever cost to their own other interests. (Hence, the Roman Catholic preference for the unbaptized fetus over its baptized mother.) But whatever the definition of a child's well-being, parents as procreators are parties to a trust, settled upon their children by God, the Creator.

The trustee model does not, however, appeal only to theists. A secular version makes the state the settlor of the trust, a *parens patriae* that may remove the natural trustee and transfer custody, guardianship, and other powers and duties to other adults. But when and how does the state establish this trust? During pregnancy? At birth? And when and how do parents undertake this alleged trusteeship?

There are two possible solutions, one from political theory, one from the law. Social contract theorists have a corresponding problem: naturalized citizens undertake political obligations at a particular time and public place, but native citizens do not. Likewise, adoptive parents publicly undertake the care of a child, but natural parents do not. The solution lies in finding actions and omissions that are the moral equivalent of a public contract. For political obligations, these include a native citizen's accepting government benefits, taking part in the political process, and not emigrating or renouncing citizenship. But for parental obligations, what actions and omissions

constitute an implicit trust agreement? Conceiving and not aborting? Caring for a child in ways that lead it and others to expect a continuation?

These acts and omissions, however, do not involve state benefits or institutions. Indeed, conception, abortion, and child rearing are covered in various degrees by judicial recognition of parental "privacy." Hence, these acts and omissions cannot be construed as parental commitments to the state.

More plausibly, they can be construed as parental commitments to the *child,* and hence can still fall under a trust model. There are two-party trusts in which settlor (the person conferring, or settling the trust on the beneficiary) and trustee are roles played by a single person. Indeed, a common example is that in which a parent settles property on a minor child. (This is the solution from the law mentioned above.)

But even two-party trusts seem to conflict with the doctrine of parental privacy and "property in their children" (as it is still put in some decisions). A person is not a trustee for his own property, but only for the property of others. But this conflict between trust and private property is resolvable. The language of the law still reflects the older view of children as their parents' chattels. Admittedly, children may still be housed, transported, and used by parents or guardians, subject only to the humane limits imposed on animal keepers. But the rationale for parental discretion in child rearing is different from that in animal husbandry. Parental privacy is not justified by the interests of parents as autonomous property holders, but as *parents.* Parents need a certain latitude in defining and scheduling child care. Were child care dictated or supervised by others, it would be more of a burden and less satisfying than it would otherwise be. And the children would suffer, as well as the parents. Parents free from intervention take more pride in, and hence more responsibility for, their children and treat them more consistently—a considerable benefit, according to current child psychologists. Close supervision, legal or otherwise, alienates a worker, and the work suffers; that is the general claim, here applied to parental work.

In a two-party trust, the trustee protects interests he has himself defined in settling the trust upon the beneficiary. A settlor-trustee is, within wide limits, a creator of benefits, rather than someone the law appoints to protect benefits already defined. Hence, the analogy captures an aspect of parenthood that the notion of guardianship does not. The parent defines and bestows benefits on the child, not as self-sacrificial fulfillment of a duty imposed by a child's state- (or God-) given right. The trust model thereby respects the metaphysical evolution of the child outlined at the outset.

A child, it was said, develops only slowly within and from the bodies and lives of its parents. Let us add some details. A child grows and develops within a world defined by its parents' prior interests, parental and non-parental. Its own interests, such as they may be, must accommodate, and be accommodated within, that world.

"Interest" is an elastic term covering both needs and desires—here, primarily the parents' desires and the children's needs. (It can be argued that very young children have no desires: until they develop the conceptual capacity for beliefs presupposed by and attributed in conjunction with desires, they merely express the discomforts and pleasures naturally linked to their needs.[2]) If a child's needs are to be met by the adults on whom it is dependent, then fulfilling those needs must simultaneously fulfill their parental desires—that is, their desire to care for a child.

As parents and child live together, there is an interplay and adjustment of need and desire. The child's needs may come to elicit parental desires to fulfill them, desires that a parent did not previously have or even foresee, desires no one else's children elicit. Conversely, parental desires may elicit new needs in a child that other children do not have, such as the need to be with and to please those particular adults.

As parents and children grow older, however, this early matching of need and desire may begin to fail. Children begin to reflect a wider world of school, friends, and other foreign influences. And parents become distracted by their non-parental interests, or become tired of parental life. And sometimes they die.

Hence, with the increasing age of child and parents, there is a mutual need they share—namely, the need for the child to be able to live a life of its own, free of its parents. A child depends on its parents for the capacity for independence.

The Model Probate Code lists, as one of the duties of a child's personal guardian, the duty "to see that he is properly trained and educated and that he has the opportunity to learn a trade, occupation or profession."[3] Personal guardianship, like parenthood, is not only temporary; it is also self-terminating, at least in the legal ideal.

This is not, however, a feature of all guardian or trust relationships, and hence, is not covered by these analogies per se. We needed the notion of a parent-guardian or parent-trustee to remind us that, although parenting is productive work, the product has distinguishable interests in need of protection. We now need to consider the *re*productive nature of parenting, subject to a temporal limit. However closely meshed a child's early needs and the guardian-gardener's desires, a child must become its own producer and guardian.

Legal and folkloric analogies have jointly brought us the following thought: a parent provides a child with the "necessaries of life," including the capacity for producing and guarding a life of its own. It is this thought that the rest of this essay will develop.

3. Parents as Providers of Life Prospects

We must first remind ourselves of a distinction we make but tend to overlook: that between "life" in a biological or zoological sense and "a life" in a biographical sense. The Greeks could mark the distinction with *zōē* and *bios*, but we make do with a syntactical distinction between *life* as a general property or state of all living things and *a life* as a particular which a person makes, loses, leads, sacrifices, takes pride in, has interrupted by prison, accident, illness, or death. But a life may end before a person dies, and a person may exist before a life begins. Indeed, children are persons before they have lives, or at least, before they have lives distinguishable from that of their parents.[4]

What distinguishes one life from another are the distinctive projects which a person pursues; the self-regarding emotions of shame, pride, and guilt associated with those projects; and the selected memories which compose his or her "story." Hence, to lead a life of one's own, a person requires various capacities

of emotion, imagination, and will. A life of one's own does not, however, require rejection of parental ways or separate domicile or occupation. It is enough that whatever the similarity and the parental influence, a child's life comes to have its own endorsement, not merely that of its parents. Parental ways and choices must, in time, become his or her ways and choices if the life to count as distinct from theirs. In principle, even Amish children may lead lives of their own in the midst of an unchanging family culture, so long as they have chosen the Amish life of their parents, rather than had it forced upon them. (See *Wisconsin v. Yoder* below, pp. 279–305).

But what are the conditions for choice? How many life possibilities must parents provide or allow their children? How much control may parents seek to exercise over the talents and opportunities which will define their children's options in life?

There are two familiar extremes. The *conservative* endorses the Amish view; a parent need not prepare a child for more than one life, that of the parent of the same sex. The *libertarian*, by contrast, would require parents to provide as many life possibilities as the child's talents and parental resources permit.

The conservative's child may embrace the parent's life, but does not choose it from a set of realizable alternatives. (There are none.) The libertarian's child has an abundance of alternatives, none of which he or she may be able to embrace fully, to the exclusion of others. But the issue is not embrace-without-choice versus choice-without-embrace. These views are extreme because they make unreasonable demands on the future. The conservative counts on a world in which a child can reproduce the parent's own life—that is, a world without cultural change. (Conservative fathers fondly imagined signs that read, "Smith & Son: Fine Carriage Makers," and ignored the Fords in their future and everyone else's. Conservative mothers dreamed of grandchildren next door and ignored the flight from marriage and the suburbs.)

The libertarian, by contrast, allows for radical changes, even in his own hopes and ideals. In setting before a child a wide range of life possibilities, libertarians in principle discount their own parental preferences, much as do family judges who in custody adjudication refer only to a child's best interests. But libertarians (and judges) thus ignore the way in which a child's interests and life choices depends on a parent's ideals, support, and own interests. In avoiding the conservative's self-reproductive ambitions, the libertarian makes parenthood a selfless, temporary service which, once rendered, allows parent and child to go their separate ways, psychologically as well as economically. The libertarian counts on a future in which the parent will approve any choice a child makes from the "life smorgasbord" the parent dutifully sets out, or at least will be indifferent. But this is to ignore the worker's just hopes; parental aims may be productive, even if not too narrowly reproductive.

The two views ignore another uncertainty, namely, the length of a parent's life. The conservative counts on a parent living long enough to train and support a child's continuation of the parental biographical lifeline. (But even if there are no Fords in the immediate future, Smith may die before it is time to hang up the carriage makers' sign, and what is Smith's son to do if he has been prepared for no extra-familial life?) By contrast, the libertarian counts on a

parent not living long enough to disapprove of a child's divergent lifeline, however sharp its angle or wavy its course. (What if a carriage maker lives long enough to see his son turn his mechanical skills and education to the design of hand-cranked automobile engines or crooked roulette wheels?)

We want, then, a principle of parenthood that will minimize rejections, resentments or disappointments, whatever the changes in culture or attitudes. We want to honor parents' productive desires and children's needs for lives of their own which neither require nor reject parental approval and support. In short, we want a principle which fosters individuation of a child's own life within its parents' life, however long or short that might be. Our question is: How self-serving may a parent be in fostering a child's life prospects? The answer must provide for individuation without rejection from either quarter.

To that end, I propose the following principle.[5] A parent must foster life prospects which

1. jointly encompass the futures the parents and those they respect deem likely, and
2. individually, if realized, would be acceptable to both parent and child.

Let us see what this Prospect Provision Principle (PPP) commits us to, morally and empirically. First, it leaves open the number of life prospects, or possibilities, a parent must foster; the number turns on the range of futures the parents and those they respect deem likely. In a community parents expect to remain highly stable and communal, the principle would permit them to foster only one life prospect. They could teach a child a single craft, so long as its mastery and exercise did not require the parents' long-term assistance. (There must be carriage makers other than Smith who would train and employ his son, should "Smith & Son: Fine Carriage Makers" fail to materialize.) If the community is to remain stable, parents and children alike must accept and remain likely to accept the life pattern: Like father, like son; like mother, like daughter. Although parents may be mistaken, they and those they respect must judge that the life pattern will persist, even though other cultural observers predict otherwise. The Amish, for example, do not have to attend to alien sociologists, so long as there is confidence within the community that the community will continue.

The principle imposes a greater burden on parents in a heterogeneous, unstable culture such as ours. There are far more respected predictors and predictions, and hence, far more futures that a parent must prepare a child for: futures with capitalist institutions and without; futures with heterosexual marriage and without; futures with a suburban car culture and without; with high energy consumption and without; with high radiation levels and without. The only relative certainty is that parents will live longer and die more slowly than before, and hence, most likely that futures will include longer parent-child relationships than in less medically advanced societies.

The more uncertain the future, the more parents are driven by PPP in the libertarian direction. But they are saved from self-denying or impersonal provision by the principle's second clause. A parent need not foster a life prospect which, if realized, would be predictably distressing. (The carriage maker need not train a son to be an auto mechanic just because the future of carriage makers is uncertain.) Nonetheless, a par-

ent in uncertain times must give more thought to the future and make wider provisions among those prospects that would, if realized, mutually satisfy parent and child.

Mutual future satisfaction is a complex matter. Among the uncertainties in a changing culture are one's own future attitudes. (Perhaps a carriage maker will gradually come to like cars and car makers.) Moreover, the more rapidly changing the culture, the more unpredictable will be relationships between generations. (Perhaps carriage makers' sons will be ashamed of their fathers' work, whatever its economic viability.) A parent must ask, Will I approve in time of a life my child may in time come to choose? And if the answer is "yes," then the parent must make *some* provision for that life prospect, even if that provision is nothing more than allowing other adults to present that life prospect favorably. (The carriage maker and his wife must let their daughter talk to the Vassar admissions officer, even if no one in the family has given serious thought to women's higher education—unless, on reflection, they are certain that a daughter so educated would cause them or herself deep distress.)

The principle does not require present agreement about what will be mutually satisfactory in the future. It allows adolescents to reject any life prospects parents favor, and it allows a child to criticize parental hopes as unrealistic. The principle does presuppose, contrary to some Freudian accounts of generational conflict, the possibility of mutually adjusted and mutually endorsed prospects. It reflects the kind of matching of parental desires and childrens' needs that their cohabitation tends to produce (in decent socioeconomic conditions).

The principle does, even in well-ordered societies, place certain burdens on parents. They must give serious thought to a world in which their children are no longer dependent, but have grown up and apart, as a result of choice or circumstance, in an unfamiliar or even alien culture. Facing that future condition is like, and may include, facing one's own death.

But whatever the cognitive and emotional burdens the PPP imposes on parents, it does not need continual legal enforcement. It merely extends the usual parental practice of looking ahead. Parenthood is prospective work from the outset; a child's current needs are generally viewed in light of future needs and desires. Parents are always taking thought for the morrow and beyond, and making speeches that begin, "You will be grateful some day that . . ."

And yet, there are various apparent violations of the principle that come into court, under child-abuse and negligence statutes. By way of further explaining and testing the principle, I will apply it to a special class of such cases—those in which parents refuse medical or surgical treatment for their children, risking life possibilities or biological survival. Medical care is counted as one of the "necessaries of life" which parents and personal guardians are expected to provide their children or wards. And yet, exceptions are made—often, it seems, when the parents' refusal does not constitute a violation of our principle.

4. Parents' Refusal of Medical Care

A moral principle shows its worth in classifying cases, as well as in deciding cases. Let us consider cases of the following kinds:

1. Children with ailments whose treatment will create life prospects they will otherwise lack, life prospects mutually acceptable to both parents and children;
2. Children for whom treatment will create life prospects the parents find intolerable (on informed reflection);
3. Children for whom treatment will provide biological survival, but no life prospects.

Some cases have come to trial, others have not. Of each, we can ask how it should have been, or should be decided if the PPP were legally recognized and decisive. (A moral principle may be legally, but not morally decisive, if there are other moral principles that override it, but none of which are legally enforced. PPP may be just such a principle.)

The case of Kevin Sampson fits the *first* category (*In re Sampson,* 317 N.Y.S. 2d 641 (1970)). The mother, a Jehovah's Witness, would not consent to blood transfusion for an operation to remove a large, disfiguring tumor of her child's head and neck. Without the operation, the child would remain secluded at home, illiterate, with no life prospects outside the family. There was no suggestion that the operation, if performed against her will, would render the child spiritually repugnant to her. The court ordered the operation (and transfusion), and thereby upheld the PPP.

The case of Martin Seiferth (309 N.Y. 80 1955, reprinted below) also involves metaphysical refusal. Martin's father insisted on trusting "natural forces of the universe," rather than surgery, to repair his son's severe cleft lip and palate. But, unlike Kevin Sampson, the child attended school, did well, and was socially accepted. The court feared that he would suffer social rejection as adolescent concern for physical appearance increased, but allowed that, even without the operation, he could survive socially until he came of age. At that point, he could, without his father's authority, have the operation. The court did not order the operation, nor did the father violate the PPP. However unreasonable by scientific standards, the father allowed for "natural healing" and saw no sacrifice of his son's life prospects by further delay.

In dissent, Judge Fuld cited Martin's right "so far as possible, to lead a normal life." By refusing the treatment, the parents were doing something "worse than beating the child or denying him food or clothing"; they were "ruining his life and any chance for a normal, happy existence." But does a child have a right to lead a normal, happy existence, so far as possible, and does it force us to recast the PPP? Do parents have a correlative duty to foster a *normal,* happy life?

I think not. Many parents do want, both for themselves and for their children, a normal life. Although a normal life, conventionally defined, may not guarantee happiness, it does make for modest social and financial rewards and harmony between generations. But to require parents to strive to provide such life prospects would be to reduce parents to guardians for the status quo and to deprive them of the special productive rewards the gardening analogy respects.

But the Seiferth case does not fully test the PPP on this point. The boy, even with an operation and therapy, will be disfigured beyond hope of a fully normal life. Moreover, he shares his father's metaphysical hope for a superior cure.

Let us contrive a case which puts the normalcy issue starkly. Suppose a dwarf woman gives birth to a child with the same congenital defect. A new treatment promises to make the child of normal size, but she and her husband refuse it; they very much want a dwarf child. Their reasons are not metaphysical, but are drawn from their experience as parents of an older child of normal size. From early infancy, their first child was too large for them to care for. They needed increasing help from larger adults, with the result that the child eventually became estranged from them, and in time ashamed of them and eager to leave the circus world in which they lived.

They agree that a child of normal size, even with the stigma of dwarf parents, might be happier than a dwarf child. But they are confident that they can raise a dwarf child to be self-reliant. They would like the child to live and work with them in the circus, but they would ensure that it had capacities for other lines of work in the increasingly tolerant outside world. Although their child would have fewer life possibilities than a normal child, there would be enough to cover the various futures they deem likely. Any of these prospects, if realized, would suit them and their child. The child will predictably wish that it were normal size, but in time—they think—it will come to respect their desire to be loving, caring parents and will appreciate the benefits of that love for it.

The parents, then, are not violating the PPP, but they are violating the child's right to a normal life—if there is such a right. I see no basis for such a right, nor do I think this case requires us to look for one. If there is such a right, we may set against it the dwarves' right to be parents. This latter right is not of course an unqualified right: parents must be able to provide "the necessaries of life," including the capacities for a life of one's own. The dwarf parents, however, are able to do so.

Let us return to two final cases, one for each of the other two classes. A publicized, but untried, case at a Baltimore hospital fits the class of children for whom treatment will create life prospects the parents find intolerable. A mother with several children gave birth to an infant with marked Down's syndrome (mongolism) and an intestinal defect which prevented food from passing through the alimentary canal. The infant could take no food by mouth without surgical repair of the defect. The mother refused permission for the surgery. The doctors concurred and allowed the infant to die of malnutrition.

Did the mother violate the PPP? Her reported reason for refusal was concern for her five other children; to care for a severely retarded child, she would have to neglect the others. I assume she rejected the offer or thought of institutional care as intolerable.

But, we ask, what is it that she finds intolerable, and for whom? Does she think that institutional care will prove intolerable to the child? Or is it rather that she thinks she cannot live with the thought of her child living its life in an institution?

She may not have drawn this distinction, but she does not have to do so. As I argued, a natural mother's special (pro)creative relation to an infant too young to have capacities for beliefs and desires entitles her to treat the child's need as identical with her parental desire. If on reflection she judges institutional existence intolerable for "her-and-the child," she commits no *conceptual*

error, even though it is the child, not she, who would live in the institution, and even though the alternative is death for the child, not her.

Nor do I think she violates the PPP. The life of an institutional ward of the state is not mutually acceptable, for it is not (and will not predictably become) acceptable to her, even if it should be acceptable to the child. There is, of course, the debatable issue of whether this infant will be capable of *accepting* or leading *any* kind of life. If its mental incapacity is severe enough, the child will have no life (in the biographical sense), either tolerable or intolerable to its mother or itself.

This is Karen Ann Quinlan's condition. The trial judge in this celebrated case refused to grant her father guardianship, hence the power to stop her artificial respiration. Given some medical opinion (which proved wrong), to grant him this power would be to allow him to deprive his daughter "of her most precious possession—life." A higher court, however, reversed this decision on the ground that biological survival without the medical possibility of "cognitive, sapient life" was of little value. To shorten the duration of her "persistent vegetative state" is not to deprive her of anything, as she herself would agree were she able to express a judgment.

So described, this is an example of the third category—that is, the case of a child for whom treatment provides biological survival but no life prospects. To refuse such treatment does not violate the PPP. Refusal could, of course, violate other moral principles, more or less stringent than the PPP. It would, for example, violate a very demanding right-to-life principle—namely, a right to whatever goods and services are needed to maintain biological functioning. The higher court recognized no such principle, nor should it have, for there is, I think, no justification for such a principle short of certain theological premises our secular legal system cannot admit.

Refusal would also violate a "respect for work" principle that allows people (in this case, physicians and nurses) to continue a project in which they have invested their efforts. Unlike a strong respect-for-biological-life principle, this 'respect-for-work' principle can be justified within secular bounds,[6] but it will not override the PPP. Indeed the Quinlans could cite such a principle to support their right, under the PPP, to discontinue a medical procedure that allows their daughter to survive as a wreck of what they and she had worked for her to become. Even though parents are often likened to gardeners, they cannot be morally required to maintain their children in a persistent vegetative state or—in the absence of yet unspecified overriding principles—morally required to permit others to do so.

There may well be overriding principles, for the PPP does not have the kind of backing we demand of ultimate moral principles. It rests, we have seen, on disputable metaphysical claims and on changeable, even if long-standing, psychological conditions. If, for example, an infant has a Platonic soul, then individuation from its parents occurs earlier and less gradually than I claim. And were infants to emerge from test tubes or with projects clearly stated and argued, then parents would have very different motives, interests, and expectations—if, indeed, there were any parents or the need for them. In such altered circumstances, the PPP would have little point.

But in our familiar world, the Prospect Provision Principle has a point. It resists our familiar and familial tendencies to become our children's masters or servants, their gardeners or guardians. It replaces biological and legal categories with those more appropriate to family relationships, and thereby allows us to say what we have known all along: the distinctive work of parenthood is life-giving, and that work, if properly done, can be uniquely life-enhancing.

The task of philosophic reflection or parenthood is to set out the political, moral, and social conditions under which parental work can be done properly. The Prospect Provision Principle is at best a start. In addition to supplementary principles about life and work, the PPP requires (as do all moral principles) a context of decent social and economic conditions for proper implementation. I will not try to sketch such conditions here. Instead, I will end with a daughter's reflection on the impact of these conditions on the ties between parents and children in two contrasting societies.

Before a trip to Cuba, Alice Walker began to dream of her father standing with an enigmatic look by a road as she moved farther and farther away. Her father had been a poor laborer in rural Georgia, supporting a family of a wife and eight children on as little as $300 a year. On arriving in Cuba, she was startled to find a man strikingly like her father in appearance and in a work history of "'Hey, boy!' jobs". But Pedro Diaz early joined the Cuban Revolution and was now a zealous historical guide for visitors. As he spoke, she noted a quality sometimes missing from her father's eyes: "the absolute assurance that he was a man whose words—because he had helped destroy a way of life he despised—would always be heard, with respect, by his children."[7]

Further reflection on the contrast between the Cuban and her father clarified both her dream and the conditions for enduring relationships between parents and children:

The transformation of Pablo Diaz from peasant to official historian deeply impressed me. I envied his children, all the children of Cuba, whose parents are encouraged and permitted to continue to grow, to develop, to change, to "keep up with" their children. To become *compañeros* as well as parents. A society in which there is respectful communication between generations is not likely, easily, to fail. Considering these thoughts, I recalled the incident that is the source of the dream I was having about my father. It is a story about economics, about politics, about class. Still, it is a very simple story, and happens somewhere in the world every day.

When I left my hometown in Georgia at 17 and went off to college, it was virtually the end of my always tenuous relationship with my father. This brilliant man—great at mathematics, unbeatable at storytelling, but unschooled beyond the primary grades—found the manners of his suddenly middle-class (by virtue of being at a college) daughter a barrier to easy contact, if not actually frightening. I found it painful to expose my thoughts in language that to him obscured more than it revealed. This separation, which neither of us wanted, is what poverty engenders. It is what injustice means.

My father stood outside the bus that day, his hat—an old fedora—in his hands; helpless as I left the only world he would every know. Unlike Pablo Diaz, there was no metamorphosis possible for him. So we never spoke of this parting, or of the pain in his beautiful eyes as the bus left him there by the side of that lonely Georgia highway,

and I moved—blinded by tears of guilt and relief—ever farther and farther away; until, by the time of his death, all I understood, *truly*, of my father's life, was how few of its possibilities he had realized, how relatively little of its probable grandeur I had known.

Notes

1. For a full account of guardians and other kinds of child-custodians, see Mnookin, "Child-Custody Adjudication: Judicial Functions in the Face of Indeterminacy," 39 *Law and Contemporary Problems,* 226 (1975).
2. Donald Davidson has drawn attention to this mutual dependence of belief and desire.
3. The Model Probate Code §§ 219, 220 (1946). Blackstone lists, as one of the "necessaries" parents must provide their children, "*education* suitable to their station in life." He observes that "it is not easy to imagine or allow, that a parent has conferred any considerable benefit upon his child by bringing him into the world; if he afterwards entirely neglects his culture and education, and suffers him to grow up like a mere beast, to lead a life useless to others, and shameful to himself. Yet the municipal laws of most countries seem to be defective in this point, by not constraining the parent to bestow a proper education upon his children. Perhaps they thought it punishment enough to leave the parent, who neglects the instruction of his family, to labor under those griefs and inconveniences which his family, so uninstructed, will be sure to bring upon him" I *Commentaries on The Laws of England* 451 (New York: Banks Law Publishing 1923, p. 165).
4. This notion of a *life* merits fuller analysis and philosophic deployment. It can do much of the work of concepts of the *soul,*

personhood, and *human existence* with more precision and fewer metaphysical shackles.

5. I am indebted to Onora O'Neill and Derek Parfit for criticizing earlier formulations, as well as to John Taurek, Amélie Rorty, and Peter Klein for provoking much of the commentary that follows.

6. Cf. my attempts to formulate this principle and a set of work-rights in medical practice in "Doctors' Rights and Work," *The Journal of Medicine and Philosophy* (forthcoming).

7. Alice Walker, "Secrets of the New Cuba," *Ms. Magazine,* vol. VI, No. 3 (1977), p. 98. Reprinted by permission.

A child's health is usually a parent's first and abiding, even obsessive, concern. But there are notable exceptions: parents may be too poor, too misinformed, or too ill to provide proper health care for a child, or the child may have a chronic malady or handicap that overtaxes a parent's resources, however devoted the parents are to the child's care. Clearly, there must be public provision of pediatric care and legal supervision of children's health. Three of the ten United Nations Declaration of the Rights of the Child cite this need.

But here as elsewhere public intervention and assistance are complicated by parental attitudes and parent-child bonds. The following case is an example. The father of a teenage child with severe facial deformity refused surgical repair, even at public expense. He had a long-standing dread and distrust of surgery, shared by his son, and both wished to rely on mental healing and the "natural forces of the universe."

If a child's life is at risk, courts usually intervene whatever the parent's desires and beliefs. But this was not an emergency, and the majority of judges upheld the father's refusal. They noted that the son shared his father's beliefs about surgery and mental healing and was unlikely to cooperate in post-surgical speech therapy. The minority held the father to be violating a child's right "so far as is possible, to lead a normal life." His refusal was, in their opinion, "far worse than beating the child or denying him food or clothing."

If there is such a right, this case makes clear that a child may well not care, or be able, to exercise it without a parent's support: outside aid may serve little purpose so long as a child reflects a parent's beliefs.

IN THE MATTER OF
SEIFERTH

In the matter of MARTIN SEIFERTH, JR., an INFANT, et al., Appellants. WILLIAM E. MOSHER, as Deputy Commssioner of Health for Erie County Health Department, Respondent. [309 N.Y. 80, July 1955] Argued before the New York Court of Appeals May 23, 1955. Decided July 8, 1955.

Summary

Parent and child—operation on child over parents' objection—proceeding for order transferring custody of child to Commissioner of Social Welfare for purpose of consenting to operation to cure child's cleft palate and harelip—child's father believes in mental healing—discretion exercised by Children's Court Judge to refuse to grant relief requested preferred over that of Appellate Division requiring child to submit to operation—application may be renewed when circumstances warrant.

In this proceeding to have a boy who has a cleft palate and harelip declared a neglected child and to have his custody transferred to the Commissioner of Social Welfare of Erie County for the purpose of consenting to such medical, surgical and dental services as may be necessary to rectify his condition, there was medical testimony to the effect that such cases are almost always given surgical treatment at an early age and that the older the patient is the less favorable are likely to be the results, but the boy's father believes in mental healing by letting "the forces of the universe work on the body." The plastic surgeon selected by petitioner declined to be precise about how detrimental it would be to defer this work for several years. He testified that although it was important to have the operation at an early age, it could be performed at any time. However, he did not attempt to view the case from the psychological viewpoint of the boy. Testimony indicated that the boy was likeable and had a newspaper route, and that his marks in school were high. The surgical procedures were explained to him, but he preferred to try for some time longer to cure his defect through "natural forces." There is no present emergency, and, in order to benefit from the operation, it will be necssary to enlist the boy's co-operation in developing normal speech patterns through a lengthy course in concentrated speech therapy. It will be almost impossible to secure his co-operation if he continues to believe as he does now. The Children's Court Judge

who saw and heard the witnesses apparently concluded that less would be lost by permitting the lapse of several more years to a time when the boy may make his own decision to submit to plastic surgery than might be sacrificed if he were compelled to undergo it now against his will. The discretion exercised by the trier of the facts is preferred to that of the Appellate Division, and the petition should be dismissed without prejudice to renewal of the application, if the circumstances warrant.

Matter of Seiferth, 285 App. Div. 221, reversed.

Appeal, by permission of the Appellate Division of the Supreme Court in the fourth judicial department, from an order of said court, entered January 12, 1955, which, by a divided court, (1) reversed, on the facts and as a matter of discretion, an order of the Children's Court of Erie County (WYLEGALA, J.), denying an application by respondent for an order declaring the infant to be a neglected child and temporarily transferring custody of him to the Commissioner of Social Welfare of Erie County for the purpose of consenting to the performance of such medical, surgical and dental services as might be necessary for the infant, and (2) granted the petition. A stated finding of fact in the decision of the Children's Court was modified and new findings of fact were made by the Appellate Division.

William G. Conable and Whitney W. Gilbert for appellants. I. New findings of fact by the Appellate Division are unsupported by the evidence. (*Matter of Vasko*, 238 App. Div. 128; *Matter of Rotkowitz*, 175 Misc. 948; *Matter of Sisson*, 152 Misc. 806; *Pierce v. Society of Sisters*, 268 U. S. 510; *Houghtaling* v. *Stoothoff*, 259 App. Div. 854; *Braisted* v.

Brooklyn & Rockaway Beach R. R. Co., 46 App. Div. 204; *Haber* v. *Paramount Ice Corp.*, 264 N. Y. 98; *Martin* v. *Martin*, 308 N. Y. 136.) II. The Appellate Division exceeded its constitutional authority in ordering an operation over the protests of the parents. (*Matter of Vasko*, 238 App. Div. 128; *People* v. *Pierson*, 176 N.Y. 201.)

Elmer R. Weil, County Attorney (*George M. Nelson* of counsel), for respondent. I. The new findings of fact by the Appellate Division are fully supported by the evidence. (*Matter of Vasko*, 238 App. Div. 128; *Matter of Rotkowitz*, 175 Misc. 948; *Matter of Sisson*, 152 Misc. 806; *Pierce* v. *Society of Sisters*, 268 U. S. 510; *Houghtaling* v. *Stoothoff*, 259 App. Div. 854; *Braisted* v. *Brooklyn & Rockaway Beach R. R. Co.*, 46 App. Div. 204; *Haber* v. *Paramount Ice Corp.*, 264 N. Y. 98; *Martin* v. *Martin*, 308 N. Y. 136; *Locklin* v. *Fisher*, 264 App. Div. 452.) II. The Appellate Division of the Supreme Court, in granting petitioner's order, exercised its constitutional powers despite the protests of the parents of the infant. (*Finlay* v. *Finlay*, 240 N. Y. 429; *People* v. *Pierson*, 176 N. Y. 201; *People ex rel. Herzog* v. *Morgan*, 287 N. Y. 317; *Prince* v. *Massachusetts*, 321 U. S. 158; *Jacobson* v. *Massachusetts*, 197 U. S. 11; *Buck* v. *Bell*, 274 U. S. 200.)

VAN VOORHIS, J. This is a case involving a fourteen-year-old boy with cleft palate and harelip, whose father holds strong convictions with which the boy has become imbued against medicine and surgery. This proceeding has been instituted by the deputy commissioner of the Erie County Health Department on petition to the Children's Court to have Martin declared a neglected child, and to have his custody transferred from his parents to the Commissioner of Social Welfare of Erie County for the purpose of consenting to such medical, surgical and dental services as may be necessary to rectify his condition. The medical testimony is to the effect that such cases are almost always given surgical treatment at an earlier age, and the older the patient is the less favorable are likely to be the results according to experience. The surgery recommended by the plastic surgeon called for petitioner consists of three operations: (1) repair of the harelip by bringing the split together; (2) closing the cleft or split in the rear of the palate, the boy being already too late in life to have the front part mended by surgery; and (3) repairing the front part of the palate by dental appliances. The only risk of mortality is the negligible one due to the use of anesthesia. These operations would be spaced a few months apart and six months would be expected to complete the work, two years at the outside in case of difficulty. Petitioner's plastic surgeon declined to be precise about how detrimental it would be to the prognosis to defer this work for several years. He said: "I do not think it is emergent, that it has to be done this month or next month, but every year that goes is important to this child, yes." A year and a half has already elapsed since this testimony was taken in December, 1953.

Even after the operation, Martin will not be able to talk normally, at least not without going to a school for an extended period for concentrated speech therapy. There are certain phases of a child's life when the importance of these defects becomes of greater significance. The first is past, when children enter grade school, the next is the period of adolescence, particularly toward the close of adolescence when social interests arise in secondary school. Concerning this last, petitioner's plastic surgeon stated: "That is an extremely important period of time. That child is approaching that age where it is very important that correction, that it is very significant that correction made at this time could probably put him in a great deal better position to enter that period of life than would otherwise. Another thing which is difficult is that we have very excellent speech facilities at the Buffalo Public Schools through grade level. At secondary school level and in higher age groups speech training facilities are less satisfactory, so that it is important that it be done at this age. However, the most important thing of all is this [is] gradually progressive with time. The earlier done, the better results. Normally the lip is repaired in early infancy, one to three years of age. Speech training would begin at school or earlier. Every year lost has been that much more lost to the boy. Each year lost continues to be lost. The time to repair is not too early." He testified that in twenty years of plastic surgery he had never encountered a child with this boy's defects who had not been operated upon at his age. Nevertheless, he testified that such an operation can be performed "from the time the child is born until he dies." In this doctor's view, the consideration bulked larger than the quality of postoperative results, that the boy's increasing social contacts required that he be made to look and to speak normally as he approached adolescence.

Everyone testified that the boy is likeable, he has a newspaper route, and his marks in school were all over 90 during the last year. However, his father did testify that recently the boy had withdrawn a little more from his fellows, although he said that "As soon as anyone contacts Martin, he is so likeable nobody is tempted to ridicule him. . . . Through his pleasantness he overcomes it."

The father testified that "If the child decides on an operation, I shall not be opposed," and that "I want to say in a few years the child should decide for himself . . . whether to have the operation or not." The father believes in mental healing by letting "the forces of the universe work on the body," although he denied that this is an established religion of any kind stating that it is purely his own philosophy and that "it is not classified as religion." There is no doubt, however, that the father is strong minded about this, and has inculcated a distrust and dread of surgery in the boy since childhood.

The Erie County Children's Court Judge caused the various surgical procedures to be explained to Martin by competent and qualified practitioners in the field of plastic surgery and orthodontia. Photographs of other children who had undergone similar remedial surgery were exhibited to him showing their condition both before and after treatment. He was also taken to the speech correction school where he heard the reproduction of his own voice and speech, as well as records depicting various stages of progress of other children. He met other children of his own age, talked to them and attended class in speech correction. Both the boy and the father were given opportunity to ask questions, which they did freely not only of the professional staff but of the different children.

On February 11, 1954, Martin, his father and attorney met after these demonstrations in Judge WYLEGALA's chambers. Judge WYLEGALA wrote in his opinion that Martin "was very much pleased with what was shown him, but had come to the conclusion that he should try for some time longer to close the cleft palate and the split lip himself through 'natural forces.'" After stating that an order for surgery would have been granted without hesitation if this proceeding had been instituted before this child acquired convictions of his own, Judge WYLEGALA summed up his conclusions as follows: "After duly deliberating upon the psychological effect of surgery upon this mature, intelligent boy, schooled as he has been for all of his young years in the existence of 'forces of nature' and his fear of surgery upon the human body, I have come to the conclusion that no order should be made at this time compelling the child to submit to surgery. His condition is not emergent and there is no serious threat to his health or life. He has time until he becomes 21 years of age to apply for financial assistance under County and State aid to physically handicapped children to have the corrections made. This has also been explained to him after he made known his decision to me." The petition accordingly was dismissed.

The Appellate Division, Fourth Department, reversed by a divided court, and granted the petition requiring Martin Seiferth to submit to surgery.

As everyone agrees, there are important considerations both ways. The Children's Court has power in drastic situations to direct the operation over the objection of parents (*Matter of Vasko*, 238 App. Div. 128, 129). Nevertheless, there is no present emergency, time is less of the essence than it was a few years ago insofar as concerns the physical prognosis, and we are impressed by the circumstance that in order to benefit from the operation upon the cleft palate, it will almost certainly be necessary to

enlist Martin's co-operation in developing normal speech patterns through a lengthy course in concentrated speech therapy. It will be almost impossible to secure his co-operation if he continues to believe, as he does now, that it will be necessary "to remedy the surgeon's distortion first and then go back to the primary task of healing the body." This is an aspect of the problem with which petitioner's plastic surgeon did not especially concern himself, for he did not attempt to view the case from the psychological viewpoint of this misguided youth. Upon the other hand, the Children's Court Judge, who saw and heard the witnesses, and arranged the conferences for the boy and his father which have been mentioned, appears to have been keenly aware of this aspect of the situation, and to have concluded that less would be lost by permitting the lapse of several more years, when the boy may make his own decision to submit to plastic surgery, than might be sacrificed if he were compelled to undergo it now against his sincere and frightened antagonism. One cannot be certain of being right under these circumstances, but this appears to be a situation where the discretion of the trier of the facts should be preferred to that of the Appellate Division (*Harrington* v. *Harrington*, 290 N. Y. 126).

The order of the Appellate Division should be reversed and that of the Children's Court reinstated dismissing the petition, without prejudice to renew the application if circumstances warrant.

FULD, J. (dissenting). Every child has a right, so far as is possible, to lead a normal life and, if his parents, through viciousness or ignorance, act in such a way as to endanger that right, the court should, as the legislature has provided, act on his behalf. Such is the case before us.

The boy Martin, twelve years old when this proceeding was begun, fourteen now, has been neglected in the most egregious way. He is afflicted with a massive harelip and cleft palate which not only grievously detract from his appearance but seriously impede his chances for a useful and productive life. Although medical opinion is agreed that the condition can be remedied by surgery, that it should be performed as soon as possible and that the risk involved is negligible, the father has refused to consent to the essential operation. His reason—which is, as the Appellate Division found, entirely unsubstantial—was that he relies on "forces in the universe" which will enable the child to cure himself of his own accord. He might consent to the operation, he said, if the boy "in a few years" should favor one.

It is quite true that the child's physical life is not at peril—as would be the situation if he had an infected appendix or a growth on the brain—but it may not be questioned, to quote from the opinion below, "What is in danger is his chance for a normal, useful life." Judge VAN VOORHIS does not, I am sure, take issue with that, but he feels that the boy will benefit, to a greater extent, from the operation if he enters the hospital with a mind favorably disposed to surgery. Therefore he counsels delay, on the *chance*—and that is all it is—on the *chance* that at some future time the boy may make his own decision to submit to plastic surgery.

It would, of course, be preferable if the boy were to accede to the operation, and I am willing to assume that, if he acquiesces, he will the more easily and quickly react to the postoperative speech therapy. However, there is no assurance that he will, either next year, in five years or six, give his consent. Quite obviously, he is greatly influenced by his father, quite plainly a victim of the latter's unfortunate delusions. And, beyond that, it must be borne in mind that there is little if any risk involved in the surgery and that, as time goes on, the operation becomes more difficult.

Be that as it may, though, it is the court which has a duty to perform (Children's Court Act, § 24), and it should not seek to avoid that duty by foisting upon the boy the ultimate decision to be made. Neither by statute nor decision is the child's consent necessary or material, and we should not permit his refusal to agree, his failure to co-operate, to ruin his life and any change for a normal, happy existence; normalcy and happiness, difficult of attainment under the most propitious conditions, will unquestionably be impossible if the disfigurement is not corrected.

Moreover, it is the fact, and a vital one, that this is a proceeding brought to determine whether the parents are neglecting the chlid by refusing and failing to provide him with necessary surgical, medical and dental service (Children's Court Act, § 2, subd. 4, cl. e).[1] Whether the child condones the neglect, whether he is willing to let his parents do as they choose, surely cannot be operative on the question as to whether or not they are guilty of neglect. They are not interested or concerned with whether he does or does not want the essential operation. They have arbitrarily taken the position that there is to be no surgery. What these parents are doing, by their failure to provide for an operation, however well-intentioned, is far worse than beating the child or denying him food or clothing. To the boy, and his future, it makes no difference that it may be ignorance rather than viciousness that will perpetuate his unfortunate condition. If parents are actually mistreating or neglecting a child, the circumstance that he may not mind it cannot alter the fact that they are guilty of neglect and it cannot render their conduct permissible.

The welfare and interests of a child are at stake. A court should not place upon his shoulders one of the most momentous and far-reaching decisions of his life. The court should make the decision, as the statute contemplates, and leave to the good sense and sound judgment of the public authorities the job of preparing the boy for the operation and of getting him as adjusted to it as possible. We should not put off decision in the hope and on the chance that the child may change his mind and submit at some future time to the operation.

The order of the Appellate Division should be affirmed.

CONWAY, Ch. J., DYE and FROESSEL, JJ., concur with VAN VOORHIS, J.; FULD, J., dissents in an opinion in which DESMOND and BURKE, JJ., concur.

Order reversed, etc.

Note

1. A "Neglected child," the Children's Court Act (§ 2, subd. 4) recites, "means a child . . . (e) whose parent, guardian or custodian neglects or refuses, when able to do so, to provide necessary medical, surgical, institutional or hospital care for such child."

Genetic engineering is no longer the science fiction prospect and project it recently was. The possibilities of recombining DNA suggest that the most beneficial, as well as the most lurid, Frankensteinian possibilities may be open to future parents. In the meantime, the less dramatic but growing use of genetic counseling, informed by amniocentesis and enforced with effective contraception or selective abortion, has given choices to some parents who previously would have faced only a genetic lottery. Such choices are particularly difficult, for they may profoundly affect, even end, the life of a child or of a family.

Life-affecting choices may also arise after a child is born. Lawrence Crocker discusses whether parents may choose their child's sexual orientation. Since nothing reliable is now known about how to do this, he has to imagine that we finally discover how to guarantee either a clearly heterosexual or a clearly homosexual orientation. (The secret lies in the early administration of Brussels sprouts.) The considerations which would be relevant in determining who may—and must—make so important a decision on a child's behalf would also be relevant in making other life-affecting decisions, including those which must be pre-parental decisions.

MEDDLING WITH THE SEXUAL ORIENTATION OF CHILDREN

LAWRENCE CROCKER

Suppose there were an inexpensive and thoroughly safe drug which, when given to a child in its first three years, would ensure that the child grew up to be (exclusively) heterosexual. Are the parents morally permitted to administer the drug? Is society morally permitted either to require its administration or to ban it?

Consider a case which most strongly suggests that the drug should be administered. That the child grows up to be heterosexual leads to the greater good for the child, the family, and the society. Homosexuals are significantly less happy than heterosexuals and cause serious problems for everyone. On no possible transformation of the society will this fail to be the case. There is a general, uncoerced, and informed belief in the society, which the parents share, that the drug ought to be administered.

Under these farfetched hypothetical conditions, are there any reasons why the drug shouldn't be administered?

The following might be suggested:

1. The drug interferes with the child's natural course of development.
2. The child is incapable of consenting to the administration of the drug.
3. If we could ask the adult who would develop from the child if the drug were not administered, he or she might object to its administration.

I. Natural and Unnatural

One reply to objection (1) is to deny that the drug interferes with the natural development of the child. Rather, it is homosexuality that is unnatural. The drug, then, simply ensures that the child will follow the natural course of development rather than getting off track. The problem with this reply is that it is not at all clear that heterosexuality is more natural than homosexuality in any sense which has the slightest moral importance. Homosexuality is, apparently, less usual than heterosexuality, but then, being red-headed or more than six foot six inches is unusual, too. Unusual and unnatural are two quite different things.

The possession of a sexual apparatus fitted to heterosexual reproduction might be thought to constitute the naturalness of heterosexuality. But then, our backbones apparently fit us better for walking on all fours or swinging in trees than for walking upright. There surely is a certain sense in which it *is* unnatural for human beings to walk on two feet or swim underwater or travel in space. But focusing, as it does, on (largely) surmountable features of our physical constitution, it seems a rather quaint

sense—more at home in jokes about old-fashioned fundamentalist preachers than in serious moral discussion.

Of course, research on the origins of sexual orientation *might* show homosexuality (or exclusive heterosexuality) to be unnatural in some fairly clear and important sense. For example, homosexuality might turn out to be the result of a pathogenic agent which destroys brain cells, leaving the victim worse off in a variety of ways as well as homosexual. Our drug, then, would simply inoculate the child against this pathogenic agent. Clearly, in such circumstances, it would be very odd to say that the drug was an unnatural interference with the child's development.

However, so far as I know, reputable researchers do not believe the causes of homosexuality to be anything like this. More likely, homosexuality is the result of a slightly different chemical balance having no other significant benefits or liabilities. Or it may simply be the result of different environmental features of no other significance. In either case, there seems to be no important respect in which homosexuality is less natural than heterosexuality.

On the other hand, it is not at all clear that administering a drug to alter a child's future sexual orientation is unnatural in any morally interesting sense, as (1) contends. Suppose that our drug works as follows. Sexual orientation is wholly determined by the average level of a certain chemical in a child's bloodstream between birth and the age of three years. The chemical is an organic complex found in several diverse foods—most abundantly in Brussels sprouts. As a result, serving Brussels sprouts as few as five times before the child is three guarantees heterosexuality. Avoiding Brussels sprouts, apricots, turnips, and wax beans during the same period guarantees homosexuality. The drug is simply concentrated essence of Brussels sprouts. Do those who administer this drug interfere unnaturally with the child's development, or do those interfere unnaturally who refrain from serving apricots, Brussels sprouts, turnips, and wax beans?

I suppose one could say that both are unnatural. What is natural would be the child's own choice of foods. Unfortunately, the child would starve if left alone to forage in any but a very special environment, and in this case, a great deal would turn on how that environment happened to be stocked. We might say that what is natural for the child's development are those foods which the parents would select if they knew nothing about the sex-orientation chemical. But this seems hopelessly silly—defining naturalness for the child in terms of ignorant and utterly arbitrary actions of the parents.

The better course, in this case, is to say that neither the development with the drug (or Brussels sprouts) nor the development without it is unnatural. This conclusion seems to me to carry over to all cases in which (*a*) The drug has no effects on behavior or consciousness except those that follow from the changed sexual orientation; (*b*) the subject loses no potentialities except those incompatible with the new sexual orientation; (*c*) the drug causes neither direct nor indirect injury to any physiological structure—all cells remain equally vigorous, etc. An unnatural development, in any sense with moral importance, must involve more than just developing differently from the way one would otherwise have developed. Johnny may develop differently if he plays the saxophone instead of chess,

but he will not, for that reason, develop unnaturally. What has to be added to change "different development" to "unnatural development," in any morally interesting sense, is some sort of injury or loss of valuable potential. So, I infer from its postulated safety that administering the drug (even if it is something other than essence of Brussels sprouts) will not cause the child to develop unnaturally. Thus, (1) fails as an objection.

Even if there were an interesting sense in which the drug caused unnatural development, that would not, by itself, be a reason to ban the drug. We do some pretty unnatural, indeed sometimes injurious, things to the human organism when we believe that they will promote long-run health and happiness. The unnaturalness of the development must at least be weighed against the advantages. So, the significant advantages postulated should outweigh any unnaturalness that might be perceived in the workings of the drug.

II. Consent and Sexual Orientation

Objections (2) and (3) have to do with the child's autonomy and give somewhat more plausible grounds for banning the drug. To alter a person's future sexual orientation is to make a fairly fundamental change in who the individual will be and what sort of life he or she will lead. Are we allowed to make such large decisions without the individual's participation?

Surely we sometimes are. An individual will lead quite a different life depending on whether he or she is crippled or not. For just this reason, we feel it is our duty to protect children against polio—without their consent. So objection (2), as it stands, seems to have little merit. Of course, in many cases, we should not benefit people without their consent. In the case of persons who cannot consent, however, and where the decision is so clearly in their interest that we could expect their consent if they were capable of giving it, we are usually permitted to perform the action in the absence of consent.

But is meddling with sexual orientation, even if it leads to a happier life, something which would definitely elicit consent if the subject could give it? Infants have no wishes one way or another about polio or about sexual preference. However, this symmetry may break down when we consider the adult who will develop from the infant. An adult who has escaped polio will be glad for the inoculation. An adult crippled by polio will wish that he or she had been inoculated. But while the heterosexual saved from homosexuality may be grateful, so may the homosexual saved from heterosexuality! The homosexual may prefer homosexuality, even believing that most heterosexuals are happier. This statistical truth needn't have much weight for the individual, since the individual may have all sorts of good evidence that his or her case would be an exception. Moreover, even with the belief that one would have been happier as a heterosexual, one still may not wish to have been a heterosexual, the thought of heterosexuality being somewhat repugnant.

So, if we look to the adult for implicit consent to alter the future sexual orientation of the infant, the answer may hinge on whether or not we do make the alteration. There are two potential adults, one having taken the drug, one not; and they disagree. Obviously, this might leave us chasing our tails. Two

different principles suggest ways out. The first is that autonomy is not violated so long as the following conditions are met: (*a*) The individual has no (even partially formed) present or past wish or desire incompatible with the action under consideration. (*b*) In the (actual) future, the individual will come to approve of this action. If this principle is correct, and assuming that people are glad to have the sexual orientation they end up having, then in the present case, we are free either to administer the drug or not, so far as the autonomy of the subject is concerned. My tendency is to feel that this gives us too much leeway. It is not a rich enough notion of autonomy if we can avoid violating it by changing the person to engineer his or her consent.

The second principle is what one who makes objection (3) may have in mind. It is that autonomy is preserved when one alters the person's development only if the development would be approved *both* by the person who would develop without the alteration *and* the person who would develop with it. So, in the present case, we cannot administer the drug on the assumption that the potential homosexual who would develop would without the drug would not approve. The potential heterosexual, of course, would disapprove of our refraining from giving the drug. But this principle, by its requirement of agreement for acting, rather than refraining, gives priority in this case to the homosexual who develops if we do not administer the drug. But surely this puts the wrong kind of moral burden on the difference between doing and refraining. Even if that distinction makes a difference with respect to the doer's or refrainer's duty or responsibility, as many philosophers believe, how can it possibly make the potential person who is the result of refraining privileged over the potential person who is the result of doing? Recall, from above, that neither of these potential persons can claim to be the more natural successor of the child.

So, our two proposed ways of avoiding tail chasing, while looking to the adult for something like implicit consent, both seem implausible. It is better to try a different tack. Imagine a rational infant—informed about the consequences of different sexual orientations (the amount and character of happiness and the like), but itself having no sexual orientation. (If infants, idealized in this way, give you conceptual problems, imagine an adult with amnesia as to his or her sexual orientation.) In the present case, this idealized infant would choose the drug since, by hypothesis, the heterosexual life is happier than the homosexual life, and the infant, unlike the potential homosexual adult, is not repelled by the idea of heterosexuality.

My conclusion, then, is that under the stated conditions, the autonomy of the child will not be infringed[1] by following what is in the best interest of the child—what the child would choose if it were rational and informed. In the case under consideration, that would set up at least a *prima facie* duty to administer the drug, thereby eliminating homosexuality in the next generation. (Recall that I have simply, and implausibly, assumed that society cannot be changed to make homosexuals as happy as heterosexuals.)

III. Who Should Judge Children's Interests?

Of course, we cannot be required to act on what really is in the best interest of the child, but only on what seems to us, on the best available evidence and rational deliberation, to be in its best interest. This raises the question, Whose judgment of the child's best interest should be followed in the case of conflicting judgments? Suppose, for example, that there is a difference of opinion between the parents and society—democratically expressed—as to whether homosexuals or heterosexuals lead the more desirable lives. May the society preempt the parents by banning or requiring the administration of a drug determining sexual orientation? Similar questions can, of course, be raised about conflicts between the judgment of parents and society with respect to other points of upbringing, such as religious or political instruction. One significant respect in which the present case differs from matters of instruction, however, is that it seems easier to change one's mind about most topics of instruction than it is to change one's sexual orientation or other deep personality structures. This is one reason that society might want to be more tolerant of the beliefs parents instill in children than of the sorts of personality they instill. We are more likely to think that parents should be permitted to fill their children's heads with nonsense (within certain limits) than that they should be permitted to saddle their children with serious psychological disabilities.

Society, then, has grounds for intervening between parent and child in the child's interests where major psychological consequences are at stake and where there is good reason to believe that the judgment of society is better than that of the parents.

But surely, there are a great many cases where the judgment of the parents is superior to that of society in assessing what is good for children. In particular, parents will know both the child and the home environment better than do those outside the family. If the question is whether a child born this year will more likely have a better life as a heterosexual than as a homosexual, the parents can at least gauge their own reaction to the two possibilities and the effect of that reaction on the child. This is only a small part of the information needed to answer the question properly, but it does give the parents a certain advantage.

Of course, there are some cases where the judgment of society is fairly clearly going to be better than that of parents. This will usually be true, for example, where parents are mentally incompetent, alcoholic, or terribly ignorant. But let me assume that such cases can be handled by some special mechanism, such as foster homes or supervision of the indicated parents. So we need not, for these sorts of reasons, let the judgment of society take precedence over that of all parents.

We might look for some guidance from a general theory of when the majority is more likely to be correct (about a factual matter) than an individual picked at random. (This is what we want to know when we are concerned solely with maximizing the number of correct answers. The two available strategies are to let everyone answer the question for himself or herself or to let the majority answer for everyone. This theory does not consider any other reputed advantages or disadvantages of democracy—such as the minimization of frustrated choices, on the one hand, or the loss of individual liberty, on the other.) Obviously, the majority has a higher probability of correctness than an individual picked at random if—and

only if—the majority believes that the proposition p is true, a non-empty minority believes that p is false, and p is in fact true. Unfortunately, we do not always know whether p is true, so we cannot always rely on this principle or make a judgment of probability in just this sense.

Frequently our most plausible course for estimating the probabilities is to base them on the beliefs of the group best qualified to assess the truth of p. (This is not always the group officially or widely recognized as best qualified on the truth of p.) If there is general agreement among the best qualified, then majority rule will maximize correctness if and only if the majority agrees with the best qualified. One case where this is likely to happen is if the question is a fairly easy one. It is sufficient indication of the appropriateness of majority rule if the person of median qualification is more likely to be right than wrong—assuming that the more qualified a person is, the more likely he or she is to be correct. On more difficult questions, there may also be a tendency for the majority to agree with the consensus of the most qualified if the latter agree more among themselves than the less qualified agree among themselves.[2]

Let us see which of these indicators of majority wisdom apply to the question at issue: Will a child born this year be more likely to have a better life as a heterosexual than as a homosexual? It seems to me that we do not know the answer to this question and that the experts are fairly badly split on it. The question is not easy. There would be, however, a great deal of agreement among those who are not particularly well qualified to answer it, as a result of the widespread irrational prejudice against homosexuality. In short, we have none of the above-mentioned indicators of the likely superiority of the majority's belief to that of an individual picked at random.[3]

To be slightly less abstract, we should, of course, think of our question being asked of a particular infant. Then the parents are not exactly randomly selected individuals. They do have the edge of knowing better their own probable reactions and influences. This, together with the fact that we have found no reason to prefer the wisdom of the majority to that of even a randomly selected individual, strongly suggests that we should not turn over to majority vote this question, or similar questions, or policy decisions which turn on answers to these questions, if our sole concern is to protect the interests of the child.

Moreover, it is a good general principle to avoid legislation in a field where there are grounds for hope that the majority will be more enlightened in the future. We don't want to impede the consequences of that enlightenment.

IV. Other Considerations

The interests and autonomy of the child are not the only things to be taken into account in deciding on the use of drugs of the sort we have been considering. There are also the interests of other parties, as well as the question of whether one party or another is a more suitable proxy for the child (independent of wisdom).

Sometimes, it is relevant, in deciding who ought to mold the character of children, to consider who will be most affected by the child, and later, the adult. One reason we think parents normally have a special right to shape children's behavior is that they are inevitably confronted with so much of that behavior. It is a necessary condition of the parents' well-being, indeed sanity, that the behavior be tolerable to them. The same principle explains some of the limits on the behaviors that parents may teach to children. If only we could, we would like to take children away from parents whose methods of upbringing create a high risk of producing a pathological murderer. Similarly, the society will usually not allow parents to raise children who routinely throw bowls of soup at strangers in restaurants. The parents' proper sphere of control over children will not always extend beyond the point where the children's behavior (present or future) begins to affect persons other than the parents significantly and detrimentally.

Another factor sometimes cited as a justification for exercising control over the child is the contribution made to the child's welfare. For parents, this often means a sacrifice of money, time, effort, and worry. A word like "investment" is out of place, since it suggests that the child is a piece of property. Still, we do believe that a parent who sacrifices to bring up a child is entitled to some assistance if the parent falls upon hard times in old age. In fact, it seems to me that their contribution properly gives parents certain control rights over children. Some control is, of course, a necessary ingredient in parental care. But I believe that it is permissible to go beyond this minimum—to insist, for example, as a prerogative stemming from their care, that teenagers do the dishes and take out the garbage.

Control rights over grown children are more speculative, especially when they represent direct demands against the grown child. (Though I am inclined to think that typical parents may morally require their children to write home occasionally.) Our case is, however, one of indirect control over the adult personality by affecting the child. Some such control might be justified (among other ways) by the parents' sacrifices and contributions. If it is inevitable that the child is to be molded one way or another on a given point, then it is not wholly implausible that those who have sacrificed for the benefit of the child should have priority as molders over those who haven't—other things being equal.

But in a dispute between parents and society over the upbringing of children, it is not altogether clear where considerations of contribution lead us, since it is not clear which party has done more for the child. Parents, typically, make greater contributions to the welfare of their child than do other individual members of the society. However, the material and cultural legacy which society has accumulated throughout history and makes (to greater or lesser degree) available to the developing child in many respects dwarfs the parents' contribution. (Think of what the very best of stone age parents could do for their offspring.)

On the other hand, it is not at all clear how much credit for the contributions and sacrifices of Aristotle, Shakespeare, Pasteur, and Edison should be thought of as vested in our current society. And, even if current society is given the credit, it is not entirely clear that the electoral majority is entitled to draw upon it.

It is, I think, wise to bypass, where possible, issues of comparative contributions and sacrifices between individuals and society. In the present case, it is not only possible but required. Other things are not equal. There are considerations which take precedence over the question of who has made the greatest sacrifices for or most benefitted the child. To give the contribution-sacrifice considerations priority over those of the child's autonomy or future welfare, for example, would surely be to claim something uncomfortably close to an investor's property right.

Certain other features of typical parent-child relations, in addition to the degree parents are affected by their children and their contribution to their children, have been thought to give rise to special parental rights of control. These include, among others, mutual affection and trust, shared experiences, common beliefs and values, and expectations of future contact. For such reasons, parents are (typically) closer to their own child than others are, and occupy a somewhat privileged position in the child's moral universe. Since, for a considerable period of time, children identify more closely with their parents than with other adults, the parents are the natural proxies for the children in the case of decisions which the children are incapable of making themselves. (Of course, they are not always the wisest proxies.)

Obviously, the moral suitability of parents as proxies reinforces the policy conclusion of our earlier finding that parents are at least as likely to choose wisely in the child's interest as is society operating democratically, when the issue is meddling with sexual orientation. The consideration of contribution by society as against parents cannot change that conclusion, since it is a lexically posterior consideration. Only the degree to which society is affected by sexual orientation, as compared to parents, remains as something that might tip the scales in society's favor. Whether they ought to be or not, parents are significantly affected by their children's sexual orientation. But then, society too will be significantly affected by the outcome of a policy decision to meddle (or to allow or to forbid meddling) with sexual orientation. Most obviously, present homosexuals would be adversely affected, at least psychologically, by the adoption of any policy intended to diminish the number of future homosexuals.

A different sort of negative effect on society would occur in the following hypothetical case. It is universally agreed that statistically homosexuals are neither better nor worse off than heterosexuals. It is also universally agreed that society benefits from a homosexual population because, for example, homosexuals tend to be more productive in certain of the arts. However, to have a homosexual child is a somewhat unhappy situation for any individual parent. Therefore, everyone hopes that (some) other people will have homosexual children. Someone suggests that we ban by law any drug which would lead to a decrease in homosexuality—all of us, then, bearing equally the risk of having homosexual children. Calculating the risk against the gain, I would be willing to take the risk, so long as others do too. (Suppose the artistic gains require a homosexual subculture. So, unless enough others take the risk, there will be no point in my taking it, because there will be no potential advantage.) Should I, then, vote for the ban? I should, only if I believe that every other potential risk taker wants the law to pass. Consider someone who does not want the law to pass because for him or her the potential gain is not worth the risk. Now, it seems to me that there are many cases where a democratic society can properly require individuals to make sacrifices which they do not wish to

make. But I do not believe that this is one of them. The artistic gain is not a weighty enough good that we can properly require reluctant parents to risk what they perceive to be a serious family hardship. A modest benefit for society ought not to be won, in matters of upbringing, at the cost of a serious loss for the family.

More generally, we have the following hierarchy with respect to upbringing and, in particular, meddling with sexual orientation. First come the interests of the child. A loss to the child can be outweighed only by a considerably greater gain to the family or a far greater gain to society. (Suppose that greater artistic productivity is bought at the cost of mild unhappiness on the part of homosexuals. This ought not to be allowed even if the artistic cost of phasing out homosexuals is considerable.) After the interests of the individual, and before the interests of society in general, come the interests of parents, family, and other closely associated persons. The rationale of the hierarchy is simply a matter of the degree to which the loss or gain is concentrated in a given individual's life. In order to save nine persons from headaches, we cannot ask the tenth to endure a headache five times more severe than he or she would otherwise have suffered.

V. Conclusions

I conclude that drugs capable of altering the future sexual orientation of children should be made available, when technically possible. They should neither be required nor banned by law unless there is very good reason to believe that the parents are not acting in the child's best interest and that the electorate is in a better position to gauge that interest. The latter condition, it seems, is not currently met.

The point of view suggested in this paper might, if it were widely shared and if the appropriate drugs were available, lead to a decrease in homosexuality in subsequent generations. But, under certain circumstances, it might also lead to and justify more sweeping changes in the sexual landscape.

Suppose, for example, that those feminist theoreticians are correct who have argued that most of the world's ills are due to genetic defects in the male personality structure—aggressiveness, violence, elitism, and the like. No genetic tinkering will remove these defects in the male, and no social revolution will ameliorate them very much. Moreover, the simple existence of two different sexes constitutes a great danger of continued sexism, just as the different races make racism so hard to avoid. Suppose, further, that the technology is available to produce and reproduce an entirely female homosexual population.

If this genetic and social theory were correct, which I am inclined to doubt, and if the joys of heterosexuality are not sufficiently great to compensate for most of the world's ills, which I am not inclined to doubt, then this extreme policy of sexual engineering would, I think, be justifiable. It would be in the interest of all (actual) persons that men be phased out by attrition, and, then, of all (actual) children that they should grow up to be homosexual.

Notes

1. I am inclined to think that hypothetical consent is the general key to the issue of paternalism. We may never, I think, intervene simply for the agent's own good. Rather, we may sometimes intervene to bring about what the agent would choose if the agent were in a better position to make a choice. (Of course, such interventions are typically thought to be beneficial to the agent, but this ought not to be the direct purpose.) By concentrating on the agent's own choice, albeit hypothetical, this general approach respects the agent's autonomy while justifying certain intuitively permissible (or obligatory) "paternalistic" interventions. Mill was right, I think, that we have good grounds for believing that pulling someone back from a danger of which he or she is unaware will not infringe on that person's autonomy.

2. We are assured that majority rule maximizes rationally expectable correctness under the following rather restrictive conditions. (a) The population can be divided by degree of qualification into some number of groups of equal size. (b) The more qualified the group, the greater the probability of a member's being correct. (c) The more qualified the group, the greater its degree of internal agreement.

3. If the split among the experts is so even that we can only assign a probability of .5 to p, then the rational expectation that the majority will be correct is the same as that for any given individual—namely, .5. Majority rule is, however, a riskier strategy, given our concern for the number of correct answers. Letting the majority answer, as it were, for everyone ensures that everyone will be correct or everyone will be wrong. It is a maximax strategy. If the only other procedure available is to let everyone decide for himself or herself, that will represent the maximin strategy. It seems to me that an argument can be made for the maximin strategy in a case like the one under consideration, but it is not a very decisive argument.

2. Child Abuse and Parental Negligence

The most publicized cases of child abuse and neglect are lurid tales of sadism and torture. But these are not the cases likely to help us to think carefully about abuse and neglect. No one doubts the need for some form of state intervention to protect children from parents (or others) who starve or batter them. Doubts arise when one considers homes which are less dramatically deficient—for example, homes which are filthy or unstimulating, or where a parent has psychiatric or other health problems or perhaps is criminal or promiscuous. Further doubts arise about the form of state intervention which should be applied in particular cases. The quality of care and life of children who are removed from their homes is often low—yet this is the "remedy" likely to be applied for many cases of neglect or abuse.

Social policies for dealing with child abuse and neglect should start with good laws. At present, the laws of different jurisdictions define child abuse and neglect in varied ways. Natalie Abrams surveys this diversity of definitions. Some refer only to the consequences of parental acts, and so must view children who, through mere good luck or resilience, weather malicious or irresponsible parental behavior as unabused and unneglected. Other definitions refer to children's best interests, and so implicitly require parents not merely to meet specific obligations to their children but also set the children's interests above all others at every point. Were this standard seriously applied, many conscientious and competent parents might be judged deficient because at some time they did not put their children first.

The common problem of these definitions, Natalie Abrams argues, is that they are framed with an eye to justifying removing children from their homes. Many less drastic remedies, including training, assisting and supervising failing parents, are then little used, even though they may be cheaper or more effective than removing children from their homes. An adequate definition of child abuse and neglect, Abrams holds, should reflect a theory of parental obligations which can be enforced by a variety of remedies, rather than trying to specify a point of crisis at which children must be removed from their homes.

PROBLEMS IN DEFINING
CHILD ABUSE AND NEGLECT

NATALIE ABRAMS

The first problem to be confronted in a philosophical consideration of child abuse and neglect is the definition of abusive or neglectful behavior itself. "The single most telling indicator that the child abuse area is at an extremely primitive level of theory construction is that there is today no widely accepted definition of child abuse. How does one investigate a phenomenon that has no widely accepted definition? Resolving this definitional dilemma must become the first item of business among workers in the child abuse area."[1] In the first two sections of this paper, I shall examine some current definitions of abuse and neglect, and try to clarify some of the possible consequences and implications of each. I shall not consider whether particular acts satisfy or fail to satisfy certain definitions, but rather, will focus on the standards set out in the definitions. In the third section, I shall recommend a new definition. In the fourth and fifth sections, I shall examine some of the implications of the suggested definition.

Abusive or neglectful behavior might be defined in terms of the agent's intentions, the consequences of the act, or the act itself. These definitions would follow traditional approaches in normative ethical theory. I shall discuss each of these definitions and some of the associated difficulties.

1. Abuse, Neglect, and Parents' Intentions

If intentions are thought to be definitive, an act would be abusive or neglectful if the agent's intention was to injure or fail to care for the child, regardless of whether or not harm actually resulted. Given this definition, parental acts would be considered benign, even if harm did result, provided the parent did not intend the consequences. Intentions should not, however, be taken as the sole criterion of whether or not a child has been abused or neglected, since they do not refer to the effect of an act on a child. Parental behavior may harm a child whether or not parents so intend. The reason it may be important to know parents' intentions is to ascertain parental responsibility and decide about possible legal sanctions. However, even when the harm to the child is thought to be intentional, the parents' behavior may manifest forms of psychopathology and be immune from criminal prosecution.[2]

2. Abuse, Neglect, and Harm to Children

Most definitions of child abuse or neglect are essentially utilitarian in that they view harmful consequences for the child as the critical factor. Only behavior which harms or is likely to harm the child is considered abusive or neglectful. The argument is made that since there is no well-established theory of parenting and no universally accepted standards for child rearing, the only rational approach to evaluating parental behavior is in terms of how the child is affected. The problem which remains for utilitarian definitions of abuse and neglect is how "harm" to the child should be conceived. There are various possibilities.

One approach is to employ the "best interest" standard. According to this standard, a child would be considered harmed, and therefore abused or neglected, if parental behavior was not in the best interest of the child. The "best interest" approach may be justifiable in custody disputes, but it does not seem appropriate in child abuse or neglect determinations. There might always be another environment which would be in some way better for the child. Furthermore, defining abuse or neglect as failure to act in the child's best interest seems to impose unreasonably demanding obligations on all parents and totally disregards competing interests or rights, such as those of parents themselves or of siblings.

Another version of a utilitarian approach is to claim that a child is harmed (and, hence, abused or neglected) if certain minimum needs are not satisfied. With this approach, it is necessary to determine, first, what needs a child has, and second, what would constitute a minimal level of satisfaction of these needs. Again, this approach focuses on consequences for the child. It would be similar to what Joel Feinberg refers to as the "unmet need" analysis of harm,[3] which views an individual as harmed if he has a need which is not met. Once all needs are satisfied, a further provision of goods would constitute unneeded benefit, and if these additional goods are not forthcoming, the individual is not benefitted but has not been harmed. One problem which Feinberg points out is that, given this analysis, a rich man would not be harmed by a small theft which left him above the minimum level. A distinction must therefore be made between actually being harmed and undergoing a change in one's condition in a harmful direction. A rich man's condition, and that of a child, might be altered in a harmful direction without falling below the minimum level—i.e. without ever reaching the state of actual injury. On the minimum needs definition of child abuse and neglect, parental behavior is abusive or neglectful only if the child's condition falls below the minimum level. Failure to realize a child's potential or even inhibiting a child's development would not be abusive, provided the child's status or level of well-being does not fall below a minimal standard.

A third consequentialist approach to defining abuse or neglect is in terms of social or community standards and specified sorts of harm. According to this approach, behavior which falls below the community norm and also results in specifiable harm would be abusive or neglectful. It is this standard which is employed in cases charging negligence. "The tort of negligence is committed when a legally protected interest of the plaintiff is invaded as a result of conduct on the part of the defendant which falls below the standard of care reasonably to be expected from ordinary members of the community, or if the defendant has some special skill or knowledge, from persons possessing such specific qualifications."[4] A physician, for example, who is charged with negligence is accused of providing medical care which results in harm and which falls below the medical community's standards. The issue, then, is whether child neglect and abuse should be conceived of as forms of parental negligence.

On the one hand, both child neglect and abuse are similar to negligence in demanding that some harm or damages result from the questionable behavior. It might be argued, therefore, that child neglect and abuse should be evaluated according to negligence standards. On the other hand, however, negligence implies inadvertence or unintentional harm, whereas the harmful consequences to children which are under discussion are frequently intended.

In addition, a number of arguments can be made against evaluating parental behavior according to community norms. For the most part, these arguments reflect differences between medicine and parenting. First, as noted before, there is no theory of parenting or body of knowledge which is widely accepted among parents, but there is a body of knowledge which is widely accepted among practicing physicians within a given community. Because there is this fairly well accepted body of knowledge, the law permits the medical profession itself, rather than a jury of laymen, to determine what is due care. "In order to prevail in a negligence suit against the doctor, the plaintiff must prove, not that what the defendant did was unreasonable, but that there is no accepted body of medical opinion according to which what the defendant did might be judged reasonable. Neither judge nor jury is entitled to determine that the practice of an 'accepted school of medicine' is itself unreasonably lax."[5]

Second, the provision of care which meets social standards might demand inordinate sacrifices for some parents in particular communities, whereas the physician receives compensation commensurate with the sacrifice. It cannot be argued that parents have necessarily accepted these sacrifices by bearing children within a given community or society, since parents cannot foresee with any degree of certainty either their fu-

ture circumstances or the future needs of their children.[6]

Third, until and unless all parenthood is voluntarily assumed, and parents accept a set of community standards just as physicians accept a set of medical standards, it is unreasonable to hold them responsible for nonadherence to those standards. Fourth, the standards employed in any community might fall below the satisfaction of minimum needs, and, also, the standards of one community might fall considerably below those of another. An appeal to social norms runs the risk, therefore, of not providing minimal care. (This fourth point, however, seems to be applicable to medical care as well.)

The criteria of best interest, minimum needs, and community standards are all attempts to determine when a child has been culpably harmed. All of these criteria hold that a child is abused or neglected only when harmful consequences are produced, whether they be physical, emotional, or psychological. A wide variety of conditions has been cited as legitimate bases for considering a child to be neglected or abused and for permitting state intervention. They include parental nonconformity (including religious nonconformity), failure to discipline, excessive discipline or cruelty, parental "immorality," failure to authorize medical treatment, excessive use of drugs or alcohol, parent's mental condition, extreme poverty, incarceration in prison or another institution, extremely low intelligence, and abandonment (including lack of financial support and/or lack of attention). In all these cases, it is supposed that the particular condition has harmed or will likely harm the child.

I claim that this emphasis on effects or consequences reflects an unrecognized purpose. These consequentialist definitions of child abuse and neglect are formulated solely to deal with the problem of state intervention.

Parents are assumed to have both the natural and the legal right to raise their children without outside interference. This right, or rather liberty of non-interference, is protected by the Fourteenth Amendment to the Constitution.[7] In certain instances, however, the state may intervene in the parent-child relationship. Specifically, the state may intervene, under the doctrine of *parens patriae,* to protect the interests either of the child or of the state itself.

Generally, state intervention is thought to be justifiable when parents or guardians fail to provide adequate care for the child, though able to do so and when parents are unable to care for the child. Children who fall in the former category are usually termed "neglected"; those in the latter category are usually termed "dependent." To apply these categories requires an interpretation of adequate care or parental behavior. This interpretation invariably refers only to harm done to or risked by the child. "By finding that a child is neglected, the court's sole focus should be whether the child is being hurt or impaired by his parent's actions and whether he is likely to be impaired if these actions continue. If the child is coming to no harm, the state has no right to intervene in the parent-child relationship through the use of neglect statutes, regardless of how despicable a character the parent may be outside of this relationship. To look at parental behavior except as it constitutes a danger to the child is to grossly abuse the *parens patriae* power which should look toward the salvation of the child, not the damnation of the parent."[8]

Since harmful consequences to the child are considered the only legitimate basis for state intervention, and since definitions of abuse and neglect have been formulated solely to permit state intervention, harmful consequences have become, in turn, the standard basis for a definition of abusive or neglectful behavior. Yet, available data demonstrate the failure of state intervention programs and of foster care facilities to improve the condition of the child substantially.[9] As a response to these data, there has been an attempt to limit the situations in which the state can intervene. This has been done by formulating very narrow and limited definitions of abuse and neglect,[10] often restricted to instances of gross physical abuse or severe deprivation.

Although harmful consequences, in particular as defined by the minimum needs criterion, may be both sufficient and necessary to justify state intervention, they do not necessarily exhaust the definition of abuse and neglect, which may be considerably broader. In addition, if harmful effects, as defined by unmet minimum needs, are taken to justify state intervention, then the child's condition is the significant factor, regardless of how or by whom the harm was caused. State intervention would be justified on behalf of any child who displayed certain traits, whether or not the behavior was thought to result from parental abuse or neglect.

3. Abuse, Neglect, and Respect for Children

I suggest that an adequately broad definition of child abuse or neglect must include reference to the kind of behavior which is abusive or neglectful, regardless of the consequences. This is the third alternative mentioned above, besides intentions and consequences, for a definition of abuse or neglect.

Such a definition would be similar to that employed in applying the concept of "battery" to conduct not involving children. "The central concept of battery is the offense to personal dignity which occurs when another impinges on one's bodily integrity without full and valid consent."[11] In order for a charge of battery to be made, it is not necessary for there to have been any damage, physical or otherwise. The affront is to an individual's dignity. It is this concept of an affront to dignity that is totally omitted in the definitions of child abuse or neglect, which focus solely on actual or risked harmful consequences. It is not enough simply to say that the harmful consequences constitute assaults on one's dignity and, therefore, that the child's dignity is indirectly being protected. Although harmful consequences must be prohibited in order to ensure the possibility of the child's development, the prevention of these harms does not amount to respect for the child's dignity, any more than it would amount to respect for adult dignity.

How might it be possible, however, to protect a child's dignity or to know when it is being violated? An affront to the dignity of an adult is protected by use of the concept of consent. Contact or "intermeddling"[12] with an adult person's body can be justified only if the person consents. Furthermore, the necessary consent must be both free and informed. In other words, an affront to the dignity of an adult is not defined by or protected by reference to some objective or social standards, but rather, by reference to that to which the individual has knowingly and freely agreed. Consent, however, does not seem to be an appropriate measure by which to respect the dignity of a child. The consent requirement presupposes the right to liberty—specifically, the right to the liberty to control what happens to and with one's own body. Children, especially young ones, do not have the right to liberty as much as the right to protection, which can often be respected *only* by violating or precluding a right to liberty—specifically, the right to liberty is restricted because it is believed that if the child had the freedom to choose, he would not necessarily choose according to his own best interest. In essence, the child's right to protection would not be respected.

An important point should be noted here. Restrictions are placed on a child's liberty because without these restrictions, the child might harm himself or not act in his own best interest. The child's liberty is not restricted simply because it is believed the child lacks the capacity for informed consent or rational decision making. "Indeed, if a person who lacked this capacity did no more harm to himself or failed to promote his own welfare no more often than a normal adult, the paternalistic justification for denying him certain legal rights to liberty could not be invoked."[13] A conflict, therefore, exists between a desire to respect the dignity of a child and a desire for the child's protection.

4. Protecting Children and Respecting Children

This conflict is extremely difficult to resolve, but I would like to suggest one possibility. If protection of the child is the sole basis for not recognizing a child's right to liberty,[14] then when protection is not an issue, recognition of this liberty should prevail. Provided the claim cannot be made that a child's welfare or development is in danger of being hindered, the child should have the right to decide matters about his own treatment or care. Parental decisions should control only those aspects of a child's life which are relevant to protecting the child's physical, emotional, and psychological development. It is legitimate to grant rights to children "provided we can predict that in the exercise of the right, the child would not do himself harm or fail to promote his own welfare or good."[15]

If this account of the respect which is due to children is built into a definition of child abuse and neglect, then parental treatment which fails to recognize or respect the child's right to make autonomous decisions in matters which are neither critical to protecting the child's basic interests, nor make claims on others, would be abusive or neglectful. These actions would essentially constitute a form of "battery" in that they would be an affront to the child's dignity. Certainly, before such an interpretation could be applied, minimum needs would have to be established, so that it would be possible to determine when the child's basic interests were in danger of being violated. Further, it would be necessary to restrict such a principle to those instances in which respecting the child's dignity by recognizing the child's right to make autonomous decisions would not make parental obligations more burdensome than would the course of action which the parent would have wanted to follow. For example, respect-

ing such dignity would not require that a parent spend additional money on a child. Rather, it would require that the money be spent as the child wishes, unless this would risk harming the child's basic physical, emotional, or psychological interests. The application of such a principle should therefore not impose additional parental obligations or increase children's claim rights. It should expand the decision-making jurisdiction of children, provided there is no increased risk to the child's well-being or development.

Obviously, a broader definition of abuse and neglect which incorporates this notion of an affront to dignity refers implicitly to the concept of consent. So, it can be applied only to children who can express their own wishes. Two points might be noted here. First, wishes can be expressed by other than verbal means. Second, it might be possible to establish standards of treatment which respect dignity, defined without reference to consent, to protect very young children. These standards should emanate from a theory of parenting, which, to my knowledge, has yet to be developed.[16] Such a theory would go beyond most contemporary writing on parenting, which focuses solely on establishing what treatment will further the child's development or the parent-child relationship. It would have to establish standards which would define violations of a child's dignity. Basically, it would have to define behavior which fails to treat children as people or as ends in themselves, rather than as mere means to their parents' futures. Given such a theory, certain types of treatment of children would be prohibited because of the behavior itself, even though harmful consequences might not result.

5. State Intervention
and Respect for Children

What is the implication of such a broader definition of abuse and neglect for the role of the state? Whereas a fully adequate definition of child abuse and neglect would have to be based on a theory of parenting and child welfare, an adequate justification for state intervention would have to be based on a social or political theory which explained the state's role in family life and its capacity to substitute for parents. It is quite possible that this definition and justification may coincide, but it does not seem to be necessary that they do. It seems reasonable, therefore, to reject the automatic connection frequently made, and discussed previously, between definitions of abuse and neglect and grounds for coercive state intervention.

Also, as noted previously, there is considerable empirical evidence of the ineffectiveness of state intervention into family life. "There is substantial evidence that, except in cases involving very seriously harmed children, we are unable to improve a child's situation through coercive state intervention. In fact, under current practice, coercive intervention frequently results in placing a child in a more detrimental situation than he would be in without intervention. This is true whether intervention results in removal of the child from his home or 'only' in mandating that his parents accept services as a condition of continued custody."[17] Increasing state intervention to protect children against parental behavior which would constitute affronts to their dignity, therefore, would certainly not be desirable. Except in extreme cases, the net effect of intervention, taking into account the child's

emotional attachment even to a psychologically unfit parent, is frequently damaging.

Based on this evidence, only failure to protect minimum interests should justify coercive state interference. Inclusion of the concept of battery or an affront to a child's dignity in a broader definition of child abuse or neglect would have no implications for the state's role. Most behavior which would produce harmful consequences for the child by not protecting minimum needs, and which would consequently justify state intervention, would also constitute abuse or neglect in this broader definition. Harmful consequences, defined by minimum needs, would therefore be a sufficient but not a necessary condition for behavior to be a violation of good parenting—i.e., abusive or neglectful.

This broader definition of abuse and neglect, which incorporates a concept of dignity and is not tailor made for justifying state intervention, could serve important functions. Using such a definition, a child might be judged abused or neglected, even if, through luck or resilience, he was able to compensate for the treatment he was receiving from his parents. A definition which emphasizes only effects classifies children with unusual capacities for resistance or compensation as neither abused nor neglected, even though treated in ways which would be considered abusive or neglectful for less resourceful children. This possibility would be eliminated by including reference to the parental behavior itself.

Furthermore, such a broader definition of abuse and neglect would help current efforts to identify potentially abusive or neglectful parents. At present, various attempts are being made to identify potential child abusers by factors such as family history, personality traits, attitude during pregnancy, and even attitude and behavior in the delivery room.[18] The hope is that if potential child abusers can be identified before abusive behavior occurs, preventive measures can be instituted. An adequate understanding of what should count as abusive behavior is essential to its prediction. Attempts at such prediction admittedly must focus on those parents who have had "unfortunate childhood experiences that could manifest as unusual child rearing practices."[19] It is not possible now, nor is there any real hope of ever identifying, potential physical abusers. These attempts at early identification must therefore be based on a broad view of what should constitute normal or acceptable child-rearing practices, one which might incorporate reference to a child's dignity. They cannot be related solely to severe physical abuse or extreme neglect.

Because these attempts at prediction cannot be related solely to severe physical abuse or extreme neglect, and hence to deprivation of minimum needs, they should not be used as a justification for coercive state intervention. By separating attempts at prediction from coercive state intervention, a number of ethical problems are precluded. The right to privacy of those labeled potential child abusers could not be invaded by state-mandated investigations. Since psychiatric attempts at predicting violent behavior do not have a high degree of accuracy, state intervention should not be permitted on this basis.

On the view which I have outlined, the traditional presumption of parental autonomy would be maintained. The state would have the right to intervene coercively only to protect minimum needs. But this limited state role would

not fully define abusive or neglectful behavior. A broader definition of abuse and neglect, which incorporates respect for a child's dignity, could form the basis for provision of voluntary services, such as preventive and therapeutic parenting programs. Such voluntary programs would not socially stigmatize or threaten their participants, but rather, would attempt to teach them proper parenting and respect for children. There need be no risk that excessive interference would follow, for the state's role in such a relationship would not be as potential guardian of children or as a threat to interfere in family life, but as educator and provider of voluntary services to promote the care of children.

Notes

I would like to thank Onora O'Neill and William Ruddick for very valuable comments on an earlier draft. The work on this essay was done while I was a Fellow of the Institute on Human Values in Medicine of the Society for Health and Human Values under National Endowment for the Humanities grant #EH-10973-74-365.

1. Edward Zigler, "Controlling Child Abuse in America: An Effort Doomed to Failure," in *Proceedings of the First National Conference on Child Abuse and Neglect*, Jan. 4–7, 1976, DHEW Pub. No. OHD 77-30094, p. 30.
2. See R. Gelles, "Child Abuse as Psychopathology: A Sociological Critique and Reformulation," 43 *American Journal of Orthopsychiatry* 3, 173, for a discussion of this widely accepted interpretation of child abuse.
3. Joel Feinberg, *Social Philosophy*, Prentice-Hall: Englewood Cliffs, N.J., 1973, p. 30.
4. Charles Fried, *Medical Experimenta-*

tion: Personal Integrity and Social Policy, American Elsevier Pub. Co.: New York, 1974, p. 14.

5. Ibid., p. 17.

6. Onora O'Neill, "Begetting, Bearing and Rearing," in the present volume, pp. 25–38.

7. "The right of a parent to be free from state interference and to raise his child in the manner that he sees fit has been described as a 'right which transcends property'" (*Denton* v. *Jones,* 107 Kansas 729, 193 Pa. 307, 1920), as an 'inalienable right' (*In re* Agor 10 C.D. 49, 1878), as a 'sacred right' (*In re* Hudson, 13 Wash. 2d 673, 126 Ped 765, 1942), as a 'natural right' (*Anguis* v. *Superior Court,* 6 Ariz. App. 68, 429 p 2d 702, 1967), and most recently as a right that has been established beyond debate as an American tradition (*Wisconsin* v. *Yoder,* 406 U.S. 205 at 232, 1972)." Brian G. Fraser, "The Child and His Parents: A Delicate Balance of Rights," in *Child Abuse and Neglect,* ed. by Ray E. Helfer and C. Henry Kempe, Ballinger Pub. Co.: Mass., 1976, p. 326.

8. Michael Sullivan, "Child Neglect: The Environmental Aspects," *Ohio State Law Journal,* vol. 29, 1968, p. 92.

9. See Michael Wald, "State Intervention on Behalf of 'Neglected' Children: A Search for Realistic Standards," *Stanford Law Review,* vol. 27, 1975, and Stephen W. Bricker, "Testimony on the Child Abuse Prevention and Treatment Act," before the Senate Sub-Committee on Child and Human Development, April 7, 1977.

10. See Theodore J. Clements, "Child Abuse: The Problem of Definition," *Creighton Law Review,* vol. 8, 1975.

11. Fried, op. cit., p. 15.

12. Ibid., p. 19.

13. See Laurence Houlgate, "Children, Paternalism, and Rights to Liberty," in the present volume, pp. 266–78.

14. Ibid.

15. Ibid., p. 14.

16. See William Ruddick, "Parents and Life Prospects," in the present volume, pp. 123–37.

17. Wald, op. cit., p. 993.

18. Ray E. Helfer, "Basic Issues Concerning Prediction," in Helfer and Kempe, op. cit.

19. Ibid., p. 363.

The conceptual disarray of abuse and neglect laws often has harsh consequences for children and parents. The U.S. District court for the Middle District of Alabama, Northern Division reviewed three closely related cases arising from the removal of a child—"Richard Roe"—from his mother. This removal was accomplished under a law (Alabama Code, Title B, nos. 350[2] and 352[4]) which in part defines a neglected child as one "who has no parental care or guardianship, or whose home by reason of neglect, cruelty or depravity on the part of parent or parents guardian or other persons in whose care he may be is an unfit and improper place . . . or is under such improper or insufficient guardianship or control as to endanger the morals, health or general welfare of such child."

The court in this case ordered the defendants (various public officials of the state of Alabama) to give up the summary removal of children not immediately endangered and to stop enforcing a "neglect" standard under which the state could remove children without demonstrating that their parents were harming them. The opinion of the judges in this case is remarkable for its thoughtful discussion of the considerations which a good abuse and neglect law should take into account and of the remedies which may be sought short of removing the child from the parent.

The removal of "Richard Roe" from his mother was instigated by a man with whom she had formerly lived who claimed to be the child's father. Under Alabama law, this man was able unilaterally to declare his paternity and impose his name on the child. "Richard Roe" and his mother were neither notified nor represented at this proceeding. The judges also enjoined those defendants who in their official capacities had enforced these provisions of the Alabama Code from further doing so. Their opinion discusses the standard which an adequate legitimation procedure must meet if the law is not to discriminate against mothers or submerge the interests of children in those of their parents.

ROE V. CONN

RICHARD ROE, etc., Plaintiff, v. L. T. CONN, etc., et al., Defendants. MARGARET ANN WAMBLES, etc., Plaintiff, v. L. T. CONN, etc., et al., Defendants. RICHARD ROE, etc., et al., Plaintiffs, v. CECIL COPPAGE et al., Defendants. Civ. A. Nos. 75–232–N, 75–233–N and 75–457–N. United States District Court, M. D. Alabama, N. D. July 6, 1976.

Summary

Class action by mother of illegitimate child challenging the constitutionality of Alabama's child neglect law and actions by child challenging the same child neglect law and state law allowing man in an ex parte proceeding to legitimize an illegitimate child by declaring himself the father and in the same proceeding to change the child's name were consolidated for trial. The Three-Judge District Court held that statute authorizing seizure of child if it appears that "the child is in such condition that its welfare requires" violates procedural due process, and the "welfare" standard is unconstitutionally vague and an unconstitutional infringement on fundamental right to family integrity; that statutory provisions for removal upon finding of "neglect" are unconstitutionally vague; that fact that white child who is part of an interracial family unit and lives in a black neighborhood may be disadvantaged socially or culturally does not rise to the level of harm to the child that is required before state can terminate parent's right to custody; that due process requires notice to mother before father may legitimate child, and that notice and opportunity to be heard must be given to mother and to child before father may change the name of the child.

Judgment for plaintiffs.

Before RIVES, Circuit Judge, JOHNSON, Chief District Judge, and VARNER, District Judge.

Opinion

These cases were consolidated for trial because of a common background of facts. *Wambles* v. *Conn,* Civil Action No. 75–233–N, is a class action challenging the constitutionality of Alabama's child neglect law, Alabama Code, Title 13, § 350 *et seq.* (1958). Plaintiff Margaret Wambles represents a class composed of mothers who have been or may be deprived of the custody of their child or children without a prior hearing where there was no showing of immediate or threatened harm, and a subclass composed of all mothers who have been or may be deprived of their child or children because they are living with men (other than relatives or boarders) to whom they are not married. *Roe* v. *Conn,* Civil Action No. 75–232–N, challenges the constitutionality of the same child neglect law from the vantage point of the child's protectable interest. Plaintiff Richard Roe represents a class composed of all children under the age of 16 who have been or may be removed from their mothers without a prior hearing, absent a showing of immediate harm or threatened harm, and all children not appointed counsel to represent their interests, and a subclass composed of all children who have been or may be removed from their mother because their mothers are living with men (other than relatives or boarders) to whom they are not married. *Roe* v. *Coppage,* Civil Action No. 75–457–N, is an action brought by Richard Roe and Plaintiff Wambles which seeks to challenge the constitutionality of the state law, Alabama Code, Title 27, §§ 11–12 (1973 Supp.), that allows a man in an *ex parte* proceeding to legitimatize an illegitimate child by declaring himself the father and in the same proceeding to change the child's name.

Defendants in these cases are Cecil Coppage; Hon. Walker Hobbie, individually and in his official capacity as Judge of Probate of Montgomery County, Alabama; L. T. Conn, individually and in his official capacity as a patrolman with the City of Montgomery Police Department; E. L. Wright, Jr., individually and as Chief of Police of the City of Montgomery Police Department; Barbara Ward, individually and as Director of the Montgomery County Youth Facility; Julia Oliver, individually and as Commissioner of the Alabama Department of Pensions and Security (DPS); Ada Kate Morgan, individually and as Director of the Montgomery County Department of Pensions and Security; and Hon. William F. Thetford, individually and as Judge of the Montgomery County Family Court. During the course of the lawsuit, Hon. John W. Davis succeeded Judge Thetford as Judge of the Montgomery County Family Court and Mr. Charles Swindall replaced Mr. Wright as Chief of the Montgomery Police Department. The successors were automatically substituted as defendants pursuant to F.R.C.P. 25(d).

A three-judge court has been convened pursuant to 28 U.S.C. § 2281 to decide these constitutional questions. After a pretrial conference at which many of the facts were stipulated, the case was submitted for decision upon the briefs and documents supplied by the parties.

Findings of Fact

Margaret Wambles is a 25-year-old white woman who has never married. On September 15, 1971, Plaintiff Wambles gave birth to a son, Richard Roe, who lived with her continuously until June 2, 1975, when he was seized by Officer L. T. Conn of the Montgomery Police Department and placed in the custody of the Montgomery County Department of Pensions and Security. This seizure was ordered by Judge Thetford of the Montgomery County Family Court without affording Plaintiff Wambles prior notice and a hearing. Such authority as

exists for this action is provided by Alabama Code, Title 13, §§ 350(2) and 352(4), which purports to permit a juvenile court judge to summarily remove a "neglected child" from its home if the judge believes the child's welfare so warrants.[1]

The investigation which led to termination of Plaintiff Wambles' parental rights was prompted by Defendant Coppage. Mr. Coppage, who is white, lived intermittently with Plaintiff Wambles from 1970 until March, 1975, and claims to have fathered Richard Roe. On June 1, 1975, Mr. Coppage contacted the Montgomery Police Department and reported that Plaintiff Wambles might be neglecting Richard Roe, that she had been evicted from her former residence because she was keeping company with black males, and that she had moved to Highland Village (a black neighborhood) where she was living with a black man. On the basis of this information, Police Officer Conn initiated an investigation of Plaintiff Wambles. The records of the Montgomery Police Department were checked but revealed no previous complaints of child neglect against Plaintiff Wambles and no adult file on her. Meanwhile, on June 2, 1975, Defendant Coppage went to the office of Barbara Ward, Director of the Montgomery County Youth Facility, and told her that he was the father of Richard Roe; that he had once lived with Margaret Wambles, who was now living with a black man and entertaining other black men; that he had reported this to the Montgomery Police Department; that he wanted to get the child out of the house; and that he wanted custody of the child.[2] Following Defendant Coppage's visit to her office, Defendant Ward conferred with Judge Thetford and then called the Montgomery Police Department. According to the police report prepared by Officer Conn, Defendant Ward advised the police to request a pick-up order if Margaret Wambles and Richard Roe were living with a man to whom Margaret Wambles was not married. Officer Conn went to the Wambles' residence, 1033–E Highland Village Drive, Montgomery, Alabama, at approximately 7:30 P.M. on June 2, 1975. Plaintiff Wambles permitted Officer Conn to enter and inspect her dwelling, which the officer found was a two-bedroom apartment, where Plaintiff Wambles and her son were living with a black man to whom she was not married. Richard Roe was clothed, clean, and in "fairly good" physical condition with no signs of physical abuse. The home was "relatively clean" and stocked with "adequate food." Upon completing his inspection, Defendant Conn left the home and called Defendant Ward and reported his findings. He was then instructed by Defendant Ward to go to the Youth Facility and get a pick-up order. The only facts about Margaret Wambles known to Judge Thetford before he issued the pick-up order were that she was unemployed and that she and her child are white and were living with a black man in a black neighborhood. Judge Thetford had no information as to how long Margaret Wambles had lived in Montgomery, where she had worked, or how long she had been unemployed.[3] He had no evidence that Richard Roe was being physically abused and no information as to the condition of the Wambles' home. Judge Thetford knew nothing about the man with whom Margaret Wambles was living, other than his race and the fact that he was not married to her. Judge Thetford testified that the race of the man with whom Plaintiff Wambles was living was relevant to his decision to order Richard Roe

removed from his mother's custody, particularly because they were living in a black neighborhood. Judge Thetford concluded that this habitation in a black neighborhood could be dangerous for a child because it was his belief that "it was not a healthy thing for a white child to be the only [white] child in a black neighborhood."

At approximately 8:30 P.M. on June 2, 1975, after obtaining the pick-up order, Defendant Conn, accompanied by two other Montgomery police officers, returned to Plaintiff Wambles' home. When Defendant Conn announced that he had come to take Richard Roe, Plaintiff Wambles picked up her child and ran to the back of the apartment. After Defendant Conn showed Plaintiff Wambles the pick-up order, she still refused to surrender the child. Thereupon, with the child crying, "No, mama, don't let him take me," Defendant Conn grabbed Plaintiff Wambles by the arm and pulled her back into the living room, took Richard Roe from her arms, and left without leaving a copy of the pick-up order. After the seizure, Defendant Conn took Richard Roe to a DPS-licensed shelter home in Montgomery.

No hearing was scheduled or held following Richard Roe's removal until July 10, 1975. No attorney was requested or appointed to represent Richard Roe, at the July 10 hearing. At the hearing in the Family Court of Montgomery County, both Defendant Coppage and Plaintiff Wambles were present and represented by counsel. Judge Thetford entered an order on July 11, 1975, wherein he awarded Defendant Coppage custody of Richard Roe after making a finding that he was the natural father of the child. The temporary custody order gave Margaret Wambles "the right to petition the court for custody of [Richard Roe] at any future date." Plaintiff Wambles' first petition for custody, filed on August 5, 1975, along with her motion for a new trial and motion for order for blood tests, was denied on August 14, 1975, by Judge Thetford as untimely filed.[4] A second petition for custody was filed by Plaintiff Wambles in November and denied by Judge John W. Davis, III, on December 22, 1975. The denial of this last petition was affirmed by the Alabama Court of Civil Appeals. *Wambles* v. *Coppage*, Civil No. 746, filed June 16, 1976.

On December 11, 1975, Plaintiff Wambles learned for the first time that Defendant Coppage had executed a declaration of fatherhood with respect to Richard Roe and had his last name changed from Wambles to Coppage. Since Margaret Wambles was unmarried at the time of Richard Roe's birth, under Title 22, § 33, he was given his mother's surname, and no information as to his father appeared on his birth certificate. The declaration of fatherhood and the name change were effected on August 22, 1975, when Cecil Coppage executed a document before Defendant Hobbie, Judge of the Probate Court of Montgomery County, pursuant to Alabama Code, Title 27, §§ 11–12 (Supp.1973). The address which appeared on Defendant Coppage's declaration of fatherhood is the Montgomery address of his attorney, although Defendant Coppage is a resident of Troy, Alabama, which is in Pike County. Neither Margaret Wambles nor Richard Roe was given notice or an opportunity to be heard relative to the August 22, 1975, declaration of fatherhood and name change. . . .

Expert Testimony

Plaintiffs Wambles and Roe have submitted the testimony of witnesses Dr. Sally A. Provence[5] and Dr. Albert J. Solnit[6] as experts in the field of child care and development. Drs. Provence and Solnit summarized their views as follows:

> 1. Summary removal of a young child from a parent who has been his major caregiver is a severe threat to his development. It disrupts and grossly endangers what he most needs, that is, the continuity of affectionate care from those to whom he is attached through bonds of love.
> 2. Summary removal should be allowed only under conditions in which physical survival is at stake.
> 3. In situations in which some interference is indicated because parents are unable to take good care of their child, there are alternatives to summary removal which should be used either singly or in combination. Among these are the following: (a) the provision in the child's home of assistance to parents with child care and with managing a household; (b) the provision of counselling to parents about how to care for a child in ways that enhance his development and well-being; (c) the provision of a day care center or day care family in which assistance to child and parent can be provided which is addressed to their specific needs; (d) the provision of a residential facility or foster family in which both parent and child can receive the nurture and guidance they may need (in extended families, relatives often supply such benevolent help, and when they are unavailable, it is one of society's responsibilities to organize and make available such assistance); and (e) the provision of 24-hour substitute care for a child, which does not cut him off from contact with his parents.

Another witness, Dr. Jonas Robitscher,[7] gave similar testimony in his deposition:

All authorities agree that there are circumstances under which summary removal of the child from his or her parent should be allowed. These circumstances would include and would be very much limited to situations in which the child was being physically abused as in the battered-child syndrome, where the child was being sexually abused as in the examples we see of stepfathers or sometimes real fathers having incestuous relationships with children, when children are brought up in an atmosphere incompatible with physical health because of neglect, lack of food and extreme uncleanliness, and when there is so little care taken of the child that the child is in danger as when small children are allowed to roam unsupervised in dangerous streets. However, most authorities agree that even psychotic or disturbed mothers can often do a good mothering job and psychotic and disturbed mothers are preferable, providing the circumstances described immediately above are not present, to institutional or impersonal care. The thrust of studies in child development then indicates that children should be summarily removed from their mothers only when their physical health and emotional health are at serious risk and only after all other alternatives to removal have been thoroughly studied.

Conclusions of Law

The fundamental right to family integrity. A district court in Iowa recently reviewed the long line of Supreme Court cases addressed to the constitutional interests at stake where various aspects of family life are threatened and concluded that there is a fundamental right to family integrity protected by the Fourteenth Amendment to the United States Constitution. *Alsager* v. *District Court of Polk County, Iowa,* 406 F.Supp. 10, 15 (S.D.

Iowa 1975). The seminal case in this constitutional development is *Meyer* v. *Nebraska,* 262 U.S. 390, 43 S.Ct. 625, 67 L.Ed. 1042 (1923), where the Supreme Court held that the "liberty" guarantee of the Fourteenth Amendment "without doubt . . . denotes . . . the right of the individual . . . to marry, establish a home and bring up children." *Id.* at 399, 43 S.Ct. at 626. The result of this decision was to uphold the right of the parents to have their children taught the German language. In *Pierce* v. *Society of Sisters,* 268 U.S. 510, 45 S.Ct. 571, 69 L.Ed. 1070 (1925), the Court again recognized this liberty of parents to direct the rearing and education of children, and in *Prince* v. *Massachusetts,* 321 U.S. 158, 64 S.Ct. 438, 88 L.Ed. 645 (1944), it said:

> It is cardinal with us that the custody, care and nurture of the child reside first in the parents, whose primary function and freedom include preparation for obligations the state can neither supply nor hinder . . . and it is in recognition of this that these decisions (*Meyer* and *Pierce*) have respected the private realm of family life which the state cannot enter. 321 U.S. at 166, 64 S.Ct. at 442.

A more recent Supreme Court decision, *Cleveland Board of Education* v. *La-Fleur,* 414 U.S. 632, 94 S.Ct. 791, 39 L.Ed.2d 52 (1974), reaffirms the constitutional nature of this interest: "freedom of personal choice in mothers [sic] of marriage and family life is one of the liberties protected by the Due Process Clause of the Fourteenth Amendment." *Id.* In addition to the "liberty" concept of the Fourteenth Amendment, the Supreme Court has been equally solicitous of the family enclave under the doctrine of privacy. See *Griswold* v. *Connecticut,* 381 U.S. 479, 85 S.Ct. 1678, 14 L.Ed.2d

510 (1965); *Eisenstadt* v. *Baird,* 405 U.S. 438, 92 S.Ct. 1029, 31 L.Ed.2d 349 (1972); *Roe* v. *Wade,* 410 U.S. 113, 93 S.Ct. 705, 35 L.Ed.2d 147 (1973). Finally in *Stanley* v. *Illinois,* 405 U.S. 645, 92 S.Ct. 1208, 31 L.Ed.2d 551 (1972), the Supreme Court declared unconstitutional the Illinois dependency statute that deprived an unmarried father of the care and custody of his natural children upon the death of their mother. In doing so, the Court held that the right to the integrity of the family unit was protected by the Fourteenth Amendment due process and equal protection clauses and by the Ninth Amendment. *Id.* at 651, 92 S.Ct. 1208.

[2] This Court is in full agreement with the conclusion of Chief Judge Hanson in *Alsager, supra,* that the Constitution recognizes as fundamental the right of family integrity. This means that in our present case the state's severance of Plaintiff Wambles' parent-child relationship and of Plaintiff Roe's child-parent relationship will receive strict judicial scrutiny. See *Roe* v. *Wade,* 410 U.S. 113, 155, 93 S.Ct. 705, 35 L.Ed.2d 147 (1973). Recognizing that fundamental right, this Court will now apply the pertinent constitutional principles to the facts of the present case.

[3] *Summary Seizure.* This Court holds that Alabama Code, Title 13, § 352(4), which authorizes summary seizure of a child "if it appears that . . . the child is in such condition that its welfare requires," violates procedural due process under the Fourteenth Amendment of the United States Constitution.

[4, 5] To determine the nature of the procedural safeguards that the Constitution mandates, the administrative needs of the State must be carefully balanced against the interests of the affected citizens.[8] There is no question that the family members will suffer a grievous loss if the State severs the parent-child relationship;[9] an interest, we have held, that is part of the liberty concept of the Fourteenth Amendment. The State of Alabama, on the other hand, does have a legitimate interest in protecting children from harm as quickly as possible. Normally, before intrusion into the affairs of the family is allowed, the State should have reliable evidence that a child is in need of protective care. In the absence of exigent circumstances, this fact-finding process, as a matter of basic fairness, should provide notice to the parents and child of the evidence of abuse and provide them with an opportunity for rebuttal at a hearing before an impartial tribunal.[10]

[6–8] The facts of this case dispel any notion that the State was faced with an emergency situation. As we earlier found, Officer Conn's investigation revealed that Richard Roe was clothed, clean, and in "fairly good" physical condition with no signs of physical abuse. The Wambles home was "relatively clean" and stocked with "adequate food." Without danger of immediate harm or threatened harm to the child, the State's interest in protecting the child is not sufficient to justify a removal of the child prior to notice and a hearing. Additionally, even in the event summary seizure had been justified, a hearing would have had to follow the seizures "as soon as practicable" and not six weeks later as it did in the present case. See *Goss* v. *Lopez, supra; Laing* v. *United States,* 161 U.S. 423, 96 S.Ct. 473, 46 L.Ed.2d 416 (decided January 13, 1976) [Brennan, *concurring*]. For these reasons, this Court is of the opinion that Alabama Code Title 13, § 352(4) violates the procedural due process clause of the Fourteenth Amendment. We also hold that the statute's "welfare" standard is un-

constitutionally vague and an unconstitutional infringement on the fundamental right to family integrity, for
reasons similar to those discussed, *infra*,
concerning removal of the child after
a hearing on the basis of a "neglect"
finding.

Removal upon a finding of "neglect."
After the hearing on July 10, 1975, Judge
Thetford ordered the termination of the
parental rights of Plaintiff Wambles to
Richard Roe on the basis that the child
was "a dependent or neglected child as
defined by the laws of Alabama." As
mentioned earlier, Alabama Code, Title
13, § 350, defines a "neglected child" as
"any child, who, while under sixteen
years of age . . . has no proper parental
care or guardianship or whose home, by
reason of neglect, cruelty, or depravity,
on the part of his parent or parents,
guardian or other person in whose care
he may be, is an unfit or improper place
for such child."[11] A co-ordinate provision
in the Code authorizes a juvenile court
to exercise the guardianship of the State
over children who fit this description of
"neglected." Id. at § 350(4); see also
§ 352.

[9–12] As discussed *supra*, the Constitution includes the right to family integrity among the fundamental rights
secured to all persons. This right is applied to the States through the Fourteenth Amendment and is accorded
strong protection from state interference. States, in the exercise of their inherent police powers, may abrogate such
rights only to advance a compelling state
interest and pursuant to a narrowly-
drawn statute restricted to achieve only
the legitimate objective. See, *e.g., Roe* v.
Wade, 410 U.S. 113, 155, 93 S.Ct. 705, 35
L.Ed.2d 147 (1973). It is not disputed
that the State of Alabama has a legitimate interest in the welfare of children.

Minor intrusions into the affairs of the
family may be permitted when the State
has reason to believe that a child's best
interest is at stake. In such cases, various
options and alternatives are available to
the State to achieve its objective of child
protection. One possibility might be a requirement that the parents attend semi-
nars and weekly counselling sessions on
child care and the responsibilities of parenthood. Another situation might warrant supervision of the parents by a welfare counselor or the placing of a neutral
person—such as an aunt—in the home to
serve as a bridge between the parents
and the child. The State's interest, however, would become "compelling" enough
to sever entirely the parent-child relationship only when the child is subjected
to real physical or emotional harm and
less drastic measures would be unavail-
ing.[12]

Here, the State offered no assistance
to Plaintiff Wambles, who was faced with
the troubling predicament of raising a
young child without the aid of a husband, nor did it explore the possibility
of accomplishing its objective of protecting Richard Roe's welfare by use of alternatives other than termination of custody.

[13] The Alabama statute defining
"neglected" children sweeps far past the
constitutionally permissible range of interference into the sanctity of the family
unit. The fact that a home is "improper"
in the eyes of the state officials does not
necessarily mean that a child in that
home is subject to physical or emotional
harm.[13]

In *Alsager* v. *District Court of Polk
County, Iowa,* 406 F.Supp. 10, 24 (S.D.-
Iowa 1975), the court held that "termination must only occur when more harm
is likely to befall the child by staying
with his parents than by being perma-

nently separated from them." This standard appears to teach that the state's burden is not only to show that the child is being disadvantaged but also to show that the child is being harmed in a real and substantial way. Accordingly, this Court declares Alabama Code, Title 13, §§ 350 and 352 unconstitutional, because it violates the family integrity of Margaret Wambles and all other mothers in the class represented by her and the family integrity of Richard Roe and all other children in the class represented by him.

[14] This Court holds, as an alternative ground, that the challenged statutory provisions are unconstitutionally vague. We adopt the reasoning and the language of the district court in *Alsager* v. *District Court of Polk County, Iowa,* supra, which states that,

> Nevertheless, Due Process requires the state to clearly identify and define the evil from which the child needs protection and to specify what parental conduct so contributes to that evil that the state is justified in terminating the parent-child relationship. 406 F.Supp. at 21.

In the present case, not only is the statutory definition of neglect circular (a neglected child is any child who has no proper parental care by reason of neglect), but it is couched in terms that have no common meaning. See *Connally* v. *General Construction Co.,* 269 U.S. 385, 391, 46 S.Ct. 126, 70 L.Ed. 322 (1956). When is a home an "unfit" or "improper" place for a child? Obviously, this is a question about which men and women of ordinary intelligence would greatly disagree. Their answers would vary in large measure in relation to their differing social, ethical, and religious views. Because these terms are too sub-

jective to denote a sufficient warning to those individuals who might be affected by their proscription, the statute is unconstitutionally vague. See *Grayned* v. *City of Rockford,* 408 U.S. 104, 108–109, 92 S.Ct. 2294, 33 L.Ed.2d 222 (1972).

[15] *Appointment of counsel for the child.* The Plaintiffs maintain that the Alabama child custody procedure violates the due process clause of the Constitution because that procedure does not provide for the appointment of independent counsel to represent a child in a neglect proceeding, and none was appointed here. We agree. Alabama Code, Title 13, §§ 350, *et seq.,* applies not only to "neglected" children but also to "delinquent" children. In this regard, it is similar to the Arizona juvenile delinquency law challenged in *In re Gault,* 387 U.S. 1, 87 S.Ct. 1428, 18 L.Ed.2d 527 (1967). Under the Arizona procedure, the parents of an infant in a juvenile delinquency proceeding could not be denied representation by counsel of their choosing, but the infant had to rely upon the parents or probation officer to protect his or her interests. The Supreme Court held that

> the Due Process Clause of the Fourteenth Amendment requires that in respect of proceedings to determine delinquency which may result in commitment to an institution in which the juvenile's freedom is curtailed, the child and his parents must be notified of the child's right to be represented by counsel retained by them, or if they are unable to afford counsel, that counsel will be appointed to represent the child. 387 U.S. at 41, 87 S.Ct. at 1451.

Much the same reasoning applies to a neglect determination proceeding. The juvenile court judge should, however, independently appoint counsel for the child, requiring the parents, if they are financially able, to pay for this legal representation.[14] If the parents are indigent, free counsel should be afforded the child. See *id.*

Consideration of race. Plaintiffs contend that there was a racial animus behind the decision to remove Richard Roe from his mother's custody.[15] It is undisputed that Judge Thetford, at the time he signed the pick-up order, knew only that Margaret Wambles was unemployed, that she and her child are white, and that they were living in a black neighborhood with a black man to whom Plaintiff Wambles was not married.

[16–18] While a white child who is part of an interracial family unit and lives in a black neighborhood may be disadvantaged socially or culturally, this fact alone does not rise to the level of harm to the child that is required before the State can terminate the parent's right to custody of the child.[16] Since race per se can never amount to sufficient harm to justify a constitutional termination, this Court finds it unnecessary to decide whether consideration of racial factors by a juvenile court judge represents prohibited racial discrimination.

Legitimation and procedural due process. Alabama Code, Title 27, § 11, provides, in pertinent part, as follows:

> The father of a bastard child may legitimate it, and render it capable of inheriting his estate, by making a declaration in writing, attested by two witnesses, setting forth the name of the child proposed to be legitimated, its sex, supposed age, and the name of the mother, and that he thereby recognizes it as his child, and capable of inheriting his estate, real and personal, as if born in wedlock; the declaration being acknowledged by the maker before the judge of probate of the county of his residence, or its execution proved by

the attesting witnesses, filed in the office of the judge of probate, and recorded on the minutes of his court, has the effect to legitimate such child. . . .

Pursuant to this statutory provision, Cecil Coppage, through his attorney, filed a document in the Probate Court of Montgomery County declaring himself to be the father of Richard Roe. No notice or opportunity to be heard was provided to either Plaintiff Roe or Plaintiff Wambles.

Defendant Hobbie testified that, when a declarant and the mother of a child appear together at the Probate Office, the mother, as well as the father, signs the declaration. When, however, the mother does not come in with the declarant, there is no formal procedure for notifying the mother. Nor is there any procedure established for the mother to appear before the probate judge and express her objections when she learns of the declaration and objects to the legitimation. Finally, there is no opportunity in this *ex parte* legitimation proceeding for the interests of the child to be heard.

Legitimation confers benefits on the child and mother by obligating the father to support the child and allowing the child to inherit from the father's estate. One would expect that the usual legitimation proceeding would thus be agreeable to the parties affected. This, however, is not the case in all situations.

The legitimation proceeding is recognized for purposes of establishing fatherhood. See *Bagwell* v. *Powell,* 267 Ala. 19, 99 So.2d 195 (1958). Thus, as a result of a § 11 declaration, the man can claim the rights of a natural father, which includes the right to withhold consent to the adoption of the child by any person, including a future stepfather. Alabama

Code, Title 27, §§ 3, 6. The status of natural father also makes the man a presumptively adequate legal guardian of the child's interests, *Kennedy v. Department of Pensions and Security*, 277 Ala. 5, 7, 166 So.2d 736 (1964), and it puts him in a strong position to claim custody of the child.

[19] Since legitimation might possibly be adverse to the interests of the mother and her illegitimate child in the exercise of their family integrity, the Fourteenth Amendment's guarantee of procedural fairness must apply. The question then becomes, what process is due? As Justice Harlan, writing in *Boddie v. Connecticut*, 401 U.S. 371, 380, 91 S.Ct. 780, 28 L.Ed.2d 113 (1971), has said, the states' obligation under the due process clause is not a fixed quantum of rights but the process due under the circumstances.

[20, 21] Here, at a minimum, due process requires notice to the mother before legitimation takes effect. Such notice should inform the mother that she has a reasonable period of time within which to notify the Probate Court if she objects to the legitimation. Upon being so notified, the Probate Court should appoint a guardian ad litem to represent the child and should conduct an informal hearing at which all interested parties could present evidence for determination of whether legitimation is in the best interest of the child.

[22] *Failure to leave a copy of the pick-up order with Margaret Wambles.* Plaintiffs assert that the failure of Defendant Conn to leave a pick-up order with Plaintiff Wambles violated Title 13, § 352(5) of the Alabama Code, which requires delivery of a summons to the custodian of the child. While undoubtedly, Defendant Conn's actions were not in conformity with the dictates of the

statute, we find that such violations do not give rise to an independent cause of action, cognizable under state law, over which this forum would have pendent jurisdiction. Plaintiffs' remedy for this violation should have been pursued in the original custody proceeding.

Name change and procedural due process. In connection with the legitimation procedure set out in Title 27, Code of Alabama, section 12 provides:

> The father may, at the same time, change the name of such child, setting in his declaration the name it is then known by, and the name he wishes it afterwards to have.

Pursuant to this provision, Defendant Coppage, as part of his declaration of fatherhood, changed Plaintiff Roe's last name from Wambles to Coppage.[17] As with the legitimation procedure, the question is whether Title 27, § 12 violates due process by permitting a declarant to change a child's name without providing the mother and/or the child notice and an opportunity to be heard.[18]

In an earlier order filed March 8, 1976, on Defendant Hobbie's motion to dismiss, this Court rejected his contention that a parent's interest in the name of a minor child does not constitute a "property" right within the meaning of the due process clause. Persuasive opinions are two Texas decisions. *Eschrich v. Williamson*, 475 S.W.2d 380 (Tex.Civ. App.1972); *Scucchi v. Woodruff*, 503 S.W.2d 356 (Tex.Civ.App.1972), which have gone so far as to hold that the notice required by due process should be read into the Texas statute allowing for the name change of a minor.

[23] The challenged statute, purporting to be concerned with the best interest of the child, at the same time

denies the opportunity to show factors bearing on that issue. The statute presumes a fact—that the child's best interest will be served by his bearing the name of the declared father—which is not necessarily or universally true. Due process requires an individual determination as to the appropriateness of the name change. To enable the probate judge to make this determination, notice and an opportunity to be heard must be given to the mother and to the child before a name change takes effect.

[24, 25] *Name change and sex discrimination.* Plaintiffs contend that Title 27, §12 works a discrimination on the basis of sex by permitting the declared father to control the child's name, irrespective of the wishes of the natural mother whose name the child has carried since birth. Surnames give an individual a personal identity and selfawareness. It seems clear that Plaintiff Roe has a "liberty" interest at stake when his name is altered. Furthermore, the name change touches on this right to maintain the integrity of established family relations. This preference for the wishes of the father cannot be said to serve a legitimate state interest in administrative convenience or avoiding confusion. See *Forbush v. Wallace,* 341 F.Supp. 217 (M.D.Ala. 1971) (three-judge court). The name change imposes the administrative burden of changing all the child's vital records, a measure which might possibly lead to confusion.[19]

[26] The Court concludes that there is no rational basis for the state's policy of giving to the declared father complete control over the child's name. For this reason, we find that Title 27, § 12 violates the equal protection clause of the Fourteenth Amendment. In changing a child's name pursuant to a declaration of father, the State should be directed not by the desires of the father but by the best interest of the child.

[27] *Failure of defendants to comply with the statute.* Alabama Code, Title 27, § 11 provides that the father of an illegitimate child must make his declaration of fatherhood before the judge of probate of "his" residence. While the statute is not altogether free from ambiguity ("his" residence could mean the child's), apparently the Legislature was referring to the residence of the father.[20] Yet, in the present case, Defendant Coppage, a resident of Pike County, Alabama, filed his declaration in the Probate Court of Montgomery County, Alabama. Plaintiffs, however, have not established that this violation of the venue provisions of Title 27, § 11 gives rise to an independent cause of action against Defendant Coppage that may be asserted in a collateral proceeding in federal court. Like the failure of Defendant Conn to leave a copy of the pick-up order, this procedural error is cognizable only in the original proceeding in the state court.

Notes

1. Title 13, § 350(2) reads in pertinent part: "The words 'neglected child' shall mean any child, who, while under sixteen years of age . . . has no proper parental care or guardianship or whose home, by reason of neglect, cruelty, or depravity, on the part of his parent or parents, guardian or other person in whose care he may be, is an unfit and improper place for such child . . . or is under such improper or insufficient guardianship or control as to endanger the morals, health or general welfare of such child . . . or who for any other cause is in need of the care and protection of the state." Sec. 350(4) pro-

vides that any child described as neglected shall be subject to the guardianship of the state and entitled to its care
and protection. Sec. 352 sets forth the
procedure to be followed in a child
neglect case. A verified complaint is
first filed with the juvenile court of the
county of the child's residence by any
person having knowledge of, or information concerning, the child. It is sufficient for the petition, after briefly stating the revelant facts, to aver that the
named child is neglected and in need of
the care and protection of the state.
Upon the filing of the petition, the
judge, clerk, or chief probation officer
of the court shall cause an examination
to be made and shall issue a summons
requiring the child to appear before the
court. Sec. 352(4) provides that, "If it
appears from the petition that . . . the
child is in such condition that its welfare requires that custody be immediately assumed, the judge of the court
may endorse upon the summons a direction that the officer serving said
summons shall at once take said child
into his custody." The statute further
provides that the custody of any child
who has been summarily seized is subject to the discretion of the judge pending hearing of the case.
2. In Montgomery County, both the Youth
Aid Division of the Police Department
and the County Department of Pensions and Security may investigate cases
of possible child neglect or dependency
and request an immediate pick-up order or file a removal petition.
3. Plaintiff Wambles had lived in Montgomery, Alabama, since 1969 and had
worked at Morrison's Cafeteria from
1969 to 1972 and again from August
1974 until May 1975.
4. The motion for a new trial had requested that blood tests be taken of the
parties involved and a new determination be made of Richard Roe's parent-
age in light of the results of those tests.
5. Dr. Sally A. Provence is professor of

pediatrics at Yale University Child
Study Center and Director of the Child
Development Unit, author of Guide to
the Care of Infants in Groups (1967),
and co-author of Infants in Institutions.
For the past 25 years, she has been involved in clinical work with children
and parents in child development research.
6. Dr. Albert J. Solnit is Sterling Professor
of Pediatrics and Psychiatry and Director of the Child Study Center at Yale
University. In this capacity, he teaches
child development, child psychiatry,
family law, and child psychoanalysis.
Dr. Solnit has published, in corrobora-
tion with Dr. Milton J. E. Senn, a textbook, Problems in Child Behavior and
Development (1968), and, in corrobo-
ration with Drs. Goldstein and Freud,
a book entitled, Beyond the Best Interests of the Child (1973).
7. Dr. Jonas Robitscher is a Henry R.
Luce Professor of Law and the Behavioral Science at Emory University
Schools of Law and Medicine.
8. See Goldberg v. Kelly, 397 U.S. 254,
262–263, 90 S.Ct. 1011, 1017–1018, 25
L.Ed.2d 287 (1970), where Justice
Brennan states that, "The extent to
which procedural due process must be
afforded the recipient is influenced by
the extent to which he may be 'condemned to suffer grievous loss,' and depends upon whether the recipient's interest in avoiding that loss outweighs
the governmental interest in summary
adjudication." (Citations omitted.)
9. The drastic nature of summary seizure
can be seen in the testimony of the experts. Drs. Provence and Solnit state
that "summary removal of a young
child from a parent who has been his
major caregiver is a severe threat to his
development [because] it disrupts and
grossly endangers what he most needs,
that is, the continuity of affectionate
care from those to whom he is attached
through bonds of love." These two doctors believe that summary seizure should

be resorted to only when the child's "physical survival" is at stake. Dr. Robitscher states that summary seizure is justified in his opinion only when the child's "physical health and emotional health are at serious risk after all other alternatives to removal have been thoroughly studied."

10. See *Goldberg* v. *Kelly*, 397 U.S. 254, 90 S.Ct. 1011, 25 L.Ed.2 287 (1970) [pretermination hearing is necessary before a welfare recipient's AFDC benefits are terminated]; *Fuentes* v. *Shevin*, 407 U.S. 67, 92 S.Ct. 1983, 32 L.Ed.2d 556 (1972) [hearing required before replevin of goods in a person's possession]; *Morrissey* v. *Brewer*, 408 U.S. 471, 92 S.Ct. 2593, 33 L.Ed.2d 484 (1972) [informal hearing required before revocation of parole rights]; *Goss* v. *Lopez*, 419 U.S. 565, 95 S.Ct. 729, 42 L.Ed.2d 725 (1975) [hearing required, absent emergency circumstances, prior to the temporary suspension of a student from public school].

11. A "dependent child" is "any child, who, while under sixteen years of age, for any reason, is destitute, homeless, or is dependent on the public for support; or who is without a parent or guardian able to provide for his support, training and education; or whose custody is the subject of controversy." Alabama Code, Title 13, § 350 (1958). Apparently, none of these apply to the present case, and Judge Thetford relied solely on the "neglected child" rubric.

12. It must be emphasized that this standard does not apply to all custody proceedings but only those where the State seeks to assume custody. In proceedings where the parties have an arguably equal right to custody, such as pursuant to a divorce, a "best interest of the child" standard is entirely appropriate.

13. Although the Alabama Department of Pensions and Security has published a Manual for Administration of Services for Children and Their Families (January, 1969), refining somewhat this definition, the manual is for administrative purposes only and is not binding on the juvenile court judges who ultimately decide these cases.

14. In a juvenile delinquency proceeding, having the parents retain counsel for the child normally does not present the same kind of potential conflict as in a proceeding where the parents are accused of abusing the child.

15. The Alabama Court of Civil Appeals in its decision, *Wambles* v. *Coppage*, Civ. No. 746, filed June 16, 1976, refused to consider the question of whether race influenced Judge Thetford's decision since the appeal was taken from Judge Davis' denial of Plaintiff Wambles' motion for modification of custody and not the original custody order.

16. Neither is the fact that the parent is living with someone to whom he or she is not married. "Immorality" of the parent, without a showing that the child is being physically or emotionally harmed in a real way, is not sufficient justification for the State to terminate a parent-child relationship.

17. Plaintiff Roe was born out of wedlock, no information relative to his father was entered on his birth certificate, and he was given the surname of his mother. Alabama Code, Title 22, § 33 (1958).

18. Title 27, § 12, has not been construed in any published cases, but the procedure followed in the present cases indicates that a notice requirement has not been read into the statute.

19. Furthermore, since Forbush was decided, the Supreme Court, in *Reed* v. *Reed*, 404 U.S. 71, 92 S.Ct. 251, 30 L.Ed.2d 225 (1971) and *Frontiero* v. *Richardson*, 411 U.S. 677, 93 S.Ct. 1764, 36 L.Ed.2d 583 (1973), has made clear that the state's interest in achieving administrative efficiency is, alone, not enough to support a sex-based classification.

20. Who would always be a "he," which is not necessarily the case with the child.

Under existing law, judges have wide discretionary authority to remove "neglected" children from their natural parents and place them in state-controlled foster care. The children are for the most part from poor families. The author describes the process by which the state can coercively remove children from their parents, and he analyzes the best interests of the child test, the legal standard courts usually employ to decide whether a neglected child should be removed from parental custody. He suggests that this standard requires predictions that cannot be made on a case by case basis and necessarily gives individual judges too much discretion to impose their own values in deciding what is best for a child. While critical of the procedural informality of the current juvenile court process, he believes additional procedural safeguards for children and their parents are in themselves unlikely to remedy the situation. He goes on to propose a new standard to limit removal to cases where there is an immediate and substantial danger to the child's health and where there are no reasonable means of protecting the child at home. In addition, a standard is proposed to ensure that prompt steps are taken to provide children who must be removed with a stable environment.

FOSTER CARE—IN WHOSE BEST INTEREST?

ROBERT H. MNOOKIN

Most American parents raise their children free of intrusive legal constraints or major governmental intervention. Although compulsory education and child labor laws indicate there are some conspicuous legal limitations on parents, it is the family, not the state, which has primary responsibility for child rearing.[1] Despite this predominant pattern, there are about 285,000 children

Research for this article was supported by grants to the Childhood and Government Project, University of California, Berkeley, from the Ford Foundation and the Carnegie Corporation of New York. For a later development of some of the ideas in this article, with greater emphasis on law and legal theory, see Robert H. Mnookin's "Child Custody Adjudication Judicial Functions in the Face of Indeterminacy," *Law and Contemporary Problems*, vol. 39, no. 3 (Summer 1975), 227–293.

From *Harvard Educational Review*, © President and Fellows of Harvard College, 43:4 (November 1973) pp. 599–638. Reprinted by permission.

under eighteen[2] among the nation's nearly 70 million[3] for whom the state has assumed primary responsibility. These children live in state sponsored foster care, a term used in this paper to include foster family homes, group homes, and child welfare institutions. For a number of the children in foster care, the state has assumed responsibility because no one else is available. Some children are orphans; others have been voluntarily given up by a family no longer willing or able to care for them. A significant number of children, however, are placed in foster care because the state has intervened and coercively removed the child from parental custody.

No national statistics are available to indicate what proportion of the children in foster care have been removed because of state coercion. When parents oppose foster care placement, a court can nevertheless order removal after a judicial proceeding if the state can demonstrate parental abuse or neglect. But if parents consent to foster care placement, no judicial action is necessary. Many foster care placements, perhaps one-half or more, are arranged by state social welfare departments without any court involvement. In California, for example, the State Social Welfare Board estimated recently that one-half of the children in state-sponsored foster care were "voluntary" placements where the parent(s) consented to relinquish custody without a formal court proceeding.[4] A study in New York City found that 58 percent of the natural parents of foster children had agreed to foster care placement.[5]

A substantial degree of state coercion may be involved in many so-called voluntary placements, making the distinction between voluntary and coercive

placement illusory. Many social welfare departments routinely ask parents to agree to give up their children before initiating neglect proceedings in court. Some parents who would have been willing to keep their children may consent to placement to avoid a court proceeding against them. If one were to use the legal standards of voluntariness and informed consent applied in the criminal law to confessions[6] and to the waiver of important legal rights,[7] many cases of relinquishment after state intervention might not be considered voluntary. On the other hand, not all court-ordered foster care placements involve coercion of the parents. Some take place with their full concurrence. In some cases, state welfare agencies require even parents who desire to place their children in foster care to go through a court proceeding. There is a financial incentive for the state to do this because under the Social Security Act, a state can be partially reimbursed by the federal government only if a court orders placement.[8]

Although it is unrealistic to make precise estimates given the complexities just outlined, I would judge that at least 100,000 children around the country are now in foster care because of coercive state intervention. Whatever their exact number, the state's role in placing them in foster care suggests a significant social responsibility. Even though state coercion can occur outside the court, judges usually have been responsible for deciding whether or not to remove children over parental objection. Law provides the principal framework to inform and constrain judicial action. This paper therefore addresses two basic questions. First, what legal standards should govern the judicial decision to remove a child over parental objections and place the child in foster care? And second, how can the law ensure developmental continuity and stability for children who must be so removed?

As background, the present legal standards for removing children, the process of intervention, and what is known about foster children and the foster care system are briefly described. I think three principles, currently violated, should govern its operation:

1. Removal should be a last resort, used only when the child cannot be protected within the home.

2. The decision to require foster care placement should be based on legal standards that can be applied in a consistent and even-handed way, and not be profoundly influenced by the values of the particular deciding judge.

3. If removal is necessary, the state should actively seek, when possible, to help the child's parents overcome the problems that led to removal so that the child can be returned home as soon as possible. In cases where the child cannot be returned home in a reasonable time, despite efforts by the state, the state should find a stable alternative arrangement such as adoption for the child. A child should not be left in foster care for an indefinite period of time.

Current legal standards for removal, under which courts increasingly purport to make individualized determinations of what is in the best interests of the child, contribute significantly to the failings of the present foster care system. My criticism is not that present standards fail to give adequate weight to parental interests, as compared to the child's interests; indeed, the focus of social concern probably should be on the child. Nor do I believe that it is always inappropriate to remove a child from parental custody for placement in foster care; in some circumstances nothing less drastic will protect a child from abusing or neglectful parents. Instead, what is wrong with the existing legal standards is that they call for individualized determinations based on discretionary assessments of the best interests of the child, and these determinations cannot be made consistently and fairly. They result in the unnecessary placement of children in foster care and do little to protect children against remaining in foster care for too long. Accordingly, substantial changes in the legal standards are needed, designed to make it more difficult to remove children initially and to provide more continuity and stability for children if removal is necessary. These changes will entail more than added procedural safeguards.

How the State Removes Children from their Parents

Source of the Power. The power of government to protect children by removing them from parental custody has roots deep in American history. And in colonial times just as today, the children of the poor were the most affected. Seventeenth century laws of Massachusetts, Connecticut, and Virginia, for example, specifically authorized magistrates to "bind out" or indenture children *of the poor* over parental objections.[9] Although it is unclear how frequently this power was exercised, the records of Watertown, Massachusetts, for instance, show that in 1671 Edward Sanderson's two oldest children were bound out as apprentices "where they may be educated and brought up in the knowledge of God and some honest calling." The reason given: poverty.[10]

By the early nineteenth century, the

parens patriae power of the state, i.e., the sovereign's ultimate responsibility to guard the interests of children and others who lacked legal capacity, was thought sufficient to empower courts to remove a child from parental custody. Significantly, the reinforcement of public morality, and not simply the protection of children from cruelty, was seen as sufficient justification for the exercise of this power. Joseph Story, the renowned Massachusetts legal scholar who sat on the Supreme Court from 1811 to 1845, stated in his treatise on equity courts:

> Although, in general, parents are intrusted with the custody of the persons, and the education of their children, yet this is done upon the natural presumption, that the children will be properly taken care of, and will be brought up with a due education in literature, and morals, and religion; and that they will be treated with kindness and affection. But, whenever this presumption is removed; whenever (for example,) it is found, that a father is guilty of gross ill-treatment or cruelty towards his infant children; or that he is in constant habits of drunkenness and blasphemy, or low and gross debauchery; or that he professes atheistical or irreligious principles; or that his domestic associations are such as tend to the corruption and contamination of his children; or that he otherwise acts in a manner injurious to the morals and interests of his children; in every such case, the Court of Chancery will interfere, and deprive him of the custody of his children, and appoint a suitable person to act as guardian, and to take care of them, and to superintend their education.[11]

Today, every state has a statute allowing a court to intervene into the family to protect a child; this authority is usually conferred on the juvenile or family court.[12] Apart from situations where the child has engaged in wrongful behavior of some sort, the statutes in most states allow the court to intrude into the child's life if, for whatever reason, he or she lacks a parent or guardian (dependent or abandoned children), if the parent has neglected properly to care for or to support him or her (neglected children), or if the parent has willfully injured the child (abused children). Frequently the terms "dependent" and "neglected" are used to describe all children subject to a juvenile court's jurisdiction who have not engaged in any wrongful behavior. In this paper, the term "neglected" is so used, and is meant to include dependent and abused children as well.

In several respects present-day legislative standards defining the circumstances where a court may intervene into the family bear a remarkable similarity to Story's nineteenth century characterization. They are vague and open-ended, they require highly subjective determinations, and they permit intervention not only when the child has been demonstrably harmed or is physically endangered but also when parental habits or attitudes are adverse to the inculcation of proper moral values. Typical statutory provisions allow court intrusion to protect a child who is not receiving "proper parental care,"[13] "proper attention,"[14] "whose home is an unfit place for him by reason of neglect, cruelty, depravity, or physical abuse,"[15] or whose parents neglect to provide the "care necessary for his health, morals or well being."[16] The Minnesota statute explicitly specifies that emotional neglect of the child is relevant to intervention.[17]

The Process of Removal. While the legal standards for court intervention are scarcely more precise today than 100 years ago, far more complex administrative processes are involved.[18] In Story's time, social workers and probation departments did not exist. Today a case usually reaches court after weaving through a complicated social welfare bureaucracy where numerous officials including social workers, probation officers, and court personnel, may have had contact with the family.

Unfortunately, very little is known about how the discretion of these various administrative officers is exercised before a case reaches court. The process is usually initiated by a report from a social worker or the police, or less frequently from a neighbor, medical professional, or school staff member.[19] Although practices vary, a member of a special unit of the social welfare or probation department is usually responsible for an initial investigation of the report. Customarily this investigation is not extensive; often it will only involve a visit to the home and a telephone conversation with the person who turned in the report. The investigator, sometimes together with a supervisor, then must decide whether to close the case, to suggest that the welfare agency informally (and noncoercively) provide services or supervision, or to file a petition in court.

Filing a petition initiates a judicial inquiry that usually has two stages. First, the court must determine whether it has jurisdiction over the child. This involves deciding on the basis of exceedingly broad and ill-defined statutory provisions whether the parents have failed to live up to acceptable social standards for child rearing. If it is determined that they have, then such jurisdiction empowers the court to intervene into the family. In the words of one juvenile court judge, "It is the ultimate finding of neglect which releases the court's wide discretionary powers of disposition, a discretion beholden to and circumscribed by the law's most challenging aphorism, 'the best interests of the child.' "[20] The second stage involves a dispositional hearing, where the judge decides the manner of intervention. Removal from the home is by no means mandatory. The court can instead require supervision within the child's own home, psychological counseling for the parents and/or the child, or periodic home visits by a social worker, probation officer, or homemaker.

No national data are available, but it appears that children are removed from parental custody in a significant percentage of the cases when the juvenile court assumes jurisdiction. In 1972, for example, the Los Angeles juvenile courts ordered removal in 1,028 out of 1,656 of the cases where jurisdiction was assumed—62 percent.[21] For San Francisco in the same year, 65 percent were ordered removed (262 out of 402).[22] Although some of these children were placed with relatives, over 80 percent of those removed were placed in foster care. Likewise, a study of dispositions in New York State during the years 1957–60 showed that the probability of removal from the home was as great as that of supervision by the probation department—each occurred in slightly over 30 percent of the neglect petitions adjudicated by the court.[23] More recently, Professor Peter Straus has estimated that in New York the child is taken from its home "in about half" of the cases of abuse or neglect.[24]

Children in Foster Care

The Characteristics of Foster Children—The Reasons for Removal. The social welfare literature provides some information about the age and economic circumstances of the children placed in foster care. Most of the chilren are quite young at the time of removal; a majority are probably six years of age or younger.[25] Their families are usually very poor, often on welfare.[26] A disproportionate number are from single parent families.[27]

Unfortunately there is very little systematic information about the circumstances that result in foster care placement over parental objections. Although some social welfare research attempts to analyze why children are placed in foster care, these studies are based on samples where many parents agreed to placement or sought it. There is no reason to assume that the circumstances leading a family to wish to give up a child are the same as those leading professionals to decide the state should compel removal. The most extensive work on reasons for foster placement has been done by Shirley Jenkins and her associates at Columbia University, published in 1966. Jenkins and Sauber analyzed 425 families whose children were placed in foster care in New York City. Using five major categories, they describe the "main reason for placement" as follows:

(1) physical illness or incapacity of child-caring person, including confinement, 29 percent; (2) mental illness of the mother, 11 percent; (3) child personality or emotional problems, 17 percent; (4) severe neglect or abuse, 10 percent; (5) 'family problems,' 33 percent. The last group includes cases of unwillingness or inability to continue

care on the part of an adult other than a parent, children left or deserted, parental incompetence, and conflicts or arrests.[28]

A later study published in 1972 by Jenkins and Norman found the following distribution of families according to reason for placement.[29] (See Table 1.)

Neither study is particularly helpful for analyzing antecedents of the legal decision to place children in foster homes. In the first study, parents were known to have objected to placement in only 10 percent of the sample cases, and the percentage distribution of reasons for placement among this subgroup is not given. While it is suggested that the "severe abuse or neglect" category included most of the objecting parents, that category, as its label shows, is no more helpful in describing the reason for the decision than the underlying statute. The

TABLE 1   Distribution of Families According to Reason for Placement

REASON FOR PLACEMENT	NUMBER OF FAMILIES	PERCENT DISTRIBUTION
Mental illness	86	22
Child behavior	63	16
Neglect or abuse	54	14
Physical illness	44	11
Unwillingness or inability to continue care	41	11
Family dysfunction	36	9
Unwillingness or inability to assume care	30	8
Abandonment or desertion	30	8
Other problems	6	1
Total	390	100

later study is also based on samples that include voluntary and nonvoluntary placements. It too uses descriptive categories lacking definitional clarity and combining situations where parents no longer want child care responsibility with those where a professional has decided the parent is not competent. Finally, as these researchers realized, more than one reason frequently can be identified for foster care placement, making the selection of a single reason difficult or inappropriate. Other social welfare research has sought to analyze the factors influencing a social worker's preference for placement outside the home as opposed to provision of services in the child's own home.[30] None, however, focuses primarily on judicial determinations.

Nor do judicial opinions or legal scholarship provide a solid basis for generalizations about the circumstances leading courts to remove children over parental objections. Legal scholarship usually is based on reported cases. It cannot be assumed these are reliable guides to the circumstances leading to removal for two reasons. First, juvenile and family court judges rarely dispose of cases with written opinions at all, much less reported ones. Second, although appealed cases often result in reported opinions, very few neglect cases are appealed. I estimate during the past six years that only one in every thousand cases where a California court has ordered foster care placement has resulted in a reported appellate opinion.[31] There is no basis for assuming these cases are representative.

Despite the paucity of data, it appears that removal over parental objections takes place most often where the court determines the parents' supervision and guidance of the child are inade-

quate, where the mother is thought to be emotionally ill, or where the child has behavior problems.[32] Although highly publicized, cases involving child battery, where a parent has intentionally abused or injured a child, are in a distinct minority.[33]

Where the Children Go. After a court decides to remove a child from home, a public agency, often the social welfare or probation department, is assigned responsibility for placing the child. In 1933 about half of the nation's neglected children were in large institutions, and a large proportion were supervised by some religiously sponsored voluntary agency.[34] In 1970 only 42,200 children lived in foster care under the auspices of voluntary agencies, while over 284,000 were under the supervision of state social service agencies. Of the state-supervised children, 243,600 lived in foster family homes, 3,600 in group homes, and only 37,300 in child welfare institutions.[35]

Foster family homes are usually licensed by the state, with regulations regarding aspects such as the size of the home, number of children, and age of foster parents. Under a contract, foster parents are paid a monthly fee for each child in their care.[36] Most foster parents, it appears, are middle- or lower-middle-class and are forty years old or older.[37] Although foster parents are responsible for the day-to-day care of the children, the contract between the agency and the foster parents usually requires the foster parents to acknowledge that "the legal responsibility for the foster child remains with the Agency," and to "accept and comply with any plans the Agency makes for the child," including "the right to determine when and how the child leaves" the foster home.[38]

How Long Do Children Remain in Foster Care? In theory, "the distinguishing aspect of foster care is that it is designed to be a temporary arrangement. The family is broken up only so that it can be put together again in a way that will be less problematic for the child."[39] It would be reassuring to know that children who enter foster care remain there only a short time, then either return to their parents or are adopted by some other family. Some children indeed do remain in foster care only a short period, but the evidence suggests that this pattern is the exception rather than the rule. Foster care is not typically short-term. On the basis of their analysis, Maas and Engler predicted that "better than half" of the more than 4,000 children they studied would be "living a major part of their childhood in foster families and institutions."[40] Similarly, in a study of 624 children under twelve who entered foster care during 1966 and were there at least 90 days, Fanshel found that 46 percent were still in foster care three and one-half years later.[41] Wiltse and Gambrill recently examined a sample composed of 772 San Francisco foster children, about one-half of that city's entire case-load. They found that 62 percent of these children were expected to remain in foster care until maturity; the average length of time in care for all the children in their sample was nearly five years.[42] One juvenile judge has written about his surprise at the beginning of his term when he found that many of the neglected children under his jurisdiction had been in "temporary" foster care for five to six years.[43]

One way the state might minimize the length of time children remain in foster care is to work intensively with the natural parents to correct the deficiency which led to coercive removal. However, natural parents are rarely offered rehabilitative services after the children are removed. In examining foster care in nine communities, Maas and Engler found that:

> More than 70 percent of the fathers and mothers of the children in this study either had no relationship with the agencies responsible for the care of their children or their relationship was erratic or untrusting. In many instances the agencies' resources were such that their staff's time was entirely consumed with the day-to-day job of caring for the children. They had no time for the kind of continuous work with the parents of the children which could affect the rehabilitation of the home. Frequently agencies fail to appreciate the dynamics of intrafamily relationships as a whole and work only with the child.[44]

Interviews during the last six months with a number of social workers in Northern California suggest that after removal, caseworkers focus attention almost exclusively on the child and the foster parents, spending little if any time with the natural parents. This may reflect lack of clarity about the parental default which must be corrected, or absence of available techniques or resources to correct the deficiencies, or both.

Whether or not rehabilitative services would help, the present reality is such that for "only a fraction of children now in foster care is there a possibility of return to their own homes."[45] Wiltse and Gambrell found in their San Francisco study that return to home was expected in only 15 percent of the cases;[46] Maas and Engler concluded on the basis of their study of 4,281 children in nine communities that for "no more than twenty-five percent" was it probable that the foster child would return home.[47]

Although many foster children never return to their natural parents, long-term plans that would provide these children with a sense of security and stability are seldom made and rarely implemented. One study concluded that "for nearly two-thirds (64 percent) of the children in foster care the public agencies reported that the only plan was continuation in foster care."[48] Moreover, because neither the foster parents nor the agency is under an obligation to keep the child where originally placed, children are often moved from one foster home to another.[49] Adoption probably provides the best chance for stability and continuity. It creates the same legal relationship between child and adult in terms of custody, support, discipline, and inheritance as exists between a parent and a biologically related, legitimate child. But very few foster children are ever adopted. In one study of foster children supervised by public agencies, only 13 percent of the children were considered likely to be adopted.[50] Social welfare agencies are frequently reluctant to place foster children for adoption because this requires final termination of the natural parents' legal rights, an act that necessitates a separate legal proceeding often involving more stringent standards than those used for the initial removal. Wishing to avoid anything drastic, and uncertain of their legal ability to act, these agencies do nothing, and, as more time goes by, adoption becomes less possible.[51] Indeed, it appears that after a child has been in foster care for more than eighteen months, the chance of either returning home or being adopted is remote.[52]

In summary, children removed by the state from the home of their parents are often destined to remain in limbo until adulthood, the wards of a largely indifferent state. On the one hand, they frequently are unable to return to their natural parents, who are offered little rehabilitative help. On the other hand, they are usually placed with a foster family and cautioned not to become too attached. These children thus grow up without a permanent and secure home.

What is Wrong with the Best Interests Standard?

We now turn to a close examination of the "best interests of the child" test, the legal standard usually employed by courts to decide whether a child should be removed from parental custody in the dispositional stage of neglect proceedings. This standard has long been used to decide matters of child custody, particularly in disputes between parents. In an opinion written nearly fifty years ago, Benjamin Cardozo described as follows the role of the judge in any child custody proceeding brought before a court of equity:

> He acts as *parens patriae* to do what is best for the interest of the child. He is to put himself in the position of a "wise, affectionate, and careful parent" . . . and make provision for the child accordingly. He may act at the intervention of a kinsman, if so the petition comes before him, but equally he may act at the instance or on the motion of any one else. He is not adjudicating a controversy between adversary parties, to compare their private differences. He is not determining rights 'as between a parent and a child'; or as between one parent and another. . . . He "interferes for the protection of infants, *qua* infants, by virtue of the prerogative which belongs to the Crown as *parens patriae*."[53]

Cardozo's description appears in a decision involving a dispute between estranged parents over who should have custody of the children. Today some version of the best interests standard is incorporated in the divorce legislation of nearly every state.[54] But Cardozo's expansive language makes it easy to understand how the test could be applied not only in disputes between parents but also in neglect proceedings. Presently, the best interests test is widely used to decide what should be done for a child over whom a juvenile court has assumed jurisdiction;[55] indeed, it is sometimes used to decide whether jurisdiction should be assumed.[56]

For the dispositional decision in neglect cases, the best interests test would appear to have much to commend it. It focuses principally on the child rather than on arbitrary legal rights of parents. It implicitly recognizes that each child is unique, and that parental conduct and home environments may have substantially different effects on different children. It also seems to require that the judge find out as much as possible about the child, the child's circumstances, the parents, and the available alternative arrangements. In fact, the best interests standard embodies what David Matza has described as a basic precept of juvenile court philosophy: the principle of "individualized justice." This principle requires each dispositional decision, in Matza's words, "to be guided by a *full understanding* of the client's personal and social characteristics and by his 'individual needs.' "[57]

Nonetheless, a careful analysis reveals serious deficiencies in the best interests test when it is used to decide whether the state should remove a child from parental custody and place the child in foster care. I will discuss some

of the test's shortcomings as it is applied in foster care cases.

Conceptual Problems with the Test. One obvious objection to the best interests of the child test is that by its very terms it ignores completely the interests of the parents. Obviously a child's parents have important interests at stake when the state seeks to intervene; a parent can derive important satisfaction and pleasures from a relationship with a child, and the destruction of this relationship can have an enormous effect on the parent, quite apart from benefits or losses to the child. I doubt whether courts ignore the effects of judicial action on parents, but the best interests of the child test disallows explicit consideration of parental interests, making the process more high-sounding, perhaps, but less honest.

But even if we assume that it is appropriate to focus attention exclusively on the child's interests, there remain conceptual difficulties with the best interests test. Its application assumes the judge will compare the probable consequences for the child of remaining in the home with the probable consequences of removal. How might a judge make this comparison? He or she would need considerable information and predictive ability. The information would include knowledge of how the parents had behaved in the past, the effect of this parental behavior on the child, and the child's present condition. Then the judge would need to predict the probable future behavior of the parents if the child were to remain in the home and to gauge the probable effects of their behavior on the child. Obviously, more than one outcome is possible, so the judge would have to assess the probability of various outcomes and evaluate the seriousness of possible benefits and harms associated with each. Next, the judge would have to compare this set of possible consequences with those if the child were placed in a foster home. This would require predicting the effect of removing the child from home, school, friends, and familiar surroundings, as well as predicting the child's experience while in the foster care system. Such predictions involve estimates of the child's future relationship with the foster parents, the child's future contact with natural parents and siblings, the number of foster homes in which the child ultimately will have to be placed, the length of time spent in foster care, the potential for acquiring a stable home, and myriad other factors.

Obviously one can question whether a judge has the necessary information. In many instances he or she lacks adequate information even about a child's life with his or her parents. Moreover, at the time of the dispositional hearing, the judge typically has *no* information about where the child will be placed if removal is ordered; he or she usually knows nothing about the characteristics of the foster family, or how long that family will want or be able to keep the child. In deciding who should raise a particular child, the court in a neglect proceeding is comparing an existing family with a largely unknown alternative. In this regard, the dispositional phase of a neglect proceeding stands in sharp contrast with a divorce custody dispute, where the best interest test is also widely employed. In a divorce custody contest, the judge is settling a dispute between two adults, usually both before the court, each of whom had a prior relationship with the child and each of whom wishes to assume full parental authority.[58] In a neglect case, the judge is deciding in a state-initiated proceeding whether to remove a child from parental custody and have the state assume responsibility by placing the child in a state-sponsored home about which the judge knows few, if any, particulars.

Even if the judge had substantial information about both the child's existing home life and the foster care alternatives, our knowledge about human behavior provides no basis for the predictions called for by the best interest standard. No consensus exists about a theory of human behavior, and no theory is widely considered capable of generating reliable predictions about the psychological and behavioral consequences of alternative dispositions. This does not imply a criticism of the behavioral sciences. Indeed, Anna Freud, who has devoted her life to the study of the child and who plainly believes that theory can be a useful guide to treatment, has warned that theory alone does not provide a reliable guide for prediction: "In spite of . . . advances," she suggests, "there remain factors which make clinial foresight, i.e., prediction, difficult and hazardous," not the least of which is that "the environmental happenings in a child's life will always remain unpredictable since they are not governed by any known laws. . . ."[59]

The limitations of psychological theory in generating verifiable predictions are suggested by the numerous studies which have attempted to trace effects of various child-rearing techniques and parental attitudes on adult personality traits. Under Sigmund Freud's influence, many psychologists have assumed the importance of a child's early years, searching for the importance of timing and techniques of nursing, weaning, toilet training, and the like. But in Sibylle Escalona's words:

The net result of a great many studies can be compressed into a single sentence: When child-rearing techniques of this order are treated as the independent variable, no significant relationship can be shown to exist between child-rearing techniques and later personality characteristics. Some parental attitudes do relate to child characteristics at school age and in adolescence, but no significant relationships have been demonstrated between parental attitudes towards a child during the first three or four years of life and the child's later characteristics.[60]

Studies that have attempted to trace personality development to specific antecedent variables have assumed that a particular practice would have the same effect on different children. This assumption is now widely questioned by experimental psychologists such as H. R. Schaffer. Schaffer and others think that infants experience in individual ways.[61] The implication of this for prediction is described very well by Arlene Skolnick: ". . . if the child selectively interprets situations and events, we cannot confidently predict behavior from knowledge of the situation alone."[62]

The difficulty of making accurate predictions is shown clearly by a study undertaken by Joan Macfarlane and her associates in Berkeley, California.[63] Using various tests and interviews, the Berkeley group studied during a thirty-year period a group of 166 infants born in 1929. Their objective was to observe the growth—emotional, mental, and physical—of normal people. As Skolnick observed:

> Over the years this study has generated several significant research findings, but the most surprising of all was the difficulty of predicting what thirty-year-old adults would be like even after the

most sophisticated data had been gathered on them as children. . . . the researchers experienced shock after shock as they saw the people they had last seen at age eighteen. It turned out that the predictions they had made about the subjects were wrong in about two-thirds of the cases! How could a group of competent psychologists have been so mistaken?

> Foremost, the researchers had tended to overestimate the damaging effects of early troubles of various kinds. Most personality theory had been derived from observations of troubled people in therapy. The pathology of adult neurotics and psychotics was traced back to disturbances early in childhood—poor parent-child relations, chronic school difficulties, and so forth. Consequently, theories of personality based on clinical observation tended to define adult psychological problems as socialization failures. But the psychiatrist sees only disturbed people; he does not encounter "normal" individuals who may experience childhood difficulties but who do not grow into troubled adults. The Berkeley method, however, called for studying such people. Data on the experience of these subjects demonstrated the error of assuming that similar childhood conditions affect every child the same way. Indeed, many instances of what looked like severe pathology to the researchers were put to constructive use by the subjects. . . .[64]

Even if accurate predictions were possible, a fundamental problem would remain. What set of values is a judge to use to determine what is in the child's best interests? Should the judge be concerned with happiness? Or should he or she worry about the child's spiritual goodness or economic productivity? Is stability and security for a child more desirable than intellectual stimulation?[65] Should the best interests of the child be viewed from a short-term or a long-term perspective? The conditions that make a person happy at age ten or fifteen may have adverse consequences at age thirty.

The neglect statutes themselves are of little help in providing guidance about the values that should inform the decision. And, our pluralistic society lacks consensus about child-rearing strategies and values. By necessity, a judge is forced to rely upon personal values to determine a child's best interests.

The Problem of Fairness. What is wrong, one may ask, with reliance on individual values and judgments? For one thing, it offends a most basic precept of law. As John Rawls wrote: the rule of law "implies the precept that similar cases be treated similarly."[66] This aspiration is not always met, but any legal test that requires impossible predictions and reliance on the decision maker's own values invites injustice.

As long as the best interests standard or some equally broad standard is used, it seems inevitable that petitions will be filed and neglect cases will be decided without any clear articulation or consistent application of the behavioral or moral premises on which the decision is based. This conclusion is supported by a simulation study which analyzed the factors influencing a judge's decision whether to provide a child with services within the child's own home or to remove the child.[67] Three judges, each with at least five years' experience, were independently given the actual files for 94 children from 50 families. Each judge was asked to decide whether the child should be removed or services should be provided. The three agreed in less than one-half of the cases (45 out of 94). Even more significantly, when the judges were asked to indicate the factors influencing their decisions, the study concluded, "Even in cases in which they agreed on the decision, the judges did not identify the same factors as determinants, each seeming to operate to some extent within his own unique value system."[68]

A judge's reliance on personal values is especially risky when class differences confound the problem. The foster care system is frequently accused of being class biased, one "in which middle-class professionals provide and control a service used mostly by poor people, with upper-lower and lower-middle class foster parents serving as intermediaries."[69] The fact that most foster children come from poor families does not, of course, prove that there is an inherent class bias in the system. There are other plausible explanations for the high proportion of poor children. The condition of poverty may lead to family breakdown and a greater likelihood that children are endangered in times of crisis. Alternatively, since poor families are more subject to scrutiny by social workers who administer welfare programs, their faults, even if no more common, may be more conspicuous. Finally, since poor families have access to few resources in the event of family crisis, their children may be forced into the foster care system because other forms of substitute care, such as babysitters, relatives, and day care centers, are not available.[70]

Although these other explanations are plausible, the fact remains that the best interests standard allows the judge to import his personal values into the process, and leaves considerable scope for class bias. An examination of available reported cases dramatically illustrates how a judge's attitude toward child rearing, sexual mores, religion, or cleanliness can affect the result of court proceedings. These cases, while not typical, clearly reveal the risks of "individualized" decisions under vague judicial standards. There are a number of reported cases, for example, where a judge has decided parental behavior was immoral and, without any systematic inquiry into how the parental conduct damaged or was likely to harm the children, the judge then determined the children to be neglected and removed them from their home.[71] A New York judge declared five small children neglected, and ordered custody to be transferred to the father on the ground that the mother "frequently entertained male companions in the apartment . . . and, on at least one occasion, one of them spent the night with the [mother] and, in fact, slept with her, to the knowledge of the children." The court openly acknowledged:

> The statutory definition of neglect, therefore, being in general terms, has resulted in a dearth of cases reported; and the tendency has been to leave it to the judge in a particular case to make his own decision as to whether or not there is neglect, based upon the particular and unique set of facts in the case at bar. It therefore has developed upon the courts to establish the moral standards to be allowed by persons to whom is entrusted the care and custody of children. And never has there been a greater need for the courts to maintain a high level of moral conduct than exists today. This court intends to give more than lip service to the principle that the fabric of our society is composed of the family unit and when the family unit is damaged, the fabric of society suffers. Our courts will continue to insist upon a high level of moral conduct on the part of custodians of children, and will never succumb to the "Hollywood" type of morality so popu-

lar today, which seems to condone and encourage the dropping of our moral guard. We have not yet reached the point where, when parents who have tired of each other's company, may be free to seek other companionship with complete disregard of the moral examples they are setting for their children. This is the crux of the case at bar.[72]

In deciding whether to remove a child from parental custody, various other judges have thought it relevant that a mother had extramarital sexual relations,[73] was a lesbian,[74] or had several illegitimate children.[75] Religion, like sex, has also triggered strong responses from judges. Religious fanaticism and unconventional beliefs of parents[76] have been considered relevant factors in neglect proceedings.

Finally, there are cases where a child is removed from his parental home because the court determines the *physical conditions* in the home are unsuitable for the child. In a recent California case, an appellate court affirmed a juvenile court decision removing children from a dirty home. The parents claimed there was no evidence showing that the children had been harmed, but the appeals court maintained that the state "was not required, as appellants assert, to prove that the conditions of the above cause 'sickness and disease of mind or body' in order to establish 'neglect' . . . the welfare of the child is of paramount concern, and a purpose of the juvenile court law is to secure for each minor such care and guidance as will serve the spiritual, emotional, mental, and physical welfare of the minor and the best interests of the state."[77] Some "dirty homes" may seriously endanger a child's growth and well-being, but most may merely offend middle-class sensibilities. One suspects courts may sometimes be enforcing middle-class norms of cleanliness where both economic and cultural circumstances make it both unfair and inappropriate.[78]

During the past ten years there have been several appellate court decisions[79] rejecting extreme attempts by trial court judges to use neglect laws "to impose middle-class mores upon families and to punish a parent's undesirable conduct unless that conduct can be shown to result in damage to the child."[80] For two reasons, however, these cases do not significantly limit the discretion of the judge who hears the case. First, the appellate decisions suggesting that specific factors are not appropriate for consideration also emphasize the continuing need for individualized determinations and wide latitude for trial judges.[81] Second, juvenile court judges can often disguise a decision based on an "improper" factor by vague recitation of general language. The real reasons may be very different than the stated ones.

David Matza thought individual treatment in juvenile court dispositions was a "mystification" and his observations have relevance to the best interests standard:

> To the extent that it prevails, its function is to obscure the process of decision and disposition rather than enlighten it. The principle of individualized justice results in a frame of relevance that is so large, so all-inclusive, that any relation between the criteria of judgment and the disposition remains obscure.[82]

The Risks of Foster Care Placement. The best interests test also makes it too easy for a judge to ignore the possible detrimental effects of removing a child from parental custody. The dangers of leaving a child at home often seem compelling, and because the judge is often unaware of or unable to evaluate the psychological risks of foster care, an individualized determination under a best interest standard may be biased in favor of removal. An assessment of the risks involved in separating children from their parents requires explicit knowledge of the foster care system. What happens to foster children? Are they happy while in foster care? What harm, both short-term and long-term, can result from being put into this system? How many chidren "fail" in foster homes?

Since predictions of how an individual child will fare in foster care have not proved reliable,[83] there is no reason to believe a judge can accurately assess the risks of placement. For the social scientist, analysis of the differential effects of foster placement on a child's development raises severe methodological problems; these include defining a control group, establishing a standard of "successful development," and isolating the factors responsible for any noticeable effects. No studies prove either that foster care benefits or harms children. The most famous longitudinal study, published in 1924, traces what happened to 910 former foster children who had spent one year or more in a foster home. The research question was, "Has the subject shown himself capable (or incapable) of managing himself and his affairs with ordinary prudence?"[84] The results of the study showed 615 subjects (67.5 percent) as "capable," 182 subjects (20.0 percent) as "incapable," and 113 subjects (12.5 percent) as of "unknown capability." Needless to say, criteria for success were defined in only the most vague and arbitrary terms. Moreover, one cannot judge whether these results were good or bad without a control group, and definition of such a group presents overwhelming problems. More recent studies have not been able to overcome the methodological difficulties nor provide definitive answers about the long-range effects of foster care.[85]

Empirical studies *do* exist, however, to illustrate the conditions of children while in foster care. These suggest there is "rather persuasive, if still incomplete, evidence that throughout the United States children in foster care are experiencing high rates of psychiatric disturbance."[86] Maas and Engler, for example, in their study, found that "forty to fifty percent or more of the children in foster care in every one of our nine communities showed symptoms of maladjustment."[87] Other studies concur with this finding.[88]

The factors responsible for the emotional problems observed in foster care are difficult to isolate. For years, the effects of "separation trauma" were studied,[89] with the argument that the "act of placement in itself creates what is known as a separation trauma" and therefore may be harmful.[90] Many psychologists would agree.

> Any child who is compelled for whatever reason to leave his own home and family and to live in foster placement lives through an experience pregnant with pain and terror for him and potentially damaging to his personality and normal growth. It is abnormal in our society for a child to be separated for any continuing length of time from his own parents and no one knows this so well as the child himself. For him placement is a shocking and bewildering calamity, the reasons for which he usually does not understand.[91]

Later, some psychologists modified this position, arguing that children who remained in their own homes with neglectful or indifferent mothers experienced greater psychological harm than children in foster homes.[92] However, when researchers observed the effects of separation on older children, concern was again expressed about the risks of removing a child for placement in foster care.[93] Although the debate is far from over, it is generally assumed that separation carries substantial risks for the child, risks that are related to the age of the child at the time of separation. Concern has been expressed particularly about children separated between six months and three years of age, at about six years of age, and at puberty.[94]

Another way the foster care system itself may cause psychological harm involves the anomalous position of a child within a foster home. "Family life can be complex indeed for the foster child."[95] The child often experiences conflict over which set of parents, natural or foster, to trust and rely on when in trouble. Moreover, the child may observe power struggles among the natural and foster parents, the social workers, and the judge, each of whom has a reason to be concerned about the child's care and future. A foster home is supposed to provide, insofar as possible, a normal family environment. But agencies often become concerned if the foster parents grow too attached to a child. In one case, the highest state court in New York approved the transfer of a child from a foster home to an unknown alternative because the foster parents "had become too emotionally involved with the child."[96] The court upheld an agency determination "that the child's best interests necessitated her placement in another environment where she would not be torn between her loyalty to her mother and her boarding parents."[97] Although the effects of ambiguous relationships are impossible to measure, there is a good theoretical argument and some suggestive evidence that a child's basic security and ability to form other relationships are shaken when he or she is torn by conflicting expectations and loyalties.[98] Lack of a solid identity, which most children acquire largely in their relationship with their parents, perhaps causes the most harm.[99] "Without an adequate conception of who he is, where he is, and why he is there, it is difficult to see how the foster child could develop well in a situation that is as complex and problematic as placement."[100]

A third psychologically detrimental factor in foster care is the instability of the system itself. As noted earlier, children are often moved from home to home,[101] and there is rapid turnover of social workers[102] and judges[103] involved in the case. Studies strongly indicate that personality problems are more frequent among children who have been moved often.[104] Maas and Engler, for example, concluded that "instability in relationships fosters personality disturbances."[105] On the other hand, the frequency of moves may depend on the child's adjustment before he or she even enters foster care: a "disturbed child who enters foster care is more likely to experience more numerous replacements, and his symptoms increase accordingly."[106] Whatever the reason, both former foster children and experienced social workers agree that moving a child from foster home to foster home is a painful and at times damaging experience.[107]

Present Legal Standards Fail to Make Removal a Last Resort. It would seem that foster care entails substantial risks of psychological harm. This does not imply that a legal standard should be adopted to make it impossible to take children from their parents and place them in foster care. But it does suggest a child's life may not be improved by removal unless the dangers of remaining at home are immediate and substantial and there are no means of protecting the child within the home.

Placing a child away from home is often referred to as a "last resort," but in fact most communities offer few preventive or protective services for children within the home while a family is helped through a crisis. Day care or babysitting services, along with parental counseling, might make removal unnecessary in a wide variety of circumstances; such services typically are unavailable. A national survey conducted by the American Humane Association in 1967 concluded that *"no state* and *no community* has developed a child protective service program adequate in size to meet the service needs of all *reported* cases of child neglect, abuse, and exploitation."[108] Even when such services are available, neglect statutes and the best interests standard do not require that before ordering removal a court conduct an inquiry into whether the child can be protected if left in parental custody.[109] Anecdotal evidence strongly suggests that children are often placed in foster care without a careful analysis of whether less drastic forms of intervention might be preferable. Thus, for instance, children have been placed in foster care because their parents' home is filthy even though a homemaker's services might have remedied the situation and done so at far less cost to the state.[110] Also, an undernourished child may be taken from the home without any prior effort to educate the parents about nutritional needs.[111] Even in child abuse cases, where removal from the home is very likely, many experts believe that the child can often be left safely at home if the parents receive appropriate treatment and support.[112]

Removal would seem appropriate only when there are no means to protect the child within the home. Given the size and quality of present institutional arrangements for children who are removed, and given the widely shared view that parents, not the state, should ordinarily be responsible for child rearing, any legal standard should incorporate a substantial presumption favoring a parent who has expressly indicated that he or she wishes to retain custody. Because of the importance of the parent-child relationship and because of the risks of removal, I believe the state should not be allowed to remove children unless less drastic means of intervention cannot protect the child.

Is Judicial Application of the Best Interests Standard the Issue? My analysis has been couched largely in terms of how *judges* behave in the *dispositional* phase of neglect proceedings. Despite problems with the best interests standard, it might be thought that the statutory standards determining when a juvenile court should assume *jurisdiction* are sufficiently stringent to exclude all but the most extreme cases from the dispositional phase of any juvenile court proceeding. But the jurisdictional phase of the court's proceeding provides no such safeguard. As already noted, some courts now appear to use the best interests standard for determining jurisdiction.[113] As indicated earlier, the statutory standards for jurisdiction are extremely vague and broad, and require findings of parental unfitness or neglect.[114] These standards provide no more guidance to a court than does best interests and do little to limit judicial discretion. Indeed, the jurisdictional provisions have been

subject to a steady barrage of criticism in the legal literature for the last two decades.[115]

Finally, and I think this is the nub of the problem, the jurisdictional decision is the same whether a court is going to supervise the child within the home or remove the child. Consequently, to assume jurisdiction need not in itself be seen as a particularly important decision. My own strong impression based on interviews and courtroom observation is that the judge and social worker consider the dispositional decision of whether to remove the child from the home as the key issue and that courts are not at all reluctant to assume jurisdiction. The fact that the juvenile courts assume jurisdiction in a very high percentage of cases suggests the same conclusion.[116]

It might be argued that social workers, probation officers, psychologists, and psychiatrists involved in the foster care system actually are the ones who decide when children should be removed, and that standards governing the judicial process therefore are of secondary importance. It may be true that judges rely on the advice of these other professionals. But deciding the direction of the causal link is no easy matter, since social workers are known to sometimes shape their recommendations according to what they think a particular judge will want to decide. In all events, the same problems that plague a judge plague these professionals too—lack of information, lack of predictive models, and the need to rely on individual values.

The Agenda for Law Reform

Is there something better than the "best interests of the child" standard?

Can an adequate legal standard be developed, given our limited knowledge of human behavior, our pluralistic value system, and the realities of present foster care arrangements? Any standard devised will necessarily involve values—values that can be questioned and attacked. But it is essential that the new standard expose for analysis what is now hidden behind the "best interests" shield. I believe any new standard must be premised on three basic principles, implicit in much of the previous discussion.

1. Removal should be only when the child cannot be protected within the home.
2. To the extent possible, the decision to require foster care placement should be based on legal standards that can be applied in a consistent and even-handed way.
3. The state should make every effort to provide children who must be removed with as much continuity and stability as possible.

Two Unlikely Solutions. Against the backdrop of these principles, it is useful to analyze why two plausible methods of legal reform hold no great promise. These are, first, stricter enforcement of criminal child neglect statutes and, second, additional procedural safeguards in neglect proceedings. Every state now has criminal child neglect, abuse, or cruelty statutes. Better articulation or enforcement of these standards of minimum parental conduct, and greater use of criminal sanctions, will not improve the foster care system and will do little or nothing to correct the causes of child neglect, and does not serve two goals of criminal law, deterrence and rehabilitation. Insofar as poverty and emotional problems are at the root of many child neglect cases, in-

creased reliance on the criminal sanction would probably be counter-productive,[117] and would have little deterrent effect. "A command impossible to fulfill does not alter the incentives of the person subject to it."[118] A jail sentence provides no rehabilitation for the parent and at the same time forces a separation between the parent and child. Retribution against the parent is achieved, but at what cost to the child?

There also have been frequent proposals in dependency and neglect cases for procedural reform.[119] Presently, neglect proceedings are highly informal. Few parents, and far fewer children, are represented by counsel; typically hearsay evidence of all sorts is admissible. The trial court often decides neglect cases without insisting on specific findings to reveal the basis for its determinations. Appellate review, infrequently sought, usually results in a rubber stamp affirmation of the trial court's decisions, particularly with regard to dispositional determinations. This procedural picture is not a happy one. Convincing arguments can be advanced that due process requires something more.[120] I believe that certain procedural reforms might have beneficial effects. If lawyers were introduced into the process, for instance, they might play a significant role in finding witnesses, presenting evidence, and suggesting alternative dispositions not considered by the state's social workers. If judges, in turn, were required to make factual findings, the involvement of lawyers in the process might make judges more self-conscious about how their values affect their decisions. Also, procedural reforms would impose higher transaction costs on an agency seeking to remove a child, perhaps reducing the number of petitions filed or limiting them to the most egregious cases.

But procedural reform alone cannot correct the fundamental fault in the system: the court's wide discretion.[121] Imagine a procedural reform guaranteeing parent and child separate legal representation in all neglect cases. How would the child's advocate determine what to advocate under a best interests standard? Ordinarily, a lawyer can look to the client for direction, and if the child is fourteen years old or even seven years old, the child is an appropriate source for information, even guidance. But a majority of children involved in neglect proceedings are younger. A lawyer with a very young client is placed in a position not dissimilar to that of the judge. He must make his own set of predictions and use his own set of values to ascertain what is in the child's best interests, and then advocate that position. The judge might agree with the lawyer's recommendation, but why should we assume the lawyer's recommendation is any more appropriate than the judge's would be? In all events, if the judge reaches some other conclusion, the chances of reversing this decision in an appellate court are slight. If the best interests standard is applied, even with additional procedural safeguards at the hearing, appellate courts will continue to give wide latitude to the trial court's individualized decision. [*Eds.* See Uviller's remarks on the "best interests" standard above, pp. 214–20.]

The Direction of Legal Change. First priority for legal reform must involve changing the underlying legal standard for removal. Although I will not attempt here to formulate a definitive legal standard, the direction of change is clear: judicial discretion to remove children should be more limited, and if possible, the standard should be made more objective. One example of such a standard would be the following:

> *A state may remove a child from parental custody without parental consent only if the state first proves: a) there is an immediate and substantial danger to the child's health; and b) there are no reasonable means by which the state can protect the child's health without removing the child from parental custody.*

Before removing the child, I would further require the court to specify in writing the basis for the conclusion that the child was immediately and substantially in danger, with an explanation of which less drastic means of intervention had been contemplated, and why these were inadequate for the child's protection. Unlike the best interests test, the proposed standard is very explicit in its value premises: children are to be left at home except when there is real danger to them. It would take courts away from evaluating parental morality or sexual conduct, except in those rare cases when the child's health was endangered by it. The test would also focus judicial inquiry on whether the child could be protected within the home. A dirty-home case would no longer justify removal, because the state could usually protect the child by sending in a homemaker or housekeeper. Similarly, a child who was malnourished because a mother did not know anything about nutritional needs could be protected either by having a social worker teach the mother about nutrition or by having someone sent into the home to prepare the child's meals.

Within the context of these new standards, additional procedural safeguards, such as separate counsel for the parents and the child, are desirable. When removal is sought, the attorney for the state would have the burden of demonstrating why the child's health is endangered and why the child cannot be protected within the home. Counsel for the parents would attempt to show why the child is not in danger, and would propose alternative methods that might allow the family to remain intact. Counsel for the child might sometimes side with the parents, other times advocate alternative services, or other times urge removal. The child's lawyer would be responsible for evaluating the case after consulting with the child and making an independent investigation.

In addition, requiring the trial judge to make findings on these issues could make appellate review of the initial determination more meaningful. Although appellate courts would not often second guess a judge's conclusions about a witness's credibility, appellate review could serve an important role in defining how much danger was sufficient to justify intervention, and how far the state would have to go in providing alternatives. Indeed, standards of general applicability could evolve by a process not unlike that of common law.

The trial judge's role under the proposed standard would still not be easy. Judges would face the problem of predicting when the risks to the child were so great that the stricter standard for removal would be met. The terms "immediate" and "substantial" are not self-defining and would require interpretation. Nevertheless, the proposed standard is much more restrictive than existing standards. The justification for a more restrictive standard was best put by Ernst Freund, who observed: "in the absence of scientific certainty it must be borne in mind that the farther back from the point of imminent danger the law draws the safety line of police regula-

tion, so much the greater is the possibility that legislative interference is unwarranted."[122]

The term "health" poses particularly difficult policy issues. When there is an immediate and substantial danger to a child's *physical* health and the child cannot be protected at home, it is reasonable to predict that his or her lot will be improved by placement in foster care. Foster care does a reasonable job of protecting a child's physical health. But there is, of course, good reason to be concerned about a child's emotional health as well. Regarding the mental health of the child, it strikes me as extraordinarily difficult to predict when a child is emotionally endangered. Moreover, there is no evidence whatsoever that foster care is psychologically therapeutic. I am therefore very concerned that individualized determinations concerning emotional health could, on balance, do more harm than good by introducing a highly speculative element into the process. On balance I think "health" should be limited to "physical health," although this is a very difficult issue and requires more thought.

Another policy problem associated with the new standard relates to the question of how far a state must go in order to demonstrate that alternatives to removal will not work. The economic questions posed here are not trivial. For example, what if the means of protecting the child in the home are extraordinarily expensive? In a dirty-home case, what if a child could be protected only if a full-time maid were available in the house? The word "reasonable" allows the court to take into account the costs of alternatives, and to consider the economic question in the context of a specific case. Two general observations should be made, however. Because the costs of foster care are substantial, always several thousand dollars per year,[123] any method of protecting the child within the home which costs less than foster care would certainly be reasonable. I do not think it would be reasonable for a state to allow the level of resources available for home-based services to vary substantially among local jurisdictions merely because their capacity to raise revenue differs.

One clear goal of the new standard is to require states to devote more resources to the protection of children within the home. It is important that certain types of services such as homemakers, housekeepers, and public health nurses be available. But one unintended consequence of the proposed standard might be that the state would neither provide services to protect children within their homes, nor remove them when they are in danger. If this were the state's response the situation might well end up worse than it is today. Children who need protection would be left in danger. Fortunately, I think this response is unlikely, both because of public concern about children and because of the vested political interest of the existing social welfare bureaucracy.

Standard for Stability. A principal objective of law reform should be to establish a legal process ensuring a greater degree of stability for the child. For children who must be removed, there should be a statutory requirement fixing the maximum length of time they can remain in "temporary" foster care. The most direct way of doing this would be to require the judge at the end of a *fixed* period (perhaps twelve or eighteen months after placement) to choose between returning the child to the parents and placing the child either in an adoptive home or some other stable long-term environment. To allow this, I would change existing laws to provide for final termination of parental rights at the end of the required period if the child could not be safely returned to the home, and if the state had made reasonable efforts to rehabilitate the parents while the child was living away from the home.

At the time of removal, I would require the state to outline to the court the services it would make available to the parents. A court hearing might be required every three months during the interim period to ensure that the social welfare agency reported on its efforts and results. I would also put the burden on the state at these interim hearings to show that the child could not be safely returned to the home.[124] If the child could not safely be returned home at the end of the statutory period, adoption would be the favored alternative. Some foster children would be difficult to place for adoption because of age, health, or behavior. Subsidized adoption would be an appropriate way to expand adoption possibilities. Short of adoption, certain other alternatives exist which are rarely employed today. Several years ago it was suggested, for instance, that social welfare agencies should encourage the grant of legal guardianship to foster parents who had a long-term interest in a child.[125] Guardians do not have a legal duty to support a child from their own funds, but unlike foster parents they do have the legal right to custody of the child and do have powers much like normal parents with regard to the everyday guidance and control over the child's life. Guardianship thus would promote a degree of continuity often lacking in foster care.

I am not prepared to state categorically what the fixed time unit should be when the court must make a permanent decision. Although no recent national data is available, Maas and Engler found that most children who are in foster care for more than eighteen months never return home. This suggests the necessity of research for the development of such criteria. It might be possible to develop different time limits for different kinds of cases. But in all events, the fixed time limit should be established at the time of removal on the basis of criteria that could be consistently and fairly applied. For example, a shorter period might be appropriate for very young children.[126] Future research might show that rehabilitative prognosis of the family in certain identifiable types of cases is sufficiently poor to allow a quick decision. The great advantage of a fixed time period rather than an openended one is that it eventually requires courts and social welfare agencies to make permanent plans. In the past, periodic review procedures have not been sufficient to break bureaucratic inertia. Instead, routine extensions have been the rule. Any fixed time period is necessarily arbitrary; a slightly longer or shorter period might be better for a particular case, and inevitably some parents' rights will be finally terminated even though with more time they might have been able to pull themselves and their families together. Nevertheless, I think this method is more desirable on balance than a system based on individualized determinations giving a judge the discretion to leave children in the limbo of foster care, granting extension after extension even though it is highly improbable that the child will return home.

The proposed standard also does much more than the present law to require the state to work with the natural parents in the home situation after re-

moval. By working with parents, social welfare agencies could acquire information to assess what should be done for the child at the end of the statutory period. This raises difficult questions of confidentiality; if the state has access to information from the parents' therapy, for example, this may in itself inhibit the therapy. On the other hand, the state has a very substantial interest in making permanent plans for the child with the best information possible.

How Reform Can Occur. Litigation has been used to challenge existing neglect statutes, on the ground that they are unconstitutionally vague[127] and on the ground that the state has ordered removal without first assessing whether the child could be protected within the home.[128] To my knowledge no court has upheld either kind of claim. But the legal arguments available for such challenges are substantial, and a victory would move the operation of the system in the right direction. Alternatively, a state court might interpret existing neglect statutes to allow removal only under the circumstances described in the new standard. Although litigation is a possible avenue for improvement, reforms along the lines outlined here can be best achieved through new legislation. The American Bar Association has spurred legislative reform recently by establishing a Juvenile Justice Standards Project. This project will make a comprehensive reassessment of laws relating to minors, reexamining among other things all the legal standards concerning dependent and neglected children.[129]

Conclusions. The standards proposed in this article are intended to limit the wide discretion presently given to the professionals involved in the foster care system. There are costs associated with limiting this discretion. Some children who would substantially benefit from placement in foster care might be excluded from the system under the new standard. Similarly, there would undoubtedly be parents whose rights would be terminated under the proposed standard who might, given more time, have been able to work things out. The underlying issue, however, is whether we would have a fairer system, and one that on balance was more helpful to children.

Although this article has been directed primarily at the problems of children who are coercively removed from their parents, the analysis has broader implications, particularly for children who are "voluntarily" placed in state-sponsored foster care with the consent of the natural parents. Usually there is no court supervision of these children, even though from the *child's* perspective, placement is no less coercive simply because the state and parents agree. While state provision of foster care for children whose parents seek it may often be desirable, it must be remembered many children voluntarily placed remain in the limbo of foster care for years. In San Francisco, for example, the average stay for these children appears to be slightly *longer* on average than for court-ordered placements.[130] Moreover, social workers have suggested in interviews that many parents who voluntarily place their children are ambivalent about wanting to raise them, but also feel guilty about waiving parental responsibility. Consequently, they often are unwilling either to keep their children at home or to allow a stable alternative to develop. Their children, like ping pong balls, are paddled back and forth between parents and the social welfare system.

In voluntary placements, consideration should be given to imposing standards similar to those suggested for court-ordered placement. Before a child is voluntarily placed, the state might offer, but not compel, alternative services to enable the parent to keep the child at home. If placement were nevertheless desired by the parent, the parent might be told that the child can remain in such care for no more than a fixed period of time. At the end of that period, if the parent were unwilling or unable to have the child return home, the state would make another permanent arrangement for the child. While not without problems requiring further analysis, such a standard might have two benefits. First, some parents might decide to keep their children at home in the first place rather than placing them unnecessarily in the foster care system. Second, both parents and the social welfare bureaucracy would be required to make a permanent decision after a reasonable period of time.

The new standard also might have implications for dispositions in juvenile court cases where jurisdiction rests not on neglect but on the wrongful behavior of the minor—i.e., in delinquency and "pre-delinquency" cases. In a delinquency case, for example, the critical question is often what the juvenile court judge does in the dispositional hearing. Although jurisdiction turns on the issue of whether the state has proved beyond a reasonable doubt that the minor has committed an act which for an adult would be a crime, the judge's analysis in that hearing very often focuses on neglect-type considerations: the quality of the child's home life, his relationship with his parents, etc. Many of the criticisms I have leveled against the use of an individualized "best interests" standard in the dispositional phase of neglect proceedings can be made with regard to dispositions in delinquency cases.[131]

Finally, the questions examined in this article are closely related to those involved in a number of other areas of the law where officials are given the power to make coercive individualized determinations even though they lack information, theoretical tools to make predictions, proven methods of therapy, and a consensus with regard to values. The use of the best interests standard poses issues analogous to those raised by discretionary sentencing in the criminal law, where the therapeutic ideal has been used to justify giving judges, probation officers, and parole boards enormous discretion.[132] Indeterminate sentences are justified on the grounds that experts should shape the length of a prison term to the time required to bring about rehabilitation, a period which may be short or extend over many years. Similar problems are raised by the involuntary "civil" commitment of those thought to be mentally ill. In all these areas, I think it would be useful to analyze closely whether additional procedural safeguards alone can ever be enough, and whether less individualized standards might not be the more important legal reform. "Ignorance, of itself, is disgraceful only so far as it is avoidable. But when, in our eagerness to find 'better ways' of handling old problems, we rush to measures affecting human liberty and human personality on the assumption that we have knowledge which, in fact, we do not possess, then the problem of ignorance takes on a more sinister hue."[133]

In closing, it is wise to acknowledge that changing the legal standard for removing children is by no means the only strategy for bringing about needed re-

forms in the foster care system. It is arguable, in fact, that political efforts for reform should be devoted not so much toward changing the law as toward improving the foster care system by securing additional resources and devising "better ways" of providing useful services. Certainly facilities should be improved; more public support also would be useful. Dramatic improvements in the operation of the foster care system of new information about its present effects might influence my conclusions. But in analyzing the present foster care system, I am impressed by the relevance of an observation made in another context by Francis Allen:

> We shall be told that progress is obstructed by the lack of public interest and support and by the absence of adequate funds. That these factors are real and their consequences devastating few would care to deny. Yet, these familiar scapegoats do not provide the most fundamental explanations. We should not overlook the fact that, in many areas, our basic difficulties still lie in our ignorance of human behavior and its infinite complexities.[134]

Notes

1. Language in several Supreme Court opinions can be read to suggest that these are constitutional underpinnings for the primary responsibility of the parental role. See, e.g., *Pierce* v. *Society of Sisters,* 268 U.S. 510, 534–35 (1925) where the court struck down an Oregon statute that required parents to send their children to public schools, stating that the statute "unreasonably interferes with the liberty of parents and guardians to direct the upbringing and education of children under their control." See also *Meyer* v. *Nebraska,* 262 U.S. 390 (1923). Com-

pare *Prince* v. *Massachusetts,* 321 U.S. 158 (1944) where the court affirmed the child labor law conviction of an aunt who had a nine-year-old niece in her custody sell Jehovah's Witness literature at night on the street in her presence. The Court emphasized that "the state has a wide range of power for limiting parental freedom and authority in things affecting the child's welfare; and that this includes, to some extent, matters of conscience and religious conviction," *id.* at 167.

2. HEW estimates that on March 31, 1970, there were 326,700 children under eighteen in foster care, approximately 284,500 of whom were under the complete or partial auspices of a public welfare agency. Of the 284,500, 243,600 were in foster family homes; 3,600 were in group homes; and 37,300 were in child welfare institutions. An additional 42,200 children were in foster care under the auspices of voluntary child welfare agencies. See U.S. Dept. of Health, Education, and Welfare, *Children Served by Public Welfare Agencies and Voluntary Child Welfare Agencies and Institutions March 1970,* Publication No. [SRS] 72-03258, March 10, 1972, Table 6.

3. U.S. Bureau of the Census, *Census of Population: 1970 General Social and Economic Characteristics, United States Summary,* PC(1)-C1 (Washington, D.C.: U.S. Government Printing Office, 1972), Table 85, pp. 1–380.

4. California State Social Welfare Board, *Report on Foster Care, Children Waiting* (Sacramento, Calif.: Department of Social Welfare, 1972), p. 7.

5. See Shirley Jenkins and Mignon Sauber, *Paths to Child Placement, Family Situations Prior to Foster Care* (New York: Community Council of Greater New York, 1966), p. 74.

6. See, e.g., *Escobedo* v. *Illinois,* 378 U.S. 478 (1964).

7. *Johnson* v. *Zerbst,* 304 U.S. 458 (1938).

8. See 42 U.S.C. §608(a).

9. See Robert Bremner, ed. *Children and Youth in America* (Cambridge, Mass.: Harvard University Press, 1970), I, pp. 64–70.

10. Bremner, p. 68.

11. Story, 2 *Equity Jurisprudence* Sec. 1341 (1857) (footnotes omitted from quote). For a discussion of the history of child neglect laws, see Mason P. Thomas, "Child Abuse and Neglect, Part I: Historical Overview, Legal Matrix, and Social Perspectives," *North Carolina Law Review,* 50 (1972), p. 293.

12. A recent collection of the citations to these provisions can be found in Sanford M. Katz, *When Parents Fail, The Law's Response to Family Breakdown* (Boston: Beacon Press, 1971), pp. 83–85.

13. See, e.g., Colo. Rev. Stat. Ann. Sec. 22-1-1 (1963).

14. See, e.g., Mass. Ann. Laws ch. 119, Sec. 24 (1965).

15. See, e.g., Cal. Welfare and Institutions Code Sec. 600 (d) (West 1972).

16. See, e.g., Ohio Rev. Code Ann. Sec. 2151.03(c) (1969).

17. See, e.g., Minn. Stat. Ann. 260.15 (b) (d) (1969).

18. For a historical description of how neglected children were cared for, see generally, Homer Folks, *The Care of Destitute, Neglected, and Delinquent Children* (New York: Macmillan, 1902). Various documents can be found in Robert Bremner, ed., *Children and Youth in America,* Vols. I, II(A) and II(B) (Cambridge, Mass.: Harvard University Press, 1970).

19. The child is sometimes taken into custody by the state at the time of this initial report—before any court hearing. The laws of many states authorize "emergency" removal from parental custody without prior court authorization by police, and sometimes social workers and doctors. In California, for example, a policeman with "reasonable

cause for believing" the child is neglected or abused can take a child into
custody without prior judicial authorization (Cal. Welfare & Institutions
Code Sec. 625). The child must be
released to the parents within forty-
eight hours, however, unless a petition
is filed to institute a juvenile court proceeding (Cal. Welfare & Institutions
Code Sec. 631). Moreover, even if a
petition is filed, the statute requires
the court to hold a detention hearing
within twenty-four hours to determine
whether the child should remain in
state custody during the pendency of
the judicial proceedings (see Cal. Welfare & Institutions Code Sec. 632),
which can often take several weeks.
Because there are situations in which
swift removal is of crucial importance
to a child's safety, the power to remove for short periods of time without
prior court approval seems plainly desirable. The important questions relating to what the standard for emergency
removals should be, and how prompt
judicial review of such interim actions
can be insured are beyond the scope
of this paper.

20. Thomas Gill, "The Legal Nature of
Neglect," *National Probation and
Parole Association Journal,* 6 (1960),
p. 14.

21. Letter dated September 25, 1973, from
Los Angeles County Department of
Public Social Services. Calculations
based on this same source suggest that
in 1972, the 3,518 juvenile court petitions filed by the Los Angeles Department of Public Social Services were
disposed of as follows:

Total Petitions	3,518
Dismissed by Department of Public Social Services before final court determination	1,480
Transferred to other jurisdictions	75
Decided by juvenile court	1,963
Dismissed by court	307
Jurisdiction assumed by court	1,656
Supervised within home	628
Removal ordered	1,028
Placed with relatives	149
Placed in foster care	879

22. Unpublished yearly statistical compilation for the San Francisco Juvenile
Court Annual Report for 1972. This
data shows that in 1972, there were
hearings in cases involving 544 children; the court transferred 22 to other
counties and dismissed 119 more without assuming jurisdiction. Of the 402
children for whom the court took jurisdiction, 141 were supervised within
their own home, 59 were ordered
placed with relatives, and 203 were
placed in foster care.

23. See N.Y. Joint Legislative Committee
on Court Reorganization: Report No.
2—The Family Court Act, McKinney's
Session Laws of New York 3428, 3443
(1962).

24. "The Relationship Between Promise
and Performance in State Intervention
in Family Life," *Columbia Journal of
Law and Social Problems,* 9 (1972)
p. 30, citing Note, "An Appraisal of
New York's Statutory Response to the
Problem of Child Abuse," *Columbia
Journal of Law and Social Problems,* 7
(1971), p. 72.

25. See, N.Y. Jt. Legislative Committee on
Court Reorganization; p. 3442. (In
neglect proceedings, 50 percent are
children under age six, 90 percent
under twelve).

26. See, e.g., Shirley Jenkins and Elaine
Norman, *Filial Deprivation and Foster
Care* (New York: Columbia Univer-
sity Press, 1972), pp. 2, 25–30; Martin
Rein, Thomas E. Nutt, and Heather
Weiss, "Foster Care: Myth and Real-
ity," in Alvin Schorr (ed.), *Children
and Decent People* (New York: Basic
Books, forthcoming). For a careful

analysis of how the judicial system treats custody decisions for the poor, see Herma Hill Kay and Irving Phillips, "Poverty and the Law of Child Custody," *California Law Review*, 54 (1966), p. 717. See also Jacobus ten Broek, "California's Dual System of Family Law: Its Origin, Development, and Present Status," *Stanford Law Review*, 16 (1964), p. 257 (Part I); p. 900 (Part II); *Stanford Law Review*, 17 (1965), p. 614 (Part III).

27. See e.g., Jenkins and Norman, *Filial Deprivation*, p. 35, indicating that only eleven percent of the foster children in their sample of 533 foster children in New York City were living with both parents at the time of placement.

28. Jenkins and Sauber, *Paths to Child Placement*, p. 80.

29. See Jenkins and Norman, *Filial Deprivation*, p. 55.

30. See Michael H. Phillips, Ann W. Shyne, Edmund A. Sherman, and Barbara L. Haring, *Factors Associated with Placement Decisions in Child Welfare* (New York: Child Welfare League of America, 1971); Bernice Boehm, "An Assessment of Family Adequacy in Protective Cases," *Child Welfare*, 41 (January 1962), pp. 10–16; Eugene Shinn, "Is Placement Necessary? An Experimental Study of Agreement Among Caseworkers in Making Foster Care Decisions," Diss., Columbia University School of Social Work, 1968.

31. In California, for example, for the period from January 1, 1967, through August 30, 1973, there are a total of fourteen reported appellate opinions for neglect cases—not one by the California Supreme Court. At the present time there are about 15,000 children in foster care for whom a court ordered removal. Most of these were first placed during that period. It seems reasonable to assume that at least as many children both entered and exited

foster care during that period as were initially placed before 1967.

32. This conclusion, based on observations of juvenile court and interviews with social workers and probation officers is consistent with the findings of Phillips, *Factors Associated with Placement*, pp. 72–79, 88, based on a simulation study of the behavior of three juvenile court judges.

33. For 1968, David Gil estimated that a total of 10,931 reports of child abuse were made under state reporting laws. *Violence Against Children, Physical Child Abuse in the United States* (Cambridge, Mass.: Harvard University Press, 1970), p. 92. At that time every state had a law requiring that child abuse be reported. For that same year HEW estimated that Juvenile Courts in the United States handled approximately 141,000 dependency and neglect cases. See United States Children's Bureau, *Juvenile Court Statistics 1968* (Statistical Series No. 95, 1970), p. 15. Although many cases of child abuse go unreported, it is reasonable to assume that most abuse cases that go to court are reported. Moreover, some reported cases of abuse do not result in juvenile court petitions. Therefore, one could reasonably estimate for that year that less than nine percent of the dependency and neglect petitions handled by juvenile courts involved child abuse. There has apparently been an increase in reported abuse cases since 1968, however, while the number of neglect cases handled by courts declined to 130,900 for 1971. See *Juvenile Court Statistics 1971*. Moreover, abuse cases are perhaps more likely to lead to removal than other cases. Based on preliminary work here in California, I would esimate that probably fifteen to twenty percent, and certainly no more than a quarter of the cases where removal is ordered involve intentional physical abuse by a parent.

34. See Alfred Kadushin, "Child Welfare: Adoption and Foster Care," in *Encyclopedia of Social Work*, Ed. R. Morris, 16th ed. (New York: National Association of Social Workers), 1971, Vol. 1, p. 104.

35. See *Children Served by Public Welfare Agencies*, at Table 6. Part of the reason for the preference for foster family care over institutional care is cost. In California, as of June, 1973, for example, the average monthly payment for residential care per child in a foster family home was $124.96; the average monthly payment for children in the institutions was $487.87. California State Department of Social Welfare, *Aid to Families with Dependent Children—Boarding Homes and Institutions Case Load Movement and Expenditure Report* (Department of Social Welfare, Sacramento, June, 1973).

36. In California the monthly rates per foster child paid to foster families are set by the county and vary widely among counties—from $72 to $160 in 1972. California State Department of Social Welfare, Aid to Families with Dependent Children. Differences in the cost of living do not justify these differentials, and one suspects that—as is true for school spending—the differences are in part related to the local wealth. Compare *Serrano* v. *Priest*, 5 Cal. 3d 584, 487 P.2d 1241 (1971). The financing of foster care is extremely complex, with funds coming from both state and federal government. The federal government, as part of the Social Security Act, reimburses states for a portion of cost of foster care for children meeting financial eligibility. See 42 U.S.C. Sec. 608(a). For a complete description of the complexities of the financing of foster care in California, see Childhood and Government Project, Earl Warren Legal Institute, University of California, Berkeley, "The Finance of Foster Care," (Staff Working Paper), 1973.

37. See, e.g., Martin Wolins, *Selecting Foster Parents* (New York: Columbia University Press, 1963), p. 201; Alfred Kadushin, *Child Welfare Services* (New York: Macmillan, 1967), p. 371.

38. Joseph Goldstein and Jay Katz, *The Family and the Law, Problems in Decision in the Family Law Process* (New York: Free Press, 1965), pp. 1021–22.

39. Kadushin, *Child Welfare Services*, p. 411.

40. Henry S. Maas and Richard E. Engler, Jr., *Children in Need of Parents* (New York: Columbia University Press, 1959), p. 356.

41. David Fanshel, "The Exit of Children from Foster Care: An Interim Research Report," *Child Welfare*, 50 (February 1971), pp. 65–81.

42. Kermit Wiltse and Eileen Gambrill, "Decision-Making Processes in Foster Care," unpublished paper, School of Social Welfare, University of California, Berkeley, Calif., 1973.

43. See Ralph W. Crary, "Neglect, Red Tape and Adoption," *National Probation and Parole Association Journal*, 6 (1960), p. 34.

44. Maas and Engler, *Children in Need*, pp. 390–91.

45. Maas and Engler, p. 383.

46. Wiltse and Gambrill.

47. Maas and Engler, p. 379.

48. Helen Jeter, *Children, Problems and Services in Child Welfare Programs* (Washington, D.C.: U.S. Government Printing Office, 1963), p. 87.

49. Jeter, p. 5; 58 percent had more than one placement; Wiltse and Gambrill state that the foster children in their sample typically had two placements.

50. Jeter, p. 87. This same study anticipated only 12 percent would return home. See also Mary Lewis, "Foster-Family Care: Has It Fulfilled Its Promise?" *The Annals*, 355 (1964), pp. 31, 36.

51. See Crary, p. 39.

52. Maas and Engler, p. 390. "In community after community it is clear

from the data in the study that unless children move out of care within the first year to year and a half of their stay in care, the likelihood of their ever moving out sharply decreases."

53. *Finlay* v. *Finlay*, 240 N.Y. 429, 433–34, 148 N.E. 624, 626 (1925).

54. Zuchman & Fox, "The Ferment in Divorce Legislation," *Journal of Family Law* 12 (1972), pp. 515, 571–576.

55. See e.g., *In Re Rocher*, 187 N.W.2d 730, 732 (Iowa, 1971): "Neither the trial court nor this one has—or claims—omniscience. It is never a pleasant task to separate parent and child. We can only take the record as we find it and reach a conclusion which appears to be for the best interest of the children. Both the statute and our previous decisions demand that we do so." *In Re East*, 32 Ohio Misc. 65, 288 N.E.2d 343 (C.P. Juv. Div. Highland County 1972); *In Re Kindis*, 162 Conn. 239, 294 A.2d 316 (1972); *In Re Johnson*, 210 Kan. 828, 504 P.2d 217 (1972); *In Re One Minor Child*, 254 A.2d 443 (Del. Sup. Ct. 1969); *In Re B.G. & V.G.*, 32 C.A. 3d 365, 108 Cal. Rptr. 121 (1973); *Hammond* v. *Department of Public Assistance*, 142 W.Va. 208, 95 S.E. 2d 345 (1956).

56. See *In Re Cager*, 251 Md. 473, 479, 248 A.2d 384, 388 (Md. Ct. App. 1968): "It is clear that the ultimate consideration in finding neglect which will serve as a basis for removing a child from its mother's custody is the best interest of the child."; *Todd* v. *Superior Court*, 68 Wash. 2d 587, 414 P.2d 605 (1966); *State* v. *Pogue*, 282 S.W. 2d 582 (Springfield Mo. Ct. App. 1955).

57. David Matza, *Delinquency and Drift* (New York: John Wiley & Sons, 1964), pp. 114–15.

58. The best interest test has been criticized in the divorce context. For a thorough review of the behavioral science research as it relates to the effects of divorce custody determinations, and an excellent argument for specific statutory presumptions for divorce custody disputes, see Phoebe C. Ellsworth and Robert J. Levy, "Legislative Reform of Child Custody Adjudication," *Law & Society Review*, 4 (1969), p. 167.

59. Anna Freud, "Child Observation and Prediction of Development—A Memorial Lecture in Honor of Ernst Kris," *The Psychoanalytic Study of the Child* (New York: International University Press, 1958), XIII, pp. 92, 97–98. After this article was submitted for publication, I discovered two fascinating essays, one by Anna Freud entitled, "The Child is a Person in His Own Right" and one by Joseph Goldstein, "The Least Detrimental Alternative to the Problem for the Law of Child Placement." Both are found in *The Psychoanalytic Study of the Child* for 1972 (New York: Quadrangle Books, 1973), and are parts of a soon-to-be published book co-authored by Freud, Goldstein, and Albert Solnit entitled *Beyond the Best Interests of the Child*. Goldstein's essay, which takes the form of a judicial opinion, suggests that courts should seek out the "least detrimental available alternative" rather than ask what is in a child's best interests in custody cases. Goldstein's analysis is consistent with my own in that it emphasizes the importance of stability and consistency in parent-child relationships; it criticizes the best interests standard for misleading judges into thinking "they have more power for 'good' than for 'bad' " in what they decide; and it suggests that courts should focus on available alternatives. Although I wonder whether in terms of information, predictions and values Goldstein's alternative standard (if applied to removing children from parental custody for initial placement in foster care) might not be subject to many of the same

criticisms as the best interest standard, I do not wish to base my judgment on the two essays alone for they are obviously part of a more elaborate analysis presented in the forthcoming book. In my expansion of this article that will be published this coming May in the *California Law Review*, I hope to analyze in some detail the Freud, Goldstein, Solnit book, which should soon be available. [New York: The Free Press, 1973.]

60. Sibylle Escalona, *The Roots of Individuality: Normal Patterns of Development in Infancy* (Chicago: Aldine, 1968), p. 13.

61. H. R. Schaffer, *The Growth of Sociability* (Baltimore: Penguin, 1971), p. 16.

62. Arlene Skolnick, *The Intimate Environment, Exploring Marriage and the Family* (Boston: Little Brown, 1973), p. 372.

63. Joan W. Macfarlane, "Perspectives on Personality Consistency and Change from the Guidance Study," *Vita Humana*, 7 (1964), pp. 115–126.

64. Skolnick, pp. 378–79.

65. See *Painter v. Bannister*, 258 Iowa 1390, 140 N.W. 2d 152 (1966).

66. John Rawls, *A Theory of Justice* (Cambridge, Mass.: Harvard University Press, 1971), p. 237.

67. Phillips *et al.*, pp. 69–84.

68. Phillips *et al.*, p. 84.

69. Rein *et al.* See also Katz, *When Parents Fail*, p. 91.

70. See Rein *et al.*

71. See generally, Michael F. Sullivan, "Child Neglect: The Environmental Aspects," *Ohio State Law Journal*, 29 (1968), p. 85.

72. *In Re Anonymous*, 37 Misc. 2d 411, 238 N.Y.S. 2d 422, 423 (Fam. Ct. Rensselaer County, 1962).

73. See *In Re Booth*, 253 Minn. 395, 91 N.W. 2d 921 (1958).

74. *In Re Tammy F.*, Cal. Dist. Ct. App., 1st Dist. Div. 2, No. 32643 (1973).

75. *In Re Three Minors*, 50 Wash. 2d 653, 314 P.2d 423 (1957). See *In re Fish*, 288 Minn. 512, 179 N.W. 2d 175 (1970).

76. See *In Re Watson*, 95 N.Y.S. 2d 798 (Dom. Rel. Ct. 1950): three children were declared neglected because their mother was "incapable by reason of her emotional status, her mental condition and her allegedly deeply religious feeling amounting to fanaticism to properly care, provide and look after the children."; *Hunter v. Powers*, 206 Misc. 784, 135 N.Y.S.2d 371 (Dom. Rel. Ct. 1954): mother, an ardent Jehovah Witness, who left the child alone while she attended Bible discussion, compelled the child to distribute religious literature on the streets during parts of the day and night; *In Re Black*, 3 Utah 2d 315, 283 P.2d 887 (1955): children removed from their parents' home because their parents believed in and practiced plural marriage which they thought to be the law of God.

77. In the Matter of Deborah Gibson, decided June 29, 1973, Cal. Court of Appeal, 2nd App. Dist., Div. 1 (2d Civil No. 40391). See *In Re Q*, 32 Cal. App. 3d 288, 107 Cal. Rptr. 646 (1973).

78. See Monrad G. Paulsen, "Juvenile Courts, Family Courts, and the Poor Man," *California Law Review* 54 (1966) p. 694.

79. See, e.g., *In Re Raya*, 255 Cal. App. 2d 260, 63 Cal. Rptr. 252 (1967): reversing neglect determination premised only on the fact that the parents were living unmarried, with new partners, because they were unable to afford divorce; *State v. Greer*, 311 S.W.2d 49, 52 (Ct. App. Mo.) (1958): reversing a juvenile court decision to remove a baby girl who was "concededly adequately housed, fed, clothed and attended, personally and medically" simply on the ground that mother had on

occasion visited taverns, had been arrested for reckless driving, and had a
child out of wedlock.

80. Katz, *When Parents Fail*, p. 69.
81. See *In re A.J.*, 274 Cal. App. 2d 199,
78 Cal. Rptr., 880 (1969).
82. David Matza, *Delinquency & Drift*,
p. 115.
83. Compare Roy Parker, *Decision in Child
Care* (London: Allen & Unwin, 1966)
with Harry Napier, "Success and Failure in Foster Care," *British Journal of
Social Work*, 2 (Summer, 1972), pp.
187–204.
84. Sophie Theis, *How Foster Children
Turn Out* (New York: State Charitable
Aid Association, 1924), p. 19.
85. Joan McCord, William McCord, and
Emily Thurber, "The Effects of Foster-
Home Placement in the Prevention of
Antisocial Behavior," *Social Service
Review* 34 (1960), pp. 415–420. This
study matched a group of nineteen
potentially delinquent boys living at
home with nineteen boys placed as a
last resort in foster care. Contrary to
their hypothesis, the results showed
that "a significantly higher proportion
of those who had been placed in foster
homes had criminal records in adulthood." See also Elizabeth Meier, "Current Circumstances of Former Foster
Children," *Child Welfare* 44 (1965),
pp. 196–206. A group of eighty-two
persons who had been in foster care
five years or more were interviewed
and their "adjustment" was evaluated.
A higher than normal incidence of
marital breakdown and a higher proportion of illegitimate births were
found. On the other hand, one-half
owned or were buying their own
homes, few needed social services, and
nearly all were self-supporting. See
also Elizabeth Meier, "Adults who
were Foster Children," *Children*, 13
(1966), pp. 16–22; Anne Roe, "The
Adult Adjustment of Children of Alcoholic Parents Raised in Foster
Homes," *Quarterly Journal of Studies*

on Alcohol, 5 (1944), pp. 378–393.
Since 1964, a research group at Columbia University has been engaged in
longitudinal research relating to foster
care. The volume on what happens to
the children in the long-run has not
yet been published.
86. Leon Eisenberg, "The Sins of the Fathers: Urban Decay and Social Pathology," *American Journal of Orthopsychiatry*, 32 (1962), p. 14.
87. Henry Maas, "Highlights of the Foster
Care Project: Introduction," *Child
Welfare*, 38 (July 1959), p. 5.
88. Gordon Trasler, *In Place of Parents:
A Study of Foster Care* (London:
Routledge & Kegan Paul, 1960);
Eugene Weinstein, *The Self-Image of
the Foster Child* (New York: Russell
Sage Foundation, 1960); Jessie Parfit,
ed., *The Community's Children: Long-
term Substitute Care: A Guide for the
Intelligent Layman* (New York: Humanities Press, 1967).
89. Ester Glickman, "Treatment of the
Child and Family after Placement,"
Social Service Review, 28 (September
1954), p. 279. See also John Bowlby,
Maternal Care and Mental Health,
Monograph No. 2 (Geneva: World
Health Organization, 1952). Ner Litt-
ner, *Some Traumatic Effects of Separation and Placement* (New York:
Child Welfare League of America,
1956).
90. Glickman, p. 279.
91. Leontine Young, "Placement from the
Child's Viewpoint," *Social Casework*,
31 (1950), p. 250.
92. See, e.g., *Deprivation of Maternal
Care; A Reassessment of its Effects*
(Geneva: World Health Organization,
1962); Lawrence Casler, *Maternal
Deprivation: A Critical Review of the
Literature*, Monograph No. 26 (Chicago: University of Chicago Press for
Research in Child Development,
1961); Anna Freud and Dorothy
Burlingham, *Infants Without Families;
The Case for and Against Residential*

Nurseries (New York: International University Press, 1944). Much of the early "separation" literature was addressed to the question of institutionalizing children—especially infants. The maternal deprivation literature began focusing on the need for a continuous relationship with the child-caring person—whether at home, in an institution, or in a foster home.

93. Martin Wolins and Irving Piliavin, *Institution or Foster Family: A Century of Debate* (New York: Child Welfare League of America, 1964). Rosemary Dinnage and M. L. Kellmer Pringle, *Foster Home Care, Facts and Fallacies: A Review of Research in the United States, Western Europe, Israel and Great Britain between 1848 and 1966* (London: Longmans, Green, 1967).

94. See Bowlby, Freud, and Napier.

95. Weinstein, p. 47.

96. *In re Jewish Child Care Ass'n*, 5 N.Y. 2d 222, 226, 156 N.E. 2d 700, 702 (1959).

97. Id. For some intriguing materials on the *Jewish Child Care Association* case see Goldstein and Katz, pp. 1027–34.

98. See Weinstein, pp. 47–57, 66–70.

99. J. Bowlby, *Forty-four Juvenile Thieves: Their Characters and Home-life* (London: Bailliere, Tindall & Cov, 1946). Bowlby concludes that children separated from their parents often develop "affection-less characters," incapable of forming lasting attachments and of adhering to society's rules. Elsewhere Bowlby states "The impairment of the capacity for successful parenthood is perhaps the most damaging of all the effects of deprivation," in *Maternal Care and Mental Health*, p. 327.

100. Weinstein, *Self-Image*, p. 66.

101. See footnote 49, and Lewis, p. 37.

102. See Lela Costin, *Child Welfare: Policies and Practice* (New York: McGraw Hill, 1972); Alfred Kadushin, *Child Welfare Services*, p. 420.

103. In many states, such as California,

judges are typically rotated through the juvenile court on a yearly basis.

104. Maas and Engler, p. 389. See Elizabeth Meier, "Adults Who Were Foster Children," *Children*, 13 (1966), pp. 16–22.

105. Maas and Engler, p. 422.

106. Wiltse and Gambrill.

107. See Young, p. 251. "One child in the process of replacement expressed his bitterness well, 'The social workers are the bat and I'm just the ball they sock from one place to another.'"

108. American Humane Association, *Child Protective Services, A National Survey* (Denver, Colo.: American Humane Association, 1967), p. 20. See Monrad G. Paulsen, "Juvenile Courts, Family Courts, and the Poor Man," *California Law Review*, 54 (1966), p. 694.

109. Minnesota is an exception for its statute provides that a child may be removed from the parents "only when his welfare or safety and protection of the public cannot be adequately safeguarded without removal." Minn. Stat. Ann. Sec. 260.011.

110. See Children's Aid Society of New York, "Nine-to-Twenty-four hour Homemaker Service Project," *Child Welfare*, Part 1, 41 (March 1962), p. 99, and Part II, 41 (April 1962), p. 103; Sue Minton, "Homemaker Classes: An Alternative to Foster Care," *Child Welfare*, 52 (March 1973), pp. 188–91.

111. See *In Re Q*, 32 Cal. App. 3d 288, 107 Cal. Rptr. 646 (1973).

112. See Ray Helfer and C. Henry Kempe, *Helping the Battered Child and His Family* (Philadelphia: Lippincott, 1972).

113. See footnote 56.

114. See pp. 601, 604–605 above.

115. See, e.g., Sullivan.

116. I think the jurisdiction/disposition division of the judicial process in neglect cases is not a useful one. Substantive standards should be established for each type of coercive intervention, with

more stringent standards for more intrusive forms of intervention. In other words, there might be one standard for a court to be able to compel protective services; a different standard for a court to allow a child to be removed from his home during the pendency of the case; and yet another standard (such as that suggested in the last section of this article) for the court to remove the child for indefinite period.

117. See Monrad G. Paulsen, "The Law and Abused Children," in *The Battered Child*, ed. Ray Helfer and C. Henry Kempe (Chicago: University of Chicago Press, 1968).

118. Richard Posner, *An Economic Analysis of the Law* (Boston: Little, Brown, 1973).

119. Since *In Re Gault*, 387 U.S. 1 (1967), held that some safeguards available in criminal trials had to be applied in juvenile court delinquency proceedings, there have been numerous articles that have advocated more stringent requirements in dependency proceedings as well. An especially thoughtful analysis of the procedural requirements appropriate in child protective cases is Robert A. Burt, "Forcing Protection on Children and their Parents: The Impact of *Wyman* v. *James*," *Michigan Law Review*, 69 (1971), p. 1259. Other articles on the subject include Thomas T. Becker, "Due Process and Child Protective Proceedings: State Intervention in Family Relations on Behalf of Neglected Children," *Cumberland-Sanford Law Review*, 2 (1971), p. 247; Dianne M. Faber, "Dependent-Neglect Proceedings: A Case for Procedural Due Process," *Duquesne Law Review*, 9 (1971), p. 651; Joseph J. Mogilner, "Admissibility of Evidence in Juvenile Court: A Double Standard or No Standard," *Journal of the State Bar Association of Colorado*, 46 (1971), p. 310; Note, "Child Neglect: Due Process for the Parent," *Colorado Law Review*, 70

(1970), p. 465; Note, "Representation in Child-Neglect Cases: Are Parents Neglected?" *Columbia Journal of Law and Social Problems*, 4 (1968), p. 230.

120. Two cases have held recently that due process requires state assigned counsel for parents when the state is seeking permanently to remove their children. See *Nebraska* v. *Caha*, decided June 8, 1973 (Neb. Sup. Ct.); *Danforth* v. *Maine Dept. of Health*, decided April 17, 1973 (Me. Sup. Ct.).

121. Lon Fuller develops a distinction between "person-oriented" and "act-oriented" legal rules which usefully explains why procedural reform is not likely to eliminate discretion if the legal standard is the best interest of a child "which by its nature cannot be rule-bound." Lon L. Fuller, "Interaction Between Law and Its Social Context," *Sociology of Law*, Summer 1971, University of California, Berkeley (bound class materials). Item 3.

122. Ernst Freund. *Standards of American Legislation* (Chicago: University of Chicago Press, 1917), p. 83.

123. See David Fanshel and Eugene B Shinn, *Dollars and Sense in the Foster Care of Children: A Look at Cost Factors* (New York: Child Welfare League of America, 1972).

124. Despite these procedural safeguards, an occasional case might arise where the state failed to make reasonable efforts to rehabilitate the parents. Termination of parental rights after the fixed time period might nevertheless be appropriate for the child's sake. Alternatively, because of the unfairness to the parent, perhaps the judge should be allowed to do everything short of termination to provide a stable environment for the child, give the parents a damage action against the state for the failure to provide past services, and compel the provision of such services for an additional period of time.

125. Hasseltine B. Taylor, "Guardianship

or 'Permanent Placement' of Children,"
California Law Review, 54 (1966),
p. 741.

126. Professor Michael Wald of Stanford
University Law School suggested to
me the possibility of a shorter time
limit for younger children.

127. See, e.g., *Minor Children of F. B.* v.
Caruthers, 323 S.W. 2d 397 (Mo. Ct.
App. St. Louis 1959); *In Re Black* 3
Utah 2d 315, 283 P.2d 887 (1955); *In
Re Cager,* 251 Md. 473, 248 A.2d 384
(Md. Ct. App. 1968).

128. See, *In Re Jeannie Q.,* 32 Cal. App. 3d
288, 107 Cal. Rptr. 646.

129. Through conversations with Professors
Michael Wald and Robert Burt of the
University of Michigan, the Reporters
for the relevant portion of the ABA
Project, after I was well into writing
this paper, I know that they were independently giving consideration to
standards that would narrow the
grounds that should justify removal
and that would establish time limits
for foster placement after removal.

130. I am grateful to Professor Kermit
Wiltse, School of Social Welfare, University of California, Berkeley, for this
finding.

131. See Matza; Edwin M. Schur, *Radical
Non-Intervention: Rethinking the De-
linquency Problem* (Englewood Cliffs,
N.J.: Prentice-Hall, 1973).

132. See American Friends Service Committee, *Struggle for Justice, A Report
on Crime and Punishment in America*
(New York: Hill and Wang, 1971).

133. Francis A. Allen, *The Borderland of
Criminal Justice* (Chicago: University
of Chicago Press, 1964), p. 13.

134. Allen, p. 12.

When children are removed from their parents, the public officials who order and perform the removal see themselves as acting in the child's interests. The law concurs, and typically no independent counsel is appointed to represent the child. When parents go to law on their child's behalf, they too see themselves as acting in the child's best interest. Again, no independent counsel is appointed to represent the child. In many such cases, the assumption that parents or public officials are the best or at least adequate guardians of a child's interests is correct; but in others, the possibly conflicting interests of parents or officials provide reasons to appoint separate counsel for children when there is litigation.

The American Civil Liberties Union has taken up many benchmark cases involving children. Typically they have acted on behalf of *parents and their children.* This dual role can, however, present conflicts of interest. In this essay, which was originally an internal memorandum for ACLU lawyers, Rena K. Uviller, head of the ACLU's Juvenile Rights Project, discusses some of the dilemmas which arise for child advocates.

If the interests of children are—as both Jeffrey Blustein and William Ruddick argue they are—neither wholly separable from nor wholy identical with those of their parents, then these are deep dilemmas. To appoint independent counsel for children risks misconstruing their interests as independent of and adversarial to those of their parents. Not to appoint independent counsel for children risks misconstruing their interests as subsumable under those of a parent or of an official charged with some aspect of child welfare. In either case, children's interests in having the interests of their families sustained are likely to be obscured.

CHILDREN VERSUS PARENTS: PERPLEXING POLICY QUESTIONS FOR THE ACLU

RENA K. UVILLER

In fulfilling its mandate as a defender of the Bill of Rights, the American Civil Liberties Union has assumed a reasonably well-defined role in asserting the rights of the individual adult against governmental excesses. With children, however, ACLU policy is less palpable. The need for a clearer children's policy has been demonstrated by the extent of recent inquiry by ACLU affiliates concerning our position on children's issues and by the disparate views and values of ACLU lawyers themselves, which have emerged in the course of litigation.

The difficulty in articulating a workable children's policy for ACLU stems principally from two causes. First, there is a potential conflict between the rights of children and those of another ACLU constituency—parents. Second, there is an extraordinary amount of ill-conceived rhetoric that suffuses the emerging "children's rights" movement, impeding analysis of the issues. For example, those who assert each child's "right" to love, security, good health, and the means to reach maturity rarely consider who is to provide this bounty. Nor do they consider how such "rights" can be converted into enforceable legal entitlements. If it is assumed that the state will be the benefactor, rarely do the proponents of greater government benefits to children consider how oppressive state control can be for parents and, ultimately, for the children themselves.

Equally unhelpful are those who would emancipate children from their families altogether, allowing them to make their own decisions. The child emancipators would, for example, give children a free choice about where and with whom to live and whether to attend school. This sort of liberation rhetoric dramatizes the perception that children often do suffer from oppressive parental control. Yet it does not account for the fact that very young children, at least, are inherently dependent upon someone. To liberate them from their parents is simply to assign them to another, potentially more oppressive protector.

There is, moreover, a growing line of Supreme Court decisions which recognize that the right of parents to the custody, care, and control of their children is a fundamental freedom upon which the state cannot infringe in the absence of compelling cause.[1] If the freedom to bear and raise children is constitutionally protected, how can these parental rights be reconciled with the absolute autonomy of children? Indeed, can parents be obliged to support children who are "liberated" from their supervision and control?

In the past, ACLU advocacy of children's rights involved youths and their parents who together were insisting that the state not treat children invidiously. Thus, in the landmark Supreme Court case of *In re Gault* (1967), the ACLU argued for a due process hearing before children accused of criminal violations could be taken from their parents and deprived of their liberty. In *Tinker v. Des Moines School Board* (1969), children and their parents successfully challenged on First Amendment grounds a school regulation that prohibited students from wearing black armbands to protest the Vietnam War. In neither *Gault* nor *Tinker* was there overt conflict between children and their parents. Dissenting in *Tinker*, however, Justice Hugo Black observed that the minors involved in the case included the thirteen- and fifteen-year-old children of parents committed to the anti-war cause. The unmistakable inference was that the freedom of speech being vindicated was that of the parents, and the children had no choice in the matter.

In recent ACLU litigation, children's rights have been more openly in conflict with those of their parents. Determining which should yield—whose interests, parent's or child's, the ACLU should advance—is difficult. Even where the child's cause is assumed, it is not easy to determine precisely what the child's interests are, particularly in cases involving infants or children too young to express their own views. Indeed, a subsidiary issue of considerable delicacy is to determine who properly represents young children in a courtroom. A lawyer's personal experience and values inevitably shape the client's legal representation; this is especially so where the client is a very young child. It is not uncommon for legal advocacy groups purporting to speak for children to challenge each other with failing to advance the child's cause in favor of the lawyer's own institutional or political agenda.

Custody

The foregoing concerns were strikingly evident in Smith v. *Organization of Foster Families for Equality and Reform* (*O.F.F.E.R.*), in which the Supreme Court in 1977 considered the constitutionality of New York laws and practices governing the removal of children from foster homes. *O.F.F.E.R.* was a class action suit brought by the New York Civil Liberties Union, initially on behalf of foster guardians who have had a particular child in their care for a year or more and on behalf of all foster children who have been with one family for a year or more. The NYCLU asserted the right of both the children and the foster guardians to a due process hearing before the defendants (public and private child care agencies) could take the children from their foster homes either to place them with new foster families or to return them to their natural parents.

The federal district court ruled that

the NYCLU could not represent both the children and the foster guardians because of a potential conflict of interest between them, and assigned a separate lawyer for the children. The lawyer assigned, however, had for many years represented the very agencies who were the defendants in the case. She was designated by the court because of her familiarity with the issues and her long-standing professional concern for children. Reflecting her own values and experience, however, she argued that the children neither desired nor needed the hearing which the NYCLU complaint sought on their behalf. Rather, she insisted that the defendant agencies could best look after the children's interests.

To complicate the matter further, a class of poor natural parents whose children were in foster care intervened in the lawsuit. They argued against a pre-removal hearing on the ground that such a hearing would constitute another bureaucratic obstacle to the return of their children to them; that their children were taken from them unfairly in the first place; and that a hearing would only prolong the separation. Even more persuasively, they argued that the very existence of the right to a hearing presupposes that their children and/or the foster guardians have a competing substantive right to each other's association that can be asserted against a fit natural parent's right to custody.

The *O.F.F.E.R.* case is an exceptional vehicle for examining the complex considerations in formulating a children's rights policy for the ACLU, especially where child custody is the issue. Do children have independent rights against their parents? In the context of *O.F.F.E.R.*, do they have a right to a hearing at which they might refuse to return to their parents, or at least delay that return? By arguing that they do have rights vis-à-vis their parents, do we encourage broad state intervention in family life, especially on behalf of very young children, who cannot express their own interests and whose cause will be zealously assumed by various child advocates, both public and private? This very much contradicts our position in other cases, in which we strongly resist state intervention for the purported benefit of children.

It may be that children's rights will be vindicated only by steadfastly resisting all state encroachment upon the authority of parents to raise their children, particularly where parents do not seek or wish the state's involvement. This is especially true for poor families, where state intervention "in the child's best interest" usually means the family's dissolution—either by incarcerating the children or by placing them in foster care. In order to stem the growing tide of familial dissolution, it may be necessary to reject the notion that children have independent interests which they or a state agency purporting to act on their behalf can assert against parents.

On the other hand, a policy of family inviolability may be prompted as much by political considerations as by a constitutional analysis of children's rights. If we urge that children do not have rights against their parents, it may be fair to say that we are not child advocates at all, but parents' advocates. How can we represent children, particularly older children, if we do not assert what they wish? If we fail to assert their wishes, however ill advised, we become just one more voice telling youths what is good for them, without regard for their own perceived self-interest.

It is well to ask, in any event, by what authority we speak for children. As lawyers, how do we purport to represent them, especially the very young ones, who can neither retain us nor tell us what they want? Are their views not derived essentially from the adults closest to them? By virtue of the inherent dependence of young children upon one benefactor or another, do we not inevitably represent the benefactor, whether it is the foster parents in *O.F.F.E.R.* or the natural parents in *Alsager* v. *District Court?* [*Eds.* Full reference is given on p. 358.]

In *Alsager,* the ACLU successfully challenged an Iowa statute that authorized the permanent termination of parental rights under a statute that was typically vague and whose application required a showing of only minimal harm to children. The evidence against the Alsager parents was that although they had a devoted and loving relationship with their children, they kept a dirty house, provided no intellectual stimulation for their mentally handicapped children, and were lackadaisical in their supervision. We argued that the state's paternalism in seeking to provide the Alsager children "with a more stimulating environment" was an unconstitutional usurpation of parental rights and necessarily discriminates against the poor.

In *Alsager,* as in *O.F.F.E.R.,* the court ruled that we could represent the parents but not the children, although there was no real conflict of interest between the two. In a period of four years, the four Alsager children had experienced more than fifteen foster placements among them. They as well as their parents had clearly suffered at the state's hands. Yet the principle that the case establishes has been criticized as being contrary to the interests of children. Properly observed, *Alsager* makes it considerably more difficult for the state to protect children against marginal parents, even where stable and permanent alternatives are available. According to the *Alsager* rationale, unless parents have been flagrantly neglectful —exposing their children to risk of death or substantial physical impairment—the state may not assume custody in order to provide children with happier surroundings. Because the highly relative "child's best interest" standard is rejected as a basis for family dissolution, our efforts in the *Alsager* case have been condemned by some child advocates.

The charge that we ignored children's interests in favor of parents was also leveled in a series of cases in which we sought to regain for Vietnamese parents the custody of children who were evacuated from South Vietnam in the closing days of the war. Various state agencies in this country placed these children for adoption with American families, usually stable, loving, and able to provide far greater material advantage than the natural families. In some instances the children, long separated from their natural families, have expressed a strong desire to remain with their foster guardians.

We believe our position in these Vietnamese cases is correct, both from a children's rights and a broader civil liberties perspective. If the right to bear and raise children is a fundamental liberty safeguarded by the Bill of Rights, then it cannot be abridged by a "best interest of the child" standard or the passage of time created by exigent circumstances such as a war. Unless parents have fallen below some minimal standard of fitness, children, too, are ultimately the losers if the state is empowered to reassign them to surrogate par-

ents on the basis of speculative psychological theories of child welfare. Critics of our position in the Vietnamese cases, however, assert that as in *Alsager*, we are not really child advocates in the clash between parent and child.

Status Offender Statutes and Curfew Laws

The potential clash between the interests of parents and children is evident in other areas as well. For example, the ACLU has consistently pressed for the repeal of status offender laws. These laws empower juvenile courts to incarcerate youngsters for "incorrigibility." The behavior typically punished, in addition to truancy, is running away from home and general disharmony between parents and children. The ACLU has opposed these laws because they permit the state to incarcerate youths in dismal institutions for non-criminal behavior. Also, their application is flagrantly discriminatory. These laws result in dramatically invidious treatment of poor children, and are used with special harshness against girls.

Yet there is one troubling implication to our resistance to status offender laws. With their abolition, parents will not be able to turn to the state to enforce even reasonable parental authority. This may not be an important consideration with regard to older adolescents. Well before the age of eighteen (the age of majority in most states), youths should be allowed to make their own decisions on a range of issues irrespective of parental consent. These might include decisions regarding medical treatment, religious practices, and education.

The abolition of status offender

laws, however, would deprive parents of one means of enforcing their judgments and values regarding younger children as well. At least symbolically, these laws represent parental control over the daily lives of children who are indisputably too young to make their own decisions. At the very minimum, non-neglecting parents need some means to ensure the child's physical presence in the home. Status offender laws, implicitly or explicitly, have been relied upon for that purpose. Their abolition may encourage the state itself to assume direct control over children, either through broader neglect laws or other means. If a young child cannot be made to stay at home or to conform to the parents' decisions regarding medical treatment, religion, and so forth, the state is invariably prompted to assume the parental role. Status offender laws are a conspicuously poor and heavy-handed means for enforcing parental authority. They have even less legitimacy when parents invoke them in order to relinquish custody of their children altogether to state institutions. Yet their abolition requires us to consider alternative means of sustaining parental judgments within the family unit lest the state fill the vacuum.

Similarly the ACLU has also challenged non-emergency curfews for minors on the theory that they impinge upon First Amendment rights of the minors as well as upon parental rights. The latter assumes that parents do not want the state to interfere with their own authority to regulate their children's hours. On the other hand, insofar as parents have a right to make these decisions for their children, it is arguable that they must have means to enforce their decisions through state authority. It may be that this can be accomplished only

through a curfew, albeit a narrowly defined one, which punishes children for not obeying the curfew set by their parents—again, a conflict between a parent's interests and those of the child.

The formulation of a children's rights policy is thus far more complex than determining policy in many other areas. Undiluted advocacy of children's rights may unintentionally invite the state to assume the parental role, wreaking havoc with principles of personal liberty and family privacy on which we otherwise stand firm. From the children's perspective, as well, broad and intrusive state intervention may be more inimical to their welfare than the palpable failings of their parents. Thus, reluctance in asserting rights of children against their parents does not necessarily stem from faith in the wisdom or beneficence of parents. Rather, it springs from a profound skepticism that the state has ever acted or is capable of acting *in loco parentis* with more wisdom or justice and less irrationality or tyranny than a child's own parents.

The most desirable approach may well be one of strong resistance to dilution of parental authority. Such a policy would conform both to a commitment to the constitutional right of family privacy and a practical recognition that social engineering for "the best interests of children" has been one of the more destructive forms of state paternalism. There are, however, three situations in which principles of family privacy should yield to other values. The most obvious, of course, is the protection of children from parents who fall below a minimally acceptable level of fitness. This involves state intervention to safeguard children from parents who subject them to serious physical abuse or the risk of loss of life itself.

There may also be a few clearly identified substantive areas that we believe are more important than family autonomy and privacy—for example, according young girls substantial self-determination regarding decisions on contraception and abortion. This is not to deny the potential for state abuse when parental control is abridged. Authorizing the sterilization of unwitting minors who are without parental guidance may be a greater hazard than withholding contraception from them in the absence of parental consultation. Yet on balance, the need for reproductive autonomy by youths may be more compelling than their need for parental protection from state abuse.

Finally, there are situations in which parents are no longer able or willing to assume the daily care of their children and transfer their custody to the state—for example, when parents seek to commit a child to a mental hospital or, in the case of status offenders, to a corrective facility. The family, or at least the parent-child relationship, is already functionally abridged in these cases. Such children *should* possess the capacity to assert independent interests and to challenge parental decisions.

Realistically, of course, the child whose parents cannot or will not keep him rarely has any alternative but the state for safekeeping. Nonetheless, it is appropriate to accord standing to the child or his advocates, even though the advocates may be state agents, to resist and oppose parental choices for the child's future. When parents are determined to relinquish custody—for valid or invalid reasons—principles of family autonomy and privacy are far less compelling, and children should be able to invoke state authority to their own advantage.

Note

1. In *Stanley* v. *Illinois* (1972), for example, the Supreme Court held that a state statute which, upon the death of a mother, interfered with an unmarried father's custody of children he raised from birth violated the Fourteenth Amendment. "It is cardinal with us," quoted Justice Byron White from an earlier line of cases, "that the custody, care and nurture of the child reside first in the parents, whose primary function and freedom include preparation for obligations the state can neither supply nor hinder" 405 U.S. at 651.

   This principle of "family integrity" has been reaffirmed by the Supreme Court with increasing frequency in recent years. See, e.g., *Moore* v. *City of East Cleveland* (1977), in which a municipal zoning ordinance was invalidated for interfering with the right of a grandmother to raise her grandchildren. Also, see *Smith* v. *Organization of Foster Families* (1977), in which the Court examined the relationship between parents, children and foster guardians. In his concurring opinion, Justice Potter Stewart observed that ". . . [i]f a State were to attempt to force the breakup of a natural family, over the objections of the parents and their children, without some showing of unfitness and for the sole reason that to do so was thought to be in the children's best interest, I should have little doubt that the State would have intruded impermissibly on the 'private realm of family life which the state cannot enter, . . .'" 53 L.Ed. 2d at 46–7.

3. Mothers and Fathers

We are all inclined to set high standards where we are most conscious of failing. By doing so, we perhaps convince ourselves that, since many fail, our own poor achievement was unremarkable. Jean-Jacques Rousseau was a conspicuous failure, indeed a non-starter, as a father, for he deposited his five infant children outside a foundling hospital. But he sets the most demanding standards for parents: "The real nurse is the mother and the real teacher is the father." There are, in Rousseau's view, only two clearly differentiated parental roles, one naturally appropriate for female and the other for male parents. Good parents do not delegate their tasks, nor do they exchange them.

It is the father who acquires the more burdensome, indeed superhuman, task: "for the training of a man one must either be a father or more than a man." Mothers nurture, but fathers support, educate, and also nurture. Rousseau would require such a father-tutor to watch solicitously over his child from birth until marriage; to share all the child's activities and shelter it from the corrupting effect of playmates and other social occasions; to foster the child's growth in knowledge and goodness; and, as the child grows older, to instruct and advise. It is hard to see how fathers who do what Rousseau requires of them would have time to carry out the other duties he lays on them. How will they find time to support their families and be good husbands if they are single-mindedly devoted to one child? How will they be adequate fathers of many children?

Perhaps some realization that what we ought to do must be something which we can do underlies Rousseau's concession that some fathers will have to delegate some of their tasks. Rousseau's imaginary pupil Emile is brought up not by his father, but by a tutor, a man who has miraculously shed all other ties and responsibilities for the twenty-five years of Emile's childhood and youth. But the relationship between Emile and his tutor remains close to filial. This tutor, like a parent, cannot resign or give up; like parents, he must work for love and not for pay; and unlike most teachers, he has but one pupil. His reward after supervising Emile's growth and education with loving, meticulous, but unobtrusive care (which Rousseau takes some four hundred pages to describe) is that when Emile is himself on the brink of fatherhood, he tells his old tutor, as new parents sometimes tell new grandparents, that this is where his job ends. Emile has turned out to be Rousseau's ideal father and will not delegate the duties of fatherhood.

EMILE

JEAN-JACQUES ROUSSEAU

Plants are fashioned by cultivation, man by education. If a man were born tall and strong, his size and strength would be of no good to him till he had learnt to use them; they would even harm him by preventing others from coming to his aid; left to himself he would die of want before he knew his needs. We lament the helplessness of infancy; we fail to perceive that the race would have perished had not man begun by being a child.

We are born weak, we need strength; helpless, we need aid; foolish, we need reason. All that we lack at birth, all that we need when we come to man's estate, is the gift of education.

This education comes to us from nature, from men, or from things. The inner growth of our organs and faculties is the education of nature, the use we learn to make of this growth is the education of men, what we gain by our experience of our surroundings is the education of things.

Thus we are each taught by three masters. If their teaching conflicts, the scholar is ill-educated and will never be at peace with himself; if their teaching agrees, he goes straight to his goal, he lives at peace with himself, he is well-educated.

Now of these three factors in education nature is wholly beyond our control, things are only partly in our power; the education of men is the only one controlled by us; and even here our power is largely illusory, for who can

hope to direct every word and deed of all with whom the child has to do.

Viewed as an art, the success of education is almost impossible, since the essential conditions of success are beyond our control. Our efforts may bring us within sight of the goal, but fortune must favor us if we are to reach it.

What is this goal? As we have just shown, it is the goal of nature. Since all three modes of education must work together, the two that we can control must follow the lead of that which is beyond our control. . . .

Everything should therefore be brought into harmony with these natural tendencies, and that might well be if our three modes of education merely differed from one another; but what can be done when they conflict, when instead of training man for himself you try to train him for others? Harmony becomes impossible. Forced to combat either nature or society, you must make your choice between the man and the citizen, you cannot train both.

. . . There remains the education of the home or of nature; but how will a man live with others if he is educated for himself alone? If the twofold aims could be resolved into one by removing the man's self-contradictions, one great obstacle to his happiness would be gone. To judge of this you must see the man full-grown; you must have noted his inclinations, watched his progress, followed his steps; in a word you must really know a natural man. When you have read this work, I think you will have made some progress in this inquiry. What must be done to train this ex-

Excerpts from Everyman edition, trans. B. Foxley. © E. P. Dutton & Co. and J. M. Dent and Sons Ltd. Pp. 6–21, 444. Reprinted by permission.

222

ceptional man! We can do much, but the chief thing is to prevent anything being done. To sail against the wind we merely follow one tack and another; to keep our position in a stormy sea we must cast anchor. Beware, young pilot, lest your boat slip its cable or drag its anchor before you know it.

In the social order where each has his own place a man must be educated for it. If such a one leave his own station he is fit for nothing else. His education is only useful when fate agrees with his parents' choice; if not, education harms the scholar, if only by the prejudices it has created. In Egypt, where the son was compelled to adopt his father's calling, education had at least a settled aim; where social grades remain fixed, but the men who form them are constantly changing, no one knows whether he is not harming his son by educating him for his own class.

In the natural order men are all equal and their common calling is that of manhood, so that a well-educated man cannot fail to do well in that calling and those related to it. It matters little to me whether my pupil is intended for the army, the church, or the law. Before his parents chose a calling for him nature called him to be a man. Life is the trade I would teach him. When he leaves me, I grant you, he will be neither a magistrate, a soldier, nor a priest; he will be a man. . . .

. . . If men were born attached to the soil of our country, if one season lasted all the year round, if every man's fortune were so firmly grasped that he could never lose it, then the established method of education would have certain advantages; the child brought up to his own calling would never leave it, he could never have to face the difficulties of any other condition. But when we consider the fleeting nature of human affairs, the restless and uneasy spirit of our times, when every generation overturns the work of its predecessor, can we conceive a more senseless plan than to educate a child as if he would never leave his room, as if he would always have his servants about him? If the wretched creature takes a single step up or down he is lost. This is not teaching him to bear pain; it is training him to feel it.

People think only of preserving their child's life; this is not enough, he must be taught to preserve his own life when he is a man, to bear the buffets of fortune, to brave wealth and poverty, to live at need among the snows of Iceland or on the scorching rocks of Malta. In vain you guard against death; he must needs die; and even if you do not kill him with your precautions, they are mistaken. Teach him to live rather than to avoid death: life is not breath, but action, the use of our senses, our mind, our faculties, every part of ourselves which makes us conscious of our being. Life consists less in length of days than in the keen sense of living. A man may be buried at a hundred and may never have lived at all. He would have fared better had he died young.

. . . Would you restore all men to their primal duties, begin with the mothers; the results will surprise you. Every evil follows in the train of the first sin; the whole moral order is disturbed, nature is quenched in every breast, the home becomes gloomy, the spectacle of a young family no longer stirs the husband's love and the stranger's reverence. The mother whose children are out of sight wins scanty esteem; there is no home life, the ties of nature are not strengthened by those of habit; fathers, mothers, children, brothers, and sisters cease to exist. They are almost strangers; how should they love one another? Each thinks of himself first. When the home is a gloomy solitude pleasure will be sought elsewhere.

But when mothers deign to nurse their own children, then will be a reform in morals; natural feeling will revive in every heart; there will be no lack of citizens for the state; this first step by itself will restore mutual affection. The charms of home are the best antidote to vice. The noisy play of children, which we thought so trying, becomes a delight; mother and father rely more on each other and grow dearer to one another; the marriage tie is strengthened. In the cheerful home life the mother finds her sweetest duties and the father his pleasantest recreation. Thus the cure of this one evil would work a wide-spread reformation; nature would regain her rights. When women become good mothers, men will be good husbands and fathers.

No mother, no child; their duties are reciprocal, and when ill done by the one they will be neglected by the other. The child should love his mother before he knows what he owes her. If the voice of instinct is not strengthened by habit it soon dies, the heart is still-born. From the outset we have strayed from the path of nature.

Would you keep him as nature made him? Watch over him from his birth. Take possession of him as soon as he comes into the world and keep him till he is a man; you will never succeed otherwise. The real nurse is the mother and the real teacher is the father. Let them agree in the ordering of their du-

ties as well as in their method, let the child pass from one to the other. He will be better educated by a sensible though ignorant father than by the cleverest master in the world. For zeal will atone for lack of knowledge, rather than knowledge for lack of zeal. But the duties of public and private business! Duty indeed! Does a father's duty come last.* It is not surprising that the man whose wife despises the duty of suckling her child should despise its education. There is no more charming picture than that of family life; but when one feature is wanting the whole is marred. If the mother is too delicate to nurse her child, the father will be too busy to teach him. Their children, scattered about in schools, convents, and colleges, will find the home of their affections elsewhere, or rather they will form the habit of caring for nothing. Brothers and sisters will scarcely know each other; when they are together in company they will behave as strangers. When there is no confidence between relations, when the family society ceases to give savor to life, its place is soon usurped by vice. Is there any man so stupid that he cannot see how all this hangs together?

A father has done but a third of his task when he begets children and provides a living for them. He owes men to

* When we read in Plutarch that Cato the Censor, who ruled Rome with such glory, brought up his own sons from the cradle, and so carefully that he left everything to be present when their nurse, that is to say their mother, bathed them; when we read in Suetonius that Augustus, the master of the world which he had conquered and which he himself governed, himself taught his grandsons to write, to swim, to understand the beginnings of science, and that he always had them with him, we cannot help smiling at the little people of those days who amused themselves with such follies, and who were too ignorant, no doubt, to attend to the great affairs of the great people of our own time.

humanity, citizens to the state. A man who can pay this threefold debt and neglects to do so is guilty, more guilty, perhaps, if he pays it in part than when he neglects it entirely. He has no right to be a father if he cannot fulfill a father's duties. Poverty, pressure of business, mistaken social prejudices, none of these can excuse a man from his duty, which is to support and educate his own children. If a man of any natural feeling neglects these sacred duties he will repent it with bitter tears and will never be comforted.

But what does this rich man do, this father of a family, compelled, so he says, to neglect his children? He pays another man to perform those duties which are his alone. Mercenary man! Do you expect to purchase a second father for your child? Do not deceive yourself; it is not even a master you have hired for him, it is a flunkey, who will soon train such another as himself.

There is much discussion as to the characteristics of a good tutor. My first requirement, and it implies a good many more, is that he should not take up his task for reward. There are callings so great that they cannot be undertaken for money without showing our unfitness for them; such callings are those of the soldier and the teacher.

"But who must train my child?" "I have just told you, you should do it yourself." "I cannot." "You cannot! Then find a friend. I see no other course."

A tutor! What a noble soul! Indeed for the training of a man one must either be a father or more than man. It is this duty you would calmly hand over to a hireling!

Can such a one be found? I know not. In this age of degradation who knows the height of virtue to which man's soul may attain? But let us assume that this prodigy has been discovered. We shall learn what he should be from the consideration of his duties. I fancy the father who realizes the value of a good tutor will contrive to do without one, for it will be harder to find one than to become such a tutor himself; he need search no further, nature herself having done half the work.

. . . People seek a tutor who has already educated one pupil. This is too much; one man can only educate one pupil; if two were essential to success, what right would he have to undertake the first? With more experience you may know better what to do, but you are less capable of doing it; once this task has been well done, you will know too much of its difficulties to attempt it a second time—if ill done, the first attempt augurs badly for the second.

It is one thing to follow a young man about for four years, another to be his guide for five-and-twenty. You find a tutor for your son when he is already formed; I want one for him before he is born. Your man may change his pupil every five years; mine will never have but one pupil. . . .

If the master is to be so carefully chosen, he may well choose his pupil, above all when he proposes to set a pattern for others. This choice cannot depend on the child's genius or character, as I adopt him before he is born, and they are only known when my task is finished. If I had my choice I would take a child of ordinary mind, such as I assume in my pupil. It is ordinary people who have to be educated, and their education alone can serve as a pattern for the education of their fellows. . . .

. . . No matter whether he has father or mother, having undertaken their duties I am invested with their rights. He must honor his parents, but he must obey me. That is my first and only condition.

I must add that there is just one other point arising out of this; we must never be separated except by mutual consent. This clause is essential, and I would have tutor and scholar so inseparable that they should regard their fate as one. If once they perceive the time of their separation drawing near, the time which must make them strangers to one another, they become strangers then and there; each makes his own little world, and both of them being busy in thought with the time when they will no longer be together, they remain together against their will. The disciple regards his master as the badge and scourge of childhood, the master regards his scholar as a heavy burden which he longs to be rid of. Both are looking forward to the time when they will part, and as there is never any real affection between them, there will be scant vigilance on the one hand, and on the other scant obedience.

But when they consider they must always live together, they must needs love one another, and in this way they really learn to love one another. The pupil is not ashamed to follow as a child the friend who will be with him in manhood; the tutor takes an interest in the efforts whose fruits he will enjoy, and the virtues he is cultivating in his pupil form a store laid up for his old age.

This agreement made beforehand assumes a normal birth, a strong, well-made, healthy child. A father has no choice, and should have no preference within the limits of the family God has given him; all his children are his alike, the same care and affection is due to all. Crippled or well-made, weak or strong, each of them is a trust for which he is responsible to the Giver, and nature is a party to the marriage contract along with husband and wife.

But if you undertake a duty not imposed upon you by nature, you must secure beforehand the means for its fulfilment, unless you would undertake duties you cannot fulfill. . . .

One morning a few months later Emile enters my room and embraces me, saying, "My master, congratulate your son; he hopes soon to have the honor of being a father. What a responsibility will be ours, how much we shall need you! Yet God forbid that I should let you educate the son as you educated the father. God forbid that so sweet and holy a task should be fulfilled by any but myself, even though I should make as good a choice for my child as was made for me! But continue to be the teacher of the young teachers. Advise and control us; we shall be easily led; as long as I live I shall need you. I need you more than ever now that I am taking up the duties of manhood. You have done your own duty: teach me to follow your example, while you enjoy your well-earned leisure.

Few children grow up with Rousseauian parents. Many families, including all those with a single parent or parent substitute and all those in which one parent is wholly taken up with activity outside the home, find that parental tasks cannot be rigidly divided into paternal and maternal ones. Most families must delegate much of their children's upbringing to others, especially to professional educators; and most children learn much not in Emile's isolation but among groups of their peers. Clearly, many of these departures from ideal Rousseauian life do not harm children; and some are commonly believed to be beneficial. So, parents who are trying to decide which sorts of parental activity they will carry out, and how they will divide these activities between them, will find the ideal that Rousseau presents unhelpful (or indeed unacceptably sexist). They need to know which parental tasks and activities they can and ought to do themselves, and which they can and perhaps ought to delegate. They need to work out how to divide parental tasks and activities when there is more than one parent or parent substitute.

Virginia Held considers the ways in which such tasks and activities ought to be allocated in families with both mothers and fathers. While there is general agreement that parents have equal obligations, it is not at all clear how parental obligations can be measured or compared. Tradition, and many legal codes, view mothers' and fathers' duties as separate but equal; fathers support their families and mothers nurture them. (Formal education is for the professionals.) This particular account of the equality of obligations does not fit well with the practice of many families, or with social changes which have led more and more mothers to work away from their homes to (help) support their children. Nor is it clear that supporting and nurturing generally make equal demands of parents. Nurturing in modern (sub)urban life can often be an isolating, day-long, and daily task which erodes longer-term work and life prospects; in other circumstances, nurturing may be a satisfying, sociable, and even creative form of life. Supporting a family is, at worst, drudgery in which health may be lost and spirit broken. At its most fortunate, it can be an absorbing sociable activity which earns success and respect but does not consume all a person's energy. Such circumstances are clearly relevant to working out what equal parental commitments and obligation would require. Virginia Held here suggests principles for allocating parental obligations which take these circumstances into account.

THE EQUAL OBLIGATIONS
OF MOTHERS AND FATHERS

VIRGINIA HELD

Over and over, one encounters the argument: if a woman chooses to become a mother, she must accept a recognized set of responsibilities and obligations that are quite different from the responsibilities and obligations of being a father. In the eyes of many people, a father is expected to contribute some of his income for the expenses his child makes necessary. A mother is expected to give up whatever other work may interfere with her availability to care for her child and to take full care of the child—cheerfully and contentedly, to whatever extent, and as long as the child needs it. And if it is thought that the child will develop problems due to early separations from a parent, it is the mother who will be thought responsible for preventing them.

Recent and still existing law, in its characteristically obtuse way in this domain, deals almost entirely with "support" of the child in the sense of paying the bills for the child's food, clothing, shelter, etc. This is thought to be the father's obligation; if he is unwilling or unable to fulfill it, it becomes the mother's. The mother, just by virtue of being a wife, has standardly been expected by the law to "render services in the home," as it is often put, and these services include, incidentally, caring for any children who happen to be in it. As summarized in a legal textbook published not long ago, *The Law of Domestic Relations,* "the husband is to provide the family with food, clothing, shelter, and as many of the amenities of life as he can manage. . . . The wife is to be mistress of the household, maintaining the home with the resources furnished by the husband, and caring for the children."[1] And as the author says, in a judgment not yet outdated, "a reading of contemporary judicial opinions leaves the impression that these roles have not changed over the last two hundred years."[2]

A few states have made some changes to bring the law in line with state equal rights amendments. And if the federal Equal Rights Amendment is adopted, it may bring about quite significant changes in the law. But courts will continue to be dominated for a long time by conservative, middle-aged men, and, more importantly, the law seldom enters into the domestic picture until there is a breakdown of a marriage. While the marriage is intact, the law leaves husband and wife great latitude to work out their domestic arrangements; when the marriage falls apart, courts decide how to divide up possessions and obligations. The possibilities of dividing parental obligations equally, even at this point, are only beginning to be explored.[3]

In the attitudes of society, "motherhood" is often taken to be an occupation (though unpaid) which women can perform the way men can be auto workers, or bankers, or professors. In a recent article by a social scientist, one comes across the following view: "Once

I am grateful to Sissela Bok, Sandra Harding, and the editors of this volume for their helpful comments.

228

these successive needs—the physical, the social-affectional, and the equal esteem or dignity needs—are sufficiently gratified, humans are not even then content: they then begin to look for that kind of activity that is particularly suited to them as unique individuals. Whether their competence is to be a ditchdigger, a powershovel operator, a construction foreman, a civil engineer or a building contractor, an architect, a mother, a writer, or a politician—they must do these things when they have become rather sure in the gratification of their even more basic physical, social and esteem needs."[4]

At least the ranking in this list is favorable. In contrast, the skill level thought to be needed by a homemaker, child-care attendant, or nursery school teacher was rated in a recent U.S. Department of Labor publication at only 878 on a scale from 1, the highest skill level, to 887, the lowest (hotel clerks were at 368).[5]

Just how ludicrous it is from the point of view of equality to see motherhood as an occupation can be seen if one substitutes "father" for "mother" in such lists. As we all know, and yet as even a rudimentary sense of equality must protest, women have routinely been asked to choose between parenthood and having an occupation (or another occupation, if one counts parenthood). Men have routinely been expected to be able to enjoy *both* parenthood *and* an occupation (or another occupation).

The common view that motherhood is one occupation among others, but virtually the only one open to mothers not driven to factory or farm labor in addition to motherhood, was shared, one regrets to note, by John Stuart Mill, despite his awareness, quite unusual

among philosophers along with nearly everyone else, that women were entitled to equal rights.[6] It has sometimes been suggested that any different view of the occupational possibilities of women had to await the development of industrialization in the nineteenth century or the development of birth control techniques later. But that this is a lame excuse for millennia of exploitation can be seen in the perfectly imaginable alternative view given by Plato, at least in *The Republic*. Plato pointed out to anyone who would notice that whether one bears or begets children is not a relevant basis on which to determine whether one is fit to govern.[7] The same argument could be applied to the whole range of occupations. Instead, the link between giving birth and caring for children is still assumed to be necessary and inevitable.

That so few have been able to imagine, much less support, the notion of both mothers and fathers caring for children and being engaged in other occupations is part of the problem of turning conceptions of equality into practice. But it is unclear, perhaps, what might be required by equality, or what parents who acknowledge each other to have equal obligations toward their children need to do to fulfill these requirements and obligations. It is this question that I shall now try to explore.

Equal Obligations

Must we suppose that equality requires both parents to do approximately the same tasks, taking approximately the same length of time, so that one parent might, for instance, be completely in charge of the children from 6 A.M. to 2 P.M., say, and the other parent completely in charge from 2 P.M. to 10 P.M., say, while both work at paid jobs to support themselves and their children in the hours they are not engaged in child care, and both take turns at whatever getting up in the night is needed? Are staggered and perhaps shorter work shifts in industry and the professions an obvious objective?

Or should we consider the possibility that if the abilities of the two parents are significantly different, the child is entitled to care "from each according to his or her ability" rather than "from each the same kind of activity for the same length of time"? It has often been supposed that women have greater natural talents for and are more skillful at taking care of small children, and that men have greater natural talents for and are more skillful at obtaining the objects and/or money with which to provide food, clothing, shelter, etc., for the child. It seems highly probable that many differences in skill levels along these lines would disappear if both parents had been brought up as equals from childhood, and if they, as parents, shared both kinds of activities. But if it should happen that some significant differences remained in particular cases, and that a given infant's mother, say, really did have much more talent than the infant's father for making the infant comfortable, happy, eager for new experiences, and friendly toward those around him, while the infant's father, say, really did have much more talent at earning the family's income, would the parents have an obligation to accept a traditional division of labor, she at home caring and he in the world earning, each working *equally hard* at contributing what they did best to the well-being of the child?

And what about preferences? If one parent greatly prefers to earn an income from outside work, rather than to take care of children, should this guide the parents' decisions on how to divide their obligations equally? Or if a child, especially at a given age, greatly prefers being taken care of by one parent rather than the other, should the parents accede to the child's wishes? Are such preferences largely the result of the habitual inequalities built into the traditional sex roles of men and women, and the expectations of children raised in sexist societies, and should they on these grounds be discounted? Or can they be legitimate preferences which should be considered when parents try to work out cooperative arrangements?

It is inadequate to consider questions of parental obligation in isolation from the social situation. Societies ought to recognize their obligations to their children. Societies ought to provide adequate levels of part-time and full-time child care, of support for parents who take care of children at home if they choose to, of medical care and education. But measures to do so are, unfortunately, in the United States, a long way off. I shall, in what follows, deal with the equal obligations of parents in terms of *given* levels, however inadequate, of social support. Doing so should certainly not be taken to imply that current social arrangements are satisfactory, only that women and men may often try to do the best they can to respect each other as equal persons within existing social structures. And the questions I shall consider are primarily moral ones. One hopes the law and social arrangements will come to reflect moral requirements, but long before they do, morally concerned persons must deal with these issues and can try to arrive at reasonable solutions of the problems involved. What I am asking, then, is: If individual women and men recognize principles of equality, as most would presumably by now profess to do, and if both really do respect each other as persons of equal worth, entitled to equal liberty[8] and justice, with equal rights to choose how to live their lives, what are the implications of this for their obligations as mothers and fathers?

Much of what is said here may apply to housework apart from child care, but I shall not discuss such applications. The difficulties of deciding how to divide housework equally are much less complex; a willingness to do so goes far, if persons living together agree on what needs to be done. But the restrictions and demands of parenthood raise complications of a different order, since the rights and interests of other human beings are involved, and since small children require someone "on duty" continually. These new complications often disrupt the equitable arrangements that might be worked out apart from children, as when it is assumed that since the mother will be home with the children anyway, she might as well do most of the housework.

Many of the activities involved in caring for children are intrinsically pleasurable. Sometimes, to be with one's child may be much closer to leisure enjoyment than to work. To play with a child for a few hours in the evening after a day of work away from home, for instance, may be a reward, not a burden, of parenthood. But providing much of what children need can be routine drudgery or emotional torment when it is done constantly, repeatedly, because of one's obligations, in a way that consumes nearly all of one's energies and time, as when a mother does nothing else than care for children and household, or a father nothing else than work at a job he hates in order to pay his fam-

ily's bills. And the burdensome aspects of these activities become all the greater when the person feels that the arrangement placing these burdens on her or on him are unjust, and that it is unfair to be required to bear them.

I shall consider, in what follows, only the obligations parents have to perform various tasks, not the activities they may share with their children for pleasure, and not the feelings with which the tasks are performed. Family and marriage texts have generally asserted that the mother's function is to provide "emotional support," to "keep the family happy," to remain calm amidst the noise and turmoil of the household, to sympathize, to be what is called the family's "heart." The father's function, on the other hand, is to be efficient and strong in dealing with the wider world, to be rational, impartial, just and firm in enforcing discipline, to be what is called the family's "head." I shall restrict the discussion that follows to the performance of specific tasks, without considering whether they include the supplying of adequate psychological or emotional benefits. And the tasks under consideration will be tasks that need doing, apart from whether or not they are done with an acceptable emotional tone or from an appropriate psychological stance.

It would certainly not be adequate to think of the relation between parents and children only or even largely in terms of obligations and rights. Children have rights to care and support, and parents have obligations to supply these when the society does not do so, but it is obviously better for children to receive more from their parents than what the mere fulfillment of the parents' obligations would require. A parent who gives love, concern, and attention to a child because it is a joy to do so is obviously a better parent than one who merely grimly meets his or her obligations to feed and safeguard the child. And it is surely of more value to the child that there be a genuine relationship of mutuality, of shared concern and respect[9] between the man and the woman who are the child's parents, than that such a relationship be absent. But I am going to limit discussion here to obligations and their equality. Parents cannot have obligations to feel emotions beyond their control, or to give children everything that would be of value to them. They can be expected to meet their equal obligations.

I shall also not discuss how parental obligations to children arise in the first place. For instance, in a case where birth control measures have failed, where neither parent wants a child, but where society compels them to become parents against their wills through laws forbidding or social practices preventing abortion, do parents have any obligations to this child, or does society alone have them? Or, if one parent wants a child and the other does not, does the parent who wants the child have greater obligations to care for the child if they have one? Possibly, in such a case, the parents might make an agreement specifying their unequal obligations to the child, which child they otherwise might not have. I shall deal only with cases where both parents voluntarily become the parents of a child, are equally responsible for becoming parents, and recognize that they are equally responsible for the child.

What Does Equality Require?

Children are entitled to support and care. To the extent that, under given so-

cial arrangements, the moral obligation to provide these falls on the parents, it falls on them collectively. From the point of view of the child, it may often not matter which parent provides what aspect of support and care in what proportion, although various studies indicate that children need fathering as much as mothering.[10]

Parents should, first of all, agree on what the child's rights and needs are, and agree on the necessity and relative importance of the tasks that are to be done before they consider which parent should do which tasks. They should try to decide how much the child's preferences will count and in which domains they will count before they discover what the child's preferences are. They should not, for instance, accept those of the child's preferences which require that the mother bear more than her otherwise fair share of the burdens of fulfilling parental obligations, and discount those of the child's preferences which would require the father to do so, although this has traditionally been standard.

Then the parents should proceed from such judgments as "the parents have an obligation to provide w, x, y, and z" to such judgments as "parent A has an obligation to provide w and z," and "parent B has an obligation to provide x and y." How people move from the former judgments to the latter has traditionally not been a matter of reasonable argument, but of little more than social prejudice. Much thinking anew and goodwill are needed to reconcile thinking about the obligations of parents with thinking about the obligations of mothers and fathers in ways that are morally plausible.

In trying to see what equality requires, it is sometimes helpful to consider its application in some other area, close enough to be relevant but different enough to be instructive. Let us consider another family context than the one of parental obligations, a context of two men able to earn income—brothers in this case—having an obligation to support an aged mother unable to be self-supporting.

If the brothers agree that their obligations are equal, what would this require? If one brother is very rich, the other very poor, it is unlikely that they would feel obligated to contribute exactly the same *amount* of money to their mother's support. Would this be a departure from their having an equal obligation? It would seem not, but rather that a requirement to contribute according to ability would be applied equally to each.

Perhaps they might consider that if one contributed more money, the other could contribute more time, visiting the aged mother more often, helping her in her garden, etc. But let us limit the debate to the question of an equal obligation to provide financial support, in terms of some monetary unit.

If, then, the brothers recognize an equal obligation to contribute to financial support, would they have to contribute an equal percentage of their income, if one is rich and the other poor? Or would equality require them to recognize a further aspect of proportionality in their ability to pay, as equality would seem to require rather than oppose a graduated income tax? I think there might be general agreement that we would hold the latter, although there might be some difficulty in specifying the amount. It would seem plausible that equality of obligation would require that the rich brother should contribute a greater amount *and* proportionately a

higher percentage of his income, because the ability to contribute is a relevant factor to consider, a greater ability requires a greater contribution, and as the ability to contribute rises, it is appropriate for the percentage contribution to rise.

The question of the brothers' obligation to earn an income in the first place might be more troublesome. Suppose that one brother has more income because he works very hard, and the other brother has less because he works very little. Both find paid work equally available, and equally unpleasant, but the one brother earns three times as much money as the other because he works three times as many hours a week. We would then have to distinguish actual ability to contribute at a given time, once income, etc., was in hand, and the effort expended, prior to this, to arrive at this actual ability. Then it would not seem that an equal obligation would require the hard-working brother to contribute three times as much as, or a much higher percentage of his income than, the lazy brother, because with an increase of effort, the lazy one could meet the difference, and contribute, himself, a sum that really would be an absolutely equal amount. If, after that, the lazy brother chose leisure over further labor, that would be his right, at least relative to his brother, although if the combined amount contributed by the two for the mother's support left her in extreme and painful poverty, the lazy brother might have an obligation to work harder, and the hard-working brother an obligation to raise the total amount.

If we suppose the earning capacity of the two brothers to be equal, and that they find the labor necessary to earn income equally unpleasant, we might think that fulfilling their obligations on a basis of equality might require each to provide half of what can be taken to be adequate to fulfill their combined obligation. Then we would be back to an absolutely equal amount, even if one brother is rich and the other is poor.

In considering cases such as these, the following principles would seem plausible: (1) In meeting their obligations, the person with the greater actual ability to contribute ought to make a proportionately larger contribution. (2) Effort is a relevant factor to consider in deciding on obligations, and obligations concerning effort take priority over obligations based on actual ability to contribute. Thus, as between two persons with an equal actual ability to contribute, one person should not be expected to expend far more effort to achieve this actual ability. And as between two persons making an equal effort, a greater resulting actual ability to contribute requires him to make a proportionately larger contribution, but if he should choose to make a further expenditure of effort, this should not be penalized by a still further increase of contribution.

If we find these principles plausible in the case of the brothers, we might extend them to the case of parental obligations. If the parents decide that the needs of the child require them to earn, say, thirty additional monetary units a week, and if, as would be likely in American society at present, the mother would have to work at a paid job almost twice as long as the father to earn the fifteen units that would seem like an equal share, then equality of obligation would not require her to provide half of the thirty units. However, if the mother wishes to work, her contribution should not be discounted just because an equal effort will bring in less money. Again, if the work the mother would have to do, even if equally paid, would be signifi-

cantly less satisfying than the work the father would have to do, and would thus be more of an effort to perform, then an equal contribution would not require the mother to expend as much time at it or to provide as much money for the child from it as the father.

In a different aspect of their obligations, if the parents decide that on a typical day the child should be given breakfast, taken on a two-hour outing with close supervision, given lunch, a bath, a story, and a long rest, that the objects the child has scattered about the house should be put away, then equal obligations would not be fulfilled if the mother, because of greater effort, did (or, when appropriate, got the child to do) all these things on the days it was her turn, while the father, because of a lesser effort, managed to get done only two or three of the five on the days, an equal number, it was his turn. But if it really was, at least temporarily, significantly more difficult for him to do these things than for her, he might be required to do fewer of them.

In making these determinations, we could raise the question of whether it is intention or success that should count in establishing when two persons are making "an equal effort." In child-care work, one person may succeed with modest effort in keeping a baby satisfied and occupied, while the other may try much harder and fail. In trying to improve one's position in outside employment, one person may try and repeatedly suffer defeat, and the other may move steadily forward with little effort. But despite the possibilities it may create for deception and self-deception, in the case of meeting one's obligations, it seems to be intention, not success, that should count.[11] But then we must assume sincerity, and that statements such as "but I *am* doing the best I can" will not be used to mask willful inefficiency.

Whenever differences of interpretation arise as to what importance to attach to what, and what guidelines to use to weigh obligations, devices to cut down distortions of perception may be helpful. Parents can acquaint themselves with all the tasks, and devise arrangements and divisions of them before knowing which tasks they themselves will perform. They can, for instance, decide whether feeding the children their evening meal should count for more than doing their laundry or count for less, before deciding which parent will do which task. And they can decide whether a typical hour of outside employment is more burdensome or more rewarding than a typical hour of child care before deciding how the hours will be divided. And so on. Differences of competence can be brought in at a later stage of discussing these arrangements, but here again, procedures to aid impartiality may be helpful. For instance, the parents might agree to evaluate each other's competence rather than their own, and to do so before knowing what arrangements their discussions will recommend. And differences of preference which make some tasks more burdensome to one parent than to the other should be considered only to the extent that the preferences of both parents are considered to an equal degree, including higher-order preferences, such as when a woman might say, "I do not now like to give lectures, but I want to get practice at it because I would like to like to."

To the charge that such "counting" of hours and such "calculation" of who is doing how much will spoil the spontaneous and harmonious relation between parents and with children, will turn family affection into the pursuit of selfishness and turn children into products, one can point to centuries of experience. Such charges have always been leveled against workers—factory workers, teachers, secretaries—who have "calculated" how many hours they were working overtime or without pay instead of failing, because of love for their companies and their work, to notice this. And such charges have routinely been used against women who have finally begun to recognize that, in addition to working all day like their husbands, they have been doing 90 percent of the evening housework. Those who have been taken advantage of have always been asked by the beneficiaries to be trusting and altruistic,[12] but the result of acquiescence in arrangements that are unfair is the growth of resentment and mistrust. The response must be that when respect and equality become habitual, calculation becomes unnecessary. Mutuality and sharing are to be sought, but on a basis of equality, not exploitation.

Can Work Be Different But Equal?

Equality of obligation would certainly not rule out *all* differences in the tasks performed by mothers and fathers. We now have, I think, no reliable empirical knowledge of any genuine differing talents and tendencies of mothers and fathers (except the dispensable and brief capacity of mothers to nurse their infants). We should be very wary of accepting any division of labor between mothers and fathers based on their differing talents at the time they become parents, since these may be due to years of sex-stereotyped preparation, in which boys are encouraged to study and work at various jobs, and girls are expected to babysit and do housework. One significant feature of parenthood is that *neither* parent has much previous training for the work, although this is often overlooked, as it is assumed that the mother will "know what to do," and hence, since it is so much "easier" for her, that she should take care of the children. Anyone who has studied, or experienced, the anxious and helpless feelings that affect women faced with a first newborn baby to care for, or the feelings of guilt and incompetence of mothers not able to handle "smoothly" the outbursts and demands of small children, has every reason to believe that fathers would be equally capable of preparing themselves for child-care work as best they could, and learning fast on the job.[13]

Still, we cannot preclude the possibility that differences of parental ability and preferences between men and women may be significant. It was suggested in a recent article by David Gutmann, a psychologist, that the differences are particularly acute among young parents, and that these differences are more than cultural. He wrote:

> . . . the vulnerability and helplessness of infants and young children seem to arouse a sense of chronic emergency in parents even under relatively affluent conditions, and fathers and mothers respond to this sense of emergency in sex-specific ways. Thus, the young father forces even more deeply into his psychic underground the receptive sensuality that might be distracting to him in his instrumental role, and hence potentially lethal to his children . . . the wife becomes an external representation of the "passive" yearnings her husband must give up in order to provide for his family. By the same token the wife concedes to her husband—and

figuratively sends out of the house with him—the aggression that might be deadly, in the emotional and even in the physical sense, to her vulnerable offspring. The standard reaction for each sex is to surrender to the other the qualities that might interfere with the provision of its own special form of security. Men, the providers of physical security, give up the sensual dependency that might inhibit their courage and endurance; and women, the providers of emotional security, give up the aggression that might frighten or hurt a vulnerable and needful child.[14]

Even if one accepts such "facts," one may doubt that they result from innate psychological dispositions. Perhaps it might be that, faced with the awesome and demanding responsibilities of new parenthood, both parents make extra efforts to conform to what society expects of them—to be, that is, what they have been induced by traditional roles to think of as "good" parents. But Gutmann considers the case for connecting different responses to parenthood with sexual differences to be strengthened by a consideration of what he calls "the sexual reversals that take place in middle-age, as children grow up and take over the responsibility of providing for their own security." As he sees it,

> A massive involution takes place in which men begin to live out directly—to own, as part of themselves—the passivity, sensuality, and tenderness, in effect the "femininity," that was previously repressed in the service of productive instrumentality. By the same token, we find (again, across a vast range of societies) the opposite effect in women, who generally become domineering, independent, and unsentimental in late middle life. . . . Grandpa

becomes sweet, affable, but rather vague, Grandma becomes tough-minded and intrusive.[15]

As a description of our social situation, this is, one must say, ludicrous, since, as one looks around at the leading positions in every important social structure—governmental, economic, legal, educational, etc.—one of its most obvious features is the almost total absence of anyone who is or ever will be a grandmother. So long as the society rewards the outside work of young fathers with promotions, pay raises, seniority, tenure, and career advancement, and asks young mothers to pay so heavily for their years of caring for children at home, to pay for the rest of their working lives with dismally restricted chances for occupational and personal development, the division of function suggested by Gutmann and those sympathetic to his point of view hardly appeals to our notions of equality.

But if, in fact, it suited our empirically given natures better for most of us to be, at different stages of our lives, successively either tenders of children or earners of income, rather than to try to keep the two in balance or to yield to one activity or the other over the whole of our lives, then possibly more mothers than fathers *would* be suited to care for small children, *and* more grandmothers than grandfathers would be suited to run the world. And the requirements of equality would not seem to be violated by life cycles that might be significantly different.

Equality of obligation, then, does not require that both parents perform exactly the same tasks, any more than equal opportunities for occupational attainment require that each person

spend his working life at exactly the same kind of work. But it does require a *starting presumption* that *all* the tasks connected with supporting and bringing up children should *each* be divided equally. Dividing the tasks equally might be done by having both parents engage in the same activities for the same periods of their lives, as when they both split their days equally between child care and outside work. Or, dividing the tasks equally might be achieved through taking somewhat longer turns, one parent working away from home for a few years for instance, while the other stayed home, and then, for the next few years, reversing the roles. These latter divisions may be especially appropriate for parents who are separated, or who must live separately at times for professional or other reasons. But women should be cautious about relying on agreements to have their years of child care "made up for later." A recent study shows that two-fifths of the divorced, separated, and single mothers legally eligible to receive child support payments from the fathers of their children "have never received even a single payment," and many of those fathers who do provide support do so irregularly and in trivial amounts.[16] Furthermore, fathers who take little part in raising their children in the early years may not be able to develop close relations with them, suddenly, later on. And it may be difficult for children to adjust to a complete shift of care from one parent to the other at different stages of their childhoods.

Equality of obligations *does* require that every departure from each parent performing the same tasks be justified in terms of relevant criteria and appropriate principles. There must be good reasons, and not merely customs and social pressures, for such departures. Simply being male or female is not a relevant ground for such departures and cannot be the basis for justifiable differences in parental roles. And equality of obligation requires that the choices to perform given tasks at given stages of our lives should be no less voluntary for one parent than for another.

For this principle to be recognized, we would have to abandon not only the view that the obligations of mothers and fathers are unequal, but also the view that they are in *any* way different. *Any* differences in tasks performed would have to be the result of voluntary agreement between the parents, arrived at on the basis of initial positions of equality, such agreements to include provisions for any later reversals of roles equality would require.

Taking care of small children for a few years of one's life is an incredibly interesting and satisfying kind of work, full of joyful as well as exhausting times. If mothers were not expected to pay so heavily in terms of their chances for self-development for choosing this kind of work, they would, I think, be eager to do it, no matter how conscious they were of the past and present exploitation of women and of their moral rights to equality.[17] In fact, women would, I think, if given the choice, be glad to agree to more than an equal share of child-care work temporarily in exchange for more than an equal share of occupational opportunity and career advancement later on. But I hardly expect that fathers would be so foolish as to let mothers get more than their fair share of the best work of young adulthood, and to let grandmothers get more than their fair share of the best work of late middle age. If fathers *would* be that

foolish, they would still be *entitled* to equality, and mothers would have an obligation to help them realize it.

Notes

1. Homer H. Clark, Jr. *The Law of Domestic Relations* (St. Paul, Minn.: West Publishing Co., 1968), p. 181.
2. Ibid.
3. See Georgia Dullea, "Joint Custody: Is Sharing the Child a Dangerous Idea?" *New York Times*, May 24, 1976, p. 24; and Charlotte Baum, "The Best of Both Parents," *New York Times Magazine*, Oct. 31, 1976, pp. 44–6.
4. Ironically, or appropriately, the quotation comes from an article called "The J-Curve of Rising and Declining Satisfaction as a Cause of some Great Revolutions and a Contained Rebellion," by James C. Davies, in *The History of Violence in America*, ed. by Hugh Davis Graham and Ted Robert Gurr (New York: New York Times Book, 1969), pp. 693–94.
5. See Ann Crittenden Scott, "The Value of Housework," *Ms.* 1(1), July, 1972, pp. 56–9.
6. See John Stuart Mill and Harriet Taylor, *Essays on Sex Equality,* ed. Alice S. Rossi (Chicago: Univ. of Chicago Press, 1970), esp. pp. 74–5 and 179–80.
7. On the distortions of Plato's argument to which his interpreters have sunk, see Christine Pierce, "Equality: *Republic V,*" *The Monist,* 57:1, January, 1973, pp. 1–11.
8. See Virginia Held, "Men, Women, and Equal Liberty," in *Equality and Social Policy,* ed. W. Feinberg (Urbana: Univ. of Illinois Press, 1978).
9. See Virginia Held, "Marx, Sex, and the Transformation of Society," in *Women and Philosophy,* ed. C. Gould and M. Wartofsky (New York: Putnam, 1976).
10. See, e.g., Vivian Gornick, "Here's News: Fathers Matter as Much as Mothers," *Village Voice,* Oct. 13, 1975, pp. 9–10.

11. For a discussion, see Michael A. Slote, "Desert, Consent, and Justice," *Philosophy and Public Affairs*, II, 4 (Summer, 1973), pp. 323–47.

12. See Larry Blum, Marcia Homiak, Judy Housman, and Naomi Scheman, "Altruism and Women's Oppression," in Gould and Wartofsky, *op. cit.*, and Virginia Held, "Rationality and Reasonable Cooperation," *Social Research*, 44:4 (Winter 1977), pp. 708–44.

13. For a perceptive discussion, see Angela Barron McBride, *The Growth and Development of Mothers* (New York: Harper, 1973).

14. David Gutmann, "Men, Women, and the Parental Imperative," *Commentary*, December, 1973, p. 62.

15. Ibid.

16. *Search* (Washington, D.C.: The Urban Institute), Spring 1977.

17. On many of these issues, see Jessie Bernard, *The Future of Motherhood* (New York: Penguin, 1975).

John Locke wrote about families for political reasons. He wanted to show that the long accepted analogies between divine, fatherly, and kingly authority, commonly appealed to in the seventeenth century to demonstrate that kings were above the law and could do no wrong, were unconvincing. In his *First Treatise of Civil Government*, his target was Robert Filmer's influential (but now unread) book *Patriarcha*. Filmer had argued that "it was God's ordinance that supremacy should be unlimited in Adam," that "Adam was father, King and Lord over his Family," and concluded that later fathers and kings too have unrestricted authority over their sons or subjects. Locke disputed both the analogy between kings and fathers and the view that fatherly authority (even Adam's fatherly authority) is unlimited. He concludes that Filmer's proof of "the Divine Rights of Kings" is quite inadequate.

This line of argument required Locke to try to give a detailed account of the authority fathers do have over their children. We have included several strands of this analysis, taken from his *Second Treatise of Civil Government*. First, there is Locke's discussion of the lack of differences between mothers' and fathers' authority. (These passages could well be read in conjunction with Virginia Held's "The Equal Obligations of Mothers and Fathers.") Second, there is Locke's argument that parental authority and consequently children's obedience are restricted in scope. Parents have authority over their children only insofar as they need it to carry out their duties to their children. Grown children owe their parents no obedience, but should honor them. (This discussion might be read in conjunction with Jeffrey Blustein's consideration of parental and filial duties, and with Jane English's account of the duties of grown children.) Third, there is Locke's account of the ending of parental authority when children become reasonable enough to make their own decisions. (These passages and others are analyzed in Edmund Leites' paper "Locke's Liberal Theory of Fatherhood." The papers by Kenneth Henley and Lawrence Houlgate explore alternative pictures of the bases of parental authority; Michael Slote provides an alternative view of the problems of outgrowing parental authority.)

On all these topics Locke has much to say. We have rearranged the order of his remarks so as to group together his views on the three topics. The paragraph numbers make it easy to refer back to the order of the original text.

PATERNAL POWER

JOHN LOCKE

On the Authority
of Mothers and Fathers

52. It may perhaps be censured as an impertinent Criticism in a discourse of this nature, to find fault with words and names that have obtained in the World: And yet possibly it may not be amiss to offer new ones when the old are apt to lead Men into mistakes, as this of *Paternal Power* probably has done, which seems so to place the Power of Parents over their Children wholly in the *Father*, as if the *Mother* had no share in it, whereas if we consult Reason or Revelation, we shall find she hath an equal Title. This may give one reason to ask, Whether this might not be more properly called *Parental Power*. For whatever obligation Nature and the right of Generation lays on Children, it must certainly bind them equal to both the concurrent Causes of it. And accordingly we see the positive Law of God every where joyns them together, without distinction, when it commands the Obedience of Children, *Honour thy Father and thy Mother*, Exod. 20. 12. *Whosoever curseth his Father or his Mother*, Lev. 20. 9. *Ye shall fear every Man his Mother and his Father*, Lev. 19. 3. *Children obey your Parents*, &c. Eph. 6. 1. is the stile of the Old and New Testament.

§ **52** *Chapter* VI. This chapter is obviously directed against Filmer, who is mentioned by

Excerpts from John Locke, *Two Treatises of Government*, edited by Peter Laslett (© Cambridge University Press, 1960, with amendments, 1963). Reprinted by permission. All references in the notes are to page and paragraph numbers in this edition.

name in § 61, and so seems clearly to belong to the original writing of 1679. Its argument is presented at greater length in the *First Treatise:* there are repetitions of phrases and of biblical citations.

1–3 Compare I, § 23, 26–9, note and references: Strauss, 1953, 221, sees in this a hint by Locke at the status of the "discourse"; see Introduction, 99, note 45.

9–21 The argument that the mother's authority is equal with that of the father is developed extensively in the *First Treatise*, and a cross-reference is given in I, § 6, 59, again in I, § 11, 35—see, in general, chapter VI of that treatise (§§ 50–73). The appeal to reason is made in I, § 55, and to revelation in I, § 61, where these four texts are cited.

11 *"Parental"*—see II, § 69, and note.

12 "right of Generation"—particularly attacked in I, § 52: in I, § 18, 20–1 and I, § 50, 22, Grotius is attacked by implication, since Filmer uses him, but there is no reason to suppose that Locke had anyone but Filmer in mind. Hobbes's similar argument in *Leviathan*, chapter 20, looks coincidental: it was attacked by Filmer, 245.

53. Had but this one thing been well consider'd without looking any deeper into the matter, it might perhaps have kept Men from running into those gross mistakes, they have made, about this Power of Parents: which however it might, without any great harshness, bear the name of Absolute Dominion, and Regal Authority, when under the Title of *Parental Power* it seem'd appropriated to the Father, would yet have sounded but oddly, and in the very name shewn the Absurdity, if this supposed Absolute Power over Children had been called *Parental*, and thereby have discover'd, that it belong'd to the *Mother* too; for it will but very ill serve the turn of those Men who contend so much for

the Absolute Power and Authority of the *Fatherhood,* as they call it, that the *Mother* should have any share in it. And it would have but ill supported the *Monarchy* they contend for, when by the very name it appeared that that Fundamental Authority from whence they would derive their Government of a single Person only, was not plac'd in one, but two Persons joyntly. But to let this of Names pass.

65. Nay, this *power* so little belongs to the *Father* by any peculiar right of Nature, but only as he is Guardian of his Children, that when he quits his Care of them, he loses his power over them, which goes along with their Nourishment and Education, to which it is inseparably annexed, and it belongs as much to the *Foster-Father* of an exposed Child, as to the Natural Father of another: So little power does the bare *act of begetting* give a Man over his Issue, if all his Care ends there, and this be all the Title he hath to the Name and Authority of a Father. And what will become of this *Paternal Power* in that part of the World where one Woman hath more than one Husband at a time? Or in those parts of *America* where when the Husband and Wife part, which happens frequently, the Children are all left to the Mother, follow her, and are wholly under her Care and Provision? If the Father die whilst the Children are young, do they not naturally every where owe the same Obedience to their *Mother,* during their Minority, as to their Father were he alive?

§ **65** 6–7 Compare I, § 100, 7–11 and Tyrrell, 1681, 16: in lines 26–7 of I, §100 Locke makes a cross reference to the *Second Treatise,* evidently with such passages in this chapter in mind.

Parents' Authority, Children's Obedience and the Filial Duties of Adult Children

63. The *Freedom* then of Man and Liberty of acting according to his own Will, is *grounded on* his having *Reason,* which is able to instruct him in that Law he is to govern himself by, and make him know how far he is left to the freedom of his own will. To turn him loose to an unrestrain'd Liberty, before he has Reason to guide him, is not the allowing him the priviledge of his Nature, to be free; but to thrust him out amongst Brutes, and abandon him to a state as wretched, and as much beneath that of a Man, as theirs. This is that which puts the *Authority* into the *Parents* hands to govern the *Minority* of their Children. God hath made it their business to imploy this Care on their Offspring, and hath placed in them suitable Inclinations of Tenderness and Concern to temper this power, to apply it as his Wisdom designed it, to the Childrens good, as long as they should need to be under it.

64. But what reason can hence advance this Care of the *Parents* due to their Off-spring into an *Absolute Arbitrary Dominion* of the Father, whose power reaches no farther, than by such a Discipline as he finds most effectual to give such strength and health to their Bodies, such vigour and rectictude to their Minds, as may best fit his Children to be most useful to themselves and others; and, if it be necessary to his Condition, to make them work when they are able for their own Subsistence. But in this power the *Mother* too has her share with the *Father.*

§ **64** 4–10 These sentiments recall Locke on *Education* (already formulated though not written when this was composed, see Introduction, 35), and even his insistence in his paper for the Board of Trade that the children of the poor must work (Introduction, 56): compare Tyrrell, 1681, 19.

67.   The subjection of a Minor places in the Father a temporary Government, which terminates with the minority of the Child: and the *honour due from a Child,* places in the Parents a perpetual right to respect, reverence, support and compliance too, more or less, as the Father's care, cost and kindness in his Education, has been more or less. This ends not with minority, but holds in all parts and conditions of a Man's Life. The want of distinguishing these two powers; viz. that which the Father hath in the right of *Tuition,* during Minority, and the right of *Honour* all his Life, may perhaps have caused a great part of the mistakes about this matter. For to speak properly of them, the first of these is rather the Priviledge of Children, and Duty of Parents, than any Prerogative of Paternal Power. The Nourishment and Education of their Children, is a Charge so incumbent on Parents for their Childrens good, that nothing can absolve them from taking care of it. . . .

68.   On the other side, *honour* and support, all that which Gratitude requires to return for the Benefits received by and from them is the indispensible Duty of the Child, and the proper Priviledge of the Parents. This is intended for the Parents advantage, as the other is for the Childs; though Education, the Parents Duty, seems to have most power, because the ignorance and infirmities of Childhood stand in need of restraint and correction; which is a visible exercise of Rule, and a kind of Dominion. And that Duty which is comprehended in the word *honour,* requires less Obedience, though the Obligation be stronger on grown than younger Children. For who can think the Command, *Children obey your Parents,* requires in a Man that has Children of his own the same submission to his Father, as it does in his yet young Children to him; and that by this Precept he were bound to obey all his Father's Commands, if out of a conceit of Authority he should have the indescretion to treat him still as a Boy?

On the Ending of Parental Authority

55.   *Children,* I confess are not born in this full state of *Equality,* though they are born to it. Their Parents have a sort of Rule and Jurisdiction over them when they come into the World, and for some time after, but 'tis but a temporary one. The Bonds of this Subjection are like the Swadling Cloths they are wrapt up in, and supported by, in the weakness of their Infancy. Age and Reason as they grow up, loosen them till at length they drop quite off, and leave a Man at his own free Disposal.

56.   *Adam* was created a perfect Man, his Body and Mind in full possession of their Strength and Reason, and so was capable from the first Instant of his being to provide for his own Support and Preservation, and govern his Actions according to the Dictates of the Law of Reason which God had implanted in him. From him the World is peopled with his Descendants, who are all born Infants, weak and helpless, without Knowledge or Understanding. But to supply the Defects of this Imperfect State, till the Improvement of Growth and Age hath removed them, *Adam* and *Eve,* and after them all *Parents* were, by the

Law of Nature, *under an obligation to preserve, nourish, and educate the Children,* they had begotten, not as their own Workmanship, but the Workmanship of their own Maker, the Almighty, to whom they were to be accountable for them.

§ **56** 4–6 Compare I, § 86, 21–4 and note.
13–16 Compare II, § 6, 11–16, note and references.

58. The *Power,* then, *that Parents have* over their Children, arises from that Duty which is incumbent on them, to take care of their Off-spring, during the imperfect state of Childhood. To inform the Mind, and govern the Actions of their yet ignorant Nonage, till Reason shall take its place, and ease them of that Trouble, is what the Children want, and the Parents are bound to. For God having given Man an Understanding to direct his actions, has allowed him a freedom of Will, and liberty of Acting, as properly belonging thereunto, within the bounds of that Law he is under. But whilst he is in an Estate, wherein he has not *Understanding* of his own to direct his *Will,* he is not to have any Will of his own to follow: He that *understands* for him, must *will* for him too; he must prescribe to his Will, and regulate his Actions; but when he comes to the Estate that made his *Father a Freeman,* the *Son is a Freeman* too.

§ **58** Tyrrell's account of the origin and nature of parental power is very similar to Locke's; see 1681, 15 and on. Both writers stress the parental duty of education, though Tyrrell is much more specific than Locke. In his diary for 1679 Locke made a note on the point from Sagard's *Canada* (1636, Appendix B, no. 72), under the title *"Pietas":* education, not generation, gave the obligation, he wrote, and compared the Hurons with the Janissaries, initialling the note

as his (compare II, § 106, 18–20 and note). The classical discussion is in Grotius (*De Jure Belli,* II, V), rejected by Filmer but characteristically close to the surface in Tyrrell: Pufendorf's commentary on the position of Grotius may well have been in Locke's mind—see especially *De Jure Naturae* (1672), VI, ii, De Protestate Patria.

11–13 Elrington (1798) uses this phrase about the understanding and will to justify the political inferiority of adults who lack intellectual attainments.

59. This holds in all the Laws a Man is under, whether Natural or Civil. Is a Man under the Law of Nature? *What made him free* of that Law? What gave him a free disposing of his Property according to his own Will, within the compass of that Law? I answer; State of Maturity wherein he might be suppos'd capable to know that Law, that so he might keep his Actions within the Bounds of it. When he has acquired that state, he is presumed to know how far that Law is to be his Guide, and how far he may make use of his *Freedom,* and so comes to have it; till then, some Body else must guide him, who is presumed to know how far the Law allows a Liberty. If such a state of Reason, such an Age of Discretion *made him free,* the same shall make his Son free too. Is a Man under the Law of *England?* *What made him free* of that Law? That is, to have the Liberty to dispose of his Actions and Possessions according to his own Will, within the Permission of that Law? A capacity of knowing that Law. Which is supposed by that Law, at the Age of one and twenty years, and in some cases sooner. If this *made* the Father *free,* it shall *make* the Son *free* too. Till then we see the Law allows the Son to have no Will, but he is to be guided by the Will of his Father or Guardian, who is to understand for him. And if the

Father die, and fail to substitute a Deputy in this Trust, if he hath not provided a Tutor to govern his Son during his Minority, during his want of Understanding, the Law takes care to do it; some other must govern him, and be a Will to him, till he hath *attained to a state of Freedom*, and his Understanding be fit to take the Government of his Will. But after that, the Father and Son are equally *free* as much as Tutor and Pupil after Nonage; equally Subjects of the same Law together, without any Dominion left in the Father over the Life, Liberty, or Estate of his Son, whether they be only in the State and under the Law of Nature, or under the positive Laws of an Establish'd Government.

60. But if through defects that may happen out of the ordinary course of Nature, any one comes not to such a degree of Reason, wherein he might be supposed capable of knowing the Law, and so living within the Rules of it, he is *never capable of being a Free Man*, he is never let loose to the disposure of his own Will (because he knows no bounds to it, has not Understanding, its proper Guide) but is continued under the Tuition and Government of others, all the time his own Understanding is uncapable of that Charge. And so *Lunaticks* and *Ideots* are never set free from the Government of their Parents; *Children, who are not as yet come unto those years whereat they may have; and Innocents which are excluded by a natural defect from ever having; Thirdly, Madmen, which for the present cannot possibly have the use of right Reason to guide themselves, have for their Guide, the Reason that guideth other Men which are Tutors over them, to seek and procure their good for them, says* Hooker,

Eccl. Pol. Lib. 1. Sect. 7. All which seems no more than that Duty, which God and Nature has laid on Man as well as other Creatures, to preserve their Offspring, till they can be able to shift for themselves, and will scarce amount to an instance or proof of *Parents* Regal Authority.

§ **60** 11–18 Keble's *Hooker*, 1836, 1, 276–7; 1676, 78, some lines after a passage copied into Locke's diary on 26 June 1681. Probably added after composition of the paragraph; see note on II, § 5, 9–28.
19–23 Compare I, § 56, 20–31.

69. The first part then of *Paternal* Power, or rather Duty, which is *Education*, belongs so to the Father that it terminates at a certain season; when the business of Education is over it ceases of it self, and is also alienable before. For a Man may put the Tuition of his Son in other hands; and he that has made his Son an *Apprentice* to another, has discharged him, during that time, of a great part of his Obedience both to himself and to his Mother. But all the *Duty of Honour*, the other part, remains never the less entire to them; nothing can cancel that. It is so inseparable from them both, that the Father's Authority cannot dispossess the Mother of this right, nor can any Man discharge his Son from *honouring* her that bore him. But both these are very far from a power to make Laws, and inforcing them with Penalties that may reach Estate, Liberty, Limbs and Life. The power of Commanding ends with Nonage; and though after that, *honour* and respect, support and defense, and whatsoever Gratitude can oblige a Man to for the highest benefits he is naturally capable of, be always due from a Son to his Parents; yet all this puts no Scepter into the

Father's hand, no Sovereign Power of Commanding. He has no Dominion over his Sons Property or Actions, nor any right, that his Will should prescribe to his Sons in all things; however it may become his Son in many things, not very inconvenient to him and his Family, to pay a Deference to it.

§ 69 1 *"Paternal* Power"—Locke seems already to have forgotten his determination in II, § 52, 11 to call it *"Parental"; compare II, § 170, 1.

  6 *"Apprentice"*—this association of the filial relationship with apprenticeship is very significant for the social structure of seventeenth-century England; compare II, § 85, 9–18.

  10–13 Compare I, § 62, 15–22.

  16–26 Compare II, § 65, 20–7 and references, especially Pufendorf.

III

GROWING
UP AND APART

Older children can do more for themselves and need less help from parents and others. They can therefore make increasing use of various liberties. Nevertheless, they often find that their legal status as minors gives them no greater liberty than they had (or needed) as infants. Others, usually their parents, may choose their place and style of life, their schooling and associates. Minors have no franchise, may not exercise full property rights, and often may be tried by courts with reduced procedural safeguards.

Parents are often more flexible than laws, and most older children claim and sometimes secure some control over various aspects of their lives. Still, this control remains at their parents' pleasure, and it falls far short of emancipation. Further, the liberties older children acquire have often more to do with the trappings than with the substance of independent adult life. Adolescent rebellion and confrontation have often focused on liberty to choose styles of hair, dress, or entertainment. These banners can serve both as the outward symbol and as a mask for the deeper battles of autonomy.

The deeper battles may be looked at from various angles and have been energetically depicted in this century. Historians of the family have chronicled the late emergence of adolescence as a separate stage of life, characterized by continued economic dependence (often guaranteed by continued schooling) which lasts beyond physical maturation. According to Philippe Ariès, adolescence was bypassed by nearly everyone before the nineteenth century; work began before physical maturation for most people. Older children might not be emancipated from their parents, but they at least shared their dependent status with large segments of the adult population.

During the nineteenth century, adolescence emerged as a middle-class preserve in industrialized nations. In this century, adolescence has become the common prerogative and problem of youth in developed countries, who find themselves for a substantial number of years physically mature but economically dependent on their parents and excluded from the world of work.

Psychologists of various persuasions have dissected the inner world of this now ubiquitous and often turbulent stage of life. Some have chronicled the stages of cognitive development through which older children pass. Others have looked at the gradual emergence of adult personality and the successive stages of maturity in moral judgment.

The complexities and details of these investigations greatly complicate any inquiry into the authority parents or others can legitimately exercise over children, and cast new light on what is involved in outgrowing these authorities and assuming adult status. It is one thing to talk about repealing compulsory schooling laws for children of fifteen, and quite another to talk of repealing all such laws. It is one thing to advocate emancipation of older adolescents, and another to seek emancipation of children whose emotional and cognitive development is at a much earlier stage. A reasoned account of the liberties which families should concede to older children and of the liberties which the state should guarantee (or deny) to older children must take into account discoveries about the stages of development which fall within the period of life which is indicated by the labels "later childhood" and "adolescence."

The essays and selections in the final section of this book look at some of the problems which arise in making decisions about the treatment of older children, both by their families and by legislators. The extract from John Stuart Mill and the essays by Kenneth Henley and Laurence Houlgate consider some of the grounds for restricting children's liberties and the conflicts which may arise between those liberties and the rights of parents. In *Wisconsin* v. *Yoder* the state's claims to educate older children for the current, secular culture are weighed against parents' rights to train them to continue simpler, religious ways of life. The authors of "Emancipating Our Children—Coming of Legal Age in America" survey the current legal restrictions and protections which affect minors in various jurisdictions within the United States. Edmund Leites and Michael Slote both look at the problems children have in outgrowing authorities to whom they have once been subject. They have, however, very different views about the course and likely outcome of adolescent battles for autonomy from parents who have recently had complete authority over their children's lives. Jane English looks beyond adolescence to grown children and asks whether and when mature and emancipated persons have duties to those who brought them up and on whom they no longer depend.

John Stuart Mill's *On Liberty* remains the classic argument against restrictions on liberty. He asserts that

> the sole end for which mankind are warranted, individually or collectively, in interfering with the liberty of action of any of their number, is self-protection. That the only purpose for which power can be rightfully exercised over any member of a civilized community, against his will, is to prevent harm to others. His own good, either physical or moral, is not a sufficient warrant. (Ch. 1: Introductory)

Both legislation and private intervention which tries to prevent others from harming themselves by acts which would harm no others are unjustifiable. One might expect Mill to claim that his principle has dramatic implications for reforming legislation which specifically affects children and for altering child-rearing practices. Many laws—for example, compulsory schooling laws and laws forbidding minors to contract—are avowedly paternalistic, and so, very obviously, are many parental interventions. But Mill draws no such conclusions. He writes roundly that his principle is meant to apply only to those who are "in the maturity of their faculties":

> We are not speaking of children, or of young persons below the age which the law may fix as that of manhood or womanhood.

Children, including older children, are therefore legitimately under parental or other authority.

The following extract from *On Liberty* contain Mill's views on compulsory schooling. He has no qualms about compelling children to be educated. He therefore advocates legislation to establish compulsory examinations in which children must demonstrate the skills they have acquired at schools parents choose (and presumably afford). Such a law would minimize interference not with children but with parents.

This conflict between parents' and children's rights was already apparent in a number of the discussions of Section II. In discussions of children's liberties, it becomes fundamental. Where parents have authority, children's liberties depend on parental concessions and may be wiped out. However, where parents *lack* authority, children do not always have liberty, for they may be subject to other (for example, to state) authority.

In this selection, two connected questions arise. The first is: When should children have which liberties, and when should they be subject to others' authority in various matters? The second is: To whose authority should children be subject in those cases where they should not have liberty?

ON LIBERTY

JOHN STUART MILL

A person should be free to do as he likes in his own concerns; but he ought not to be free to do as he likes in acting for another, under the pretext that the affairs of the other are his own affairs. The State, while it respects the liberty of each in what specially regards himself, is bound to maintain a vigilant control over his exercise of any power which it allows him to possess over others. This obligation is almost entirely disregarded in the case of the family relations, a case, in its direct influence on human happiness, more important than all others taken together. The almost despotic power of husbands over wives needs not be enlarged upon here, because nothing more is needed for the complete removal of the evil than that wives should have the same rights, and should receive the protection of law in the same manner, as all other persons; and because, on this subject, the defenders of established injustice do not avail themselves of the plea of liberty, but stand forth openly as the champions of power. It is in the case of children that misapplied notions of liberty are a real obstacle to the fulfillment by the State of its duties. One would almost think that a man's children were supposed to be literally, and not metaphorically, a part of himself, so jealous is opinion of the smallest interference of law with his absolute and exclusive control over them; more jealous than of almost any interference with his own freedom of action: so much less do the generality of mankind value liberty than power. Consider, for example, the case of education. Is it not almost a self-evident axiom, that the

From "On Liberty," Chap. v, "Applications."

State should require and compel the education, up to a certain standard, of every human being who is born its citizen? Yet who is there that is not afraid to recognize and assert this truth? Hardly anyone indeed will deny that it is one of the most sacred duties of the parents (or, as law and usage now stand, the father), after summoning a human being into the world, to give to that being an education fitting him to perform his part well in life towards others and towards himself. But while this is unanimously declared to be the father's duty, scarcely anybody, in this country, will bear to hear of obliging him to perform it. Instead of his being required to make any exertion or sacrifice for securing education to his child, it is left to his choice to accept it or not when it is provided gratis! It still remains unrecognized, that to bring a child into existence without a fair prospect of being able, not only to provide food for its body, but instruction and training for its mind, is a moral crime, both against the unfortunate offspring and against society; and that if the parent does not fulfill this obligation, the State ought to see it fulfilled, at the charge, as far as possible, of the parent.

Were the duty of enforcing universal education once admitted there would be an end to the difficulties about what the State should teach, and how it should teach, which now convert the subject into a mere battlefield for sects and parties, causing the time and labor which should have been spent in educating to be wasted in quarreling about education. If the government would make up its mind to require for every child a good education, it might save itself the trouble of providing one. It might leave to parents to obtain the education where and how they pleased, and content itself with helping to pay the school fees of the poorer classes of children, and defraying the entire school expenses of those who have no one else to pay for them. The objections which are urged with reason against State education do not apply to the enforcement of education by the State, but to the State's taking upon itself to direct that education; which is a totally different thing. That the whole or any large part of the education of the people should be in State hands, I as far as anyone in deprecating. All that has been said of the importance of individuality of character, and diversity in opinions and modes of conduct, involves, as of the same unspeakable importance, diversity of education. A general State education is a mere contrivance for moulding people to be exactly like one another: and as the mould in which it casts them is that which pleases the predominant power in the government, whether this be a monarch, a priesthood, an aristocracy, or the majority of the existing generation; in proportion as it is efficient and successful, it establishes a despotism over the mind, leading by natural tendency to one over the body. An education established and controlled by the State should only exist, if it exist at all, as one among many competing experiments, carried on for the purpose of example and stimulus, to keep the others up to a certain standard of excellence. Unless, indeed, when society in general is in so backward a state that it could not or would not provide for itself any proper institutions of education unless the government undertook the task: then, indeed, the government may, as the less of two great evils, take upon itself the business of schools and universities, as it may that of joint stock companies, when private enterprise, in a shape fitted for undertaking great works of industry, does not exist in the country. But in general, if the country contains a sufficient number of persons qualified to provide education under government auspices, the same persons would be able and willing to give an equally good education on the voluntary principle, under the assurance of remuneration afforded by a law rendering education compulsory, combined with State aid to those unable to defray the expense.

The instrument for enforcing the law could be no other than public examinations, extending to all children, and beginning at an early age. An age might be fixed at which every child must be examined, to ascertain if he (or she) is able to read. If a child proves unable, the father, unless he has some sufficient ground of excuse, might be subjected to a moderate fine, to be worked out, if necessary, by his labor, and the child might be put to school at his expense. Once in every year the examination should be renewed, with a gradually extending range of subjects, so as to make the universal acquisition, and what is more, retention, of a certain minimum of general knowledge virtually compulsory. Beyond that minimum there should be voluntary examinations on all subjects, at which all who come up to a certain standard of proficiency might claim a certificate. To prevent the State from exercising, through these arrangements, an improper influence over opinion, the knowledge required for passing an examination (beyond the merely instrumental parts of knowledge, such as languages and their use) should, even in the higher classes of examinations, be confined to facts and positive science exclusively. The examinations on religion, politics, or other disputed topics should not turn on the truth or falsehood of opinions, but on the matter of fact that such and such an opinion is held, on such grounds, by such authors, or schools, or churches. Under this system, the rising generation would be no worse off in regard to all disputed truths than they are at present; they would be brought up either churchmen or dissenters as they now are, the State merely taking care that they should be instructed churchmen, or instructed dissenters. There would be nothing to hinder them from being taught religion, if their parents chose, at the same schools where they were taught other things. All attempts by the State to bias the conclusions of its citizens on disputed subjects are evil; but it may very properly offer to ascertain and certify that a person possesses the knowledge requisite to make his conclusions, on any given subject, worth attending to. A student of philosophy would be the better for being able to stand an examination both in Locke and in Kant, whichever of the two he takes up with, or even if with neither: and there is no reasonable objection to examining an atheist in the evidences of Christianity, provided he is not required to profess a belief in them. The examinations, however, in the higher branches of knowledge should, I conceive, be entirely voluntary. It would be giving too dangerous a power to governments were they allowed to exclude any one from professions, even from the profession of teacher, for alleged deficiency of qualifications: and I think, with Wilhelm von Humboldt, that degrees, or other public certificates of scientific or professional acquirements, should be given to all who present themselves for examination, and stand the test; but that

such certificates should confer no advantage over competitors other than the weight which may be attached to their testimony by public opinion.

It is not in the matter of education only that misplaced notions of liberty prevent moral obligations on the part of parents from being recognized, and legal obligations from being imposed, where there are the strongest grounds for the former always, and in many cases for the latter also. The fact itself, of causing the existence of a human being, is one of the most responsible actions in the range of human life. To undertake this responsibility—to bestow a life which may be either a curse or a blessing—unless the being on whom it is to be bestowed will have at least the ordinary chances of a desirable existence, is a crime against that being. And in a country either over-peopled, or threatened with being so, to produce children, beyond a very small number, with the effect of reducing the reward of labor by their competition, is a serious offense against all who live by the remuneration of their labor. The laws which, in many countries on the Continent, forbid marriage unless the parties can show that they have the means of supporting a family, do not exceed the legitimate powers of the State: and whether such laws be expedient or not (a question mainly dependent on local circumstances and feelings), they are not objectionable as violations of liberty. Such laws are interferences of the State to prohibit a mischievous act—an act injurious to others which ought to be a subject of reprobation, and social stigma, even when it is not deemed expedient to superadd legal punishment. Yet the current ideas of liberty, which bend so easily to real infringements of the freedom of the individual in things which concern only himself, would repel the attempt to put any restraint upon his inclinations when the consequence of their indulgence is a life or lives of wretchedness and depravity to the offspring, with manifold evils to those sufficiently within reach to be in any way affected by their actions.

When we compare the strange respect of mankind for liberty, with their strange want of respect for it, we might imagine that a man had an indispensable right to do harm to others, and no right at all to please himself without giving pain to any one. . . .

In bringing up children and educating them, parents and others interfere in children's lives in ways which would be quite unacceptable intrusions into the lives of other adults. We are so used to this sort of interference that it may not appear as such until we see a case of its misapplication: for example, the woman who, steeped in motherhood, turned to her neighbor at a dinner party and cut up his meat.

In "The Authority to Educate," Kenneth Henley considers various reasons given for intervening in children's lives. His argument brings out two sorts of limitations in these reasons. First, there are conflicts between different reasons cited for interfering in children's lives. For example, parents' rights to determine their child's schooling and religious observance may conflict with (older?) children's rights to standard constitutional guarantees of freedom in these matters; children's interests in receiving an education of a certain sort may be incompatible with parents' rights to choose certain forms of life. Second, there are (partly because of these conflicts) limits to the amount and kind of interference which can be justified, however benevolent the motives of those who would intervene. No case can therefore be made for a blanket denial of adult liberties to those who are supposed not to be "in the maturity of their faculties."

THE AUTHORITY TO EDUCATE[1]

KENNETH HENLEY

Introduction:
Education and Liberty

None of us is born into the condition of Adam. As Locke wrote: "Adam was created a perfect man . . . and so was capable, from the first instant of his being, to provide for his own support and preservation, and govern his actions according to the dictates of the law of reason. . . . From him the world is peopled with his descendants, who are all born infants, weak and helpless, without knowledge or understanding."[2] Adam came into the world already socialized. But actual human beings must be slowly socialized, by way of education. I use "education" in its broadest sense, and education in this sense begins at birth. Most of this education is informal, and a good deal of it even unintentional on the part of the "educators." And there is also that formal part of the child's education which I will call "schooling." If we were born already socialized adults, either the now distinctive normative problems which arise in socializing children would be replaced by a special set of normative problems under the general topic of genetic engineering, or, if we had no control over the initial character of the adults born into our society, we would come to look upon the initial character of new persons as a mere accident of birth. The characters of such Adams would change only through mutation or reeducation. But actual human societies do not have to wait for character mutations or undertake reeducation to change the socialization of the members of the society. We can *attempt* to socialize infants as we wish.

Adam could play no role in the action which gave him both physical and mental maturity, since that action was his creation. But actual human beings inevitably play some role in their own education. Although both state and parents may wish to be as God to children, neither can succeed; for though we are not born into the condition of Adam, neither are we born into the condition of the dust from which Adam was made. We are born, instead, into an intermediate condition. Infants can be molded, but not into just any form, and never without themselves contributing to the final shape they take. Children display volition before they display articulated thought, and articulated thought before they have achieved fully acceptable socialization. So there will usually be some conflict between socializing agents and the child. Paternalism toward children seems unavoidable, for we cannot always await their consent to the sometimes painful steps of growing up. The moral and legal liberties of children must be limited by the right of others to socialize them.

If the child is to become a responsi-ble member of society, there *must be* socializing agents; but it is not clear what legitimizes a particular socializing agent. There are two basic normative questions concerning the authority to educate: who has legitimate authority? and what is the extent of each authority's legitimate control over education? Each of these questions can be raised from a legal and from a moral viewpoint. Since many of the moral assumptions on which I will depend are also found in our law, I shall proceed at first without distinguishing between the moral and legal viewpoints.

At the birth of a child, there are only two candidates who might act as authorities over education: the family (whether natural or adoptive) and agencies of the state. This much restricted list of possible authorities is not meant to apply to all societies, for clearly there are societies in which children are not so much born into a family as born into a community, and there are societies in which it makes no sense to speak of "the state." But in our society, any legal authority which a community has over a child derives from the authority of the child's parents or guardians. I will not here question the individualist presuppositions of our society, but rather work within them. Our form of social organization, like any other, limits the possible authorities over education. Although it is an important question whether radically different forms of social organization are preferable to ours, the question of legitimate authority over education *within* our form of social organization is the prior question for us. Not only must we, at least temporarily, live within the social organization we have, we must also get to any new social organization from where we are. Since control over education is an important means of achieving social change, we need to know where authority over education should reside.

I will discuss six considerations relevant to the problem of the authority to educate. There are three parties affected by decisions about this authority: the child, the parents or guardians, and society (represented by the state). The interests of each party can be interpreted in at least two ways: as interests in maximizing subjective satisfactions, or as interests in having certain liberties (whether or not having those liberties leads to a maximization of subjective satisfactions).

1. Satisfying the Child

It might seem plausible to say that authority to educate must be based on the child's own need to be educated in order that his life be more satisfying than it would otherwise have been. Both parents and state would have the authority to educate, and its legitimate exercise would be constrained by the desirability to the child of the sort of life his education makes possible for him. Resolution of any conflicts between parents and the state would depend upon a determination, presumably by a court, of the education most likely to please the child in the long run.

Great weight in any such deliberation should be given to the young child's need for the sustained intimate relationships found almost exclusively in families. Such relationships are themselves educative, and a source of great satisfaction to the child. It seems likely that continuity of intimate relationships is necessary for normal development.[3] This need would support the moral and legal

presumption that the child will normally be under the immediate authority of his parents. As the child matures, however, there is a competing need to develop an independent adult identity. These two competing needs can be satisfied by maintaining the privacy of the family while legally requiring parents to send children to schools which give scope to the child's growing independence.

No sense can be given to the central idea of desirability to the child in a large and important range of cases. Whether a certain sort of life would please a child often depends upon *how* he has been socialized, and so we cannot decide whether to socialize him for that life by asking whether that kind of life would please him. We can in such cases ask whether that kind of life would be desirable *for* him, but this is not a question simply about his present or future preferences. Of course, the idea of desirability to the child does make sense in another range of cases—those in which the choice is between more or less of something that is either valued or disvalued by almost everyone. But even here, we should not underestimate the power of socialization. Some children do learn an attitude to poverty and its attendant unpleasantness which fits them for a life of *satisfied* poverty. Once the child has been socialized to the point at which it makes sense to speak of him as deciding and deliberating, we can make sense of the idea of desirability to him by reference to the pattern of satisfaction and dissatisfaction which he displays. But this pattern might not itself be good *for* him; and it is neither fully natural nor self-chosen, but the result in part of his early education. We cannot resolve the problem of the authority to educate merely by considering the subjective interests of the child.

2. Satisfying the Parents

In our society, some parents consider their children an important source of emotional satisfaction, and, when things go wrong, of dissatisfaction. Not only do parents often enjoy the affection and companionship of their children, they often identify so closely with the lives of their children that the child's life, as perceived by the parent, comes to play a central role in the parent's life. And so, it might be claimed that the parents derive at least some authority over the education of their children from the subjective interest they have in that education. After all, until the child leaves home, the parents will be affected by his behavior more than anyone else will; and even after the child becomes an adult, the parents are often more seriously affected by his behavior than anyone else, except his own new family (if he has one). The child is a part of the life of the parents, and people have authority to arrange their lives to please themselves.

Not many parents would wish to rest their authority to educate on this consideration alone. For to educate the child *merely* in order to satisfy the parents is to treat the child like a pet or a slave. But in unreflective moments, people do speak of children, even their own, as if the point of a child were to please parents, relatives, and other adults. We are all parts of each other's lives to the extent that we impinge upon each other; but no authority over another person can rest upon the mere fact that there is such a connection. It is reasonable for parents to claim authority over the education of their children in order to fit the child into their life only to the extent that there are no other considerations. Parental desires only justify authority

which leaves largely untouched the interests of the child and of society: authority over indifferent domestic arrangements, and over matters which require a decision but in which there must be an element of arbitrariness. Any broader authority which parents have to integrate the child into their lives must rest on the child's need for intimate relationships and society's interest in emotionally healthy new members. The parents' own need for the intimate relationships of child rearing could not alone justify any broad authority over another person.

3. Satisfying Society

The child must come to understand which kinds of interference in the lives of others are prohibited and which are allowed. This learning is needed for social life; its detail will vary from society to society and from time to time. In a technologically complex society such as ours, many of the prohibitions cannot be understood without basic technological literacy. Thus, a relatively sophisticated education may be necessary in our society in order for children to come up to the socially required standard of behavior. The state, since charged with the protection of the public interest, has authority to educate children in order to do so. In our society, it is not feasible for government or community agencies to oversee the early, informal education of children, so parents must accept responsibility for their early socialization. Continuity of intimate relationships must be provided in any case, for otherwise, socialization is unlikely to be successful.[4] By having children, parents commit themselves to act *in loco societatis* toward their children; and the state has the authority to remove the child from the parents if they do not, or cannot, provide a socialization which is minimally acceptable to society.

But the same difficulty, writ large, arises with this consideration that arose with the account of satisfying the child. For a large and important range of cases, what counts as harmful to the members of a society depends upon what their socialization has been. For instance, deprivation of personal property, if it results neither in actual nor in potential worsening of the life of the owner, will be counted as a harm only by someone who has internalized a certain attitude toward personal property. Given an internalized attitude of possessiveness, there may be actual emotional turmoil on the part of someone who has been deprived of something which he *knows* he would never have used. Teaching a child respect for property rights is not simply a way of protecting the independently identifiable interests of the members of society. It is also a way of perpetuating a form of society which, like all forms of society, creates interests that otherwise would not have existed. This difficulty might be overcome by arguing that there is a form of society which allows for more human satisfaction on balance than any other form, and so, that the interests which rest on socialization in that society would themselves have an ultimate justification based on the satisfaction of interests which can be specified independently of socialization. But to show that a form of society is optimal seems very difficult; even procuring a reasonably exhaustive account of possible forms of social life has obvious theoretical difficulties. However, there may be such an optimal form of society; and within that society, the full socialization of children could be justified without vicious circularity by

reference to the interests of the society's members.

Non-optimal societies, and optimal societies without good grounds for thinking that they are optimal, cannot justifiably claim blanket authority for society or the state to educate children to satisfy society, unless the claim rests on more than a simple appeal to satisfy the desires of the society. In a well-run slave society, in which slaves are properly socialized into their roles, satisfaction of the desires of all members of society, including slaves, might be maximized by continuing to socialize children into the roles found in the society. It is important to unveil the logic of the claim that every society, whether or not it satisfies human interests as fully as other sorts of society, has full, unrestrained authority to socialize children in order to maximize satisfactions within that sort of society. This claim is not grounded on an appeal to the satisfaction of human interests, but is rather a disguised claim that society or the state has arbitrary authority over its minor citizens.

In societies without a well-grounded claim to be optimal, a restricted authority to educate can be grounded on a non-circular appeal to the interests of the members of the society. This restricted authority encompasses socialization which protects just those interests of the members of society which are independent of their socialization. It is also reasonable to assert that the state has authority to socialize children in order to satisfy even the socially created interests of the members of society, as long as no other consideration (for instance, the interest of the child in having certain liberties) is in conflict with these socially created interests. It seems clear that while the interest of the child in having certain liberties, and perhaps even the child's interest in maximizing his own satisfactions, might be morally and legally important enough to outweigh the interest of the society in maximizing satisfactions, the parents' interest in maximizing their own satisfactions could never outweigh the interests of society. For the parents' satisfaction does not have the privileged position conferred on the satisfaction of the child by the fact that it is paternalism toward the *child* which is being justified. I shall consider an appeal to the interests of the parents in having a protected liberty in the education of their children in Section 5.

4. Protecting the Liberty of the Child

We may wish to have moral and legal rules which confer upon minors at birth rights to basic liberties. I will not discuss the reasons for having such rules; I am concerned here with the implications of having them. In our society, public argument presupposes that we are born with certain rights. Locke speaks for our society when he writes: "Thus we are born free, as we are born rational; not that we have actually the exercise of either; age that brings one, brings with it the other too."[5] If children have rights from birth, then the authority to educate the child must be circumscribed by a respect for those rights. Thus, there is legitimate authority to educate the child into rationality, and also to educate the child to respect the rights of others, since no one is born with the right to violate the rights of others. But once the child is capable of rational deliberation, and once he has internalized the prohibition against violating the rights of others, there is no le-

gitimate authority to educate him further against his will.

The standard used to judge whether he has accomplished both of these tasks must not be more stringent than that which is applied to adults. Since there must be a general legal rule to decide whether a child can choose for himself whether to be educated in a certain way, the age specified by the rule would certainly have to be much earlier than is usually found in state statutes. The average fourteen-year-old has accomplished these tasks as well as the average sixteen-year-old. It could be argued that these tasks are accomplished as well as they ever will be, for most people, at an even younger age. Since the state is the final protector of the rights of individuals against other individuals, the state will have final authority over the education of children, protecting the child against his parents' tendency to extend the period of their authority over him beyond its proper limits. The state might reasonably delegate its authority to parents (especially in the early years of the child's informal education), but whenever there is a challenge to parental exercise of this delegated authority, the state must act as protector of the rights of the child. The state must also protect the child from the tendency of his parents to educate him into the kind of life which *they* want for him, for there can be no parental authority to do this unless the child is born without rights which are independent of the parent-child relationship. For, as Locke pointed out, parental powers are "to speak properly of them, the . . . privilege of children, and duty of parents, than any prerogative of paternal power."[6]

It might be argued that since the child is born with the right to become, so far as he is able, a fully functioning citizen, the state has authority to educate him to be a citizen capable of making reasonable decisions when exercising his rights (in voting, for instance). And this authority, it might be argued, will last longer than into the fourteenth or even sixteenth year. But this argument is an amalgam of very different sorts of consideration. The state does have authority to prepare children for responsible citizenship. But this authority must come to an end at some point, or else the state would claim paternalistic authority over its citizens throughout their lives. We cannot set the end to this authority simply by the test of whether the child has become a responsible citizen, since this test would be failed by an overwhelming majority of adult citizens. Since it is clearly possible for the state to educate children so that by the age of fourteen (or even younger) they have the skills with which they *may* subsequently become responsible citizens, there is no need to claim an extended authority to educate in order to prepare children for exercising their rights as citizens. There are good reasons for setting the voting age later than the age at which the child is free from coercive education, but that is another matter. Of course, in our society, the state and the parents sometimes do not fulfill their responsibility to educate children so that basic skills are mastered at an early age; but in those cases, such skills are usually not mastered at a later stage, either. The incompetence of our educational system should not be used to justify an extended period of coercive education.

5. Protecting the Liberty of the Parents

Parents often claim a right to educate their children as they wish, and claim this right as if it were not merely the right to protect the rights and interests of the children. Indeed, the Supreme Court has recognized a legally protected "liberty of parents and guardians to direct the upbringing and education of children under their control."[7] And the Court has explicated this liberty in a way which establishes a legal right of parents to socialize their children into lives which the parents want for the children, lives full of obligations which go beyond those of a member of society and a citizen: "the child is not the mere creature of the state; those who nurture him and direct his destiny have the right, coupled with the high duty, to recognize and prepare him for additional obligations."[8] The additional obligations immediately intended by the Court are religious obligations. It is also often asserted—for instance, in public debate concerning school busing—that parents have a *moral* right to educate their children as they please, and those who assert this right usually mean to assert more than that the parents have a right to protect the rights and interests of their children.

Such a liberty of parents to educate their children is clearly in conflict with the liberty of the children. For it makes no sense to say that a child is born, for instance, with religious liberty, but that the child's parents have a protected liberty to coerce the older child to fulfill the religious obligations which the parents choose for him. In the early years of the child's socialization, he will be surrounded by the religious life of his parents. Since the parents have a right to live such religious lives, and on the assumption that children will normally be raised by their parents, parental influence on the child's religious life is both legitimate and unavoidable. But at such an early stage, it can hardly be said that coercion is involved; the child simply lives in the midst of a religious way of life and comes to share in it. But surely, the assertion that the child is born with religious liberty must entail that parents are under at least moral constraints not to *force* their religious beliefs upon the child once he is capable of forming his own views. By the time the child begins formal schooling, he is perhaps already in some sense a believer in the religion of his parents—and normally, there will have been no need for coercion by the parents in order to accomplish this. But if the child has religious liberty, those in authority over him have a duty to prepare him for the exercise of it. Thus, he must at least not be intentionally isolated as he grows older from all ways of life other than those of his parents' co-religionists. And nonreligious parents have a duty not to isolate their children from religious ways of life. Are the parents morally and legally free to send the child to a religious school entirely closed to the pluralistic society? The parents are legally free, for the courts have recognized the right of parents to prepare their children for "additional obligations." But the courts have also insisted that constitutional rights apply to children as well as to adults.[9] What happens to the religious liberty of the child if the parents are allowed to isolate him from the larger community, not only in his early years but through the whole of his schooling? Even if we hesitate to say that the law should protect the religious liberty of children against encroachments by parents—for such legal protection would involve us in conflicts with the privacy of the lives of both the parents and the children—is it not clear that we must either give up talking about the child as

if he were a person with all of the same basic liberties as any other person, *or* we must admit that parents are under a moral obligation to protect the religious liberty, and the other liberties, of the child? A parent who recognizes such a moral obligation will not consider himself at liberty to force upon his child any obligations other than those which the child has as a member of the social community. The parent will attempt to prepare the child to exercise the religious liberty with which he was born by making it easy for the child, as he matures, to learn of the variety of religious and non-religious ways of life. A parent who sees himself as trustee of the child's liberties will not feel free to choose the child's schooling so as to limit drastically the child's access to both experience and knowledge. Though it may be in the child's interest to share in a family life committed to values additional to those required by society, the maturing child surely has the right to learn well before the present age of majority that these additional values are not socially obligatory. Parents have a duty to provide the child with a family life committed to basic social values, such as honesty and justice, and this life should never be portrayed as optional. In some families, *no* additional values might be recognized. I see no reason why such traditional liberal values cannot suffice to structure a meaningful life. The maturing child in such a family has the right to learn that additional values are socially *permissible*.

If we are to say that children are born with liberties, then they are neither mere creatures of the state nor mere creatures of the state and the parents combined. Chief Justice Burger has gone so far as to suggest that the state has no authority to intervene on the child's behalf if, against parental wishes, an Amish child expressly desires to continue his schooling beyond an eighth-grade Amish education.[10] The legal rights of the child, on this view, seem not so much in trust as non-existent. The Supreme Court has recognized that each child has a property right in the public schooling which is provided by the states.[11] This property right seems unprotected if a parent can, on his own personal religious grounds, decide that his child cannot choose to exercise it. In cases less extreme than the Amish, it seems that the child's property right in the education provided by the state is arbitrarily violated by parents who decide to send their children to makeshift private schools in order to avoid, for instance, school busing or integration. Surely the states have a legal duty to license only those private schools which offer educational opportunities at least roughly comparable to those of the public schools. Otherwise, parents are allowed to decide that the exercise of the child's property right to a public education will be replaced by the exercise of a purchased right to an inferior property. But the courts have not consistently protected the rights of children, even such explicitly recognized and specific rights as the property right in public education. The courts have failed to protect children because they insist on recognizing a liberty of parents so extensive that it is incompatible with the rights of the children.

There would be no conflict with the right to privacy of both the parents and the child if the state generally required either public schooling or schooling in private schools which offer equivalent educational opportunity and variety of social experience. For such a general requirement would not mandate that the state inquire into the private lives of parents and children. But to insure that the parents' choice of private schooling for their child would not constitute a deprivation of the child's property right in public education, the licensing requirements for schools which enroll minors under compulsory education laws would have to be quite strict. It is plausible that one of the licensing requirements must be that the private school admit children of all racial, ethnic, and religious backgrounds, since children will otherwise have a restricted social experience.[12] Surely no school could be licensed which refuses to teach scientific theories on the grounds that they contradict religious revelation. It is a difficult question whether religious objections to scientific theories should be discussed in schools; such discussions would tend to be partisan and would encourage the view that science and religion are competitors—a view considered confused by many religious people. Parents will be free to insist on religious doctrine in the privacy of the home—*legally* free, that is, for I do not think that they are morally free to *require* belief of older children. But surely parents cannot have the legal right to prevent their children from coming into contact with current scientific knowledge. It might be claimed that some traditional ways of life—for instance, that of the Amish—could not survive the requirement that older children be allowed to go to school with children from the larger community and to learn about science and technology. *If* this claim is true, then such traditional ways of life have no right to survive, for their survival is at the expense of the liberty of the children who are born into them.

6. Protecting the Liberty of the Members of Society

If we conceive of the state as a mere protector of the interests and rights of the citizens, rather than as an entity with rights of its own, independent of its function as protector, then there is no need to consider the liberty of the state. But there is a need to consider the liberty of the members of society, for this consideration is quite different from that of satisfying members of society. While there is clearly conflict between protecting the legitimate liberty of the child and satisfying the members of society, there is no conflict between protecting the legitimate liberty of the child and protecting the legitimate liberty of the members of society. For the legitimate liberties of each member of society are circumscribed by the legitimate liberties of each other member of society, and provided we specify these liberties consistently, the child will never be free to constitute or cause an invasion of the liberties of others. Here also the state is the final protector of the rights of individuals, and has authority to educate children into respect for the rights of the other members of society—but this educating is at the same time, of course, an educating of the child into an understanding of his own rights.

There would be a serious conflict between the rights of the state over the child and the rights of the child himself if the state asserted a right to socialize the child into whatever role it saw fit. Just as the child can be viewed as the property of the parents, he may be viewed as the property of the state. Both of these claims to own the child conflict with the claim that the child has rights and subjective interests which merit consideration. The claim of the parents is also in potential conflict with the claim of the members of society to have their subjective interests satisfied and their liberties protected. In this confrontation, the property claim of the parents must give way. The recognition of the basic liberties of all citizens is more deeply embedded in our law and in our morality than is the recognition of the special right of parents to oversee the upbringing of their children as they wish—and these competing rights cannot both be consistently maintained. If the state limits its claim upon the child to the right to socialize the child in the interests of society only when others' liberties so require or when the liberty of the child is not at issue, then the authority of the state over the child's education will in no way conflict with the child's rights. And since the state is also the final protector of the interests and liberty of the child, its authority over the child's education would then be doubly established.

The state can best exercise this ultimate authority as *parens patriae*[13] by supporting the immediate authority of parents over the early and informal education of children, and by requiring schooling under strong licensing provisions which protect the maturing child's right to grow into an independent adult. The privacy of the family fosters the continuing intimate relationships so essential to the child's well-being, while the school's openness establishes the older child within the larger society.

Notes

1. An earlier version of this paper was presented at a meeting of the Society for Philosophy and Public Affairs in New Orleans on April 30, 1976. I am indebted to Onora O'Neill, Jeffrey Blustein, and Michael Bayles for their helpful comments.
2. John Locke, *Second Treatise of Government*, section 56. [*Eds.* Pp. 241–42 above.]
3. See Joseph Goldstein, Anna Freud, and Albert Solnit, *Beyond the Best Interests of the Child* (New York: The Free Press, 1973), Chaps. 2 and 3.

4. For evidence that continuous intimate relationships with parents (and others) can perhaps be provided even in collective child rearing, see R. Kahane, "The Committed: Preliminary Reflections of the Impact of the Kibbutz Socialization Pattern on Adolescents," *The British Journal of Sociology*, Vol. XXVI, No. 3, Sept., 1975. This article also suggests that successful socialization is possible with little coercion except that offered by peer pressure.

5. John Locke, *Second Treatise of Government*, section 61.

6. John Locke, *Second Treatise of Government*, section 67.

7. *Pierce* v. *Society of Sisters*, 268 U.S. 510, 534–535 (1924).

8. *Pierce* v. *Society of Sisters*, 268 U.S. 510, 535 (1924).

9. See the many citations listed by Mr. Justice Douglas in his dissent to *Wisconsin* v. *Yoder*, 406 U.S. 205, 243–246 (1972). For perhaps the most important recognition of the constitutional rights of children see *In re Gault*, 387 U.S. 1 (1966). [*Eds.* See pp. 304–5 below.]

10. *Wisconsin* v. *Yoder*, 406 U.S. 205, 230–234 (1972). Mr. Chief Justice Burger, in the majority opinion, claims that this issue is not before the Court. Nevertheless, he seems to suggest that the right of Amish parents to oversee the education of their child might well override the rights and expressed interests of the child in such a case.

11. *Brown* v. *Board of Education,* 347 U.S. 483 (1954) and *Goss* v. *Lopez,* 419 U.S. 565 (1975).

12. After this paper was first presented, the Supreme Court held that *non-sectarian* private schools may not exclude students on the basis of race and reaffirmed that "while parents have a constitutional right to send their children to private schools . . . they have no constitutional right to provide their children with private school education unfettered by reasonable government regulation" (*Runyon* v. *McCrary*, 96 S. Ct. 2586, at 2598 (1976). The decision to prohibit racial discrimination was based on the equal right of all to enter into contracts, rather than on the broader issues which I have raised. Only racial discrimination was in question. The decision expressly leaves untouched even *racial* exclusion if it is based on religious grounds. But it nevertheless recognizes broad state power to regulate private schools, and argues that such power does not infringe on parental privacy. My argument would support much broader state regulation, and the application of such regulation to sectarian schools.

13. For an important discussion of the state's authority as *parens patriae*, see *Prince* v. *Massachusetts*, 321 U.S. 158 (1944).

Kenneth Henley's discussion of the limits of justifiable intervention in children's lives assumed that children had at least some liberty rights which parents and state should respect. But most jurisdictions explicitly deny to children a variety of liberty rights which adults in the same jurisdiction possess. In "Children, Paternalism, and Rights of Liberty," Laurence Houlgate considers the most common grounds for such denials of liberty. He takes the traditional arguments for paternalism, as deployed by John Stuart Mill and many others, and considers whether it is reasonable to hold that children (and others not "in the maturity of their faculties") should be denied liberties which they might misuse to their own detriment.

The weakness of such paternalism has always been that we are *all* likely to misuse liberties to our own detriment. There is no plausible way of demarcating a class of minors and incompetents containing all and only those who would misuse their liberty. Once one has seen this problem of demarcation, one might move in various directions in trying to state the limits of paternalistic denial of liberty.

Some people have believed that since we are all likely to harm ourselves if given liberty to do so, none of us should have liberty. The best polity is a benevolent despotism in which all citizens are as children to the state; they lack liberty but receive what is best for them. On the other hand, libertarians of various sorts have looked at the same difficulties of demarcation and concluded that everyone should be legally emancipated. The slight and unsystematic differences in capacity between persons cannot provide grounds for denying liberties to some. In recent years, Thomas Szasz has argued for abolishing involuntary hospitalization of persons held to lack "normal" mental capacities, and Ivan Illich has argued in *Deschooling* for repealing compulsory schooling laws. Some of the writers who have advocated "children's rights"—for example, John Holt—have also been concerned with extending adult liberties to children. Others are more concerned with seeing that children's claims are met than with extending their liberties.

Houlgate takes a more probing and piecemeal approach than either benevolent despots or libertarians. He considers just which inabilities of children are supposed to make them unfit for liberty, and then whether all whose liberties the law limits on grounds of their minority really have these inabilities. He questions whether lack of these abilities really does make misuse of liberties to one's own detriment more likely. He considers how lack of liberty to choose and try and make mistakes can produce or sustain the very incapacities which are thought to justify the lack. If liberties are to be denied children for their own protection, the denial should reflect an accurate account of the capacities children have or lack at various stages of their development and of the likelihood that specific incapacities will lead children to harm themselves if allowed certain liberties.

CHILDREN, PATERNALISM, AND RIGHTS TO LIBERTY

LAURENCE D. HOULGATE

1. Should Children Have Rights to Liberty?

Are there any legal rights to liberty possessed by sane, competent adults that ought not to be possessed by children? If there are such rights, then what arguments have been or can be invoked in refusing to grant them to children? Are these arguments sound?

Although there are some who would extend all adult rights to children, the answer to the first question appears to be a nearly unanimous "yes," and several examples of rights that many believe we should deny to children are cited. Thus, it is held that a child ought not to have the legal right to choose his own place of residence, to choose whether or not to attend school, to be in public places during certain late night and early morning hours, to purchase alcoholic beverages, to drive an automobile, to be "unruly" or disobedient to his parents, to engage in certain kinds of sexual activity (especially if female), to read certain books, or to attend a whole range of public entertainments. There are many other examples,[1] but this short list should suffice to convince that although there are some legal rights to liberty that are shared by children and adults, there is a large number of such rights that most persons think ought not to be possessed by children.

I have referred to these as "rights to liberty." They are rights to act or not act as one chooses, and in this paper, I shall discuss only such rights. A person has a right to liberty if he has a claim to certain *forbearances* of others and they have a duty to *refrain* from interfering with him in certain ways. I shall not be considering rights that we might grant to children such as the right to receive an education, to obtain adequate medical care, or to be secure economically and emotionally, all of which imply that a child has a claim to *specific actions* by particular persons who have a duty to *do* something.[2]

Second, I shall be concerned primarily with one argument that has been used to justify legal restrictions on the freedom of action of children. This is the argument from paternalism, the argument that justifies denials of rights to liberty to children on the ground that such denials either prevent them from doing harm to themselves or promote their good or welfare. There are, of course, a number of other considerations that a legislator would use in deciding whether or not to grant a particular liberty right to children,[3] but I shall concentrate on paternalism because it seems to me to be the argument that is most often appealed to in discussions of children's rights and yet has been subjected to the least amount of critical attention.

Of course, there have been a number of philosophical discussions of paternalism as a liberty-limiting principle, either in general[4] or as it applies to medical interventions.[5] There have been no detailed examinations of the way in which paternalistic arguments have been or should be used to deny liberty rights to children. I hope to provide this, principally by examining the crucial assumption of such arguments that children "lack the capacity for rational choice." I shall also discuss the moral basis for legal paternalism, but will show that the moral principles which I believe ultimately justify some paternalistic interferences in the lives of others cannot be used to deny legal rights to *all* persons now legally classified as children.

I shall use the word "child" ("infant," "minor") in this paper as it is presently used in the law—i.e., to describe a person under the age of eighteen years, or under twenty-one years for some purposes, although it seems obvious that this classification blurs the large differences among children of different ages and the striking similarities between older children and adults.[6] I shall show how these differences and similarities are crucial when we come to make decisions about the legal rights that ought to be possessed by children.

2. The Argument from Paternalism

The argument from paternalism for denying children certain legal rights to liberty can be stated as follows:

1. Children are likely to do harm to themselves or fail to promote their own good or welfare if granted certain legal rights to liberty (e.g., the right to purchase alcoholic beverages).
2. It is morally justifiable to deny legal liberty rights to a class of persons whenever members of the class are likely to do harm to themselves or to fail to promote their own good or welfare if granted those rights.

Therefore,

3. It is morally justifiable to deny certain legal liberty rights to children.

I shall refer to this as the "standard version" of the argument from paternalism. There are a number of points of clarification to make about the argument. First, the phrase invoked in premises 1 and 2 mentions two alternatives: preventing harm or promoting good or welfare. It would have been possible to state the case more simply by referring only to the promotion of a child's good, but it is useful to distinguish cases in which we interfere with a child's liberty for the good of protecting him from harm from cases in which the good is some positive benefit we hope to achieve. That is, not being harmed is assuredly a benefit, but there are some benefits we can achieve for a child over and above his not being harmed.[7] For example, compulsory school attendance laws are justified partly on the ground that it is to the child's positive benefit that he is made to go to school. This is not just another way of saying that he will be harmed if he does not attend (though this may be an indirect result of his not receiving the benefit).

Second, premise 1 is a prediction about what will happen to children under certain conditions. As such, it can be proved true by gathering the relevant statistical evidence. This is rarely, if ever, done. Usually, a claim of the sort specified in premise 1 is derived from a more general empirical claim about a child's lack of capacity for rational choice. That is, the following subarguments are offered:

4. Persons who do not have the capacity for rational choice are likely to do harm to themselves or to fail to promote their own good or welfare if granted certain legal rights to liberty.
5. Children do not have the capacity for rational choice.

Therefore,

6. Children are likely to do harm to themselves or to fail to promote their own good or welfare if granted certain legal rights to liberty.

Finally, the argument from paternalism does not employ the notion of "consent" of the person whose liberty of action is denied. The justification of interference is stated entirely in terms of the child's own good, regardless of whether or not he wants or desires to have his own good promoted. Nor does the argument imply any statement about the "hypothetical consent" of the person whose freedom is restricted. It may be that the child interfered with would want us to do what we are now doing if he were capable of rational choice, but the argument is silent about such claims and we need not infer them from it.

Both premise 2 of the argument from paternalism and premise 5 of its sub-argument are open to objection. I shall discuss the latter premise in the next section and follow with a discussion of premise 2.

3. The Capacity for Rational Choice

Do children lack the capacity for rational choice? In order to answer this question, we must clarify what is meant by the phrase "rational choice." The concept is importantly ambiguous. Consider the following example. Smith, despondent over the recent death of a loved one, commits suicide. We can ask two questions about his choice. (a) What made him commit suicide? (b) Given the facts at his disposal, was his choice to commit suicide reasonable or correct? It is clear that question (a) would re-

ceive a different answer than question (b). The latter question calls for an *assessment* of Smith's choice, not, as with (a), a *description* of the way in which he arrived at his choice. The difference is important. The question "Was Smith's choice rational?" may mean either "Was his choice reasoned, thoughtful?" or it may mean "Was his choice reasonable?"[8] It is obvious that a person may think for a long time about a practical problem and yet make an unreasonable or incorrect decision. For example, a mature, informed businessman may ponder for days about a potential investment and yet make a financially disastrous choice.[9] It is equally clear that a person may sometimes make a correct decision without deliberating at all; for example, a happy-go-lucky gambler impulsively bets a few dollars on a horse and wins. In either case, we may call the choice "irrational," indicating respectively either that a person's thinking or reasoning has been faulty or that he simply failed to think at all about the situation before choosing.

I shall refer to a choice that is rational in the descriptive sense a *reasoned* choice. I shall call a choice that is rational in the evaluative sense a *reasonable* choice. In what sense, if any, is it true to say that children lack the capacity for rational choice?

First, the claim that children lack the capacity for "reasoned" choice surely applies only to very young children, those whom Inhelder and Piaget describe as in the "sensorimotor" stage of development (0–2 years) and those in the early period of the "preoperational" stage (2–7 years).[10] It certainly cannot be said of children beyond the age of, say, seven years that they are unable to reason or choose on the basis of reasons, or that most of their choices (like that of the suicidal man in the preceding example) are caused by the varying emotional states from which all of us are prone on occasion to suffer.

Let us assume, then, that to say that children do not have the capacity for rational choice means that they are unable to make "reasonable" choices. We are to suppose, that is, that although children over the age of seven years can have reasons for choosing as they do, they have bad or incorrect reasons, and this is evidenced by the generally poor choices that they make if left unrestricted. I suspect that it is this sense of "irrational" that people usually have in mind when they refer to the choices of children as irrational. They are making the value judgment that children's choices are usually bad or incorrect.

In order to decide whether this claim has any empirical basis, we must first clarify what makes a choice good or bad. This, of course, is an enormously complex task, depending on the construction of a general view about the capacities which it is desirable for people to possess, an "ethical opinion about the 'true' nature of Man."[11] Nonetheless, there may be some rough guidelines that can be developed. Let us suppose that survival is a proper end of human activity. Then we may refer to most choices that put a person in danger of losing his life or risking serious harm or injury as unreasonable choices. Are children generally unreasonable in this sense? Are they prone to put themselves in situations in which their survival or bodily integrity is put at risk?

If the latter question is to be answered in the affirmative, then either it will have to be statistically proved that children usually behave in ways that put them at risk or we will have to derive this claim from some more general empirical observation about children. As for the first alternative, existing empirical research does not seem to prove very much. First, experimental work in child psychology is usually done in a laboratory setting that does not reflect the real social situations in which the child may find himself.[12] Second, existing statistical studies on causes of death in the U.S. population, although more relevant to our question, are inconclusive. They show that whereas accidents are the leading cause of death among children over the age of one year, accidents rank fourth in causes of death among the total population (National Center for Health Statistics, 1976). Are we to conclude from this that children are more prone to put themselves in situations in which their survival or bodily integrity is put at risk? Or shall we conclude that children are not as susceptible as the rest of the population to heart disease, cancer, and stroke (the three leading causes of death)? This is not to deny that some young children, when left unattended, will ride tricycles in the street, play with matches, and drink strange substances which turn out to be poison. But we can no more conclude from this that *all* persons legally classified as children are prone to do such things than we can conclude that all adults are prone to endanger themselves from the fact that some adults chain-smoke, sky-dive, or climb mountains.

The general empirical judgments that are usually appealed to in order to prove that children are prone to make (would make) unreasonable (dangerous, risky) choices are: (6) those who do not know that there is a risk of harm involved in some of the courses of action open to them are prone to make self-harm risking choices; (7) those who lack the cognitive capacity to under-

stand that there is a risk of harm involved in a particular choice are prone
to make self-harm risking choices; and
(8) those who are unable to defer the
gratification of a desire for very long
are prone to make self-harm risking
choices. We then couple each of these
general judgments with the following
particular judgments: (9) children lack
information about the risks of harm involved in many of their choices; (10)
children lack the cognitive capacity to
understand that there is a risk of harm
involved in many of their choices; (11)
children are unable to defer gratifying
their desires for very long. From each
pair of judgments (i.e., 6 and 9, 7 and
10, 8 and 11), we derive the conclusion
that children are prone to make self-
harm risking choices. Moreover, if it is
agreed that this proneness is a sufficient
condition for the lack of capacity for
rational choice, then premise 5 of the
sub-argument of the argument from paternalism has been proved true.

Suppose that the statement that
someone is "prone" to act in ways that
may cause harm to himself is, at least
in part, a comparative judgment—i.e., it
implies a comparison between himself
and some subset of the class of human
beings. For example, to say that persons
who lack information about the risk of
harm involved in some of the choices
available to them are prone to make self-
harm risking choices is to imply the comparative judgment that such persons are
more likely to choose the dangerous alternative than persons who *do* have such
information. If this is granted, then it
seems to me that the claims made in
(6), (7), and (8) are true. That is, each
of them states a "safe" prediction, given
what we know about human behavior
and the general desire to survive and
avoid pain.

However, I would strongly object to
the claims made in (9), (10), and (11).
There is either no evidence available to
support the claim in each case,[13] or the
evidence that is available will support
the claim only if qualified to apply to
very young children. For example, if the
ability to discriminate shape is present
in a child from as early as six months of
age,[14] then it is difficult to believe the
claim in (10) that children (i.e., all persons from 0–18 years) lack the cognitive
capacity to understand that there is a
risk of harm involved in a choice that is
available to them. Second, the psychological studies of the behavior of children
in games indicates a capacity at a very
young age to defer immediate gratification of a desire. Indeed, children in the
five-to-seven-year age range "come to see
the necessity for rules and sometimes
set up much stricter regulations governing their own activities than those established by adults."[15] The strong urge to
gratify a desire to take a ball and run is
resisted by the child who knows that the
rules of the game do not allow this.
Third, the proposal in (9) that children
lack the information about the risks involved in many of their choices is undoubtedly true about a larger age range
of children than the range for which the
claims in (10) and (11) are true.

However, since there are no studies
available to indicate precisely what sorts
of informational lacks exist at specific
age ranges, there is not much more to
be done than to make educated guesses
about the age ranges. At what age, for
example, do children acquire the information that there are risks involved in
being in certain areas of large American
cities at night? At what age do they
learn that there are hazards involved in
operating certain kinds of machinery?
The answer to these questions often de-

pends upon the extent to which adults have chosen to withhold such information from them. Nonetheless, it is difficult to believe that most city children beyond the age of say, ten years, are ignorant of the former fact and that most farm children of the same age are ignorant of the latter fact.

I conclude that because the claims made in (9), (10), and (11) are unfounded, the arguments in which these claims occur as premises are unsound, and subsequently, they cannot serve as grounds for the claim in (5) that children do not have the capacity for rational choice.

4. Freedom and Self-realization

Let us repair the argument from paternalism so that it applies only to those children who clearly lack the capacity for rational (reasonable) choice. For example, we shall assume for purposes of argument that we have the statistical evidence to show that premise 5 (and therefore, premise 1) is true for most children under the age of twelve years. Does it follow that it is justifiable to restrict their freedom of action by denying them certain rights to liberty?

The answer to this question depends upon whether we should also accept premise 2. There are cases which give us reason to reject it. Suppose, for example, that mountain climbing is likely to cause death or serious injury to the unchaperoned adult amateur climber. Although we might very well agree that the state should continually confront potential climbers with the facts so that there is no escaping the knowledge of the risks they are taking, there are many persons who would resist the suggestion that the state would be justified in re-

fusing to grant such persons the right to climb mountains on the mere ground that this is likely to lead to self-harm.

Still, we might conjecture why anyone would be inclined to accept premise 2. A possible answer is that it is derived from the moral principle of beneficence. This principle, which some philosophers would claim to be a "basic" moral principle, asserts that we have a duty to promote good and prevent or avoid doing harm.[16] Thus, if we believe that we can either advance the good of a person or prevent him from doing harm to himself by restricting his liberty, then, by the principle of beneficence, it is morally right to restrict his liberty.

And yet, it would appear that such restrictions are sometimes unjustifiable. It is at least debatable that the state should legally restrict the adult amateur mountain climber, or indeed, any competent person who is capable of making an informed choice prior to engaging in a potentially self-harmful activity. One reason for this can be traced to the principle of beneficence itself, and was first stated by John Stuart Mill: an attempt to restrict the liberty of action of an individual for his own good is likely to produce more harm than the harm it is introduced to avoid. Specifically, the harms that Mill had in mind were to the interests of all persons in their growth and self-realization. "Self-realization consists in the actualization of certain uniquely human potentialities, the bringing to full development of certain powers and abilities."[17] In order to accomplish this, one must constantly practice making difficult choices:

> The human faculties of perception, judgment, discriminative feeling, mental activity, and even moral preference are exercised only in making a choice. He who does anything because it is the

custom makes no choice. He gains no practice either in discerning or in desiring what is best. The mental and moral, like the muscular, powers are improved only in being used.[18]

Since freedom of choice is necessary to the attainment of self-realization, it follows that granting rights to liberty to competent, fully informed adults would have the tendency to promote the good of the person who is given the liberty, even if this freedom permits him to make dangerous or foolish mistakes. It follows, then, that the most that the state is justified in doing when there is substantial risk and the individual is capable of rational choice is to *educate* the person to the existence and nature of the risk, or even to temporarily *enjoin* him in order to make certain that his subsequent choice is "calm and cool," but never to *coerce* him from choosing the risky course of action altogether.

On the other hand, Mill would argue, if we remove the legal barrier to a child's exercise of the choice to perform a potentially self-harmful action, this would only reveal a *natural* obstacle in the form of that child's lack of capacity to make a rational choice. Mill does not use the latter phrase. Instead, he writes of children not being "in the maturity of their faculties." But his point is clear: children are not yet "capable of being improved by free and equal discussion."[19] As such, it would be useless to attempt to educate or inform the child about the existence or nature of a risk involved in his conduct, and anyway, it is doubtful that the child would stand to gain anything (by way of developing his character or intellect) that would offset the potential for harm that is inherent in many of the choices that the law now denies to him.

My objection to this line of reasoning is simply that I doubt that the facts would support the empirical claim that restrictions on liberty stunt an individual's process of growth or "self-realization." Although it may be true that large-scale legal restrictions on freedom of action would produce some retardation in the development of the average person's intellect or character, I doubt that this claim can be made about *particular* restrictions, and it is particular restrictions which are our present concern. For example, I doubt that we would witness a stunting in the growth of the average person's process of self-realization if the state decides to deny all persons the legal right to smoke tobacco. Hence, this could not be the justification for our thinking that it would be wrong to deny adults this right, and if this is so, we cannot amend premise 2 of the standard version of the argument from paternalism in the way suggested by Mill's remarks. I conclude, then, that because of the deficiencies in both premises 1 and 2, we must reject the argument from paternalism for denying certain liberty rights to children.

5. Justice and Paternalism

The principle of beneficence justifies too much interference in people's lives; that is, it has been seen to lead to restrictions on freedom of action that are intuitively unjustifiable. And yet, I see no reason to reject the suggestion that promoting the good of others or preventing or avoiding harm that might be done to them is *a* moral duty. It is, rather, that beneficence cannot be the whole story of our moral life. We need some other moral principle which can supplement the principle of beneficence but which will not lead us to justify paternalistic interferences in the lives of those who are capable of rational choice.

One principle that comes to mind is that of justice. In this section, I want to examine the suggestion that it is justifiable to paternalistically restrict the liberty of *some* children (those who lack the capacity for rational choice), but not that of other children and most adults, because it is *just* to do so.

The formal principle of justice is to "treat like cases alike and different cases differently." The material principle of relevant likenesses and differences that modern society attaches to this is that of equality: *prima facie* human beings are entitled to be treated alike. If we treat them differently, it is only because they are seen to differ in some "morally relevant" respect.

This immediately poses a dilemma. It might be (and has been) suggested that chronological age is not a morally relevant respect justifying differences in treatment. Surely a person cannot help being the age he is, any more than he can help being a particular sex or race. If so, then it is as unjust to discriminate on the basis of being under eighteen years of age as it is to discriminate on the basis of being female or black.

I think that this argument is unsound. It is true that we treat people equally when we attend only to morally relevant similarities or dissimilarities among them. But I do not think it follows that it is unjust to place certain legal restrictions on some children that we do not place on other children and most adults. In order to see this, we must first specify what makes a similarity or dissimilarity morally relevant. I accept William Frankena's suggestion that "those that are relevant are the ones that bear on the goodness or badness of people's lives."[20] A person's sex or race has nothing to do with how (naturally) good or bad his life is. Hence, these are not morally relevant similarities or dissimilarities, and we think that it is unjust when the state discriminates against people on these bases when distributing burdens or benefits. On the other hand, a person's (natural) abilities and needs are morally relevant. We would make a just distribution of benefits among persons if we help in proportion to their needs, for by doing so, we give them an equal chance with others of enjoying a good life. "That, for instance, is why justice calls for giving extra attention to handicapped people."[21] Only with such attention can they have something comparable to an equal chance with others of achieving the best life they are capable of achieving.

The concept of need furnishes us the clue to the explanation of differences in the way that the law should treat some children—namely, those who clearly lack the capacity for rational choice. It may be said that persons who lack this capacity have a particular sort of need (a handicap) that prevents them from having an equal chance with others of enjoying a good life. If left to their own devices, they would be unable to provide for themselves in an extraordinarily complex society. Hence, we sometimes restrict their liberty, *not* to impose a *burden* on them enjoyed by others but to provide them with a *benefit* of protection and guidance, a benefit that uniquely attends to their special needs and helps them to achieve the best lives they are capable of achieving. It is therefore just to restrict the liberty of this class of children because, having a greater initial burden or deficit (e.g., the burden of being unable to guard against harm), this restriction brings them up to the same level as other children and most adults.

This analysis solves the dilemma posed above. It is true that age is not a morally relevant difference justifying differences in treatment under the law. But the capacity for rational choice is, and the age of a person is believed to correlate with his capacity for rational choice (although, as I have argued, there are as yet no empirically based guidelines that show the precise correlations). Hence, we do not treat children under a certain age unjustly when we deny them certain rights to liberty accorded to other children and most adults, for they are not being unequally treated by being denied such rights. It was the belief that this sort of discrimination led to unequal treatment that was the source of the dilemma.

Finally, the principle of egalitarian justice provides the supplement to the principle of beneficence that is required to avoid excessive interferences with the freedom of action of persons resulting from an application of the latter principle. For unless we can establish the existence of need or another natural characteristic bearing on the goodness or badness of people's lives, then we have insufficient grounds for paternalistic interference. It follows that if the paternalistic purpose of a law restricting the right to liberty of children is not based on a clearly established need, then the law is unjustifiable.

6. Paternalism and Legal Reform

I am hesitant to make specific recommendations for legal reform for two reasons. First, I have examined only one argument that is currently used for legally restricting the freedom of action of children. There are considerations other than those of paternalism that a legislator would appeal to in deciding whether or not to enact a liberty-limiting statute, and I have not discussed these here. Second, although I believe that the age of majority is set much too high for engaging in most of the activities now denied to children, I have no empirical basis for asserting that only children under some specific age (say, twelve years) ought to be paternalistically restricted from engaging in certain activities. One of my main points is that those who have set the age of majority at eighteen years have no such basis either. Thus, they unjustly restrict the liberty of many persons under the age of eighteen when their sole reason for the restriction is preventing them from harming themselves or promoting their good.

Nonetheless, it would be useful to show how the limited form of paternalism that I have defended in the preceding section would work in actual practice. I shall conclude with a discussion of a particularly controversial kind of law—juvenile curfew statutes—in order to indicate the sorts of considerations to which an ideal legislator would attend in deciding whether or not certain liberty-limiting laws are to be adopted for children.

A typical juvenile curfew statute has the following wording in its pertinent part:

> It is unlawful for a person less than 18 years of age to be present at or upon any public assembly, building, place, street, or highway at the following times unless accompanied and supervised by a parent, legal guardian or other responsible companion at least 21 years of age approved by a parent or legal guardian or unless engaged in a business or occupation

which the laws of this State authorize a person less than 18 years to perform:

1. Between 12:01 A.M. and 6:00 A.M. Saturday;
2. Between 12:01 A.M. and 6:00 A.M. Sunday;
3. Between 11:00 P.M. on Sunday to Thursday, inclusive, and 6:00 A.M. on the following day.[22]

Traditionally, the incentive for passing juvenile curfew ordinances has been the hope of city officials that a curfew would keep children apart from "evil influences" found in a city at night and also help police to prevent juvenile delinquency by giving them authority to command nighttime gatherings of youngsters to disperse.[23] Hence, such statutes do not restrict a child's liberty only for paternalistic purposes; the social good of safety and order in the community is another goal they hope to achieve.[24]

A second paternalistic end of such statutes is that of promoting the child's interest in being secure from bodily harm. This seems especially important in large metropolitan communities, where the danger of being on the street late at night is sometimes substantial. And yet, it would be difficult to maintain that juvenile curfew statutes have no bad consequences. There is at least one evil they are said to inflict on children: the loss of freedom to move about in public whenever they choose to do so prevents the child from entering into invaluable social relationships and from the effective exercise of public speech and public religious assembly:

When a person walks out into public he removes the barriers that inhibit ready association and communication by him and his fellow citizens. Only when he is in public may he enjoy the most meaningful exercise of his freedom of speech, his freedom of association, his freedom peaceably to assemble with others, and his freedom of religion.[25]

These are freedoms secured by the First Amendment to the U.S. Constitution and, it might be argued, their loss is at least as great an evil for the child as the possible benefits of being protected from "evil influences" and bodily harm.

The complex questions that an ideal legislator must ask in assessing such statutes on paternalistic grounds now begin to emerge. First, he must establish the probability that the goods and evils cited will occur. If there is a relatively small chance that the goods would be promoted and a substantial chance that the evils will occur, then he has good reason for rejecting the statute. Second, supposing the probabilities of occurrence to be identical, he must ask about the relative value of the goods to be promoted and the evils inflicted. Is it more important that children be free to move about in public places whenever they choose to do so than that they be secure from the sorts of "evil influences" and bodily harms to which they might be subjected? The answer to this question will depend upon the age of the child. The freedom to speak in public is undoubtedly less important to a five-year-old than it is to a sixteen-year-old child.

Let us suppose that the goods and evils cited do in fact occur, and that enacting and enforcing juvenile curfew statutes promote as great a balance of good over evil for children as the alternative of not enacting or enforcing them. We must still ask whether the statutes are *just* in the way in which they *distribute* the goods and evils they promote and inflict on all. I have argued that the egalitarian principle that is to be applied in answering this question is that of *need*. Thus, if the curfew statute is just, there must be adequate proof that the persons to whom it applies actually need the benefit of protection it provides. It seems to me extremely doubtful that this can be shown for *all* children affected by the statute—i.e., all those under eighteen years of age. The only way to establish the factor of need is to show that all children under eighteen years lack the sort of capacity for rational choice that is necessary to contend with the "evil influences" and other harms to which they might be subjected at night in public places. But as I have continually stressed, this claim has no empirical basic whatsoever. Hence, it cannot be just to treat *all* children under eighteen years of age differently than we treat adults by subjecting the former to juvenile curfew statutes (although it may very well be just to restrict the liberty of *some* children in this way).

A final thought. The principle of egalitarian justice establishes that the state has a duty to meet the need of some as yet unspecified age group of children for protection when they are in public places during certain hours. We should note that the principle is silent as to the specific way in which the state is required to meet this need of children for protection. Hence, it could conceivably respond in either of two ways: enact a law prohibiting children from being in public places during the "dangerous" hours *or* give children adequate police protection when they are in public places during these hours. The reason that the state does not opt for the latter alternative is that it is "impractical." The principle that seems to dictate this choice may be worded as follows: when justice requires that we respond to the need(s) of a class of persons and the

only practical way of doing this is to restrict their liberty, then we are justified in restricting their liberty. The problem I have in accepting this principle is due to the ambiguity of the word "practical." It sometimes means "effective," and when it means this, I am sympathetic to the legislator who claims that even a greatly enlarged police force would not be adequate to protect children at night in a large metropolitan area. However, I suspect that "practical" is usually construed to mean "less costly," and the choice that the legislator is asked to make is between asking his constituents to pay higher taxes in order to strengthen the community police force and the far less costly alternative of enacting a juvenile curfew statute. It is not surprising that the average (non-ideal) legislator will vote for the latter alternative.

The ideal legislator, unencumbered by the need to please voters, can pose the following question: which of these alternatives is the greater evil? There are no absolute criteria to which he might appeal in answering this question, but the following consideration may be of some help. If the class of children affected by the statute is restricted to those who clearly need the benefit of protection it provides, then the freedom to travel in or to public places unaccompanied by a parent or legal guardian during the special hours *may* be relatively unimportant. If this is true, then in this sort of limited circumstance, economic considerations may receive a higher priority in making the legislative decision.

Notes

1. There is an excellent account of the legal status of the child, including rights

to liberty, in Alan Sussman, *The Rights of Young People* (New York: Avon, 1977).

2. Nor shall I include "rights to security" in my account—e.g., the right not to be abused, to have one's affairs kept secret or one's reputation undamaged. However, I believe that the theory I propose below can be applied to what Hohfeld refers to as "powers"—i.e., the legal capacity of a person to alter at will some of the rights, duties, powers, etc. of another person. Examples of powers include: the right to execute a will or a contract, to marry, and to vote. See W. N. Hohfeld, *Fundamental Legal Conceptions* (New Haven: Yale University Press, 1919).

3. One of the central considerations would be whether granting the right to liberty would promote the social good. Another would be whether granting a legal right to liberty recognizes a morally basic right of autonomous, rational persons. The former consideration is in the tradition of utilitarianism, the latter in the tradition of deontological ethics.

4. Michael D. Bayles, "Criminal Paternalism," in *The Limits of Law*, ed. by Roland J. Pennock and John W. Chapman (New York: Lieber-Atherton, 1974); Gerald Dworkin, "Paternalism," in *Morality and the Law*, ed. by R. Wasserstrom (Belmont, Calif.: Wadsworth, 1971); Joel Feinberg, "Legal Paternalism," *Canadian Journal of Philosophy*, Vol. 1 (1971), and *Social Philosophy* (Englewood Cliffs, N.J.: Prentice-Hall, 1973), pp. 45–51; Donald H. Regan, "Justifications for Paternalism," in *The Limits of Law*, op. cit.

5. Bernard Gert and Charles W. Culver, "Paternalistic Behavior," *Philosophy and Public Affairs*, Vol. 6 (1976).

6. Hilary Rodham, "Children Under the Law," in Harvard Educational Review (ed.), *The Rights of Children* (Cambridge, Mass., 1974).

7. Bayles, op. cit., p. 176.

8. I owe this distinction to J. Kemp, *Reason, Action and Morality* (New York: Humanities Press, 1964), Ch. VII.

9. I owe this and the next example to Thomas Hill, Jr.

10. B. Inhelder and J. Piaget, *The Growth of Logical Thinking* (New York: Basic Books, 1958).

11. Stephen Toulmin, "The Concept of Stages in Psychological Development," in T. Mischel (ed.), *Cognitive Development and Epistemology* (New York: Academic Press, 1971), pp. 25–71.

12. Another sense of "reasonable" is suggested by Dworkin (op. cit.): a person makes a reasonable choice just in case it can be shown to be consistent with his overall life plan. But see the discussion of this in Bayles, op. cit., p. 182. For another review of the various senses of "rational," see Herbert Fingarette, *The Meaning of Criminal Insanity* (Berkeley: University of California Press, 1972), pp. 185–197.

13. Arlene Skolnik argues that American developmental psychology "has tended to emphasize laboratory studies in which the child performs an unfamiliar task in a strange situation with a strange adult." The bits of information that we get from such studies are so isolated that they do not reflect the real social situations from which they were supposedly derived. A. Skolnik, "The Limits of Childhood," *Law and Contemporary Problems*, Vol. 39 (1975), p. 53.

14. B. C. Ling, "Form discrimination as a learning cue in infants," *Comparative Psychological Monographs*, Vol. 17, No. 2, pp. 519–520. Ling's subjects were fifty children, six to fifteen months of age. They identified and isolated a property of an object—its triangularity, for example—which served to differentiate it in form from some other object. They then ascribed that property to other forms (triangles), where appropriate, even when those forms were larger or smaller than the first, or upside down. The concepts of size, space, time,

number, life, self, and other persons that children possess at various age levels have been clearly established. Such information has been utilized in determining age norms for various concepts in intelligence tests. L. M. Terman and M. A. Merrill, *Measuring Intelligence* (New York: Houghton Mifflin, 1937). At the nine-year-old level, for example, the child should be able to tell how the objects in each of the following pairs are alike and how they are different: honey and glue, pencil and pen, banana and lemon, shoe and glove. By the age of eleven years, he is expected to define such abstract words as "connection" and "obedience." W. E. Martin and C. B. Stendler, *Child Behavior and Development* (New York: Harcourt, 1959), p. 524.

15. Martin and Stendler, ibid., p. 559.
16. William Frankena, *Ethics* (Englewood Cliffs, N.J.: Prentice-Hall, 1973), p. 45. Frankena argues that the principle of utility presupposes the principle of beneficence. "We have a prima facie obligation to maximize the balance of good over evil only if we have a *prior* prima facie obligation to do good and prevent harm."
17. Joel Feinberg, *Social Philosophy,* op. cit., p. 21.
18. John Stuart Mill, *On Liberty* (New York: Liberal Arts Press, 1956), p. 71.
19. Ibid., p. 14.
20. Frankena, op. cit., p. 51.

21. Ibid.
22. *Ill. Rev. Stat.,* 1973, ch. 23, par. 2371.
23. Note, "Curfew Ordinances and the Control of Nocturnal Juvenile Crime," *Univ. of Pennsylvania Law Review,* Vol. 107 (1958), pp. 66–68.
24. This manner of justifying juvenile curfew statutes strikes me as particularly invidious. Justice surely dictates that we choose the narrowest restriction on freedom of action from the available alternatives, consistent with achieving the goal of protecting others from harm to their person or property. Juvenile curfew statutes do not meet this test. There are narrower restrictions on freedom that the state can and already does impose on juveniles—namely, the prohibitions announced by the existing criminal laws on assault, murder, theft, arson, etc. It follows that the entire justificatory burden of juvenile curfew statutes must, in the end, rest on their paternalistic purpose.
25. *People* v. *Chambers,* 335 N.E. 2d 612. This is one of the few cases in which a juvenile curfew law has been struck down on constitutional grounds (as a violation of the Fourteenth Amendment). However, in the first federal case of its kind, the constitutionality of a curfew ordinance was recently upheld by the Third Circuit Court of Appeals. A petition of *certiorari* has just been filed in the United States Supreme Court.

Parents must educate their children for adult life, but how and for which adult life? Various court cases have defined these matters for American parents. Parents may no longer educate children at home, but they may send them to state-certified private schools that better reflect parental values than do public schools. Military and religious schools are noted examples, so too are race- and class-selective schools. Whatever the ideological differences, these schools seek to prepare children for adult life in the general community, or in special parts of it.

Wisconsin v. *Yoder* raises the issue of parents who live outside the general community and wish their children to do likewise. The Old Order Amish try to preserve a simple, rural, religious farm life, relatively free of modern secular concerns. They send their children to public elementary schools to acquire literacy necessary for farming and Bible-reading. But they reject public high school as a threat to the continuity of their families and way of life. Hence, they refuse to send their children to school beyond the age of 14, two years short of the state requirement.

The Court upheld their parental right to do so, under the Constitutional protection of free exercise of religion. They make clear that they do not thereby give comfort to groups "claiming to have recently discovered some 'progressive' or more enlightened process for rearing children for modern life." Nor do they encourage secular rejections of modern life: Thoreau's "philosophical and personal" critique would not keep children out of high schools. But despite this narrow ruling, the *Yoder* decision can and has been cited in defense of parental control in less original contexts.

In dissent, Justice Douglas objects to the Court's indifference to the Amish childrens' opinions in the matter. (Only one of the three involved was interviewed: she seems to endorse her parents' desires.) The Chief Justice replies that the children were not parties to the case, but makes clear that even if they had wanted to attend public school, he would have hesitated to allow the State to force the parents to send them. To do so would be (in the language of *Pierce* v. *Society of Sisters*) to deny parents "the right, coupled with the high duty, to recognize and prepare him [the child] for additional obligations." This preparation is here understood to include "the inculcation of moral standards, religious beliefs, and elements of good citizenship."

Several justices note that children who do leave the Amish world manage to "survive" in modern society without welfare assistance. Some even go on to higher learning and secular professions.

However, no mention is made of those who would like to leave the Amish world, but who understandably fear to do so for want of secular, "modern" skills, even in farming. Nor does the Court address general questions about a parent's right to prepare a child for no other way of life than the parent's own, however worthy that life may be. It may be true, as the Chief Justice says, that young Amish people will not become "burdens on society because of educational shortcomings" since they have "practical agricultural training and habits of industry and self-reliance." But we might wonder whether their prospects in the non-Amish world include more than menial labor, and, if not, whether the Court's standard is too low.

WISCONSIN V. YODER

WISCONSIN v. YODER et al. Certiorari to the Supreme Court of Wisconsin 406 U.S. 205 (1972). Argued before the United States Supreme Court December 8, 1971. Decided May 15, 1972.

Summary

Respondents, members of the Old Order Amish religion and the Conservative Amish Mennonite Church, were convicted of violating Wisconsin's compulsory school-attendance law (which requires a child's school attendance until age 16) by declining to send their children to public or private school after they had graduated from the eighth grade. The evidence showed that the Amish provide continuing informal vocational education to their children designed to prepare them for life in the rural Amish community. The evidence also showed that respondents sincerely believed that high school attendance was contrary to the Amish religion and way of life and that they would endanger their own salvation and that of their children by complying with the law. The State Supreme Court sustained respondents' claim that application of the compulsory school-attendance law to them violated their rights under the Free Ex-

ercise Clause of the First Amendment, made applicable to the States by the Fourteenth Amendment. *Held:*

1. The State's interest in universal education is not totally free from a balancing process when it impinges on other fundamental rights, such as those specifically protected by the Free Exercise Clause of the First Amendment and the traditional interest of parents with respect to the religious upbringing of their children. [Pp. 284–85.]

2. Respondents have amply supported their claim that enforcement of the compulsory formal education requirement after the eighth grade would gravely endanger if not destroy the free exercise of their religious beliefs. [Pp. 285–87.]

3. Aided by a history of three centuries as an identifiable religious sect and a long history as a successful and self-sufficient segment of American society, the Amish have demonstrated the sincerity of their religious beliefs, the interrelationship of belief with their mode of life, the vital role that belief and daily conduct play in the continuing survival of Old Order Amish communities, and the hazards presented by the State's enforcement of a statute generally valid as to others. Beyond this, they have carried

the difficult burden of demonstrating the adequacy of their alternative mode of continuing informal vocational education in terms of the overall interests that the State relies on in support of its program of compulsory high school education. In light of this showing, and weighing the minimal difference between what the State would require and what the Amish already accept, it was incumbent on the State to show with more particularity how its admittedly strong interest in compulsory education would be adversely affected by granting an exemption to the Amish. [Pp. 287–91, 293–94.]

4. The State's claim that it is empowered, as *parens patriae,* to extend the benefit of secondary education to children regardless of the wishes of their parents cannot be sustained against a free exercise claim of the nature revealed by this record, for the Amish have introduced convincing evidence that accommodating their religious objections by forgoing one or two additional years of compulsory education will not impair the physical or mental health of the child, or result in an inability to be self-supporting or to discharge the duties and responsibilities of citizenship, or in any other way materially detract from the welfare of society. [Pp. 291–93.]

49 Wis. 2d 430, 182 N. W. 2d 539, affirmed.

BURGER, C. J., delivered the opinion of the Court, in which BRENNAN, STEWART, WHITE, MARSHALL, and BLACKMUN, JJ., joined. STEWART, J., filed a concurring opinion, in which BRENNAN, J., joined, *post,* p. 237. WHITE, J., filed a concurring opinion, in which BRENNAN and STEWART, JJ., joined, *post,* p. 237. DOUGLAS, J., filed an opinion dissenting in part, *post,* p. 241. POWELL and RHENQUIST, JJ., took no part in the consideration or decision of the case.

John W. Calhoun, Assistant Attorney General of Wisconsin, argued the cause for petitioner. With him on the briefs were Robert W. Warren, Attorney General, and William H. Wilker, Assistant Attorney General.

William B. Ball argued the cause for respondents. With him on the brief was Joseph G. Skelly.

Briefs of *amici curiae* urging affirmance were filed by Donald E. Showalter for the Mennonite Central Committee; by Boardman Noland and Lee Boothby for the General Conference of Seventh-Day Adventists; by William S. Ellis for the National Council of the Churches of Christ; by Nathan Lewin for the National Jewish Commission on Law and Public Affairs; and by Leo Pfeffer for the Synagogue Council of America et al.

MR. CHIEF JUSTICE BURGER delivered the opinion of the Court.

On petition of the State of Wisconsin, we granted the writ of certiorari in this case to review a decision of the Wisconsin Supreme Court holding that respondents' convictions of violating the State's compulsory school-attendance law were invalid under the Free Exercise Clause of the First Amendment to the United States Constitution made applicable to the States by the Fourteenth Amendment. For the reasons hereafter stated we affirm the judgment of the Supreme Court of Wisconsin.

Respondents Jonas Yoder and Wallace Miller are members of the Old Order Amish religion, and respondent Adin Yutzy is a member of the Conservative Amish Mennonite Church. They and their families are residents of Green County, Wisconsin. Wisconsin's compulsory school-attendance law required them to cause their children to attend public or private school until reaching age 16 but the respondents declined to send their children, ages 14 and 15, to public school after they completed the eighth grade.[1] The children were not enrolled in any private school, or within any recognized exception to the compulsory-attendance law,[2] and they are conceded to be subject to the Wisconsin statute.

On complaint of the school district administrator for the public schools, respondents were charged, tried, and convicted of violating the compulsory-attendance law in Green County Court and were fined the sum of $5 each.[3] Respondents defended on the ground that the application of the compulsory-attendance law violated their rights under the First and Fourteenth Amendments.[4] The trial testimony showed that respondents believed, in accordance with the tenets of Old Order Amish communities generally, that their children's attendance at high school, public or private, was contrary to the Amish religion and way of life. They believed that by sending their children to high school, they would not only expose themselves to the danger of the censure of the church community, but, as found by the county court, also endanger their own salvation and that of their children. The State stipulated that respondents' religious beliefs were sincere.

In support of their position, respondents presented as expert witnesses scholars on religion and education whose testimony is uncontradicted. They expressed their opinions on the relationship of the Amish belief concerning school attendance to the more general tenets of their religion, and described the impact that compulsory high school attendance could have on the continued survival of Amish communities as they exist in the United States today. The history of the Amish sect was given in some detail, beginning

with the Swiss Anabaptists of the 16th century who rejected institutionalized churches and sought to return to the early, simple, Christian life de-emphasizing material success, rejecting the competitive spirit, and seeking to insulate themselves from the modern world. As a result of their common heritage, Old Order Amish communities today are characterized by a fundamental belief that salvation requires life in a church community separate and apart from the world and worldly influence. This concept of life aloof from the world and its values is central to their faith.

A related feature of Old Order Amish communities is their devotion to a life in harmony with nature and the soil, as exemplified by the simple life of the early Christian era that continued in America during much of our early national life. Amish beliefs require members of the community to make their living by farming or closely related activities. Broadly speaking, the Old Order Amish religion pervades and determines the entire mode of life of its adherents. Their conduct is regulated in great detail by the *Ordnung,* or rules, of the church community. Adult baptism, which occurs in late adolescence, is the time at which Amish young people voluntarily undertake heavy obligations, not unlike the Bar Mitzvah of the Jews, to abide by the rules of the church community.[5]

Amish objection to formal education beyond the eighth grade is firmly grounded in these central religious concepts. They object to the high school, and higher education generally, because the values they teach are in marked variance with Amish values and the Amish way of life; they view secondary school education as an impermissible exposure of their children to a "worldly" influence in conflict with their beliefs. The high school tends to emphasize intellectual and scientific accomplishments, self-distinction, competitiveness, worldly success, and social life with other students. Amish society emphasizes informal learning-through-doing; a life of "goodness," rather than a life of intellect; wisdom, rather than technical knowledge; community welfare, rather than competition; and separation from, rather than integration with, contemporary worldly society.

Formal high school education beyond the eighth grade is contrary to Amish beliefs, not only because it places Amish children in an environment hostile to Amish beliefs with increasing emphasis on competition in class work and sports and with pressure to conform to the styles, manners, and ways of the peer group, but also because it takes them away from their community, physically and emotionally, during the crucial and formative adolescent period of life. During this period, the children must acquire Amish attitudes favoring manual work and self-reliance and the specific skills needed to perform the adult role of an Amish farmer or housewife. They must learn to enjoy physical labor. Once a child has learned basic reading, writing, and elementary mathematics, these traits, skills, and attitudes admittedly fall within the category of those best learned through example and "doing" rather than in a classroom. And, at this time in life, the Amish child must also grow in his faith and his relationship to the Amish community if he is to be prepared to accept the heavy obligations imposed by adult baptism. In short, high school attendance with teachers who are not of the Amish faith—and may even be hostile to it—interposes a serious barrier to the integration of the Amish child into the Amish religious community. Dr. John Hostetler, one of the experts on Amish society, testified that the modern high school is not equipped, in curriculum or social environment, to impart the values promoted by Amish society.

The Amish do not object to elementary education through the first eight grades as a general proposition because they agree that their children must have basic skills in the "three R's" in order to read the Bible, to be good farmers and citizens, and to be able to deal with non-Amish people when necessary in the course of daily affairs. They view such a basic education as acceptable because it does not significantly expose their children to worldly values or interfere with their development in the Amish community during the crucial adolescent period. While Amish accept compulsory elementary education generally, wherever possible they have established their own elementary schools in many respects like the small local schools of the past. In the Amish belief higher learning tends to develop values they reject as influences that alienate man from God.

On the basis of such considerations, Dr. Hostetler testified that compulsory high school attendance could not only result in great psychological harm to Amish children, because of the conflicts it would produce, but would also, in his opinion, ultimately result in the destruction of the Old Order Amish church community as it exists in the United States today. The testimony of Dr. Donald A. Erickson, an expert witness on education, also showed that the Amish succeed in preparing their high school age children to be productive members of the Amish community. He described their system of learning through doing the skills directly relevant to their adult roles in the Amish community as "ideal" and perhaps superior to ordinary high school education. The evidence also showed that the Amish have an excellent record as law-abiding and generally self-sufficient members of society.

Although the trial court in its careful findings determined that the Wisconsin compulsory school-attendance law "does interfere with the freedom of the Defendants to act in accordance with their sincere religious belief" it also concluded that the requirement of high school attendance until age 16 was a "reasonable and constitutional" exercise of governmental power, and therefore denied the motion to dismiss the charges. The Wisconsin Circuit Court affirmed the convictions. The Wisconsin Supreme Court, however, sustained respondents' claim under the Free Exercise Clause of the First Amendment and reversed the convictions. A majority of the court was of the opinion that the State had failed to make an adequate showing that its interest in "establishing and maintaining an educational system overrides the defendants' right to the free exercise of their religion." 49 Wis. 2d 430, 447, 182 N. W. 2d 539, 547 (1971).

I

There is no doubt as to the power of a State, having a high responsibility for education of its citizens, to impose reasonable regulations for the control and duration of basic education. See, e. g., *Pierce* v. *Society of Sisters*, 268 U. S. 510, 534 (1925). Providing public schools ranks at the very apex of the function of a State. Yet even this paramount responsibility was, in *Pierce*, made to yield to the right of parents to provide an equivalent education in a privately operated system. There the Court held that Oregon's statute compelling attendance in a public school from age eight to age 16

unreasonably interfered with the interest of parents in directing the rearing of their offspring, including their education in church-operated schools. As that case suggests, the values of parental direction of the religious upbringing and education of their children in their early and formative years have a high place in our society. See also *Ginsberg* v. *New York*, 390 U. S. 629, 639 (1968); *Meyer* v. *Nebraska*, 262 U. S. 390 (1923); cf. *Brown* v. *Post Office Dept.*, 397 U. S. 728 (1970). Thus, a State's interest in universal education, however highly we rank it, is not totally free from a balancing process when it impinges on fundamental rights and interests, such as those specifically protected by the Free Exercise Clause of the First Amendment, and the traditional interest of parents with respect to the religious upbringing of their children so long as they, in the words of *Pierce*, "prepare [them] for additional obligations." 268 U. S., at 535.

It follows that in order for Wisconsin to compel school attendance beyond the eighth grade against a claim that such attendance interferes with the practice of a legitimate religious belief, it must appear either that the State does not deny the free exercise of religious belief by its requirement, or that there is a state interest of sufficient magnitude to override the interest claiming protection under the Free Exercise Clause. Long before there was general acknowledgment of the need for universal formal education, the Religion Clauses had specifically and firmly fixed the right to free exercise of religious beliefs, and buttressing this fundamental right was an equally firm, even if less explicit, prohibition against the establishment of any religion by government. The values underlying these two provisions relating to religion have been zealously protected, sometimes even at the expense of other interests of admittedly high social importance. The invalidation of financial aid to parochial schools by government grants for a salary subsidy for teachers is but one example of the extent to which courts have gone in this regard, notwithstanding that such aid programs were legislatively determined to be in the public interest and the service of sound educational policy by States and by Congress. *Lemon* v. *Kurtzman*, 403 U. S. 602 (1971); *Tilton* v. *Richardson*, 403 U. S. 672 (1971). See also *Everson* v. *Board of Education*, 330 U. S. 1, 18 (1947).

The essence of all that has been said and written on the subject is that only those interests of the highest order and those not otherwise served can overbalance legitimate claims to the free exercise of religion. We can accept it as settled, therefore, that, however strong the State's interest in universal compulsory education, it is by no means absolute to the exclusion or subordination of all other interests. *E. g., Sherbert* v. *Verner*, 374 U. S. 398 (1963); *McGowan* v. *Maryland*, 366 U. S. 420, 459 (1961) (separate opinion of Frankfurter, J.); *Prince* v. *Massachusetts*, 321 U. S. 158, 165 (1944).

II

We come then to the quality of the claims of the respondents concerning the alleged encroachment of Wisconsin's compulsory school-attendance statute on their rights and the rights of their children to the free exercise of the religious beliefs they and their forebears have adhered to for almost three centuries. In evaluating those claims we must be careful to determine whether the Amish religious faith and their mode of life are, as they claim, inseparable and interdependent. A way of life, however virtuous and admirable, may not be interposed as a

barrier to reasonable state regulation of education if it is based on purely secular considerations; to have the protection of the Religion Clauses, the claims must be rooted in religious belief. Although a determination of what is a "religious" belief or practice entitled to constitutional protection may present a most delicate question,[6] the very concept of ordered liberty precludes allowing every person to make his own standards on matters of conduct in which society as a whole has important interests. Thus, if the Amish asserted their claims because of their subjective evaluation and rejection of the contemporary secular values accepted by the majority, much as Thoreau rejected the social values of his time and isolated himself at Walden Pond, their claims would not rest on a religious basis. Thoreau's choice was philosophical and personal rather than religious, and such belief does not rise to the demands of the Religion Clauses.

Giving no weight to such secular considerations, however, we see that the record in this case abundantly supports the claim that the traditional way of life of the Amish is not merely a matter of personal preference, but one of deep religious conviction, shared by an organized group, and intimately related to daily living. That the Old Order Amish daily life and religious practice stem from their faith is shown by the fact that it is in response to their literal interpretation of the Biblical injunction from the Epistle of Paul to the Romans, "be not conformed to this world. . . ." This command is fundamental to the Amish faith. Moreover, for the Old Order Amish, religion is not simply a matter of theocratic belief. As the expert witnesses explained, the Old Order Amish religion pervades and determines virtually their entire way of life, regulating it with the detail of the

Talmudic diet through the strictly enforced rules of the church community.

The record shows that the respondents' religious beliefs and attitude toward life, family, and home have remained constant—perhaps some would say static—in a period of unparalleled progress in human knowledge generally and great changes in education.[7] The respondents freely concede, and indeed assert as an article of faith, that their religious beliefs and what we would today call "life style" have not altered in fundamentals for centuries. Their way of life in a church-oriented community, separated from the outside world and "worldly" influences, their attachment to nature and the soil, is a way inherently simple and uncomplicated, albeit difficult to preserve against the pressure to conform. Their rejection of telephones, automobiles, radios, and television, their mode of dress, of speech, their habits of manual work do indeed set them apart from much of contemporary society; these customs are both symbolic and practical.

As the society around the Amish has become more populous, urban, industrialized, and complex, particularly in this century, government regulation of human affairs has correspondingly become more detailed and pervasive. The Amish mode of life has thus come into conflict increasingly with requirements of contemporary society exerting a hydraulic insistence on conformity to majoritarian standards. So long as compulsory education laws were confined to eight grades of elementary basic education imparted in a nearby rural schoolhouse, with a large proportion of students of the Amish faith, the Old Order Amish had little basis to fear that school attendance would expose their children to the worldly influence they reject. But

modern compulsory secondary education in rural areas is now largely carried on in a consolidated school, often remote from the student's home and alien to his daily home life. As the record so strongly shows, the values and programs of the modern secondary school are in sharp conflict with the fundamental mode of life mandated by the Amish religion; modern laws requiring compulsory secondary education have accordingly engendered great concern and conflict.[8] The conclusion is inescapable that secondary schooling, by exposing Amish children to worldly influences in terms of attitudes, goals, and values contrary to beliefs, and by substantially interfering with the religious development of the Amish child and his integration into the way of life of the Amish faith community at the crucial adolescent stage of development, contravenes the basic religious tenets and practice of the Amish faith, both as to the parent and the child.

The impact of the compulsory-attendance law on respondents' practice of the Amish religion is not only severe, but inescapable, for the Wisconsin law affirmatively compels them, under threat of criminal sanction, to perform acts undeniably at odds with fundamental tenets of their religious beliefs. See *Braunfeld v. Brown*, 366 U. S. 599, 605 (1961). Nor is the impact of the compulsory-attendance law confined to grave interference with important Amish religious tenets from a subjective point of view. It carries with it precisely the kind of objective danger to the free exercise of religion that the First Amendment was designed to prevent. As the record shows, compulsory school attendance to age 16 for Amish children carries with it a very real threat of undermining the Amish community and religious practice as they exist today; they must either abandon belief and be assimilated into society at large, or be forced to migrate to some other and more tolerant region.[9]

In sum, the unchallenged testimony of acknowledged experts in education and religious history, almost 300 years of consistent practice, and strong evidence of a sustained faith pervading and regulating respondents' entire mode of life support the claim that enforcement of the State's requirement of compulsory formal education after the eighth grade would gravely endanger if not destroy the free exercise of respondents' religious beliefs.

III

Neither the findings of the trial court nor the Amish claims as to the nature of their faith are challenged in this Court by the State of Wisconsin. Its position is that the State's interest in universal compulsory formal secondary education to age 16 is so great that it is paramount to the undisputed claims of respondents that their mode of preparing their youth for Amish life, after the traditional elementary education, is an essential part of their religious belief and practice. Nor does the State undertake to meet the claim that the Amish mode of life and education is inseparable from and a part of the basic tenets of their religion—indeed, as much a part of their religious belief and practices as baptism, the confessional, or a sabbath may be for others.

Wisconsin concedes that under the Religion Clauses religious beliefs are absolutely free from the State's control, but it argues that "actions," even though religiously grounded, are outside the protection of the First Amendment.[10] But our decisions have rejected the idea that religiously grounded conduct is always outside the protection of the Free Exercise Clause. It is true that activities of individuals, even when religiously based, are often subject to regulation by the States in the exercise of their undoubted power to promote the health, safety, and general welfare, or the Federal Government in the exercise of its delegated powers. See, e. g., *Gillette v. United States*, 401 U. S. 437 (1971); *Braunfeld v. Brown*, 366 U. S. 599 (1961); *Prince v. Massachusetts*, 321 U. S. 158 (1944); *Reynolds v. United States*, 98 U. S. 145 (1879). But to agree that religiously grounded conduct must often be subject to the broad police power of the State is not to deny that there are areas of conduct protected by the Free Exercise Clause of the First Amendment and thus beyond the power of the State to control, even under regulations of general applicability. E. g., *Sherbert v. Verner*, 374 U. S. 398 (1963); *Murdock v. Pennsylvania*, 319 U. S. 105 (1943); *Cantwell v. Connecticut*, 310 U. S. 296, 303–304 (1940). This case, therefore, does not become easier because respondents were convicted for their "actions" in refusing to send their children to the public high school; in this context belief and action cannot be neatly confined in logic-tight compartments. Cf. *Lemon v. Kurtzman*, 403 U. S., at 612.

Nor can this case be disposed of on the grounds that Wisconsin's requirement for school attendance to age 16 applies uniformly to all citizens of the State and does not, on its face, discriminate against religions or a particular religion, or that it is motivated by legitimate secular concerns. A regulation neutral on its face may, in its application, nonetheless offend the constitutional requirement for governmental neutrality if it unduly burdens the free exercise of religion. *Sherbert v. Verner, supra*; cf. *Walz v. Tax Commission*, 397 U. S. 664 (1970). The Court must not ignore the danger

that an exception from a general obligation of citizenship on religious grounds
may run afoul of the Establishment
Clause, but that danger cannot be allowed to prevent any exception no matter how vital it may be to the protection
of values promoted by the right of free
exercise. By preserving doctrinal flexibility and recognizing the need for a
sensible and realistic application of the
Religion Clauses

> we have been able to chart a course
> that preserved the autonomy and free-
> dom of religious bodies while avoiding
> any semblance of established religion.
> This is a "tight rope" and one we have
> successfully traversed. *Walz* v. *Tax
> Commission, supra,* at 672.

We turn, then, to the State's broader
contention that its interest in its system
of compulsory education is so compelling that even the established religious
practices of the Amish must give way.
Where fundamental claims of religious
freedom are at stake, however, we cannot accept such a sweeping claim; despite its admitted validity in the generality of cases, we must searchingly
examine the interests that the State seeks
to promote by its requirement for compulsory education to age 16, and the impediment to those objectives that would
flow from recognizing the claimed Amish
exemption. See, *e. g., Sherbert* v. *Verner,
supra; Martin* v. *City of Struthers,* 319
U. S. 141 (1943); *Schneider* v. *State,* 308
U. S. 147 (1939).

The State advances two primary
arguments in support of its system of
compulsory education. It notes, as
Thomas Jefferson pointed out early in
our history, that some degree of education is necessary to prepare citizens to
participate effectively and intelligently

in our open political system if we are to
preserve freedom and independence.
Further, education prepares individuals
to be self-reliant and self-sufficient participants in society. We accept these
propositions.

However, the evidence adduced by
the Amish in this case is persuasively to
the effect that an additional one or two
years of formal high school for Amish
children in place of their long-established
program of informal vocational education would do little to serve those interests. Respondents' experts testified at
trial, without challenge, that the value of
all education must be assessed in terms
of its capacity to prepare the child for
life. It is one thing to say that compulsory education for a year or two beyond
the eighth grade may be necessary when
its goal is the preparation of the child
for life in modern society as the majority
live, but it is quite another if the goal of
education be viewed as the preparation
of the child for life in the separated
agrarian community that is the keystone
of the Amish faith. See *Meyer* v. *Nebraska,* 262 U. S., at 400.

The State attacks respondents' position as one fostering "ignorance" from
which the child must be protected by the
State. No one can question the State's
duty to protect children from ignorance
but this argument does not square with
the facts disclosed in the record. Whatever their idiosyncrasies as seen by the
majority, this record strongly shows that
the Amish community has been a highly
successful social unit within our society,
even if apart from the conventional
"mainstream." Its members are productive and very law-abiding members of
society; they reject public welfare in any
of its usual modern forms. The Congress
itself recognized their self-sufficiency by

authorizing exemption of such groups as the Amish from the obligation to pay social security taxes.[11]

It is neither fair nor correct to suggest that the Amish are opposed to education beyond the eighth grade level. What this record shows is that they are opposed to conventional formal education of the type provided by a certified high school because it comes at the child's crucial adolescent period of religious development. Dr. Donald Erickson, for example, testified that their system of learning-by-doing was an "ideal system" of education in terms of preparing Amish children for life as adults in the Amish community, and that "I would be inclined to say they do a better job in this than most of the rest of us do." As he put it, "These people aren't purporting to be learned people, and it seems to me the self-sufficiency of the community is the best evidence I can point to—whatever is being done seems to function well."[12]

We must not forget that in the Middle Ages important values of the civilization of the Western World were preserved by members of religious orders who isolated themselves from all worldly influences against great obstacles. There can be no assumption that today's majority is "right" and the Amish and others like them are "wrong." A way of life that is odd or even erratic but interferes with no rights or interests of others is not to be condemned because it is different.

The State, however, supports its interest in providing an additional one or two years of compulsory high school education to Amish children because of the possibility that some such children will choose to leave the Amish community, and that if this occurs they will be ill-equipped for life. The State argues that if Amish children leave their church they should not be in the position of making their way in the world without the education available in the one or two additional years the State requires. However, on this record, that argument is highly speculative. There is no specific evidence of the loss of Amish adherents by attrition, nor is there any showing that upon leaving the Amish community Amish children, with their practical agricultural training and habits of industry and self-reliance, would become burdens on society because of educational shortcomings. Indeed, this argument of the State appears to rest primarily on the State's mistaken assumption, already noted, that the Amish do not provide any education for their children beyond the eighth grade, but allow them to grow in "ignorance." To the contrary, not only do the Amish accept the necessity for formal schooling through the eighth grade level, but continue to provide what has been characterized by the undisputed testimony of expert educators as an "ideal" vocational education for their children in the adolescent years.

There is nothing in this record to suggest that the Amish qualities of reliability, self-reliance, and dedication to work would fail to find ready markets in today's society. Absent some contrary evidence supporting the State's position, we are unwilling to assume that persons possessing such valuable vocational skills and habits are doomed to become burdens on society should they determine to leave the Amish faith, nor is there any basis in the record to warrant a finding that an additional one or two years of formal school education beyond the eighth grade would serve to eliminate any such problem that might exist.

Insofar as the State's claim rests on the view that a brief additional period of formal education is imperative to enable the Amish to participate effectively and intelligently in our democratic process, it must fall. The Amish alternative to formal secondary school education has enabled them to function effectively in their day-to-day life under self-imposed limitations on relations with the world, and to survive and prosper in contemporary society as a separate, sharply identifiable and highly self-sufficient community for more than 200 years in this country. In itself this is strong evidence that they are capable of fulfilling the social and political responsibilities of citizenship without compelled attendance beyond the eighth grade at the price of jeopardizing their free exercise of religious belief.[13] When Thomas Jefferson emphasized the need for education as a bulwark of a free people against tyranny, there is nothing to indicate he had in mind compulsory education through any fixed age beyond a basic education. Indeed, the Amish communities singularly parallel and reflect many of the virtues of Jefferson's ideal of the "sturdy yeoman" who would form the basis of what he considered as the ideal of a democratic society.[14] Even their idiosyncratic separateness exemplifies the diversity we profess to admire and encourage.

The requirement for compulsory education beyond the eighth grade is a relatively recent development in our history. Less than 60 years ago, the educational requirements of almost all of the States were satisfied by completion of the elementary grades, at least where the child was regularly and lawfully employed.[15] The independence and successful social functioning of the Amish community for a period approaching almost three centuries and more than 200 years in this country are strong evidence that there is at best a speculative gain, in terms of meeting the duties of citizenship, from an additional one or two years of compulsory formal education. Against this background it would require a more particularized showing from the State on this point to justify the severe interference with religious freedom such additional compulsory attendance would entail.

We should also note that compulsory education and child labor laws find their historical origin in common humanitarian instincts, and that the age limits of both laws have been coordinated to achieve their related objectives.[16] In the context of this case, such considerations, if anything, support rather than detract from respondents' position. The origins of the requirement for school attendance to age 16, an age falling after the completion of elementary school but before completion of high school, are not entirely clear. But to some extent such laws reflected the movement to prohibit most child labor under age 16 that culminated in the provisions of the Federal Fair Labor Standards Act of 1938.[17] It is true, then, that the 16-year child labor age limit may to some degree derive from a contemporary impression that children should be in school until that age. But at the same time, it cannot be denied that, conversely, the 16-year education limit reflects, in substantial measure, the concern that children under that age not be employed under conditions hazardous to their health, or in work that should be performed by adults.

The requirement of compulsory schooling to age 16 must therefore be viewed as aimed not merely at providing educational opportunities for children, but as an alternative to the equally undesirable consequence of unhealthful child labor displacing adult workers, or, on the other hand, forced idleness.[18] The two kinds of statutes—compulsory school attendance and child labor laws—tend to keep children of certain ages off the labor market and in school; this regimen in turn provides opportunity to prepare for a livelihood of a higher order than that which children could pursue without education and protects their health in adolescence.

In these terms, Wisconsin's interest in compelling the school attendance of Amish children to age 16 emerges as somewhat less substantial than requiring such attendance for children generally. For, while agricultural employment is not totally outside the legitimate concerns of the child labor laws, employment of children under parental guidance and on the family farm from age 14 to age 16 is an ancient tradition that lies at the periphery of the objectives of such laws.[19] There is no intimation that the Amish employment of their children on family farms is in any way deleterious to their health or that Amish parents exploit children at tender years. Any such inference would be contrary to the record before us. Moreover, employment of Amish children on the family farm does not present the undesirable economic aspects of eliminating jobs that might otherwise be held by adults.

IV

Finally, the State, on authority of *Prince* v. *Massachusetts*, argues that a decision exempting Amish children from the State's requirement fails to recognize the substantive right of the Amish child to a secondary education, and fails to give due regard to the power of the State as *parens patriae* to extend the benefit of secondary education to children regardless of the wishes of their parents. Taken at its broadest sweep, the Court's language in *Prince*, might be read to give

support to the State's position. However, the Court was not confronted in *Prince* with a situation comparable to that of the Amish as revealed in this record; this is shown by the Court's severe characterization of the evils that it thought the legislature could legitimately associate with child labor, even when performed in the company of an adult. 321 U. S., at 169–170. The Court later took great care to confine *Prince* to a narrow scope in *Sherbert* v. *Verner*, when it stated:

> On the other hand, the Court has rejected challenges under the Free Exercise Clause to governmental regulation of certain overt acts prompted by religious beliefs or principles, for "even when the action is in accord with one's religious convictions, [it] is not totally free from legislative restrictions." *Braunfeld* v. *Brown*, 366 U. S. 599, 603. The conduct or actions so regulated have invariably posed some substantial threat to public safety, peace or order. See, *e. g.*, *Reynolds* v. *United States*, 98 U. S. 145; *Jacobson* v. *Massachusetts*, 197 U. S. 11; *Prince* v. *Massachusetts*, 321 U. S. 158. . . . 374 U. S., at 402–403.

This case, of course, is not one in which any harm to the physical or mental health of the child or to the public safety, peace, order, or welfare has been demonstrated or may be properly inferred.[20] The record is to the contrary, and any reliance on that theory would find no support in the evidence.

Contrary to the suggestion of the dissenting opinion of Mr. Justice Douglas, our holding today in no degree depends on the assertion of the religious interest of the child as contrasted with that of the parents. It is the parents who are subject to prosecution here for failing to cause their children to attend school, and it is their right of free exercise, not that of their children, that must determine Wisconsin's power to impose criminal penalties on the parent. The dissent argues that a child who expresses a desire to attend public high school in conflict with the wishes of his parents should not be prevented from doing so. There is no reason for the Court to consider that point since it is not an issue in the case. The children are not parties to this litigation. The State has at no point tried this case on the theory that respondents were preventing their children from attending school against their expressed desires, and indeed the record is to the contrary.[21] The State's position from the outset has been that it is empowered to apply its compulsory-attendance law to Amish parents in the same manner as to other parents—that is, without regard to the wishes of the child. That is the claim we reject today.

Our holding in no way determines the proper resolution of possible competing interests of parents, children, and the State in an appropriate state court proceeding in which the power of the State is asserted on the theory that Amish parents are preventing their minor children from attending high school despite their expressed desires to the contrary. Recognition of the claim of the State in such a proceeding would, of course, call into question traditional concepts of parental control over the religious upbringing and education of their minor children recognized in this Court's past decisions. It is clear that such an intrusion by a State into family decisions in the area of religious training would give rise to grave questions of religious freedom comparable to those raised here and those presented in *Pierce* v. *Society of Sisters*, 268 U. S. 510 (1925). On this record we neither reach nor decide those issues.

The State's argument proceeds

without reliance on any actual conflict between the wishes of parents and children. It appears to rest on the potential that exemption of Amish parents from the requirements of the compulsory-education law might allow some parents to act contrary to the best interests of their children by foreclosing their opportunity to make an intelligent choice between the Amish way of life and that of the outside world. The same argument could, of course, be made with respect to all church schools short of college. There is nothing in the record or in the ordinary course of human experience to suggest that non-Amish parents generally consult with children of ages 14–16 if they are placed in a church school of the parents' faith.

Indeed it seems clear that if the State is empowered, as *parens patriae*, to "save" a child from himself or his Amish parents by requiring an additional two years of compulsory formal high school education, the State will in large measure influence, if not determine, the religious future of the child. Even more markedly than in *Prince*, therefore, this case involves the fundamental interest of parents, as contrasted with that of the State, to guide the religious future and education of their children. The history and culture of Western civilization reflect a strong tradition of parental concern for the nurture and upbringing of their children. This primary role of the parents in the upbringing of their children is now established beyond debate as an enduring American tradition. If not the first, perhaps the most significant statements of the Court in this area are found in *Pierce* v. *Society of Sisters*, in which the Court observed:

Under the doctrine of *Meyer* v. *Nebraska*, 262 U. S. 390, we think it entirely plain that the Act of 1922 unreasonably interferes with the liberty of parents and guardians to direct the upbringing and education of children under their control. As often heretofore pointed out, rights guaranteed by the Constitution may not be abridged by legislation which has no reasonable relation to some purpose within the competency of the State. The fundamental theory of liberty upon which all governments in this Union repose excludes any general power of the State to standardize its children by forcing them to accept instruction from public teachers only. The child is not the mere creature of the State; those who nurture him and direct his destiny have the right, coupled with the high duty, to recognize and prepare him for additional obligations. 268 U. S., at 534–535.

The duty to prepare the child for "additional obligations," referred to by the Court, must be read to include the inculcation of moral standards, religious beliefs, and elements of good citizenship. *Pierce,* of course, recognized that where nothing more than the general interest of the parent in the nurture and education of his children is involved, it is beyond dispute that the State acts "reasonably" and constitutionally in requiring education to age 16 in some public or private school meeting the standards prescribed by the State.

However read, the Court's holding in *Pierce* stands as a charter of the rights of parents to direct the religious upbringing of their children. And, when the interests of parenthood are combined with a free exercise claim of the nature revealed by this record, more than merely a "reasonable relation to some purpose within the competency of the State" is required to sustain the validity of the State's requirement under the First

Amendment. To be sure, the power of the parent, even when linked to a free exercise claim, may be subject to limitation under *Prince* if it appears that parental decisions will jeopardize the health or safety of the child, or have a potential for significant social burdens. But in this case, the Amish have introduced persuasive evidence undermining the arguments the State has advanced to support its claims in terms of the welfare of the child and society as a whole. The record strongly indicates that accommodating the religious objections of the Amish by forgoing one, or at most two, additional years of compulsory education will not impair the physical or mental health of the child, or result in an inability to be self-supporting or to discharge the duties and responsibilities of citizenship, or in any other way materially detract from the welfare of society.

In the face of our consistent emphasis on the central values underlying the Religion Clauses in our constitutional scheme of government, we cannot accept a *parens patriae* claim of such all-encompassing scope and with such sweeping potential for broad and unforeseeable application as that urged by the State.

V

For the reasons stated we hold, with the Supreme Court of Wisconsin, that the First and Fourteenth Amendments prevent the State from compelling respondents to cause their children to attend formal high school to age 16.[22] Our disposition of this case, however, in no way alters our recognition of the obvious fact that courts are not school boards or legislatures, and are ill-equipped to determine the "necessity" of discrete aspects of a State's program of compulsory education. This should suggest that courts must move with great circumspection in performing the sensitive and delicate task of weighing a State's legitimate social concern when faced with religious claims for exemption from generally applicable educational requirements. It cannot be overemphasized that we are not dealing with a way of life and mode of education by a group claiming to have recently discovered some "progressive" or more enlightened process for rearing children for modern life.

Aided by a history of three centuries as an identifiable religious sect and a long history as a successful and self-sufficient segment of American society, the Amish in this case have convincingly demonstrated the sincerity of their religious beliefs, the interrelationship of belief with their mode of life, the vital role that belief and daily conduct play in the continued survival of Old Order Amish communities and their religious organization, and the hazards presented by the State's enforcement of a statute generally valid as to others. Beyond this, they have carried the even more difficult burden of demonstrating the adequacy of their alternative mode of continuing informal vocational education in terms of precisely those overall interests that the State advances in support of its program of compulsory high school education. In light of this convincing showing, one that probably few other religious groups or sects could make, and weighing the minimal difference between what the State would require and what the Amish already accept, it was incumbent on the State to show with more particularity how its admittedly strong interest in compulsory education would be adversely affected by granting an exemption to the Amish. *Sherbert* v. *Verner, supra.*

Nothing we hold is intended to un-

dermine the general applicability of the State's compulsory school-attendance statutes or to limit the power of the State to promulgate reasonable standards that, while not impairing the free exercise of religion, provide for continuing agricultural vocational education under parental and church guidance by the Old Order Amish or others similarly situated. The States have had a long history of amicable and effective relationships with church-sponsored schools, and there is no basis for assuming that, in this related context, reasonable standards cannot be established concerning the content of the continuing vocational education of Amish children under parental guidance, provided always that state regulations are not inconsistent with what we have said in this opinion.[23]

Affirmed.

Notes

1. The children, Frieda Yoder, aged 15, Barbara Miller, aged 15, and Vernon Yutzy, aged 14, were all graduates of the eighth grade of public school.
2. Wis. Stat. § 118.15 (1969) provides in pertinent part:
"118.15 *Compulsory school attendance*
"(1) (a) Unless the child has a legal excuse or has graduated from high school, any person having under his control a child who is between the ages of 7 and 16 years shall cause such child to attend school regularly during the full period and hours, religious holidays excepted, that the public or private school in which such child should be enrolled is in session until the end of the school term, quarter or semester of the school year in which he becomes 16 years of age. . . .
"(3) This section does not apply to any child who is not in proper physical or mental condition to attend school,

to any child exempted for good cause by the school board of the district in which the child resides or to any child who has completed the full 4-year high school course. The certificate of a reputable physician in general practice shall be sufficient proof that a child is unable to attend school.

"(4) Instruction during the required period elsewhere than at school may be substituted for school attendance. Such instruction must be approved by the state superintendent as substantially equivalent to instruction given to children of like ages in the public or private schools where such children reside.

"(5) Whoever violates this section . . . may be fined not less than $5 nor more than $50 or imprisoned not more than 3 months or both."

Section 118.15 (1) (b) requires attendance to age 18 in a school district containing a "vocational, technical and adult education school," but this section is concededly inapplicable in this case, for there is no such school in the district involved.

3. Prior to trial, the attorney for respondents wrote the State Superintendent of Public Instruction in an effort to explore the possibilities for a compromise settlement. Among other possibilities, he suggested that perhaps the State Superintendent could administratively determine that the Amish could satisfy the compulsory-attendance law by establishing their own vocational training plan similar to one that has been established in Pennsylvania. Supp. App. 6. Under the Pennsylvania plan, Amish children of high school age are required to attend an Amish vocational school for three hours a week, during which time they are taught such subjects as English, mathematics, health, and social studies by an Amish teacher. For the balance of the week, the children perform farm and household duties under parental supervision, and keep a

journal of their daily activities. The major portion of the curriculum is home projects in agriculture and homemaking. See generally J. Hostetler & G. Huntington, Children in Amish Society: Socialization and Community Education, c. 5 (1971). A similar program has been instituted in Indiana. *Ibid.* See also Iowa Code § 299.24 (1971); Kan. Stat. Ann. § 72–1111 (Supp. 1971).

The Superintendent rejected this proposal on the ground that it would not afford Amish children "substantially equivalent education" to that offered in the schools of the area. Supp. App. 6.

4. The First Amendment provides: "Congress shall make no law respecting an establishment of religion, or prohibiting the free exercise thereof. . . ."

5. See generally J. Hostetler, Amish Society (1968); J. Hostetler & G. Huntington, Children in Amish Society (1971); Littell, Sectarian Protestantism and the Pursuit of Wisdom: Must Technological Objectives Prevail?, in Public Controls for Nonpublic Schools 61 (D. Erickson ed. 1969).

6. See *Welsh* v. *United States*, 398 U. S. 333, 351–361 (1970) (Harlan, J., concurring in result); *United States* v. *Ballard*, 322 U. S. 78 (1944).

7. See generally R. Butts & L. Cremin, A History of Education in American Culture (1953); L. Cremin, The Transformation of the School (1961).

8. Hostetler, *supra*, n. 5, c. 9; Hostetler & Huntington, *supra*, n. 5.

9. Some States have developed working arrangements with the Amish regarding high school attendance. See n. 3, *supra*. However, the danger to the continued existence of an ancient religious faith cannot be ignored simply because of the assumption that its adherents will continue to be able, at considerable sacrifice, to relocate in some more tolerant State or country or work out accommodations under threat of criminal prosecution. Forced migration of reli-

gious minorities was an evil that lay at the heart of the Religion Clauses. See, e. g., *Everson* v. *Board of Education,* 330 U. S. 1, 9–10 (1947); Madison, Memorial and Remonstrance Against Religious Assessments, 2 Writings of James Madison 183 (G. Hunt ed. 1901).

10. That has been the apparent ground for decision in several previous state cases rejecting claims for exemption similar to that here. See, e. g., *State* v. *Garber,* 197 Kan. 567, 419 P. 2d 896 (1966), cert. denied, 389 U. S. 51 (1967); *State* v. *Hershberger,* 103 Ohio App. 188, 144 N. E. 2d 693 (1955); *Commonwealth* v. *Beiler,* 168 Pa. Super. 462, 79 A. 2d 134 (1951).

11. Title 26 U. S. C. § 1402 (h) authorizes the Secretary of Health, Education, and Welfare to exempt members of "a recognized religious sect" existing at all times since December 31, 1950, from the obligation to pay social security taxes if they are, by reason of the tenets of their sect, opposed to receipt of such benefits and agree to waive them, provided the Secretary finds that the sect makes reasonable provision for its dependent members. The history of the exemption shows it was enacted with the situation of the Old Order Amish specifically in view. H. R. Rep. No. 213, 89th Cong., 1st Sess., 101–102 (1965).

The record in this case establishes without contradiction that the Green County Amish had never been known to commit crimes, that none had been known to receive public assistance, and that none were unemployed.

12. Dr. Erickson had previously written: "Many public educators would be elated if their programs were as successful in preparing students for productive community life as the Amish system seems to be. In fact, while some public schoolmen strive to outlaw the Amish approach, others are being forced to emulate many of its features." Erickson,

Showdown at an Amish Schoolhouse: A Description and Analysis of the Iowa Controversy, in Public Controls for Nonpublic Schools 15, 53 (D. Erickson ed. 1969). And see Littell, *supra,* n. 5, at 61.

13. All of the children involved in this case are graduates of the eighth grade. In the county court, the defense introduced a study by Dr. Hostetler indicating that Amish children in the eighth grade achieved comparably to non-Amish children in the basic skills. Supp. App. 9–11. See generally Hostetler & Huntington, *supra,* n. 5, at 88–96.

14. While Jefferson recognized that education was essential to the welfare and liberty of the people, he was reluctant to directly force instruction of children "in opposition to the will of the parent." Instead he proposed that state citizenship be conditioned on the ability to "read readily in some tongue, native or acquired." Letter from Thomas Jefferson to Joseph Cabell, Sept. 9, 1817, in 17 Writings of Thomas Jefferson 417, 423–424 (Mem. ed. 1904). And it is clear that, so far as the mass of the people were concerned, he envisaged that a basic education in the "three R's" would sufficiently meet the interests of the State. He suggested that after completion of elementary school, "those destined for labor will engage in the business of agriculture, or enter into apprenticeships to such handicraft art as may be their choice." Letter from Thomas Jefferson to Peter Carr, Sept. 7, 1814, in Thomas Jefferson and Education in a Republic 93–106 (Arrowood ed. 1930). See also *id.,* at 60–64, 70, 83, 136–137.

15. See Dept. of Interior, Bureau of Education, Bulletin No. 47, Digest of State Laws Relating to Public Education 527–559 (1916); Joint Hearings on S. 2475 and H. R. 7200 before the Senate Committee on Education and Labor 75th Cong., 1st Sess., pt. 2, p. 416.

Even today, an eighth grade education fully satisfies the educational requirements of at least six States. See Ariz. Rev. Stat. Ann. § 15–321 (B) (4) (1956); Ark. Stat. Ann. § 80–1504 (1947); Iowa Code § 299.2 (1971); S. D. Comp. Laws Ann. § 13–27–1 (1967); Wyo. Stat. Ann. § 21.1–48 (Supp. 1971). (Mississippi has no compulsory education law.) A number of other States have flexible provisions permitting children aged 14 or having completed the eighth grade to be excused from school in order to engage in lawful employment. *E. g.,* Colo. Rev. Stat. Ann. §§ 1 123–20–5, 80–6–1 to 80–6–12 (1963); Conn. Gen. Stat. Rev. §§ 10–184, 10–189 (1964); D. C. Code Ann. §§ 31–202, 36–201 to 36–228 (1967); Ind. Ann. Stat. §§ 28–505 to 28–506, 28–519 (1948); Mass. Gen. Laws Ann., c. 76, § 1 (Supp. 1972) and c. 149, § 86 (1971); Mo. Rev. Stat. §§ 167.031, 294.051 (1969); Nev. Rev. Stat. § 392.110 (1968); N. M. Stat. Ann. § 77–10–6 (1968).

An eighth grade education satisfied Wisconsin's formal education requirements until 1933. See Wis. Laws 1927, c. 425, § 97; Laws 1933, c. 143. (Prior to 1933, provision was made for attendance at continuation or vocational schools by working children past the eighth grade, but only if one was maintained by the community in question.) For a general discussion of the early development of Wisconsin's compulsory education and child labor laws, see F. Ensign, Compulsory School Attendance and Child Labor 203–230 (1921).

16. See, *e. g.,* Joint Hearings, *supra,* n. 15, pt. 1, at 185–187 (statement of Frances Perkins, Secretary of Labor), pt. 2, at 381–387 (statement of Katherine Lenroot, Chief, Children's Bureau, Department of Labor); National Child Labor Committee, 40th Anniversary Report. The Long Road (1944); 1 G. Abbott, The Child and the State 259–269, 566 (Greenwood reprint 1968); L. Cremin, The Transformation of the School, c. 3 (1961); A. Steinhilber & C. Sokolowski, State Law on Compulsory Attendance 3–4 (Dept. of Health, Education, and Welfare 1966).

17. 52 Stat. 1060, as amended, 29 U. S. C. §§ 201–219.

18. See materials cited n. 16, *supra;* Casad, Compulsory Education and Individual Rights, in 5 Religion and the Public Order 51, 82 (D. Giannella ed. 1969).

19. See, *e. g.,* Abbott, *supra,* n. 16, at 266. The Federal Fair Labor Standards Act of 1938 excludes from its definition of "[o]ppressive child labor" employment of a child under age 16 by "a parent . . . employing his own child . . . in an occupation other than manufacturing or mining or an occupation found by the Secretary of Labor to be particularly hazardous for the employment of children between the ages of sixteen and eighteen years or detrimental to their health or well-being." 29 U. S. C. § 203 (*l*).

20. Cf. *e. g., Jacobson v. Massachusetts,* 197 U. S. 11 (1905); *Wright v. DeWitt School District,* 238 Ark. 906, 385 S. W. 2d 644 (1965); *Application of President and Directors of Georgetown College, Inc.,* 118 U. S. App. D. C. 80, 87–90, 1 F. 2d 1000, 1007–1010 (in-chambers opinion), cert. denied, 377 U. S. 978 (1964).

21. The only relevant testimony in the record is to the effect that the wishes of the one child who testified corresponded with those of her parents. Testimony of Frieda Yoder, Tr. 92–94, to the effect that her personal religious beliefs guided her decision to discontinue school attendance after the eighth grade. The other children were not called by either side.

22. What we have said should meet the suggestion that the decision of the Wisconsin Supreme Court recognizing an exemption for the Amish from the State's system of compulsory education constituted an impermissible establishment of religion. In *Walz v. Tax Com-*

mission, the Court saw the three main concerns against which the Establishment Clause sought to protect as "sponsorship, financial support, and active involvement of the sovereign in religious activity." 397 U. S. 664, 668 (1970). Accommodating the religious beliefs of the Amish can hardly be characterized as sponsorship or active involvement. The purpose and effect of such an exemption are not to support, favor, advance, or assist the Amish, but to allow their centuries-old religious society, here long before the advent of any compulsory education, to survive free from the heavy impediment compliance with the Wisconsin compulsory-education law would impose. Such an accommodation "reflects nothing more than the governmental obligation of neutrality in the face of religious differences, and does not represent that involvement of religious with secular institutions which it is the object of the Establishment Clause to forestall." *Sherbert* v. *Verner,* 374 U. S. 398, 409 (1963).

23. Several States have now adopted plans to accommodate Amish religious beliefs through the establishment of an "Amish vocational school." See n. 3, *supra.* These are not schools in the traditional sense of the word. As previously noted, respondents attempted to reach a compromise with the State of Wisconsin patterned after the Pennsylvania plan, but those efforts were not productive. There is no basis to assume that Wisconsin will be unable to reach a satisfactory accommodation with the Amish in light of what we now hold, so as to serve its interests without impinging on respondents' protected free exercise of their religion.

Mr. Justice Powell and Mr. Justice Rehnquist took no part in the consideration or decision of this case.

Mr. Justice Stewart, with whom Mr. Justice Brennan joins, concurring.

This case involves the constitutionality of imposing criminal punishment upon Amish parents for their religiously based refusal to compel their children to attend public high schools. Wisconsin has sought to brand these parents as criminals for following *their* religious beliefs, and the Court today rightly holds that Wisconsin cannot constitutionally do so.

This case in no way involves any questions regarding the right of the children of Amish parents to attend public high schools, or any other institutions of learning, if they wish to do so. As the Court points out, there is no suggestion whatever in the record that the religious beliefs of the children here concerned differ in any way from those of their parents. Only one of the children testified. The last two questions and answers on her cross-examination accurately sum up her testimony:

> Q. So I take it then, Frieda, the only reason you are not going to school, and did not go to school since last September, is because of *your* religion?
> A. Yes.
> Q. That is the only reason?
> A. Yes. (Emphasis supplied.)

It is clear to me, therefore, that this record simply does not present the interesting and important issue discussed in Part II of the dissenting opinion of Mr. Justice Douglas. With this observation, I join the opinion and the judgment of the Court.

Mr. Justice White, with whom Mr. Justice Brennan and Mr. Justice Stewart join, concurring.

Cases such as this one inevitably call for a delicate balancing of important but conflicting interests. I join the opinion and judgment of the Court because I cannot say that the State's interest in requiring two more years of compulsory education in the ninth and tenth grades outweighs the importance of the concededly sincere Amish religious practice to the survival of that sect.

This would be a very different case for me if respondents' claim were that their religion forbade their children from attending any school at any time and from complying in any way with the educational standards set by the State. Since the Amish children are permitted to acquire the basic tools of literacy to survive in modern society by attending grades one through eight and since the deviation from the State's compulsory-education law is relatively slight, I conclude that respondents' claim must prevail, largely because "religious freedom—the freedom to believe and to practice strange and, it may be, foreign creeds—has classically been one of the highest values of our society." *Braunfeld* v. *Brown*, 366 U. S. 599, 612 (1961) (BRENNAN, J., concurring and dissenting).

The importance of the state interest asserted here cannot be denigrated, however:

> Today, education is perhaps the most important function of state and local governments. Compulsory school attendance laws and the great expenditures for education both demonstrate our recognition of the importance of education to our democratic society. It is required in the performance of our most basic public responsibilities, even service in the armed forces. It is the very foundation of good citizenship. Today it is a principal instrument in awakening the child to cultural values, in preparing him for later professional

training, and in helping him to adjust normally to his environment. *Brown* v. *Board of Education*, 347 U. S. 483, 493 (1954).

As recently as last Term, the Court re-emphasized the legitimacy of the State's concern for enforcing minimal educational standards, *Lemon* v. *Kurtzman*, 403 U. S. 602, 613 (1971).[1] *Pierce v. Society of Sisters*, 268 U. S. 510 (1925), lends no support to the contention that parents may replace state educational requirements with their own idiosyncratic views of what knowledge a child needs to be a productive and happy member of society; in *Pierce*, both the parochial and military schools were in compliance with all the educational standards that the State had set, and the Court held simply that while a State may posit such standards, it may not pre-empt the educational process by requiring children to attend public schools.[2] In the present case, the State is not concerned with the maintenance of an educational system as an end in itself, it is rather attempting to nurture and develop the human potential of its children, whether Amish or non-Amish: to expand their knowledge, broaden their sensibilities, kindle their imagination, foster a spirit of free inquiry, and increase their human understanding and tolerance. It is possible that most Amish children will wish to continue living the rural life of their parents, in which case their training at home will adequately equip them for their future role. Others, however, may wish to become nuclear physicists, ballet dancers, computer programmers, or historians, and for these occupations, formal training will be necessary. There is evidence in the record that many children desert the Amish faith when they come of age.[3] A State has a legitimate interest not only in seeking to develop the latent talents of its children but also in seeking to prepare them for the life style that they may later choose, or at least to provide them with an option other than the life they have led in the past. In the circumstances of this case, although the question is close, I am unable to say that the State has demonstrated that Amish children who leave school in the eighth grade will be intellectually stultified or unable to acquire new academic skills later. The statutory minimum school attendance age set by the State is, after all, only 16.

Decision in cases such as this and the administration of an exemption for Old Order Amish from the State's compulsory school-attendance laws will inevitably involve the kind of close and perhaps repeated scrutiny of religious practices, as is exemplified in today's opinion, which the Court has heretofore been anxious to avoid. But such entanglement does not create a forbidden establishment of religion where it is essential to implement free exercise values threatened by an otherwise neutral program instituted to foster some permissible, nonreligious state objective. I join the Court because the sincerity of the Amish religious policy here is uncontested, because the potentially adverse impact of the state requirement is great, and because the State's valid interest in education has already been largely satisfied by the eight years the children have already spent in school.

Notes

1. The challenged Amish religious practice here does not pose a substantial threat to public safety, peace, or order; if it did,

analysis under the Free Exercise Clause would be substantially different. See *Jacobson* v. *Massachusetts*, 197 U. S. 11 (1905); *Prince* v. *Massachusetts*, 321 U. S. 158 (1944); *Cleveland* v. *United States*, 329 U. S. 14 (1946); *Application of President and Directors of Georgetown College, Inc.*, 118 U. S. App. D. C. 80, 331 F. 2d 1000, cert. denied, 377 U. S. 978 (1964).

2. "No question is raised concerning the power of the State reasonably to regulate all schools, to inspect, supervise and examine them, their teachers and pupils; to require that all children of proper age attend some school, that teachers shall be of good moral character and patriotic disposition, that certain studies plainly essential to good citizenship must be taught, and that nothing be taught which is manifestly inimical to the public welfare." *Pierce* v. *Society of Sisters*, 268 U. S. 510, 534 (1925).

3. Dr. Hostetler testified that though there was a gradual increase in the total number of Old Order Amish in the United States over the past 50 years, "at the same time the Amish have also lost members [of] their church" and that the turnover rate was such that "probably two-thirds [of the present Amish] have been assimilated non-Amish people." App. 110. Justice Heffernan, dissenting below, opined that "[l]arge numbers of young people voluntarily leave the Amish community each year and are thereafter forced to make their way in the world." 49 Wis. 2d 430, 451, 182 N. W. 2d 539, 549 (1971).

MR. JUSTICE DOUGLAS, dissenting in part.

I

I agree with the Court that the religious scruples of the Amish are opposed to the education of their children beyond the grade schools, yet I disagree with the Court's conclusion that the matter is within the dispensation of parents alone. The Court's analysis assumes that the only interests at stake in the case are those of the Amish parents on the one hand, and those of the State on the other. The difficulty with this approach is that, despite the Court's claim, the parents are seeking to vindicate not only their own free exercise claims, but also those of their high-school-age children.

It is argued that the right of the Amish children to religious freedom is not presented by the facts of the case, as the issue before the Court involves only the Amish parents' religious freedom to defy a state criminal statute imposing upon them an affirmative duty to cause their children to attend high school.

First, respondents' motion to dismiss in the trial court expressly asserts, not only the religious liberty of the adults, but also that of the children, as a defense to the prosecutions. It is, of course, beyond question that the parents have standing as defendants in a criminal prosecution to assert the religious interests of their children as a defense.[1] Although the lower courts and a majority of this Court assume an identity of interest between parent and child, it is clear that they have treated the religious interest of the child as a factor in the analysis.

Second, it is essential to reach the question to decide the case, not only because the question was squarely raised in the motion to dismiss, but also because no analysis of religious-liberty claims can take place in a vacuum. If the parents in this case are allowed a religious exemption, the ineviable effect is to impose the parents' notions of religious duty upon their children. Where the child is mature enough to express potentially conflicting desires, it would be an invasion of the child's rights to

permit such an imposition without canvassing his views. As in *Prince* v. *Massachusetts,* 321 U. S. 158, it is an imposition resulting from this very litigation. As the child has no other effective forum, it is in this litigation that his rights should be considered. And, if an Amish child desires to attend high school, and is mature enough to have that desire respected, the State may well be able to override the parents' religiously motivated objections.

Religion is an individual experience. It is not necessary, nor even appropriate, for every Amish child to express his views on the subject in a prosecution of a single adult. Crucial, however, are the views of the child whose parent is the subject of the suit. Frieda Yoder has in fact testified that her own religious views are opposed to high-school education. I therefore join the judgment of the Court as to respondent Jonas Yoder. But Frieda Yoder's views may not be those of Vernon Yutzy or Barbara Miller. I must dissent, therefore, as to respondents Adin Yutzy and Wallace Miller as their motion to dismiss also raised the question of their children's religious liberty.

II

This issue has never been squarely presented before today. Our opinions are full of talk about the power of the parents over the child's education. See *Pierce* v. *Society of Sisters,* 268 U. S. 510; *Meyer* v. *Nebraska,* 262 U. S. 390. And we have in the past analyzed similar conflicts between parent and State with little regard for the views of the child. See *Prince* v. *Massachusetts, supra.* Recent cases, however, have clearly held that the children themselves have constitutionally protectible interests.

These children are "persons" within the meaning of the Bill of Rights. We have so held over and over again. In *Haley* v. *Ohio,* 332 U. S. 596, we extended the protection of the Fourteenth Amendment in a state trial of a 15-year-old boy. In *In re Gault,* 387 U. S. 1, 13, we held that "neither the Fourteenth Amendment nor the Bill of Rights is for adults alone." In *In re Winship,* 397 U. S. 358, we held that a 12-year-old boy, when charged with an act which would be a crime if committed by an adult, was entitled to procedural safeguards contained in the Sixth Amendment.

In *Tinker* v. *Des Moines School District,* 393 U. S. 503, we dealt with 13-year-old, 15-year-old, and 16-year-old students who wore armbands to public schools and were disciplined for doing so. We gave them relief, saying that their First Amendment rights had been abridged.

> Students in school as well as out of school are "persons" under our Constitution. They are possessed of fundamental rights which the State must respect, just as they themselves must respect their obligations to the State. *Id.,* at 511.

In *Board of Education* v. *Barnette,* 319 U. S. 624, we held that schoolchildren, whose religious beliefs collided with a school rule requiring them to salute the flag, could not be required to do so. While the sanction included expulsion of the students and prosecution of the parents, *id.,* at 630, the vice of the regime was its interference with the child's free exercise of religion. We said: "Here . . . we are dealing with a compulsion of students to declare a belief." *Id.,* at 631. In emphasizing the important and delicate task of boards of education we said:

> That they are educating the young for citizenship is reason for scrupulous protection of Constitutional freedoms of the individual, if we are not to strangle the free mind at its source and teach youth to discount important principles of our government as mere platitudes. *Id.,* at 637.

On this important and vital matter of education, I think the children should be entitled to be heard. While the parents, absent dissent, normally speak for the entire family, the education of the child is a matter on which the child will often have decided views. He may want to be a pianist or an astronaut or an oceanographer. To do so he will have to break from the Amish tradition.[2]

It is the future of the student, not the future of the parents, that is imperiled by today's decision. If a parent keeps his child out of school beyond the grade school, then the child will be forever barred from entry into the new and amazing world of diversity that we have today. The child may decide that that is the preferred course, or he may rebel. It is the student's judgment, not his parents', that is essential if we are to give full meaning to what we have said about the Bill of Rights and of the right of students to be masters of their own destiny.[3] If he is harnessed to the Amish way of life by those in authority over him and if his education is truncated, his entire life may be stunted and deformed. The child, therefore, should be given an opportunity to be heard before the State gives the exemption which we honor today.

The views of the two children in question were not canvassed by the Wisconsin courts. The matter should be explicitly reserved so that new hearings can be held on remand of the case.[4]

III

I think the emphasis of the Court on the "law and order" record of this Amish group of people is quite irrelevant. A religion is a religion irrespective of what the misdemeanor or felony records of its members might be. I am not at all sure how the Catholics, Episcopalians, the Baptists, Jehovah's Witnesses, the Unitarians, and my own Presbyterians would make out if subjected to such a test. It is, of course, true that if a group or society was organized to perpetuate crime and if that is its motive, we would have rather startling problems akin to those that were raised when some years back a particular sect was challenged here as operating on a fraudulent basis. *United States* v. *Ballard*, 322 U. S. 78. But no such factors are present here, and the Amish, whether with a high or low criminal record,[5] certainly qualify by all historic standards as a religion within the meaning of the First Amendment.

The Court rightly rejects the notion that actions, even though religiously grounded, are always outside the protection of the Free Exercise Clause of the First Amendment. In so ruling, the Court departs from the teaching of *Reynolds* v. *United States*, 98 U. S. 145, 164, where it was said concerning the reach of the Free Exercise Clause of the First Amendment, "Congress was deprived of all legislative power over mere opinion, but was left free to reach actions which were in violation of social duties or subversive of good order." In that case it was conceded that polygamy was a part of the religion of the Mormons. Yet the Court said, "It matters not that his belief [in polygamy] was a part of his professed religion: it was still belief, and belief only." *Id.*, at 167.

Action, which the Court deemed to be antisocial, could be punished even though it was grounded on deeply held and sincere religious convictions. What we do today, at least in this respect, opens the way to give organized religion a broader base than it has ever enjoyed; and it even promises that in time *Reynolds* will be overruled.

In another way, however, the Court retreats when in reference to Henry Thoreau it says his "choice was philosophical and personal rather than religious, and such belief does not rise to the demands of the Religion Clauses." That is contrary to what we held in *United States* v. *Seeger*, 380 U. S. 163, where we were concerned with the meaning of the words "religious training and belief" in the Selective Service Act, which were the basis of many conscientious objector claims. We said:

> Within that phrase would come all sincere religious beliefs which are based upon a power or being, or upon a faith, to which all else is subordinate or upon which all else is ultimately dependent. The test might be stated in these words: A sincere and meaningful belief which occupies in the life of its possessor a place parallel to that filled by the God of those admittedly qualifying for the exemption comes within the statutory definition. This construction avoids imputing to Congress an intent to classify different religious beliefs, exempting some and excluding others, and is in accord with the well-established congressional policy of equal treatment for those whose opposition to service is grounded in their religious tenets. *Id.*, at 176.

Welsh v. *United States*, 398 U. S. 333, was in the same vein, the Court saying:

In this case, Welsh's conscientious objection to war was undeniably based in part on his perception of world politics. In a letter to his local board, he wrote: "I can only act according to what I am and what I see. And I see that the military complex wastes both human and material resources, that it fosters disregard for (what I consider a paramount concern) human needs and ends; I see that the means we employ to 'defend' our 'way of life' profoundly change that way of life. I see that in our failure to recognize the political, social, and economic realities of the world, we, *as a nation*, fail our responsibility *as a nation*." *Id.*, at 342.

The essence of Welsh's philosophy, on the basis of which we held he was entitled to an exemption, was in these words:

"I believe that human life is valuable in and of itself; in its living; therefore I will not injure or kill another human being. This belief (and the corresponding 'duty' to abstain from violence toward another person) is not 'superior to those arising from any human relation.' On the contrary: *it is essential to every human relation*. I cannot, therefore, conscientiously comply with the Government's insistence that I assume duties which I feel are immoral and totally repugnant." *Id.*, at 343.

I adhere to these exalted views of "religion" and see no acceptable alternative to them now that we have become a Nation of many religions and sects, representing all of the diversities of the human race. *United States* v. *Seeger*, 380 U. S., at 192–193 (concurring opinion).

Notes

1. Thus, in *Prince* v. *Massachusetts*, 321 U. S. 158, a Jehovah's Witness was convicted for having violated a state child labor law by allowing her nine-year-old niece and ward to circulate religious literature on the public streets. There, as here, the narrow question was the religious liberty of the adult. There, as here, the Court analyzed the problem from the point of view of the State's conflicting interest in the welfare of the child. But, as MR. JUSTICE BRENNAN, speaking for the Court, has so recently pointed out, "The Court [in *Prince*] implicitly held that the custodian had standing to assert alleged freedom of religion . . . rights of the child that were threatened in the very litigation before the Court and that the child had no effective way of asserting herself." *Eisenstadt* v. *Baird*, 405 U. S. 438, 446 n. 6. Here, as in *Prince*, the children have no effective alternate means to vindicate their rights. The question, therefore, is squarely before us.

2. A significant number of Amish children do leave the Old Order. Professor Hostetler notes that "[t]he loss of members is very limited in some Amish districts and considerable in others." J. Hostetler, Amish Society 226 (1968). In one Pennsylvania church, he observed a defection rate of 30%. *Ibid.* Rates up to 50% have been reported by others. Casad, Compulsory High School Attendance and the Old Order Amish: A Commentary on State v. Garber, 16 Kan. L. Rev. 423, 434 n. 51 (1968).

3. The court below brushed aside the students' interests with the offhand comment that "[w]hen a child reaches the age of judgment, he can choose for himself his religion." 49 Wis. 2d 430, 440, 182 N. W. 2d 539, 543. But there is nothing in this record to indicate that the moral and intellectual judgment demanded of the student by the question in this case is beyond his capacity. Children far younger than the 14- and 15-year-olds involved here are regularly permitted to testify in custody and other proceedings. Indeed, the failure to call

the affected child in a custody hearing is often reversible error. See, *e. g., Callicott v. Callicott,* 364 S. W. 2d 455 (Civ. App. Tex.) (reversible error for trial judge to refuse to hear testimony of eight-year-old in custody battle). Moreover, there is substantial agreement among child psychologists and sociologists that the moral and intellectual maturity of the 14-year-old approaches that of the adult. See, *e. g.,* J. Piaget, The Moral Judgment of the Child (1948); D. Elkind, Children and Adolescents 75–80 (1970); Kohlberg, Moral Education in the Schools: A Developmental View, in R. Muuss, Adolescent Behavior and Society 193, 199–200 (1971); W. Kay, Moral Development 172–183 (1968); A. Gesell & F. Ilg, Youth: The Years From Ten to Sixteen 175–182 (1956). The maturity of Amish youth, who identify with and assume adult roles from early childhood, see M. Goodman, The Culture of Childhood 92–94 (1970), is certainly not less than that of children in the general population.

4. Canvassing the views of all school-age Amish children in the State of Wisconsin would not present insurmountable difficulties. A 1968 survey indicated that there were at that time only 256 such children in the entire State. Comment, 1971 Wis. L. Rev. 832, 852 n. 132.

5. The observation of Justice Heffernan, dissenting below, that the principal opinion in his court portrayed the Amish as leading a life of "idyllic agrarianism," is equally applicable to the majority opinion in this Court. So, too, is his observation that such a portrayal rests on a "mythological basis." Professor Hostetler has noted that "[d]rinking among the youth is common in all the large Amish settlements." Amish Society 283. Moreover, "[i]t would appear that among the Amish the rate of suicide is just as high, if not higher, than for the nation." *Id.,* at 300. He also notes an unfortunate Amish "preoccupation with filthy stories," *id.,* at 282, as well as significant "rowdyism and stress." *Id.,* at 281. These are not traits peculiar to the Amish, of course. The point is that the Amish are not people set apart and different.

There is more to growing up than growing older and finally attaining one's majority. Legal emancipation must, if it is to have a purpose, be coupled with an inner emancipation which allows a person to decide for himself how to use the liberties which majority confers. But the two emancipations often do not go hand in hand. The history of strong voices speaking out against oppression testifies to inner emancipation which has no legal counterpart. Outer emancipation without inner strength is shown by many still dependent and timid adults in jurisdictions which confer on them liberties they do not use. If we are concerned that children (and others) have liberty rights, we must be equally concerned that they acquire the autonomy which makes these rights valuable. If they do not, they will, after all, still be acting at others' behest, and the point of liberty is lost.

The next two essays take up the problem of inner emancipation. In the first, Edmund Leites looks at Locke's account of bringing up children for autonomy. Locke claims that parents should exercise firm authority with young children, but that if they do so in a reasonable way, then the children will gradually transfer allegiance from the parent personally to the standards of reason the parent presents. Such a child, when grown, will not kowtow to further authorities; such a parent will respect intimations of reason as they first appear in the child. In Locke's view, permissive child rearing does not help children to acquire autonomy, but rather hinders their development of self-control. Parental authority is essential to bring up persons who have the autonomy and reasoning ability to enjoy liberty; but it is equally essential that this authority be temporary and used only until children can be their own masters.

LOCKE'S LIBERAL THEORY OF PARENTHOOD

EDMUND LEITES

Parents today are sometimes uneasy about their right to exercise authority over their children; they are not sure they have any real right to command their children's obedience. Mothers and fathers who are unsure of their right to govern may nonetheless require submission from their children, at least, in some matters. They may come to this out of a despairing conviction that things will just not work out at home if they do not exercise some rule. But the underlying insecurity about the legitimacy of parental authority can remain.

Mothers and fathers may regard the use of parental authority as bad because they think it encourages "authoritarian" attitudes in their children. If parents bring up their child to be submissive to their wills, is it not likely that he will become an adult who is willing to be ruled in a similar way by political figures? He will submit to a similar authoritarian rule in the wider world, outside the family, and expect others to do likewise. And as he grows older, he will find or seek to find a powerful, commanding, and awesome father in the nation's capital to take the psychological role once filled by his own father. Writings of Wilhelm Reich, A. S. Neill, and members of the Frankfurt School (Max Horkheimer, Theodor Adorno, Herbert Marcuse, and others) sustain these suspicions about the political implications of parental authority.

There are opposing views, however, about the parental right to command children. These views ought to be examined with care, especially if they are supported by considerable philosophical and psychological insight. For this reason, John Locke's views on the legitimacy of parental authority and its political meanings are well worth our attention.

Although Locke remained a bachelor without children throughout his life, he had much experience in raising and educating children. From 1660 to 1666, as part of his duties as lecturer in Greek at Christ Church, Oxford, Locke had students under his care and tuition. His tutorial duties, writes James Axtell, "consisted primarily of ministering to the intellectual and domestic needs of up to ten pupils ranging in age from thirteen to eighteen." He was truly *in loco parentis*. His account book indicates that he spent money on one pupil's behalf for "door keys, paper, laundry, bedmaker, butler, caution money, nurses, doctors and medicine for illnesses, and tutor's fees" (Locke, 1968: 38).

Locke's interest and studies in medicine led to his meeting Anthony Ashley Cooper, Lord Ashley (later the first Earl of Shaftesbury) in 1666. Ashley took a liking to Locke and in that same year invited him to London, to be his medical advisor and general aide. At Exeter House, the London home of Lord Ashley, Locke took on both pediatric and pedagogical duties. He was given full educational and medical charge of Ashley's fifteen-year-old son and sole heir, who was of sickly constitution. Later, after the son's marriage (in a match arranged by Locke himself), he supervised the education and general upbringing of the seven children, male and female, of this marriage. The eldest son, and heir (who became the third Earl of Shaftesbury and a philosophical luminary of late seventeenth-century England), was put under Locke's particular charge. Shaftesbury writes that Locke had "the absolute direction of my education." Locke did more than raise and educate Shaftesbury; he even assisted at his birth, in his capacity as household physician (Locke, 1968: 45).

In 1675, after the first Earl of Shaftesbury had lost his government offices, Locke left Exeter House and traveled in France. But this was not the end of his career as an educator and guardian of youth. After a year and a half in France, at the behest of Shaftesbury and his friend Sir John Banks, he undertook the care of Banks's son, Caleb, "to let him see the manners" of the French. From 1677 to 1679, Caleb was in his charge in Paris and other parts of France; only snow in the Alps prevented their visiting Rome. After 1679, Locke never again had children or young men under his personal supervision; but by this time, as Axtell puts it, he "had passed through a whole spectrum of gentlemanly educational experience—Oxford don, pediatrician, private tutor, and travelling governor on the grand tour" (Locke, 1968: 47).

II

Locke was never a parent; but as is evident from the foregoing, he had much experience acting in the place of parents. His interest and experience in political matters is well known. In the following pages, I shall explore his views on the duties parents have toward their children, the authority they rightly have over them, and the implications of their authority for political life.

In the second of his *Two Treatises of Government,* Locke writes that "all *Parents*" are, "by the Law of Nature," *"under an obligation to preserve, nourish, and educate their Children,"* who are "the Workmanship" of God. He defines parental responsibility in matters of education in these broad terms: parents must give "such vigor and rectitude" to their children's minds as will make them "most useful to themselves and others" as adults. More specifically, they must prepare their children for the freedom to which they have a right as adults. For while children are not born in freedom, they are "born to it." Young children's want of judgment makes them stand in need of restraint and discipline; parents therefore have a right to govern them. But a child ends his nonage when he "comes to the use of *his Reason.*" This permits him to know "the Law of Reason," which ought to govern all his acts. He then has a right to act according to his own will by the light of his

own understanding of this common "Law of Nature" (*Treatises,* II, §§55–57, 64, 173, 174).[1]

If the child and his father live "under the positive Law of an Establish'd Government," he now has the capacity to know these laws as well, and to rule his will in accordance with them. So, he now has a liberty, equal to his father's, "to dispose of his Actions and Possessions according to his own Will, within the Permission of that Law." Moreover, he now has a relation to the law of the established government which he did not have as a child. He has the ability to ascertain whether the government and its laws conform to the higher law of reason, which defines and limits the purposes and powers of civil government; for government has a rightful claim to his obedience only if it does so. As an adult, he should evaluate his government for himself in the light of this higher law; in this, as in all other matters, he should govern his *"Will"* by his *own* "Understanding" (*Treatises,* II, §§59, 149–51, 55).

What must parents do to bring up children who will be self-reliant in this way? We should not expect a full theory of childhood education from Locke in his *Two Treatises,* since it is a work on government. However, what we do get is curious. Locke tells us that since a child is born into the world "in an Estate, wherein he has not *Understanding* of his own to direct his *Will;* he is not to have any Will of his own to follow: He that understands for him, must will for him too; he must proscribe to his Will, and regulate his Actions" (*Treatises,* II, §55). At first, it is hard to see how Locke's method of education makes it likely that children will become adults who will be self-reliant in judgment and masters of their own will. Children are to have no will of their own, and are to subject their will in all things to the understanding of their parents; how does this prepare them for the freedom and responsibilities of adulthood?

Yet, Locke does think that this regime, *as part of a larger scheme of childhood education,* will lead children to become adults who will govern their conduct by judgments they have made for themselves. For a full statement and explanation of his belief, we must turn to his *Thoughts concerning Education.* There, he says that a resolution of the natural struggle between *parent* and *child* which establishes the full authority of the parents can help greatly to resolve the natural struggle between *reason* and *willfulness* that also occurs, *within* the child, as he moves toward adulthood.[2]

The struggle between parents and child begins early, for a child loves "*Dominion*" even more than he loves "*Liberty*. . . . And this is the first Original of the most vicious Habits, that are ordinary and natural. This love of *Power* and Dominion shows it self very early, . . . Children as soon almost as they are born . . . cry, grow peevish, sullen, and out of humor, for nothing but to have their *Wills.* They would have their Desires submitted to by others." This love of dominion leads a child to contend with his parents "for Mastery." The parents must win, for if they do not, they will not only end up his slave but make him a slave to his own willfulness. "When their Children are grown up," parents who did not take their children in hand when young "complain, that the Brats are untoward and perverse." They should not be surprised. Since their children had their way with parents and tutors when young, why should they not continue to be willful when older?

(*Thoughts,* §§103–104, 38, 78, 35). But if parental mastery is achieved *in the name and spirit of reason,* it allows the child to grow into an adult who will turn to his own reason for guidance in matters of conduct and belief. The rigorous rule of a young child is therefore justified because it enables him to rule himself as an adult.

The same willfulness, the same demand to have whatever one desires, which is expressed in children's desire to have their own way over their parents, is at work within their souls. There, its opponent is their own good judgment, weakly developed, and at first having little power over their conduct. How shall they develop the habit of giving the reins to reason, rather than to their willful desires?

Locke does not believe that a power sufficient to command conduct will accrue to children's reason without help from adults. Modern parents sometimes suppose that children are most likely to grow up to be adults who will regulate themselves if they are left to regulate themselves as children, without parental interference. The earlier adults call upon children to govern themselves by the use of their own reason, the better. Parental interference is thus seen as a check upon the growth of a child's self-governing habits. Locke observes that rationality attracts children at an early age, for the growth of their rational capacities is a sign to them of their maturity, their growth toward adulthood. "If I mis-observe not," he writes, "they love to be treated as Rational Creatures sooner than is imagined" (*Thoughts,* §81). To treat them in this way is to begin to give them some of the dignity of adults. But their attraction to their own rationality is a weak force compared to the power of other desires—including, above all, their desire to have their own way, no matter what. Hence, their own reason is at first, and must remain for some time, a weak opponent. Parents cannot expect their child's own rationality to command the field against his desires. On their own, children *cannot* tame themselves in the name of reason.

Parents must therefore tame their children's will for them, in the name and spirit of a reasonableness which is too weak in the children themselves. To tame this willfulness in one's children is to create within them a firm and unswerving habit of submission to reason, even if it is, at the outset, the reason of the parents. But "he that is not used to submit his Will to the Reason of others, *when* he is *Young,* will scarce hearken to submit to his own Reason when he is of an Age to make use of it" (*Thoughts,* §36).

Parents should not gain this submission by a general use of corporeal punishment, but by creating, as soon as possible, a sense of awe in their children which will lead them willingly to conduct themselves as their parents wish. "Every one will judge it reasonable, that their Children, *when little,* should look upon their Parents as their Lords, their Absolute Governors, and, as such stand in Awe of them." This ought to give parents their "first power" over their children's minds (*Thoughts,* §51, 77, 41, 42). A child's experience of the affection which his parents naturally have for him, and his experience of their conscientious concern for his good, which they ought to have, will make it easier for him to submit to their will. He will love them. But awe consists of more than love. There must also be a certain distance between parents and their

child, and he must deeply fear offending them (*Thoughts,* §99). With awe of his parents as a basis, his submission to parental judgment can be gradually transformed into a willing submission to his own reason.

Readers may object that Locke's method of training is authoritarian; that children who are not permitted to judge for themselves are not likely to become adults who will habitually govern their conduct by their own reason. But Locke says that children (and adults) have a natural desire to act as they see fit. If a parental regime is not too harsh, children's spirits will not be broken; they will retain this desire. They will be submissive to their parents, but wish for the freedom of adults. Yet, this desire cannot be left untouched, for if it is, submissive children may become adults who simply do what they like, however unreasonable their actions may be. If they are to become adults who rely on their reason to govern their conduct, parents must offer the proper example. Children want to be adults; their idea of adulthood is formed largely by the behavior of those who govern them. If parents govern not only their children but also *themselves* in the name and spirit of reason, they will give their children a strong desire to govern themselves by reasonable means. They need not fear that their example will go to waste. Even at an early age, children can often perceive when adults are acting in the spirit of reason.[3]

Locke grants that a child's attraction to the use of reason is not based solely on an emulation of parental example. In some way (Locke does not make clear how) children come to the idea that the use of reason is an essential element of maturity, whether or not their parents make much use of it. Parents who fail to be rational thus may rightly fear their children's disrespect. "Frequent, and especially, passionate *Chiding*," Locke writes, is of "ill consequence. It lessens the Authority of the Parents and the Respect of the Child: For . . . they distinguish early betwixt Passion and Reason: And as they cannot but have a Reverence for what comes from the latter, so they quickly grow into a contempt of the former; . . . natural Inclination will easily learn to slight such Scare-crows, which make noise, but are not animated by Reason" (*Thoughts*, §77).

But the child's natural respect for rationality, as an element of maturity, competes with another idea of adult life: grown-ups are free to do whatever they want, reasonable or not. Parents must regulate their conduct in the name and spirit of reason, if they wish the former idea to mean more to their child than the latter. Counseling fathers on the upbringing of a son, Locke writes,

> If anything scape you, which you would have pass for a Fault in him, he will be sure to shelter himself under your Example, and shelter himself so as that it will not be easie to come at him, to correct it in him the right Way. If you punish him for what he sees you practice your self, . . . he will be apt to interpret it, the Peevishness, and Arbitrary Imperiousness of a Father, who, without and Ground for it, would deny his Son the Liberty and Pleasures he takes himself. Or if you assume to your self the liberty you have taken, as a Privilege belonging to riper Years, to which a Child must not aspire, you do but add new force to your Example, . . . For you must always remember, that Children affect to be Men earlier than is thought: And they love

Breeches, not for their Cut, or Ease, but because having them is a Mark or Step towards Manhood. (*Thoughts*, §71)

If children are habitually willful, their emulation of rationality in adults, strong as it is, will not be able to match the power of their habit of self-indulgence. But if their willfulness has been tamed by their parent's rule, their desire to govern themselves as their parents do can meet with success, for their own reason can manage their already tamed desires. Hence, as they grow older, they can gradually become self-reliant adults. Locke says that once a child easily submits to the reasonable rule of his parents, they should prepare him for his freedom by encouraging him to rely on his own judgment in matters within the reach of his understanding. As children "grow up to the Use of Reason," the rigor of parental government should be "gently relaxed" (*Thoughts*, §41). It should be relaxed

> . . . as fast as their Age, Discretion, and Good Behavior . . . allow it; even to that degree, that a Father would do well, as his Son grows up, and is capable of it, to talk *familiarly with* him; nay, *ask his advice*, and *Consult* with him, about those things wherein he has nay knowledge, or understanding. By this, the Father will put . . . serious Considerations into his Son's Thoughts, . . . The sooner *you treat him as a Man*, the sooner he will begin to be one. . . . (*Thoughts*, §95)

Once children are in proper awe of their parents, their faults should be dealt with by calm words and reasons adapted to their understanding. Locke does not suppose that girls and boys "in Hanging-Sleeves" should have "the Reason and Conduct of Councellors." Yet, apart from obstinacy, which may require physical punishment, "there will never want such Motives, as may be sufficient to convince them" or "the Vertue they should be excited to" or "Fault they should be kept from." If no other reasons seem suited to their minds, "these will always be intelligible, and of force to deter them from any Fault, fit to be taken notice of in them, (*viz.*) That it will be a Discredit and a Disgrace to them, and displease you" (*Thoughts,* §§39, 81).

When obstinacy is the source of a child's misbehavior, however, physical punishment may be used if words do not work, but only if there is some hope that the child will become truly more willing to obey his parents. If whippings do not have this effect, Locke asks, "to what purpose should they be any more used?" (*Thoughts,* §§78, 87).

Even if we grant that Locke's method of education may create adults who look to their own reason for guidance, we may still find Locke's method of child rearing rather harsh. Hence, it should be noted that he thinks the use of parental authority is a delicate matter. Mastery of impulse is essential to virtue, but energy and spirit must also be strong in anyone who is to do much for himself or others. Too harsh a parental regime, even in the name of reason, will break the mind or spirit of a child. He will be a *"low spirited moap'd Creature"* who, when grown, will be of as little use to himself as he is to his friends. "The true Secret of Education," Locke writes, is to know "how to keep up a Child's Spirits, easy, active and free; and yet, at the same time, to restrain him from many things he has a Mind to, and to draw him to things that are uneasy to him" (*Thoughts,* §§51, 65; also see §46).

Curiosity and a spirit of playful inquiry are not encouraged by the heavy hand of parental authority, but Locke thinks these motives should play a large part in the intellectual growth of a child. Therefore, when it comes to the learning of reading, writing, and other elements of a proper curriculum, he contends that parental commands should ordinarily not be used to force a young child to study. The right way to teach children reading, writing, foreign languages, etc., "is to give them a Liking and Inclination to what you propose to them to be learn'd; and that will engage their Industry and Application" (*Thoughts,* §72).

III

Locke says that by his methods, children will gain "an ingenuous Education" (*Thoughts,* §45). This means, on the one hand, an education designed to bring up a child to be "noble in . . . character . . . , generous . . . high-minded"; on the other hand, it may also mean an "education befitting a free-born person" or "one of honorable station" (*Oxford English Dictionary.* Today we might say that Locke's object is a *liberal* education; see the *OED,* and see Garforth, in Locke, 1964: 60). These two distinct senses of "ingenuous" raise problems, however. For is Locke's method of education suited to those who find themselves in such dependent social positions that a reliance on their own judgment of what is permitted by law, civil or moral, will only make their lives miserable, if they survive at all? Shall day laborers, wholly dependent upon the economic good will of others, speak and act their mind as gentlemen do? Shall servants who live in the family, and are considered to be under the paternal authority of the master of the house, have this self-reliance? Shall women, even gentlewomen, govern themselves as gentlemen do? Is his method really suited, or meant, for *all* children?

We can raise these same questions in the light of the unequal distribution of *political* rights in late seventeenth-century England. Locke is no democrat; he does not advocate the extension of suffrage to poor adult males or to women. Can we suppose that he nonetheless thinks that all should be educated so that they will act in the light of their own judgment of what the law requires? Why would Locke believe that this education is suited to all if he thinks that most must rest content to be ruled by others, in politics, marriage, and work?

Such questions might lead us to conclude that his system of moral education was meant only for the *sons* of *gentlemen*. As adults, they could make good use of a self-reliant attitude in moral and legal matters. Politics would be open to them. They would be nobody's servant or humble wife, and their economic well-being would free them from having to act in a servile manner in order to make a living. This conclusion would be reinforced by Locke's own statements concerning the purpose of this book.

Locke introduces the *Thoughts* by saying that it is aimed at *"our* English *Gentry,"* for he is concerned *"that the young Gentlemen should be put into (that which every one ought to be solicitous about) the best way of being formed and instructed."* If those of the rank of gentlemen *"are by their Education once set right, they will quickly bring all the rest into Order."* He concludes his book by saying that he desired only to present *"some general*

Views, in reference to the main End, and aims in Education, and those designed for a Gentlemen's Son" (*Thoughts*, The Epistle Dedicatory, §216).

I would nonetheless argue that Locke believes his method of moral education is fit for all. Locke's statements concerning the purpose of his book are made with reference to the *whole book;* but it does not mean he believes that only gentlemen would benefit from the methods described. Some are particularly suited to gentlemen (or their betters), but the fundamental elements of moral training have wider application.

Young gentlemen require "Breeding"; they need to be taught the carriage and manners which will prepare them to act and feel in a manner suitable to their station in life. They should not be given the manners suitable to a "Prince" or "Nobleman," nor should they be given the breeding suitable to someone of lower station. Gentlemen are in the middle of the social hierarchy. They must know how to conduct themselves with appropriate dignity in the presence of their equals, their inferiors, and their superiors (*Thoughts*, §§216, 141–43; also see §94).

Gentlemen must also be given an education fit for the leisure they will have as adults. Thus, their tutors should introduce them to science, mathematics, philosophy, and other subjects which they may pursue more deeply, if they wish, as adults. Their leisure will also permit them to take a responsible part in public life; to do so is their proper calling (*Thoughts*, §94). Hence, a gentleman's child must learn sufficient history, law, and political theory, and have sufficient experience in political life (when he is of a suitable age to gain it), to play an intelligent part in the public world (see "Some Thoughts Concerning Reading and Study for a Gentleman," in Locke, 1968, 397–404). In his private affairs, he may be faced with substantial matters of business, investment, finance, and the like; therefore, he must be prepared, "step by step," for these things as well. It is of more import for a son to learn how to "manage his affairs wisely" than it is for him to learn to speak Greek and Latin (*Thoughts*, §94).[4]

All these things should be taught to those who will be gentlemen. However, the chief object of education, the creation of a virtuous character, which must include moral self-reliance, is not reserved for gentlemen, noblemen, or princes. *This* is an object that should guide the education of anyone, high or low, male or female. Reflecting on the education of a son, Locke writes, "I place Vertue as the first and most necessary of those endowments that belong to a *Man* or a Gentleman, . . . Without that I think, He will be happy neither in this, nor in the other World" (*Thoughts*, §135; my italics).

Women deserve no less. Locke writes that "the principal aim of his . . . Discourse is, how a young Gentleman should be brought up from his Infancy, which, in all things will not so perfectly suit the Education of Daughters; though where the Difference of Sex requires different Treatment 'twill be no hard Matter to distinguish" (*Thoughts*, §6). It does not affect Locke's methods of moral education. His *Some Thoughts concerning Education* is based on a set of letters he wrote to Edward Clarke concerning the education of his son, Edward, Jr. At one point in the correspondence, Mrs. Clarke requested Locke to counsel her on the education of their daughter, Elizabeth. In response, Locke wrote, "since . . . I acknowledge no

difference in your mind relating . . . to truth, virtue and obedience, I think well to have no thing altered in it from what is [writ for the son]" (Locke, 1968, 344). We should also note that in illustration of his thesis that parents must not brook obstinacy on the part of their children, Locke praises the *mother* "who was forced to whip her little *Daughter* at first coming home from Nurse, eight times successively the same morning, before she could master her Stubbornness and obtain a compliance in a very easie and indifferent matter" (*Thoughts*, §78; my italics).

IV

Does Locke's theory of parental responsibility have a political implication? It does. Parents must gain absolute submission from their child so that when he is grown, he shall see none of his superiors as fathers or mothers, to whom he owes the obedience he owed his parents when he was young. Locke will not have the initial relation between parents and children be a model for relations found outside the family (*Treatises*, II, §§77–86; see also §2).[5]

In so doing, he goes against a common seventeenth-century English practice: any relation of superiority and subordination was thought to be like that of parent and child. The religious teaching of the Church of England,

    . . . existing without an interruption at least from the reign of Edward VI, consisted of a social and political interpretation of the duty to obey parents enjoined by the Decalogue; the simple requirement to "Honor thy father and mother" was expanded to include loyalty and obedience to the king and all magistrates, as well as to masters, teachers, and ministers. This reading of the Fifth Commandment appeared in

. . . the catechism, which . . . all members of the Church of England had to learn. (Schochet, 1975, 6)

Children in New England were by no means exempt. "Puritan children, studying the famous catechism prepared by John Cotton, learned to answer the question '*Who are here* in the fifth commandment *meant by Father and Mother?*' with the words, 'All our Superiors, whether in Family, School, Church, and Common-wealth'" (Cotton, 1656, 4; quoted in Morgan, 1966, 19).

Of course, those who used the fifth commandment in this way were not required to suppose that the duties and rights of magistrate, or clergyman, or landlord were *in all respects* like that of a father or mother to their children; each office could be understood to have its distinct duties and privileges (see Schochet, 1975, 78–81). What all superiors had in common was that they were set over their inferiors by God's will and law, as parents were set over children by His law; all of them deserved "Reverance and Obedience, Service and Maintenance, Love and Honor" (Brailsford, 1689, 40; quoted in Schochet, 1975, 80–81), just as parents did.

The family was thus seen as the natural and appropriate place to prepare children to take part in larger social realities. For the relation of parent to child within the family was like those which the child would encounter throughout his life; it was but the first. One Puritan preacher wrote that

. . . a family is a little Church, and a little Common-wealth, . . . whereby tryall may be made of such as are fit for any place of authority, or of subjection in Church or Common-wealth. Or rather it is as a school wherein the first

principles and grounds of government and subjugation are learned: whereby men are fitted to greater matters in Church or Commonwealth. (William Gouge, *Of Domesticall Duties*, first published in 1622; quoted by Haller, 1941–42; 246)

This use of the relation between parents and children had support from the Stuart kings, for they believed it would reinforce their own claim to the loyalty of their subjects. The Stuart kings were not alone in the view that a willingness to submit to parental power was the best preparation for obedience to a strong monarch. In 1639, a French royal declaration stated that "the natural respect of children toward their parents is the bond of the legitimate obedience of subjects to their sovereigns" (quoted in Stone, 1975, 55). Paternal power was particularly favored by the "new Renaissance State" in France and England. The Stuart and Bourbon kings sought to centralize power in their own hands and direct all political loyalty to the throne. Thus, they were firm opponents of loyalties to cousins and distant kin, especially among the aristocracy. Such networks of allegiance were "a direct threat to the States' own claim to prior loyalty." But a stress on the subordination of children to their *own* father within the smaller nuclear family was no such threat. Indeed, it was seen as a basis for a firm and unswerving obedience to the sole and absolute rule of the monarch. "The seventeenth-century State was as supportive of the patriarchal family as it was hostile" to the family oriented to kin (Stone, 1975, 24, 55).

Locke rejects the view that the family is a microcosm of the larger social world. The attitude that young children should have toward their parents is not the attitude they should have as adults to political, or any other, superiors. The powers of kings, or of any magistrates of the civil order, are not forms of *"Parental Power."* Hence, Locke rejects Filmer's claim that kings have a right to command the obedience of their subjects because they are the proper heirs to the paternal power which Adam had over his children. "The right which . . . Parents have by Nature, and which is conferred to them by the 5*th* Commandment, cannot be . . . political Dominion," Locke says, for it "contains nothing of the Magistrate's Power in it" (*Treatises*, II, §§52, 63; see also §66). In my concluding remarks, I shall outline some of Locke's reasons for saying this, especially those which bear upon his notions of child rearing.

The law of reason and nature gives parents the right to command their young children and sets limits upon the use of this authority. But parents cannot expect that their young children will give them the obedience which the law of reason requires *out of an ultimate loyalty to the law itself*. Children must begin their moral growth with a firm and *ultimate* allegiance to their own parents. It must go no further than that. If parents embody the spirit of rationality in their own acts and speech, in time the law of reason can become detached in a child's mind as a *separate* object of deep devotion. This loyalty to an abstraction cannot take place at first, however. In the beginning, parents should not seek to distinguish the authority of reason from the authority of their own persons. Their children should experience them as *one*.

But this is just what should *not* take place in civil society. The powers of a magistrate should never be seen as inhering in his very person, for law, either natural or civil, is the sole source of the legitimate powers of any element of civil government. Subjects should see civil authority in this way. The "Allegiance" which they should give to the executor of the laws established by their legislature should be "nothing but an Obedience according to Law." They should be careful to distinguish the executor's *person* from the laws themselves. Their loyalty to the latter alone should lead them to obey him. If he violates the law, "he has no right to Obedience, nor can claim it otherwise than as the publick person vested with the Power of the Law, and so is to be considered as the Image, Phantom, or Representative of the Commonwealth, . . . declared in its Laws; and thus he has no Will, no Power, but that of the Law" (*Treatises*, II, §151).

The executor of the laws has power by virtue of the laws of the commonwealth. These laws themselves must be made by legislators who act on its behalf. But the members of the commonwealth should no more give their ultimate allegiance to their legislators than they should to the executor of the laws; for legislators can lose their legitimacy as well. They do so when they go against the rational purpose of a legislature, which is to protect the rights and liberties of all subjects. Therefore, the people must make a sharp distinction between the persons of the legislators and the rational purposes which may justify their rule:

> The Legislature being only a Fiduciary Power to act for certain ends, there remains still *in the People a Supream Power* to remove or *alter the Legislature*, when they find the *Legislature* act contrary to the trust reposed in them. . . . Thus the *Community* perpetually

retains a Supream Power of saving themselves from the attempts and designs of any Body, even of their Legislators, whenever they should be so foolish, and so wicked, as to lay and carry on designs against the Liberties and Properties of the Subject. (*Treatises*, II, §149)

A parent may rightfully govern the will of his young children without their consent, for the law of nature or reason gives this power to parents "for the Benefit of their Children during their Minority, to supply their want of Ability, and understanding how to manage" themselves. But "*Voluntary Agreement*" alone "*gives . . . Political Power to Governors*" (*Treatises*, II, §173). In the ordinary course of affairs, this consent to their rule is implicitly given by our very use of the freedoms which they sustain —for example, by our ownership of land which they protect, or even by our use of the roads of the commonwealth (*Treatises*, II, §§119–22). But this consent may properly be withdrawn when they no longer rule in accord with the law, civil or natural, which sustains their authority. Children must give their ultimate allegiance to the persons of their parents, for they cannot govern themselves by their knowledge of the laws they are under. But adults must give their ultimate allegiance to no other person; they must not find other "mothers" and "fathers." Their knowledge of law alone should command their obedience to civil authorities.

By rejecting a familial model for the political order, Locke gives up a most convenient way to integrate the family and the larger social world. The awe which parents can command from their children can easily be transferred in later life to other social superiors.

Readers of the *Two Treatises* may well wonder how Locke proposes to bridge this gap between family and polity. In this essay, I have sought to show how he thinks childhood awe can lead to the rule of law.

Notes

Discussions on Locke with Paul Desjardins (of Haverford College) have been of great use. I have benefited from F. W. Garforth's intelligently edited and abridged version of Locke's *Thoughts on Education* (Locke, 1964).

1. Locke's *Two Treatises* was first published in 1689, with a publication date of 1690 on the title page. I quote throughout from Peter Laslett's edition of the Treatises (1963), which is based on the third printing (1698), as corrected by Locke. "II" indicates the *Second Treatise*. I refer to the sections of this *Treatise*, rather than to pages of Laslett's edition, for the convenience of readers who use other editions.

2. *Some Thoughts concerning Education* is based on a set of letters which Locke wrote to Edward Clarke in 1684 and 1685, in answer to Clarke's request for counsel on the education of his son, Edward, Jr. It was first published in 1693. I quote throughout from James Axtell's edition of the *Thoughts* (1968), which is based on the fifth edition, published in 1705. This was the last edition to undergo revisions by Locke, who died in 1704. I refer to sections of the *Thoughts* for the convenience of readers who do not have ready access to Axtell's edition.

3. We must distinguish two senses of rationality to understand what Locke means when he says that even young children can perceive the rationality of many adult actions. An act is rational *in spirit* if it is guided by considerations

genuinely thought to be reasonable by the agent. But an act is *substantively* rational if it is truly appropriate, when judged from a rational point of view. Locke believes that very young children can often tell when their parents' conduct toward them is rational in spirit, even if they cannot judge its substantive rationality. Addressing parents, Locke explains that when he says that children "must be *treated as Rational Creatures,*" he means that "you should make them sensible by the Mildness of your Carriage, and the Composure even in your Correction of them, that what you do is reasonable in you, and useful and necessary for them: And that is not out of *Caprichio,* Passion or Fancy, that you command or forbid them any Thing. This they are capable of understanding" (*Thoughts,* §81).

4. "*Wisdom* . . . in the popular acceptation," writes Locke, "is a Man's managing his Business abley, with forsight in this World" (*Thoughts,* §140).

5. For that matter, Locke will not use the relation between parents and children as a model for other relations *within* the family, such as husband and wife. More generally, he rejects *any* use of the family as a model for relations in the larger society.

References

Brailsford, Humphrey, *The Poor Man's Help.* London, 1689.

Cotton, John, *Spiritual Milk for Boston Babes.* Cambridge, Mass., 1956.

Haller, William and Malleville, "The Puritan Art of Love," *Huntington Library Quarterly,* V (1941–42), 235–72.

Locke, John, *Two Treatises of Government,* ed. by Peter Laslett, rev. ed., New American Library, New York, 1963.

Locke, John, *The Educational Writings of John Locke,* ed. by James L. Axtell, Cambridge University Press, Cambridge, 1968.

Morgan, Edmund S., *The Puritan Family,* rev. ed., Harper, New York, 1966.

Schochet, Gordon J., *Patriarchalism in Political Thought,* Basil Blackwell, Oxford, 1975.

Stone, Lawrence, "The Rise of the Nuclear Family in Early Modern England: The Patriarchal Stage," in *The Family as History,* ed. Charles G. Rosenberg, University of Pennsylvania Press, Philadelphia, 1975, pp. 13–57.

The psychoanalytic tradition has done as much as any movement or discovery in this century to alter our perception of childhood. Even though it has not produced a generally accepted account of the emergence of adult personality, it has taught us to look much further back for the roots of that personality, to suspect that things are not always what they seem, and to look for surviving "childish" demands and desires just beneath an "adult" surface of rationality. This tradition leads us to suspect that the transformation of an obedient child into an autonomous citizen may not be as smooth as Locke and Leites suggest, and that the obedient and deferential child may survive within his adult successor.

In "Obedience and Illusions," Michael Slote looks at the darker and more difficult side of the transition to autonomy. Children who once submit to strong parental authority do not, he argues, easily overcome habits of obedience and deference. Autonomy is not only, as Locke argued, attractive to children, but also threatening, so that some children find dependency tempting and desirable even when grown. Only such an undercurrent of longing for childish dependency can explain the elaborate rationalizations of parental (and other) authority which are often given. In Slote's opinion, the enlightenment view of personality development, which Locke typifies, cannot account for the unresolved conflicts between desires for autonomy and for dependence which dog so many people into adulthood.

OBEDIENCE AND ILLUSIONS

MICHAEL A. SLOTE

1. Obligations to Obey

Not long ago, the following reasoning would to many people have seemed compelling, if not inescapable:

> We are all God's children. He has done for us what parents do for their children: created us and given us all we have. We owe Him a debt of gratitude of the kind children owe to (good) parents, and therefore owe Him the kind of obedience children owe to parents.

Today, most of us live in a world where reasoning like this has lost its power to persuade. Has the widespread loss of belief in God made the difference? In some measure, perhaps. But I think the change is also largely the result of the way our thoughts about childhood have matured. I shall spend much of this paper explaining the implications and significance of this last remark. I shall talk about authority and childhood, about divine authority and the important ways it resembles parental authority. Although I shall in no way be attacking religion or theism per se, I shall argue that both divine authority and parental authority are underlaid by illusions that must be shed in order to complete the process of growing up, and that the very knowledge that this is so is part of the ongoing maturation of our culture and ourselves.

The argument given at the beginning of the paper can be "stood on its head" in two different ways. First, it can be used to prove the very opposite of what it purports to prove. To many of us, it seems obvious that children have no *obligation* to obey their parents, any more than they have duties of *filial piety*. So any force there is to the analogy between God's creation and parental begetting can, for modern ways of seeing, tend to show that we have no duty to obey God, if He exists.

Moreover, one can reach this conclusion without necessarily holding that children have *no* obligations, owe *nothing*, to their parents. It may well be that good parents are owed a debt of gratitude—though the notion of "debt" here is probably somewhat loose and metaphorical, since it is difficult to believe that one has any moral *duty* to show gratitude for benefits one has not requested. Perhaps children also have a moral obligation to care for their parents when they become sick or infirm. But in neither case does anything seem to follow about debts or duties of obedience. If a stranger, unasked, gives me the money for a college education, I at most owe him a debt of gratitude, not of obedience. And why should it be any different with parents?

Furthermore, it seems entirely gratuitous to suppose that *very young children* have any moral obligations at all, even to their parents. Such obligations,

it would seem, exist, if at all, only when moral concepts are firmly implanted. But, on the other hand, if we think of older children—say, adolescents—duties of obedience seem to vanish in another direction. Young children seem to be too young to have any *obligations* or *duties* of obedience or anything else. But older children, precisely because they are more mature, seem to possess a right to determine for themselves how they should live, and this seems to undermine any duty of *obedience* to parents. After reaching a certain age, children, e.g., on a family farm may have duties of cooperation; at least, they have no right to a share of the farm produce unless they cooperate. And such cooperation may entail doing what their more knowledgeable parents tell them to do. But it is unlikely that this constitutes any duty of obedience. Even if the child has a duty to cooperate, and cooperation, in a particular instance, requires doing what a more knowledgeable parent says to do, it does not follow that the child has any general obligation to follow parental instructions or any duty to *obey* his parents in the particular instance.

In addition, I have emphasized that the obligation to cooperate exists, if at all, only to the degree that the older child wants or demands some share in the goods produced by the family. There is, I think, no duty of fair play that requires him to stay with the family and share in its life and benefits because of his parents' past beneficence. The duty of fair play presumably exists only where benefits are voluntarily accepted within a cooperative scheme, and we can hardly suppose that a child has voluntarily accepted his role in (the cooperative scheme of) family life. The (older) child, then, may always opt out of his whole family situation, and we have, in all, found no reason to believe that any child has a duty to obey his parents.

The reasoning at the beginning of this paper needs to be stood on its head in another sense, because it implies an inverted picture of the nature and causality of parental and divine authority. It implies that our acknowledgment of or submission to parental (or divine) authority is (often) powered by our sense of the moral validity of such authority, and just the reverse seems to me to be the case. I believe that moral arguments for duties of obedience to authority are typically epiphenomena: secondary rationalizations of deeper feelings, habits, and (illusory) ideas connected with authority. People do not submit to authority because they recognize a duty to do so on the basis of abstract moral reasoning. Rather, they are, first, under the yoke of such authority—in certain matters feeling, for example, that they have no choice but to do what God or their parents tell them—and only then, or on that basis, make an intellectual accommodation with that authority.

I shall now argue that we are faced with (at least) two levels of illusion when we consider the nature of authority. Submission to authority, by its very nature, involves certain illusions about matters other than the nature of authority itself. However, such submission also typically gives rise to ideological support and reinforcement for the first illusions in the form of illusions *about what authority is*, and the illusion that parental authority (causally) derives from a moral sense of its legitimacy is a good example of such derivative "ideology of authority." We need to understand both these levels of illusion and their modes of interaction.

2. Illusions of Authority

Most parents have some legal authority over their children, but they almost always also have that "aura" of authority that makes their children accept most of their dictates unquestioningly. It is this sort of submission to parental authority that I mean to refer to when I speak hereafter of parental authority, and I believe that parental authority, in this sense, is closely related to the acceptance of divine authority by the devoutly religious.

When people submit to divine authority, they seem to think that they have no choice but to obey God. And I believe that when a devout person, confronted by what he takes to be God's will, thinks, "I have no choice in the matter," he represents himself as a mere object that lacks choice and will altogether—a mere instrument of divine purposes. No doubt, it will immediately be replied that in thinking this way, a devout person may simply be using a harmless metaphor and thus be under no illusion about what he is. But the devout person who thinks or says this sort of thing is typically not, at that moment, clear in his own mind about the merely metaphorical nature of his utterance. If my wife wants me to stay in bed in the morning, and I tell her, "I have no choice in the matter; I have to get to work," I speak in all *seriousness* and in order to *justify* my departure. I need to be *reminded* that what I am saying is not literally true, and am not, therefore, like someone who says that his wife has a heart of gold and never suffers any initial unclarity or confusion about the literal falsity of what he says. Similarly, I think someone who believes he has no choice once God has spoken is not, at least initially, as clear in his own mind about the literal falsity of what he says as is the person who says his wife has a heart of gold. And this gives us at least some reason to claim that religious people, at some point and at some level, actually imagine they lack choice and are mere instruments or things. I think, moreover, that having such illusory thoughts is part of what it is fully to accept God's authority. To see clearly that one has a choice—perhaps a coerced and threatened choice, but a choice, nonetheless—about whether to do as God asks is precisely *not* to submit to divine authority in the manner of the devout.

Important additional evidence for the existence of these illusions comes from the fact that someone who submits to divine authority invariably feels that the presence of God in the universe makes an automatic and total difference to his life and its meaning. The difference he supposes God to make does not seem to consist *merely* in the fact that if God exists, there is a totally wise and good being in the world from whom one can learn; nor can it simply involve God's ability to get us to do what He wants or to impose dire punishments if we do not. And it is very difficult to explain why so many religious people think God makes a total difference to life and its meaning. But we *can* explain this belief if we say that those who hold it are under the illusions we have discussed. For if we are choiceless things because of God's presence in the universe, then that presence clearly does make a total difference to one's life, since it in effect destroys human life and replaces it with the existence of a mere thing. If, by virtue of the divine presence, we are mere instruments of God's purposes, then our lives have no meaning (of their own), and surely it makes

a total difference to the meaning of a human life whether that life has or lacks meaning (of its own).[1]

What we have just said about submission to divine authority carries over, in great part, to the authority of parents. I think that children, like the devout, feel their submission to their parents as a loss of will. The child under effective parental authority feels that he has no choice or will of his own in certain matters where his parents have prescribed. And there is every reason to believe that if devout people are under illusions about whether they have choice and wills (or purposes) of their own, children who accept parental authority are under similar illusions. I shall now attempt to explain why children come to have such illusions of choicelessness and willlessness.

Many things can stand in the way of a child's development of autonomy. To learn to think and act for himself, he must also, along the way, rely heavily on his parents or parental substitutes; he must take some things for granted. The child is thus subject to a number of conflicting pressures. He seeks autonomy and is constantly tugging against parental bonds, and yet he needs his parents and has to depend on them for many things. And even as far as the drive for autonomy itself is concerned, parents represent both opportunity and threat. They themselves subject the child to conflicting pressures, wanting the child to grow up and mature, but almost always also seeking to impose more intellectual, moral, and emotional baggage on the child than he needs to make his own way in the world.

But parents are not the only threat to a child's developing autonomy. Autonomy has its own risks, anxieties, and frustrations, and these can frighten a child and cause him to regress into dependency. Such a child may then desire to be taken care of again like an infant, to have others make his choices, to lose autonomy. Alternatively, if the parents themselves seek to block the child's autonomy with prohibitions, threats, or hostile accusations of ingratitude, the child may become panicky about the impending loss of his autonomy. And rather than fight his parents, who may seem practically omnipotent in his eyes, he may acquiesce in their domination. Faced with a losing battle, the child may try, defensively, to convince himself that he really didn't want to be autonomous in the first place. Or he may reason that he really has nothing to lose from his parents' domination because he has, in fact, no will of his own to be thwarted. He may welcome the loss of autonomy or imagine he never had any autonomy that could be taken away, in order to console himself for, or reconcile himself to, the loss he so greatly fears. That fear is not so much destroyed by these devices as kept out of direct awareness.

Such phenomena are not psychologically atypical or rare. It is, for example, a truism of psychiatry and a fact ordinary people are commonly aware of that an overwhelming anxiety in the face of impending death may give rise to the defensive thought-feeling that one doesn't really care if one dies, or even that one welcomes death. Similarly, when things take a dramatic turn *for the better*, people often say: I must be dreaming all this. And the explanation is fairly obvious. One tries to convince oneself that it is all a dream, and thus, that one has nothing to lose, in order to counteract and submerge one's fears of losing what one has suddenly gained and to soften the blow if one *does* lose it.

And this is very close to what happens when a child who faces a loss of autonomy imagines he has no will of his own.

I think, then, that when children accept parental authority without question, even after they have arrived at a stage where they desire considerable autonomy for themselves, a kind of regression has occurred as a means of alleviating anxiety—anxiety at the frustrations of autonomy itself, anxiety over parental attempts to thwart the child's desires for autonomy, and perhaps other forms of anxiety as well. This regression involves an attempt to retreat to the stage of infancy where decisions were made for one and life was a blissful ease of dependency.[2] And to do this, one erects psychic structures of indifference to the loss of autonomy, either welcoming the loss one thinks will occur or denying that there is anything to lose. The acceptance of parental authority in such circumstances, then, is an easy retreat from threats and frustration, but it involves the illusion that one has no choice or will of one's own, a repudiation of one's real and persisting desires to be autonomous, and a certain amount of internal conflict as a result.

What I have just said, moreover, indicates that the threat power of parents lies behind, even if it is not the same as, their authority. It is their power to circumvent or coerce the child's will, their power to deprive it of the autonomy it seeks, that sends some children scurrying into the defenses and illusions that constitute submission to parental authority.[3] So, we must contrast living in fear of parental attempts to limit one's autonomy, which may involve no illusions at all, with submitting to those attempts, or to parental authority, which does. Since, in addition, the illusions involved in acquiescing in parental authority are part of the way children cope with and allay powerful anxieties, we should expect that they would resist exposure. To see that they were illusions would be to become partly free of them and thus no longer able to "use" them as part of one's psychological defenses. To protect the illusions involved in submission to authority, people often develop complicated and clever secondary rationalizations of such authority. This is the derivative "ideology of authority" I mentioned earlier. The illusions of authority can be defended from discovery and preserved by means of a distorted intellectual picture of what submission to authority actually is. One will, for example, moralize about authority using the reasoning at the beginning of this paper. One will somehow be convinced that it is morality, and the rational acknowledgment of moral requirements, that powers one's submission to parental authority. So, the illusions intrinsic to authority naturally give rise to illusions *about* (submission to) authority—illusions that, in effect, deny the illusory character that submission to authority actually has. And these illusions about illusions serve to perpetuate the illusions they are about.[4]

3. Being Adult

What can we conclude from the fact that people so often seek an authority that involves illusions? To begin with, it may well be true that children in some measure *need* to submit to parental authority during childhood if they are later to have successful or satisfying adult lives. Perhaps the illusions of authority are "noble lies" of childhood, and it is good for children to believe

such lies the way it is good for them to believe the fairy tales they hear.

But even if we need to have illusions about parental authority as children, it hardly seems likely that we are better off having such illusions when we become older. I have said that the child who submits to parental authority out of fear of parental threats to his autonomy is in a state of conflict. He retreats into dependence on his parents, yet never really loses his desire for autonomy; so, he both needs and resents his parents. He will not show that resentment for fear of retaliation, and if his parents continue to impose upon him well into adulthood, he may never get over his fearful submission to them. He will then frequently become the kind of parent his parents were to him—displaying to his children an aggression he could never vent against his parents. The "authoritarian personality" that often develops with submission to parental authority tends to perpetuate itself, generation after generation, and what is most clear about such continuing cycles of submission and domination is that *no one* has grown up completely.* The dominating authoritarian parent acts as he does as a result of his own illusory and childish submissiveness to his parents. To become fully an adult, one has to cease submitting to the authority of one's parents—to become one's own parent, as it is said—and gain that autonomy that parents who seek to impose authority on a child may *seem to have* and that children themselves seek, but often permanently give away, before fully attaining it. If what I have been saying here is correct, the person who gains such autonomy will have to

* Witness the last paragraph of *Emile,* above, p. 226. [Eds.]

free himself from various illusions of authority, and from the inordinate fear of his parents that results in defensive submission to their authority and in internal conflicts between a desire for autonomy and a desire for dependence. That person will unequivocally accept his autonomy despite its risks and frustrations, and he fulfills (a great part of) my idea of what it is to be, morally speaking, an adult.[5]

Finally, I think that our culture has itself grown up to the degree that it has freed itself from various illusions of authority. There is evidence of this maturation, for example, in the present powerlessness of the argument with which we began. That we no longer see any need to believe in the child's moral obligation to obey his parents shows, it seems to me, that our culture no longer encourages as much submission to parental authority as it used to. Some of the illusions of parental authority are now harder to foster and maintain. Perhaps the development and spread of political democracy has aided the discovery of the illusions of parental and divine authority. When the authority of kings came into question, it perhaps became easier to recognize the illusions, rationalizations, and conflicts inherent in other kinds of submission to authority. I hope, however, that I am under no illusions about the "progress" that has been made in discarding the illusions connected with authority. I do not doubt that the insights that have been developed are very frail reeds, pawns to future history and to the very needs and fears that so often give rise to submission to authority. I do not, then, believe that further progress in this area is inevitable, and sadly enough, it seems quite possible that our insight into the illusions of authority and our greater pres-

ent freedom from submission to authority should someday, somehow, be lost.[6]

Notes

1. Of course, in using this explanation, we assume that the belief that God can or does make an automatic total difference to our lives is as illusory as the beliefs that explain it. But I think it is impossible to specify a way in which God actually could make an automatic total difference to human life and its meaning; let the reader try for himself, if he will. So, I think the religious assumption that God can make such a difference is as illusory as the assumptions about choicelessness, etc., that are needed to explain it.

   Perhaps the first philosopher to hold that submission to authority involves illusions was Sartre in *Being and Nothingness* and in his play "The Flies." But Sartre's conception of the content of those illusions differs considerably from what I have been saying here and is open to serious criticism. (On this, see my "Existentialism and the Fear of Dying," *American Philosophical Quarterly* 12 (1975) p. 27.) Most significantly of all, perhaps, Sartre does not see that the illusory religious belief that God can make a total difference provides some of the best evidence for the illusory character of submission to divine, or parental, authority. (In fact, in his essay "Existentialism Is a Humanism," Sartre comes close to *endorsing* the idea that God makes a total difference to human life.)

2. It is conventional psychiatric wisdom that if one's infancy was *not* very happy or tranquil, one will seek to regress to infancy when life is frustrating, in order to *make up for*, or *overcome*, that earlier lack of satisfaction.

3. Submission to authority need not, I think, imply that there *is* an authority to whom one submits. However, it is not clear whether we should want to say that

parents *lack* the authority that children attribute to them because they cannot take away their children's choice in the way children imagine; or whether we should not, instead, say that parents *have* authority over submissive children because to have authority is just to be in a position where others have certain habits and illusions. But whatever we decide to say about this question, we needn't conclude that there is any *validity* to parental authority of the kind we are focusing on. Authority cannot, I think, be valid when it *has to be* based on false beliefs or illusions. Cf. my "Morality and Ignorance," *Journal of Philosophy*, LXXIV (1977), pp. 745–767, for a lengthy elaboration of this and related themes.

4. In many ways, my account of the desire for autonomy and of the ways we regress into dependency when it is threatened derives from Erich Fromm's *Escape from Freedom* (New York: Holt, 1941). But, more in the manner of Sartre, I have emphasized the illusions of authority. And Fromm not only ignores this aspect of authority but sometimes seems *himself* to fall under some of the illusions of authority I have described. He often says that when we submit to authority, we give up our freedom and individuality. And he speaks of both the annihilation and the loss of the self, in this connection. (See *Escape from Freedom*, pp. 140f., 154f., 185f., 206.) At the very least, he does not distinguish clearly enough between the *illusion* that we have no self or will of our own, an illusion involved in submitting to authority, and the (impossible) state of affairs that that illusion is *about*.

5. To the degree, moreover, that submission to divine authority—as opposed to simple belief in or fear of God—involves similar illusions, resentments, and conflicts, adulthood may be incompatible with religious submissiveness of the sort I have been describing.

6. I am indebted to Arthur Fine, the editors of this book, and, especially, Hans Kleinschmidt and David Levin, for helpful criticisms and suggestions.

The Twenty-sixth Amendment to the U.S. Constitution gave persons over eighteen the right to vote. Even so, persons under twenty-one are still hedged by many restrictions and disabilities, while those under eighteen are subject to laws which give parents (and others) control over most aspects of their lives, including even the use of the children's earnings. Modern parents often waive control over older children. Even so, their children are not guaranteed standard adult liberty rights until they reach their majority at the age of twenty-one.

The essays by Kenneth Henley and Laurence Houlgate discussed some of the principles which are important in determining which restrictions of liberty should be placed on which children, even though they are not placed on adults. Applying these principles to existing (or proposed) legislation would be a long and intricate task.

In this article, Sanford Katz, William Schroeder, and Lawrence Sidman review current legislation and litigation which determine minors' liberty and paretal authority in various U.S. jurisdictions. Their survey documents the extent, variety, and complexity of restrictions on minors' liberty, and the rarity of legal emancipation before age twenty-one. Anyone who seeks a reasoned restructuring of children's liberties and parental authority will have to bring principles such as those proposed by Henley and Houlgate to bear on the web of restrictions which Katz, Schroeder, and Sidman depict. Success in this task might show that the concept of the "age of majority" has little use, for we need to attend to a variety of ages—or rather, stages—beyond which specific liberties may or should be conferred on children.

EMANCIPATING OUR CHILDREN— COMING OF LEGAL AGE IN AMERICA

SANFORD N. KATZ, WILLIAM A. SCHROEDER, AND LAWRENCE R. SIDMAN

I. Introduction

Emancipation, a basic tenet of family law,[1] has generally been viewed as a highly technical legal concept with limited social implications.[2] Discussion, whether the emancipation resulted from judicial or legislative action, tended to be narrow in scope and overly functional in emphasis.[3] Little consideration

From *Family Law Quarterly* VII:3 (1973) pp. 211–41. Reprinted by permission of Sanford N. Katz, Editor-in-chief.

has been given to the assumptions implicit in the term "emancipation" and
the historical context in which it developed.

In colonial America children occupied the lowest rungs of the social lad-
der. Various enactments of the Massachusetts Bay Colony suggest that children and servants were treated similarly
before the law[4] and were subject to the
harshest punishments for relatively trivial offenses.[5] Apprenticeship "was often
merely a specialized form of servitude."[6]
Children owed the strictest obedience
toward parents and were expected to assume completely subservient positions
within the family unit. Since child labor
was crucial to the economic system, the
parental right to a minor child's services
and wages was also a practical necessity.[7] In such a hierarchical and tightly
structured system, breaking the tie of
duty and obligation between parent and
child was unthinkable.[8]

While there are scattered instances
early in the nineteenth century of courts
severing that tie,[9] the doctrine of emancipation was not extensively employed
until after the turn of this century, when
the Industrial Revolution led to the un-
precedented use of child labor. The
abuses to which minors were subjected
resulted eventually in major protective
child labor legislation.[10] Simultaneously,
the belief in the ability of the individual
to strike out on his own and through
hard work and persistence become a
"success" reached its zenith. In this atmosphere, the family lost some of its
cohesiveness. The legal sanctioning of
some limited mobility out of the family
was compatible with and even respon-
sive to the economic needs and cultural
tenor of the times.

Emancipation from 1900 to the
early 1960s was almost exclusively judicial and conformed closely to the dominant societal attitudes during that period. The Progressive and New Deal
eras brought many social reforms based
on the philosophy that the State knew
what was best for its citizens. The
growth of the *parens patriae* principle,[11]
under which the State could intervene
in the affairs of the family to safeguard
the best interests of the child, was mir-
rored in the increased willingness of
courts to issue emancipation decrees, releasing children from their filial ties
where circumstances so warranted. The
approach to judicial emancipation was
on a case by case basis, and the doctrine
was often manipulated by the courts to
conform with a judge's own values
rather than with the best interests of
the child.

Inquiry into the policy bases of
emancipation is particularly appropriate
at this time. For, as a consequence of
disintegrative forces which have caused
the divorce rate to spiral[12] and influenced the "running away" of thousands
of teen-agers,[13] the nuclear family seems
less stable than at any other period in
American history.[14] At the same time
there has been major legislative action,
including the ratification of the Twenty-
sixth Amendment[15] and the lowering of
the age of majority in many jurisdictions.[16] This study of the legal machinery, both judicial and statutory, used
presently and in the past to emancipate
children, should provide important insights into the law's response to the
changing nature of the parent-child relationship.

II. Judicial Emancipation

In American law[17] judicial emancipation refers to the termination of cer-

tain rights and obligations attaching to the parent-child relationship during the child's minority. It is different from the proceedings or actions which precede the freeing of a child for adoption. In the latter all rights and obligations, including inheritance, are legally terminated. The parent-child relationship is thus completely and permanently severed.

As a result of statutory and common law developments, the American parent is generally held responsible for his child's financial support, health, education, morality, and for instilling in him respect for people and authority.[18] To facilitate the performance of these obligations, the parent is vested with the custody and control of the child, including the requisite disciplinary authority.[19] And, under a heritage of the past, the parent is also entitled to the child's services[20] and, by derivation, to his or her earnings.[21] When a child is adjudicated a fully emancipated minor, these reciprocal rights and responsibilities are extinguished and are no longer legally enforceable:[22] the emancipated child is thus legally treated as an adult.[23]

Partial Emancipation. Not all decrees of judicial emancipation result in the total termination of mutual responsibilities, however. The courts distinguish between complete and partial emancipation.[24] A partial emancipation may result in freeing a child from all of his parents' rights in him for a part of the period of minority; freeing a child from only some of the parents' rights for the remaining period of minority; or freeing the child from some of the parents' rights for only a portion of the infant's minority.[25] As a result a partially emancipated child is occasionally able to assert rights normally incident to com-

plete emancipation while still able to enforce parental obligations. Thus, for example, a minor child who has been allowed to retain his or her wages may still be eligible to receive child support on the theory that, since only a partial emancipation took place, the child could revert to an unemancipated status at any time prior to attaining the age of majority.[26] On the other hand, a partially emancipated child may be barred from bringing certain causes of action open to a completely emancipated child.[27]

The determination of whether a partial or complete emancipation has occurred is contingent upon three major factors: whether there has been an express or implied emancipation; the nature of the acts alleged to have emancipated the child; and, perhaps most importantly, the legal setting in which the claim of emancipation is raised.

Complete Emancipation. The clearest instance of a complete emancipation occurs where there is an express agreement by which the parents relinquish their rights in their child in exchange for the child's relieving them of their financial obligations.[28] In such a situation the positions of the respective parties are clearly fixed. Moreover, the agreement is consistent with the rule that emancipation must be accomplished by the act of the parent, not by the act of the child.[29] Unfortunately from an analytical standpoint, very few cases involving such an express arrangement have been litigated. In one such case, *Carricato v. Carricato*,[30] the Kentucky Court of Appeals found evidence of an "understanding" between parent and child that the daughter would be "on her own" after reaching age eighteen. While the court held the daughter to be completely emancipated, its conclusion rested heavily upon evidence extrinsic to the agreement. Whether the paucity of express emancipation decisions is attributable to the unambiguous nature of such an agreement or to the fact that such arrangements are generally informal and thus not litigated is uncertain. Where express emancipations exist, however, they will almost invariably be held to be complete and absolute.[31]

A complete emancipation is much less likely to be found where the emancipation is implied merely from the conduct of the parties. In these instances courts depart from adherence to the strict rule that emancipation must be by parental act and look to the totality of the circumstances. If it is apparent that the minor occupies a status which is clearly inconsistent with that of a subordinate family member, emancipation may well be implied.[32] Unless there is compelling evidence of complete independence,[33] however, courts will generally hold that the emancipation is only partial.[34] In *Detwiler* v. *Detwiler*,[35] for example, a Pennsylvania court held that even though an eighteen-year-old son was paying board, working outside for independent employers and using his earnings as he saw fit, he was only a partially emancipated minor. This reluctance to imply complete emancipation is consistent with the presumption that a minor *ipso facto* is not emancipated and that the burden of proving emancipation is upon the party asserting it.[36] Perhaps more fundamentally, it reflects a judicial reluctance to tamper with the rights and responsibilities normally incident to the parent-child relationship. In that sense implied partial emancipation may be viewed more as legal recognition of the precariousness of a family structure than as an alteration of that structure.

The combinations and permutations of factual patterns which may lead a court to conclude that a child is or is not emancipated are almost infinite. Only marriage[37] and enlistment in the armed services[38] are generally deemed sufficient in themselves to constitute emancipation.[39] The rationale for holding these acts to be presumptive evidence of emancipation is that they reflect such a radical change in his position in the family unit that it would be entirely inconsistent to continue to view the minor as unemancipated. Moreover, these acts entail new legal responsibilities and rights inconsistent with those of a child. As one court has said:

> When a minor enlists in the military service of this country, he ceases to be a part of his father's family, and puts himself under the control of the government, and is consequently emancipated so long as this service continues.[40]

Interestingly, marriage or enlistment resulting in a minor's emancipation does not sharply clash with the view that it is the parent's acts and not the minor's that are controlling on the issue of emancipation. Since minors can neither enlist nor marry without parental consent, that consent operates as an emancipating parental act.

Absent marriage or enlistment, determinations of emancipation are made by evaluating all of the surrounding circumstances on a case by case basis. This is generally a question for the jury,[41] but the court may enter a judgment notwithstanding the verdict if, as a matter of law, the jury's findings of fact do not comport with its conclusion regarding emancipation.[42]

> It is a question for the jury to determine the facts when an issue is raised of a minor's emancipation. It is a ques-

tion of law for the court to determine whether the facts so established constitute a complete emancipation of a minor.[43]

Among the most frequently considered factors are: whether the child is living at home,[44] whether the child is paying room and board if living at home,[45] whether the parents are exercising disciplinary control over the minor,[46] whether the child is independently employed,[47] whether the child has been given the right to retain wages and spend them without parental restraints,[48] whether the child is responsible for debts incurred and the extent of the parents' contributions toward the payment of outstanding bills,[49] whether the child owns a major commodity such as a car,[50] and whether the parent has listed the child as a dependent for tax purposes.[51] Age, of course, is also a critical element. None of these factors, however, is conclusive:

> A minor child may live away from the home of its parents and receive his wages for the week, and pay his own expenses therefrom, and yet not be freed from the authority and control of his father and entitled to the earnings from his services.[52]

More important than any single one of these factors, however, is the legal setting in which the claim of emancipation is raised. Indeed, the nature of the claim and the context in which it is brought are often paramount in determining whether emancipation will be decreed. Thus, where the causes of action differ,[53] a court faced with nearly identical fact situations may reach different results. And it is here that basic judicial values concerning the child's place in the family are revealed.

Intra-family Torts. By far the greatest number of cases involving emancipation is in the area of intra-family torts, with the issue being whether the intra-family tort immunity rule will be applied so as to bar the suit.[54] Where such immunity has not been abrogated,[55] the rule is that tort actions may not be maintained either by parents against their children, or conversely by children against their parents. Courts have consistently held, however, that where the minor is emancipated, either party may bring an action.[56] The emancipation must be complete before the action can be brought; such suits will still be barred where the minor is only partially emancipated.[57]

Historically, the intra-family tort immunity rule appears to be an offshoot of the inter-spousal tort immunity which barred husband and wife from suing each other.[58] This doctrine survived into modern times as a legacy of the medieval notion of husband and wife as "of one flesh";[59] one does not sue oneself in tort. More contemporary theorists supporting the rule have reasoned that it is essential to the solidarity of the marital relationship,[60] really a rephrasing of the "one flesh" concept, and that it is needed to prevent collusive suits.[61] Opponents have argued that the doctrine in fact subverts the marital relationship by denying the integrity of the spouses as independent human beings who should not be placed under civil disability simply because of their married status.[62] The collusion argument has been countered by claims that insurance, virtually a necessity in our society, mitigates the dangers of suits not prosecuted in good faith.[63]

The modern bases of intra-family tort immunity are similar. It is said that suits between parent and child will foster acrimony and destroy the unity of the nuclear family. "[S]uch actions are disruptive of family peace and destructive of filial discipline."[64] But this view rests on the assumption that family stability can only be achieved where the lines of authority are clearly drawn, where children are prohibited from challenging parental authority even if only to seek relief for a wrong committed against them. One wonders whether this view too does not derive from our medieval heritage which cast children in the role of chattel or servants[65] rather than persons entitled to vindicate their rights.

It is not surprising then that jurisdictions unsympathetic toward the intra-family tort immunity rule have been willing to strain to find emancipation so as to allow the suit. In an early and oft-cited case, *Dunlap* v. *Dunlap*,[66] the New Hampshire Supreme Court found that a sixteen-year-old boy, living at home and attending high school, was sufficiently emancipated to sue his father for negligence. The boy had been working on building construction for his father during summer vacation, receiving the same wages as other workmen less a deduction for board, when he was injured by the collapse of the staging upon which he was working. Rather than concentrating upon the boy's independence, the court thoroughly reviewed the history of denying recovery to children in similar situations. It rejected the notion that immunity is necessary to bolster parental discipline:

> The danger that insubordination will arise from possible knowledge of a right to complain of willful wrong has been magnified out of all proportion to the facts of life. . . . In this age it can hardly be necessary or even desirable that the child be reared in the atmos-

phere of one under the control of an absolute tyrant.[67]

The court felt that immunity should only insulate the parent from suit in connection with actions incident to his or her status as a parent and should not extend to other spheres. Here the court perceived the relationship to be more like master-servant than parent-child and concluded that:

> Emancipation is an answer to this defense because the father's act has so changed the situation that it is everywhere conceded that there is no longer valid reason for denying recovery. When the right of discipline and family association have been surrendered, a rule intended to preserve their integrity is not applicable.[68]

The *Dunlap* court's use of emancipation as a vehicle for eroding the intra-family tort immunity rule is even more impressively illustrated in a series of California decisions. In *Martinez* v. *Southern Pacific Company*,[69] the California Supreme Court, following other jurisdictions, allowed an emancipated minor to sue her parent for negligence. Very shortly thereafter the same court held that unemancipated minor daughters could sue their father for willful or malicious misconduct:[70]

> While it may seem repugnant to allow a minor to sue his parent, we think it more repugnant to leave a minor child without redress for the damage he has suffered by reason of his parent's willful or malicious misconduct. A child, like every other individual, has a right to freedom from such injury.[71]

Finally in 1971 the California Supreme Court abrogated the intra-family tort immunity doctrine.[72] Acknowledging that the *Martinez* case had been the opening wedge, the court permitted an unemancipated minor son to sue his father in negligence:

> We have concluded that parental immunity has become a legal anachronism, riddled with exceptions and seriously undermined by recent decisions of this court. Lacking the support of authority and reason, the rule must fall.[73]

There is a line of cases where directed verdicts (or judgments notwithstanding the verdict), based upon rulings of no emancipation, were reversed on appeal. These cases illustrate how findings of emancipation may depend on a court's attitude toward the intra-family immunity doctrine. In *Wurth* v. *Wurth*,[74] a nineteen-year-old daughter, living at home although employed, brought a negligence action against her father for injuries sustained in an automobile accident. The girl used her wages to pay board. The jury's award to the minor was nullified when the trial court entered judgment notwithstanding the verdict, on the grounds that the minor was unemancipated as a matter of law and that no action would lie. In affirming the trial court's action, the Missouri Court of Appeals revealed its view of emancipation and intra-family tort immunity:

> Merely to show the plaintiff, while residing at her parents' home, was employed outside and used her moderate earnings to pay board and other bills does not completely rebut the cautionary presumption with which the law protects the parent in the enjoyment of the normal parental relations. The preservation of the peace, harmony and security so vital to the family and home cannot so easily be accommodated to meet the ends of expediency.[75]

On appeal, the Missouri Supreme Court reversed and reinstated the jury verdict in favor of the girl.[76] Looking at the identical fact pattern, the court found the girl to be emancipated. Absent from its decision was any reliance on the immunity doctrine as savior of the family. Other state supreme courts have adopted similar approaches where lower courts have adhered strictly to the immunity rule.[77]

Interestingly, courts have shown less reluctance to find emancipation where the parent is suing the mature minor child in tort.[78] In *Gillikin* v. *Burbage*,[79] for example, the North Carolina Supreme Court upheld a mother's right to bring negligence action against her nineteen-year-old daughter. The minor was living at home and generally deferred to her parents' requests. She did, however, pay one-third of the household expenses, worked at several jobs and retained her own earnings, owned an automobile, and had no curfews. The court's analysis proceeded in an objective, factual manner designed to determine whether the child was really self-sufficient. It did not, however, enter into a discussion of intra-family tort immunity or the policy reasons behind insulating a child from suit. It is unclear whether this different approach signifies that courts do not indulge in a presumption against emancipation when the parent is suing the child, but do so only when the child is suing the parent. If this were the case,[80] emancipation would be a sword wielded by the parent rather than a shield for the child.

In general, recent court decisions have been fairly liberal in finding emancipation in the intra-family tort immunity area.[81] This is consistent with the trend toward judicial abrogation of the doctrine, which has already taken place in twelve jurisdictions.[82] Whether these emancipation cases merely reflect hostility toward parent-child immunity, or whether they signal affirmative judicial action in utilizing old doctrines to carve out adult rights and responsibilities for minors, can only be determined by investigating other situations in which emancipation arises.

Minor's Wages and Damages. Emancipation questions have also been frequently raised in connection with actions to recover a minor's wages[83] or to recover damages for the loss of a minor's services.[84] These actions stem, of course, from the parent's common law right to the services of his or her child. Since it has long been held that emancipation terminates the right,[85] the resolution of that issue is often conclusive.

In the leading case on the right to recover minors' wages, *Rounds Brothers* v. *McDaniel*,[86] the son had commenced work when he was fourteen years old and was residing with his father and an aunt. He moved at age sixteen and received no support from his father until the action was brought. In the interim the boy had been earning his wages and spending them as he pleased. When the minor was eighteen, the father demanded of his son's employer that his son's wages be paid directly to him; the employer refused and the father sued. The Supreme Court of Kentucky denied recovery on the grounds that the son was emancipated by implication and that, in any event, the father was estopped from claiming his son's wages at such a late date:

> But where the child leaves home and goes out to make his own living under the assumption that his parent has emancipated him, his rights to his services and earnings are not absolute, as

in the case of an express emancipation, and the parent may, by taking timely action, resume parental authority and reclaim the services of his child, but he must not delay until his implied emancipation has ripened into an express relinquishment, or wait until it would be hurtful to the best interest of the child to interfere with his individual aims and plans.[87]

The application of the "best interests of the child" test in relation to emancipation reflects a flexible concern for the welfare of the minor rather than a rigid doctrinal adherence.

The *Rounds Brothers* court's willingness to find emancipation so as to allow the minor to retain his earnings foreshadowed a weakening of the parental right to a child's wages. Due to a changed economic climate and altered perceptions of the parent-child relationship, the predominant cultural expectation is increasingly that the child be allowed to keep his or her earnings and decide how to expend them.[88] Indeed, actions for recovery of a child's wages have become something of a rarity. Nevertheless, collateral actions for loss of a child's time and impairment to his or her earning capacity are still brought by parents. Curiously, in such actions, courts, when confronted between an award to the minor to compensate for injuries sustained by him or an award to the parents, have occasionally found for the parents, holding the minor to be unemancipated even though the facts might well have supported a finding of emancipation.[89] Whether such decisions are aberrations or desperate efforts to retain some vestige of the old common law rule remains to be seen.

Child Support. Emancipation is often a defense to a claim for child support payments. The contention is that emancipation terminates parental obligations as well as rights, including the duty of support. It is interesting, however, that courts have demonstrated a marked lack of willingness to accept this argument. Rather they have generally held the parent responsible for the child's support[90] and in doing so have resorted to a number of approaches to avoid cutting off the minor's support. The most straightforward method has simply been to hold that the alleged parental acts were insufficient to constitute an emancipation of the child.[91] Emancipation would not be implied absent "proof of an intention of the mother [father] to renounce permanently her [his] right as a parent."[92] In *Turner* v. *Turner*,[93] the Kentucky Court of Appeals held that a father was required to pay child support to his twenty-year-old daughter, even though she had previously been employed and supported herself, so she could resume her education. In reaching its result, the court appeared to concede that while the child was partially emancipated she was nonetheless entitled to support on the grounds that the parental duty of support revives if the child undergoes a change in status making her dependent once again.[94] The *Turner* court further departed from emancipation doctrine by implying that the child, as well as the parent, had power to revoke the emancipation.[95]

Judicial hesitation in finding emancipation in child support situations is exemplified by the recent New York case of *Bates* v. *Bates*.[96] There a twenty-year-old son petitioned the court to modify his support award from $30 per week to $300 per week. The evidence indicated that the son was living in Florida, had been in and out of several colleges, and was something of a playboy. Despite

this independent existence and despite the judge's obvious displeasure with the boy's lifestyle, the court balked at making a finding of emancipation. While the father's failure to protest the original support order and the father's claiming of the son as a dependent for income tax purposes provided some basis for a finding of no emancipation, the court's biggest conceptual problem arose from the divorce context:

> [F]or a parent to effectively emancipate his child, the latter must first be under his control and supervision. . . . Here the father has no control over the petitioner-son since custody has been and is in the mother. . . . Absent control over the infant, the latter, [by his conduct] cannot be regarded as having adopted an inconsistent status.[97]

The court obviously had difficulty with a situation where custody and control were vested in one parent and the obligation of support was vested in another parent. Instead of taking the approach it did, however, the court could have inquired into whether the mother, by her acts, had emancipated the child. If so, logically the child would be emancipated as to the father as well, and the father's support duty would therefore cease. In the *Bates* case, in contrast to others in this area, it was the court's strict adherence to the principle that emancipation must be by parental act which led to a finding of no emancipation.

The results in the child support cases are susceptible to several interpretations. Courts may think it unfair to deprive a child of support where he or she has already been subject to the trauma of family breakdown. One court has hinted at such a reservation. "We entertain serious doubt that the doctrine of emancipation has application at all in situations whereby the usual family relationship has been disrupted by divorce."[98] While theoretically if a child were truly independent the fact of parental divorce should not matter to him or her, there may be a feeling that the dissolution of marriage had formed the background for the emancipation and that the child should not be penalized for the acts of the parents. Underlying this view may be the belief that the parents, by divorcing, breached their duties to their children and should not be rewarded by being relieved of support obligations as well.[99]

Another explanation for the results in these support cases is simply that the courts wish to make sure that the child is in fact capable of self-support before stripping him or her of the right to support. This view is corroborated by language from other cases:

> The limitation of this emancipating power . . . does not extend to releasing the father from the responsibilities which the law imposes upon him. The rights of the child are protected and may not be impaired. But his disabilities may be removed by the act of the father.[100]

Carried to its logical conclusion, this position would mean that emancipation is a doctrine for children, enabling a minor to vindicate certain rights that he would otherwise be barred from asserting, yet cloaking him with the continuing protection afforded by parental obligations. The majority view, however, is that emancipated minors cannot have their cake and eat it.[101] Nevertheless, there has been a general recognition of the unique importance to the child of the duty of support. When the issue is squarely raised, courts, acting for the

State in its capacity as *parens patriae,* will be reluctant to decree emancipation unless presented with a very clear fact pattern.

Emancipation of Infants. A similarly protective version of emancipation emerges from those cases dealing with emancipation of infants. These decisions stand on a different footing from all other emancipation situations. While the emancipation of eighteen- to twenty-year-old minors is often a legal recognition of the fact that the child's position has become totally inconsistent with that of a subordinate member in the family, the emancipation of young children is designed to permit an infant to escape from an insupportable family relationship and to have a chance at a stable and healthy upbringing. Indeed, the emancipation of infant cases clearly resemble those arising under relinquishment and termination of parental right statutes for purposes of adoption.[102] Because emancipation in such cases is designed to effect rather than recognize a change in the parent-child relationship, its use in this context is conceptually confusing and should probably be dropped.

The issue of emancipation of infants arises most frequently in litigation between counties, cities, or towns concerning settlement for poor relief purposes. In such cases the question is which unit of local government is to have the responsibility for supporting poor children. Because the child's settlement is derived from that of the father or, if the child is illegitimate, from that of the mother, shifts in the parent's residence mean changes in the child's settlement. If the child is emancipated, however, the settlement becomes fixed at the place of emancipation. In a typical case where an unwed mother has relinquished her child to an agency and has then proceeded to live in several new locations,[103] the question of support, if the child should become a public charge, is likely to be litigated between the county of the mother's most recent residence and the county where the relinquishment occurred. Generally the outcome of this litigation will depend upon whether the child was emancipated by the relinquishment.

It has been held that the abandonment and relinquishment of an infant child to an adoption agency[104] or a grandparent[105] constitutes an emancipation. While some courts have used the test of independence generally applied in emancipation cases,[106] most have applied far more stringent criteria before finding emancipation of infants and have held that:

> [I]t must appear that his parents have absolutely transferred all their right to the care and control of the infant; and all their right to his services, and that the person to whom such rights are transferred has accepted the infant as his own and agreed to stand in loco parentis.[107]

Moreover, even where these conditions have been fulfilled and emancipation decreed, the courts have held that the parent remains obligated to furnish necessaries for the child and to contribute to the public support provided by the town or county. This result has been justified on the grounds that a relinquishment under the circumstances creates only a partial emancipation;[108] but it would be more candid and helpful to admit that emancipation of infants is a special case and that therefore ordinary rules of emancipation are simply not controlling.

Emancipation and Third Parties.
Courts have also been confronted with numerous cases in which emancipation has been raised in connection with third parties. Courts have nearly all held that judicial emancipation is a family law doctrine basically concerned with the extinguishment of parental rights and obligations and not with the removal of disabilities in general, and that third parties could not avail themselves of its benefits. In *Vaupel v. Bellach*,[109] for example, a tortfeasor brought an action against a nineteen-year-old boy seeking contribution for injuries received by the boy's mother in an automobile accident. The son had been working on a farm since he was seventeen and had been employed for a time in a factory, during which period he had lived in his own apartment. At the time of the accident the child was nineteen, collecting unemployment compensation, and was living at home, where he was not paying room and board. The Iowa Supreme Court dismissed the suit on the theory that the child was not emancipated and therefore, since the boy's mother could not have sued him, no action for contribution would lie. Given the fact pattern connoting considerable independence and self-sufficiency, one wonders whether the court would have reached a similar conclusion if a third party had not been involved and the mother had sued the child directly.

The greatest concentration of third party emancipation cases has been in the area of contractual liability. The general rule is that "emancipation does not remove or affect a minor's incapacity to subject himself to contractual liability for things which are not necessaries."[110] Thus, even though a minor may judicially be emancipated, he or she retains the right to disaffirm a contract entered into during minority.[111] In *Kiefer* v. *Fred Howe Motors, Inc.*[112] the Wisconsin Supreme Court was asked to adopt a new rule making eighteen-year-old emancipated minors liable for their contracts and preventing them from disaffirming. In that case a twenty-year-old boy, married and the father of a child, brought an action to recover the purchase price of a used car after disaffirming his contract when the seller refused to make an adjustment. The court was clearly disturbed by the old rule and suggested a variety of legislative approaches to modify or abolish it, but still felt constrained, even on these facts, to allow disaffirmance.

Although the principle against extending emancipation to affect the rights of minors vis-à-vis third parties is well-established, it is not absolute. In *Merrick* v. *Stephens*,[113] the plaintiff brought an action to recover payments made on a mortgage which he had executed when he was a nineteen-year-old emancipated minor and disaffirmed shortly after reaching the age of majority. There was evidence that the boy misrepresented his age at the time of execution. While recognizing the general rule that "emancipation does not, in and of itself, operate to make the infant sui juris,"[114] the Missouri court utilized the idea of emancipation to expand the doctrine of necessaries:

> [I]f we have a combination of emancipation with necessity there is often an enlarged and more extended necessity. If the minor is emancipated and does not have the parental roof of shelter, and if he is married (or marrying), with a wife for whom he is obligated to furnish shelter and lodging, the purchase or lease of a home can . . . become a necessity.[115]

Voter Registration. Recently the issue of emancipation has surfaced within the novel context of voter registration and residency requirements.[116] Following the passage of the twenty-sixth amendment granting the right to vote to eighteen-year-olds, voter registrars in many states refused to register students and other eighteen- to twenty-one-year-olds living away from home on the grounds that their residence was that of their parents and that they therefore had to register to vote in the district where their parents resided. In ordering a writ of mandamus requiring voting officials to register young people where they resided, the California Supreme Court relied heavily on the doctrine of emancipation:

> Specifically, under California law a minor may be emancipated partially or completely by his parents or by operation of the law. It is possible that a minor of 18 years of age or older, living apart from his parents, will be emancipated for all purposes; it is substantially probable that he will be emancipated for purposes of residence; and the minor is necessarily emancipated for all purposes relating to voting when he is given the vote in his own right, without regard to the consent of his parent or guardian.[117]

The California court's conclusion, that "the emancipated child is in all respects his own man . . . with the same independence as though he had attained the age of majority,"[118] is especially significant. It marks a radical departure from the idea that the minor is emancipated only as against his or her parents,[119] replacing it with the principle that the minor is emancipated as against the whole world. This concept directly contradicts the decisions in the cases involving contractual liability to third parties discussed above. One way to reconcile the two is to view the California decision as merely implementing the express statutory emancipation for voting purposes conferred on eighteen-year-olds by the twenty-sixth amendment. Read more broadly, however, it may be seen as a landmark decision in which judicial emancipation is used to remove disabilities of minority, thus obliterating the traditional distinction between judicial and statutory emancipation.

III. Statutory Emancipation

Statutory emancipation, unlike judicial emancipation, is concerned with the removal of the disabilities of minority. The manner in which those disabilities are removed distinguishes the first type of statutory emancipation, an equitable proceeding in which the minor petitions the court to be relieved of the disabilities of non-age, from the second type, a special statutory enactment removing specific disabilities of minority.

Equitable Proceeding. In the first type of statutory emancipation the minor, through his parents or next friend, petitions the court to be relieved of the disabilities of minority. If the petition is approved, the court issues a decree affording the petitioner all the rights and responsibilities of an adult subject to any conditions which the court may attach. Although this proceeding, because it entails a judicial hearing, has often been called judicial emancipation, the entire process is governed by statute, and it seems conceptually clearer to

deem it statutory emancipation, distinguishing it from the emancipation situations discussed above.

Only eight states, Alabama, Arkansas, Kansas, Louisiana, Mississippi, Oklahoma, Tennessee and Texas, provide such statutory procedures for emancipation.[120] Judging by the sparseness of reported case law, the frequency with which these procedures are utilized may not be great. Moreover, the utility of these statutes is limited by the restrictions placed on young people seeking to avail themselves of the procedures and by a judicial hostility toward emancipation reflected in the courts' strict construction of the statutes.[121]

In four of these statutory emancipation jurisdictions, the minor must be 18-years-old or more before he may file a petition to be relieved of the disabilities of minority.[122] Arkansas has made one exception to this rule by allowing sixteen-year-old females to file for emancipation,[123] while Tennessee has a similar exception for sixteen-year-old married minors.[124] It is interesting to note in connection with the statutes in these four states that with the recent trend toward lowering the age of majority from twenty-one to eighteen, the emancipation procedure may well be inoperative aside from the exception.[125]

In general, if a decree of emancipation is issued to a child who has not yet attained the minimum statutory age, the decree is void and is subject to collateral attack.[126] In *Hutchinson* v. *Till*,[127] an action to remove the cloud on a title to real estate, both parties claimed under deed from an eighteen-year-old emancipated minor. The boy had obtained one decree removing the disability of minority, conveyed the land in question to respondent, and then moved to vacate that decree on the ground that he had been mistaken about his age and was in fact not yet eighteen. He subsequently obtained a second decree of emancipation and executed a new deed for the same land to the complainant. The court, clearly relying on the equities of the case, held that, while the boy might be permitted to set aside the initial decree, he was estopped from doing so where it would adversely affect rights vested under it.

In the states where no minimum statutory age is set out, the courts appear free to exercise their discretion in issuing emancipation decrees to younger minors. Indeed, in one Mississippi case, the court held that a thirteen-year-old girl had been validly emancipated by court decree.[128] While that girl might have been exceptionally mature for her age, one is compelled to wonder whether this is not too young to confer full adult rights and duties. The issue of how early emancipation may properly be decreed looms important as states lower the age of majority from twenty-one to eighteen, and thereby eliminate from the operation of the doctrine the eighteen- to twenty-one-year-old span where it previously had its greatest efficacy. Aside from age there are other requirements for obtaining an emancipation decree. Thus, residency requirements require the minor to file in the county in which he resides or, in some cases, where his parents reside.[129] Some jurisdictions require the minor to aver that he or she has been a bona fide resident of the county in which the petition has been filed for one year.[130] Half of the statutory emancipation jurisdictions also have special provisions for non-resident minors owning real property in a county, who may wish to be emancipated for purposes of making a

conveyance or otherwise contracting with respect to the property.[131]

Perhaps the most formidable impediment to obtaining a decree of emancipation is the consent requirement. In only two of the eight states, Kansas and Oklahoma, is it clear that the consent of a parent, guardian or other relative is not a prerequisite to obtaining a decree. In those two states the minor need only file a petition by his or her next friend setting out age, residency and reasons for emancipation. If the court finds that emancipation is warranted, it shall so decree. In Arkansas, the statute does not detail the procedure for petitioning the court. One might assume that such legislative silence implies no need for parental consent, but that is far from certain.[132] In the remaining statutory emancipation jurisdictions the consent of the parent(s), other adult kin, or a guardian is required before a decree of emancipation can be entered.[133] In some instances, the parents are joined as defendants in a quasi-adversary proceeding.[134] Where the basis for the petition is ill treatment, refusal to support, or corrupt examples, parental consent may be dispensed with in at least one state.[135] In Alabama the minor may not himself petition the court to be emancipated unless he has no parents or guardian, they are insane, or the child has been abandoned for over one year; otherwise his parents must file the petition.[136] In addition to the specific consent requirements, all of these jurisdictions have provisions for publication of notice of the emancipation proceedings to give any person who wishes to oppose the petition ample opportunity to appear.[137]

Except where a child is illegitimate, in which case the consent of the putative father at least prior to *Stanley* v. *Illinois*, was customarily dispensed with,[138] the courts have interpreted consent requirements extremely strictly. Thus a decree of emancipation was held to be void where no special tutor had been appointed to consent to it.[139] Similarly, in *Emancipation of Dupuy*,[140] the father and special tutor assented to the petition for emancipation but the mother refused. Since the parents were separated with custody of the child in the mother, the court held that it could not entertain the petition without the mother's consent. This case appears to treat consent as a jurisdictional fact, meaning that a decree without the proper consents may be subject to collateral attack.

The statutory and judicial insistence upon parental consent reflects a feeling that, while the primary purpose of statutory emancipation is the removal of disabilities of minority, it also, like judicial emancipation, entails severing parental and filial ties. The following statement is characteristic of the courts' cautious concern in this area:

> [O]ur law does not favor the displacement of parental authority without the consent of the parents. . . . [P]arental control is the fundamental principle that lies at the foundation of society. . . .[141]

Thus, even when confronted with a statutory procedure designed to free the child from his or her subordinate position as a minor, the courts will continue to indulge in presumptions favoring the stability of the family unit, an approach which, if carried to extremes, could frustrate the purpose of statutory emancipation.

Apart from the factors discussed above, the principal criterion for granting a minor's petition for emancipation is that the issuance of the decree be in the best interests of the child.[142] This is the test generally used by the courts in adoption and custody proceedings and calls for case by case determinations based upon a consideration of all the circumstances involved. Two states, Kansas and Oklahoma, stipulate that the petitioner must be of sound mind.[143] Along with Louisiana, they also mandate that the minor must be capable of transacting his own affairs.[144] This concern for the fiscal status of the minor is consistent with the economic considerations which play such a significant role in judicial emancipation cases. If the minor is economically self-sufficient, the chances of his or her obtaining an emancipation decree are substantially increased.

As is true in instances of judicial emancipation, statutory procedure may result in either complete or partial emancipation. Generally, the statutes declare that a decree of emancipation enables the minor to sue and be sued, to contract, to buy and sell real estate, and to perform all other acts which a person over twenty-one may lawfully do. However, they also empower the courts to attach such conditions and limitations upon the emancipation as are deemed appropriate, which limitations are usually set out in the final decree.[145] An indication of how narrowly a court may construe the effect of an emancipation decree is provided by *Howard v. McMurchy*.[146] In that case, the plaintiffs sued for partition of land and cancellation of a mortgage on the ground that a decree relieving the minor of the disabilities of non-age did not confer the power to execute a mortgage. Even though the decree expressly stated that the girl would be empowered to buy and sell real estate as if she were twenty-one, the Mississippi Supreme Court held that this did not include the power to mortgage:

> A minor is incapable of contracting un-less and until his disabilities of minority are removed and then only to the ex-tent provided in the decree removing them, and, where the words of the decree are plain and unambiguous, the power thereby conferred cannot be ex-tended beyond the plain meaning of the language used.[147]

If there are specific statutory pro-visions conflicting with a decree of emancipation, the decree is not likely to be accorded overriding weight. In *Landsberg* v. *Board of Examiners*,[148] a seventeen-year-old girl who had been emancipated in a statutory proceeding sought a writ of mandamus compelling the school board to certify her as a teacher. According to state law, an ap-plicant had to be eighteen years old be-fore a teaching certificate could be issued. The court denied the petition, holding that the emancipation had "no effect whatever" upon the minimum age qualification. An even more interesting case would be presented if an emanci-pated minor were arrested for violating a curfew applying only to persons under twenty-one. The due process problems raised by such a case would force courts to confront squarely the effect to be given to an emancipation decree.

Statutory Removal of Disabilities. In contrast to the limited number of jurisdictions having individualized statu-tory emancipation procedures, almost all fifty states have enacted legislation re-lieving all minors above a certain age from specific disabilities of minority. The second kind of statutory emancipa-tion differs from the first in that it is by

definition only partial and extends to the entire underage population rather than to specific individuals under twenty-one. It is also a relatively new phenome-non, the great bulk of the statutes having been passed within the last five years.

Medical Treatment. Perhaps the most significant movement in legislative emancipation was the ratification of the Twenty-sixth Amendment, conferring voting rights on eighteen- to twenty-one-year-olds. The right to vote will almost surely bring about more rapid change in other areas involving legislative emanci-pation, including the vitally important area of medical treatment for minors. Prior to the passage of laws enabling minors to consent to medical treatment for various problems, a minor had to obtain parental consent before he or she could receive medical treatment. Since minors can disaffirm their contracts, physicians who risked treatment of chil-dren without parental consent also risked not getting compensated for their efforts. This situation often resulted in minors' not receiving medical care when needed and created grave perils in emergency cases. The entire situation worsened in the 1960s with the increas-ing incidence of drug abuse and venereal disease among the country's youth. As juveniles were particularly reluctant to disclose their involvement with sex and drugs to their parents, they were not ob-taining treatment. The result was a crisis in both individual and public health.

State legislatures responded by passing laws enabling minors to consent to medical treatment for various prob-lems, thereby removing one disability of minority.[149] All but five states now per-mit minors to consent to treatment for ve-nereal disease.[150] The language of these statutes varies, however, and while some provide that all persons under twenty-one may consent to treatment,[151] others require that the minor be at least twelve-years-old before such consent can be effective.[152] Moreover, some of the statutes focus on insulating the physicians from liability[153] while others specifically state that the consent shall not be subject to disaffirmance by reason of minority.[154] Finally, the statutes differ as to whether they contain a mandatory reporting clause compelling physicians to inform the parents that their children are being treated for venereal disease;[155] a clause which, if present, may discourage a minor from seeking treatment.

Many of the states providing for minors' consent to treatment for venereal disease also enable the minor to obtain other medical services. A growing number of jurisdictions permit minors to consent to treatment for drug abuse or dependency.[156] Most states now allow minors over eighteen to donate blood without parental consent.[157] In some states, a minor may also obtain emergency medical treatment without parental consent where a delay would endanger his or her health.[158] In California, minors fifteen or over may consent to hospital, medical, surgical or dental care provided they are living apart from their parents and managing their own affairs;[159] and in Connecticut minors over eighteen may consent to the full array of health services without any further qualifications.[160]

Educational Support. The field of higher education is another major area of legislative emancipation. Due to the prohibitive costs of colleges and universities, most students require some form of financial assistance. Where there is parental opposition to children's continuing their education beyond high school, such students must have some

independent access to scholarship or loan funds. To meet these needs, legislation has been adopted allowing for easier availability of educational funds. As part of that program, most states have declared that minors over sixteen may contract for higher education loans, and any obligations arising from those transactions will not be subject to disaffirmance by reason of minority.[161]

Contractual Competence. Other aspects of minor's contractual disability have also come under legislative scrutiny. In Kentucky, for example, minors not less than fifteen may execute contracts for insurance which cannot be "rescinded, avoided or repudiated" by reason of minority.[162] Under California law, contracts for artistic or creative services and professional sports contracts may not be disaffirmed by reason of minority provided they have court approval.[163] In Massachusetts, minors eighteen and over may contract for the repair, purchase, or sale of automobiles and will be held liable on those contracts if made with parental consent.[164]

What is unique about the statutory removal of disabilities is that it is based more upon changing social and cultural demands than economic capability. In the other areas of emancipation, the minor's financial status plays a large if not determinative role, and major shifts in the economic nature of the parent-child relationship are often reflected in changes in the legal nature of that relationship. Here, on the other hand, minors are being emancipated for certain purposes without regard to economic criteria. Indeed, such emancipation is being accomplished in spite of the continuing financial dependence of the child upon the parent which results from such factors as the high costs of living, the increasing number of young people in higher education, and the extended adolescence found in post-industrial society. This most recent phase of statutory emancipation must thus be seen as a direct response to the cultural and political movements among young people in the past decade, with the emancipation legislation discussed here playing a prominent role in bringing the young "into the system" on an equal basis with others.

IV. A Concluding Note

The theme of this article has been that by studying the development of the doctrine of judicial emancipation and noting the recent shift in emphasis from judicial to statutory emancipation, we may observe the changing status of the child within the family and in American society. It is important to bear in mind that resort to the courts in order to establish emancipation presupposes some parent-child conflict, or problem of legal responsibility, insoluble within the family itself. Such conflicts or problems may arise from factors purely economic, or psychological, or from a combination of these with social factors.

Since 1967 there has been a quantum jump in the enactment of statutes removing certain disabilities of minority from all "older" children within a jurisdiction. These new laws represent a decision to accord mature minors certain advantages as a matter of right rather than privilege, and as a group or class rather than as individuals. Such laws represent a philosophy about children which rejects the basic theoretical premises of judicial emancipation. The ultimate extension of this process is the lowering of the age of majority, noted

earlier, which has already taken place in eighteen states with several more expected to follow suit shortly. While it is still too early to predict what the eventual social consequences of such a development will be, it is likely that, with the twenty-sixth amendment as a catalyst, the age of adulthood for legal purposes will be fixed at eighteen in all states before the end of the decade.

Notes

1. As early as 1818, the Supreme Judicial Court of Massachusetts used the emancipation doctrine to protect a minor's right to receive compensation for his services. In *Nightingale* v. *Withington*, 15 Mass. 272, 274 S.75 (15 Tyng) (1818), the court said: "But where the father has discharged himself of the obligation to support the child, or has obliged the child to support himself, there is no principle, but that of slavery, which will continue his right to receive the earnings of the child's labor. . . . [T]he law will imply an emancipation of the son. . . ."

2. In Professor Homer Clark's family law treatise, H. Clark, *Domestic Relations* 240 (1968), the author refers to emancipation as "this peculiar and fortunately, unimportant corner of the law."

3. There have been no major law review articles on the topic. Some background treatment is provided in H. Clark, *Domestic Relations* 240–44 (1968). There is a lengthy annotation in Annot., 165 A.L.R. 723 (1946). There is also a comprehensive note in 59 Am. Jur. 2d, *Parent and Child*, §§ 93–100 (1971), and a similar one in 67 C.J.S., *Parent and Child* §§ 86–90 (1950).

4. The Stubborn Child Law enacted in Massachusetts in 1654 punished "divers children and servants [who] behave themselves too disrespectively, disobediently and disorderly toward

their parents, masters and governors."
See 3 N. Shurtleff, *Records of the Governor and Company of Massachusetts Bay Colony in New England* 355 (1853–54).

The constitutionality of this law, still on the books, was recently upheld in *Commonwealth* v. *Brasher,* 1971 Mass. Adv. Sh. 907, 270 N.E.2d 389. For a critical analysis of the decision, see Katz and Schroeder, *Disobeying a Father's Voice: A Comment on Commonwealth* v. *Brasher,* 57 Mass. L. Q. 43 (1972), and Sidman, *The Massachusetts Stubborn Child Law: Law and Order in the Home,* 6 Fam. L. Q. 33 (1972).

5. The death penalty was possible for violation of the early Stubborn Child Law.
6. I *Children and Youth in America* 104 (R. Bremner ed. 1970).
7. A good analysis of the economic function of children in colonial America is found in E. Morgan, *The Puritan Family* (1966).
8. Interestingly, however, laws were enacted to insure the children were gainfully employed, even if that meant taking them away from parents for a period of time and apprenticing them to more "industrious" persons. See W. Whitmore, *The Colonial Laws of Massachusetts* 25 (1887).
9. See note 1 *supra.*
10. See the history of *Hammer* v. *Dagenhart,* 247 U.S. 351 (1918), striking down federal child labor laws. The decision was overruled more than twenty years later in *United States* v. *Darby,* 312 U.S. 100 (1941).
11. For a good discussion of *parens patriae,* see A. Platt, *The Child Savers* (1969). See also *Prince* v. *Massachusetts,* 321 U.S. 158 (1944).
12. Recent statistics indicate that approximately 42 percent of all marriages end in divorce. In some states, such as California, the figure is hovering at the 50 percent mark.

13. The best insights into this phenomenon were produced over a decade before it actually began to occur. See P. Goodman, *Growing Up Absurd* (1956).
14. Arguably, this is related to the post-World War II technological revolution and, while no single volume has as yet related that revolution to family breakdown, several do begin the process. In particular see A. Toffler, *Future Shock* (1970); M. Mead, *Culture and Commitment—A Study of the Generation Gap* (1970); and J. Ellul, *The Technological Society* (1964).
15. The twenty-sixth amendment became law in 1971 after ratification by three quarters of the state legislatures. It reads:

> The right of citizens of the United States, who are eighteen years of age or older, to vote shall not be denied or abridged by the United States or by any State on account of age.

16. Eighteen states have lowered the age of majority from 21 to 18. They are California *(Cal. Civ. Code,* § 25 (Supp. 1971)); Connecticut (Conn. Pub. Act 127 (1972)); Illinois (*Ill. Ann. Stat.,* c.3, § 131 (Smith-Hurd Supp. (1971)); Kentucky *(Ky. Rev. Stat.,* tit. 2.015 (1966)); Maine (Me. Spec. Sess. c.598 1972)); Michigan (*Mich. Stat. Ann.,* § 25.244 (51) (1971)); New Jersey Reg. Sess., c. 296 (1972); New Mexico *(N.M. Stat. Ann.,* § 13–13–1 (Supp. 1971)); North Carolina (*N.C. Gen Stat.,* § 48A–1 (Supp. 1971)); North Dakota (N.D. Code Ann., § 14–10–02 (1971)); Oklahoma (Okla. Reg. Sess., c.221 (1972)); Rhode Island *(R.I. Gen. Laws,* §§ 15–12–1 (1972)); Tennessee *(Tenn. Code. Ann.,* S.1.–113 (Supp. 1971)); Vermont *(Vt. Stat. Ann.,* tit. 1, § 173 (1972)); Washington (*Wash. Rev. Code, App.* 1.292x (Supp. 1971)); West Virginia (*W. Va. Code,* § 2–2–10(a) (Supp. 1972)); Wisconsin (Wis. Reg. Sess., c.213 (1972)); and

Wyoming (*Wyo. Stat. Ann.*, § 14–11 (Supp. 1971)). In addition, three states have lowered the age of majority to 19. They are Alaska (*Alaska Stat. Ann.*, tit. 25.20.010 (1965)); Iowa (Iowa Reg. Sess. 261 (1972)); and Montana (*Mont. Rev. Code*, § 64–101 (1971 Supp.)). Five states set the age of majority at 21 for males and 18 for females: Arkansas (*Ark. Rev. Stat.*, tit. 57, § 134 (1971)); Idaho (*Idaho Code Ann.*, § 32–101 (1948)); Nevada (*Nev. Rev. Stat.*, § 129.010 (1963)); South Dakota (*S.D. Code*, § 43.0101 (1939)); and Utah (*Utah Code Ann.*, § 15–2–1 (1953)).

17. The doctrine of emancipation appears to be unknown to the common law but has become an established part of American jurisprudence. See *In re* Sonnenberg, 256 Minn. 571, 575, 99 N.W. 2d 444, 447 (1959).

18. S. Katz, *When Parents Fail* 9 (1971).

19. *Id.* at 18.

20. H. Clark, *supra* note 2, at 234.

21. See *Weeks* v. *Holmes*, 66 Mass. 215 (12 Cush.) (1853).

22. See, e.g., *Wurth* v. *Wurth*, 322 S.W. 2d 745 (Mo. 1959).

23. *Rounds Bros.* v. *McDaniel*, 133 Ky. 669, 676, 118 S.W. 956, 958 (1909).

24. See *Perkins* v. *Robinson*, 140 Cal. App. 2d 536, 295 P.2d 972 (1956).

25. *Vaupel* v. *Bellach*, 261 *Iowa* 376, 379–80, 154 N.W.2d 149, 150–51 (1967).

26. *Turner* v. *Turner*, 441 S.W.2d 105 (Ky. Ct. App. 1969).

27. Compare *Perkins* v. *Robinson*, 140 Cal. App. 2d 536, 295 P.2d 972 (1956) with *Wood* v. *Wood*, 135 *Conn.* 280, 63 A.2d 586 (1948).

28. A good discussion of express emancipation is found in *Rounds Bros.* v. *McDaniel*, *supra* note 23.

29. This principle is most forcefully stated in *Bates* v. *Bates*, 62 Misc. 2d 498, 310 N.Y.S.2d 26 (1970).

30. 384 S.W.2d 85 (Ky. Ct. App. 1964).

31. See note 28, *supra*. See also *Parker* v. *Parker*, 230 S.C. 28, 94 S.E.2d 12 (1956).

32. *Wood* v. *Wood*, 135 Conn. 280, 283, 63 A.2d 586, 588 (1948).

33. See *Gillikin* v. *Burbage*, 263 N.C. 317, 139 S.E.2d 753 (1965).

34. *Vaupel* v. *Bellach*, *supra* note 25, offers a good example of how courts will find only partial emancipation even where there is strong evidence of almost complete independence.

35. 162 Pa. Super. 383, 57 A.2d 426 (1948).

36. *Allen* v. *Arthur*, 139 Ind. App. 460, 463, 220 N.E.2d 658, 660 (1966).

37. *Id.*

38. See, e.g., *Iroquois Iron Co.* v. *Industrial Commission*, 294 Ill. 106, 128 N.E. 289 (1920).

39. Of course, attaining the age of majority also works a complete emancipation. See *Fitzgerald* v. *Valdez*, 77 N.M. 769, 427 P.2d 655 (1967).

40. *Iroquois Iron Co.* v. *Industrial Commission*, 294 Ill. 106, 109, 128 N.E. 289, 290 (1920).

41. In *Wood* v. *Wood*, 135 Conn. 280, 63 A.2d 586 (1948), the trial court had directed a verdict for the defendant on the grounds that the suit was barred by the intra-family tort immunity rule. The Connecticut Supreme Court reversed, holding that the trial court should have allowed the issue of emancipation to go to the jury. See also *Parker* v. *Parker*, 230 S.C. 28, 94 S.E. 2d 12 (1956).

42. *Wurth* v. *Wurth*, 313 S.W.2d 161 (Mo. Ct. App. 1958). Interestingly, the Missouri Supreme Court later reversed the intermediate appellate court, noting that entry of judgment n.o.v. was improper on the facts. *Wurth* v. *Wurth*, 322 S.W.2d 745 (Mo. 1959).

43. 313 S.W.2d at 165.

44. *Fitzgerald* v. *Valdez*, 77 N.M. 769, 427 P.2d 655 (1967).

45. *Wurth* v. *Wurth*, 322 S.W.2d 745 (Mo. 1959).

46. *Gillikin* v. *Burbage*, 263 N.C. 317, 139 S.E.2d 753 (1965).
47. *Schoenung* v. *Gallet*, 206 Wis. 52, 238 N.W. 852 (1931).
48. *Lufkin* v. *Harvey*, 131 Minn. 238, 154 N.W. 1097 (1915).
49. *Carricato* v. *Carricato*, 384 S.W.2d 85 (Ky. Ct. App. 1964).
50. *Parker* v. *Parker*, 230 S.C. 28, 94 S.E. 2d 12 (1956).
51. *Wadoz* v. *United National Indemnity Co.*, 274 Wis. 383, 80 N.W.2d 262 (1957).
52. *Gillikin* v. *Burbage*, 263 N.C. 317, 323, 139 S.E.2d 753, 758 (1965).
53. Compare *Carricato* v. *Carricato*, 384 S.W.2d 85 (Ky. Ct. App. 1964) with a later decision in the same jurisdiction, *Turner* v. *Turner*, 441 S.W.2d 105 (Ky. Ct. App. 1969).
54. See W. Prosser, *Law of Torts* 864–868 (4th ed. 1971); McCurdy, *Torts Between Persons in Domestic Relations*, 43 *Harv. L. Rev.* 1030, 1072–1077 (1930).
55. The intra-family tort immunity rule has been abrogated in at least 11 jurisdictions. For a listing of these states, see note 82 *infra*.
56. See, e.g., *Glover* v. *Glover*, 319 S.W. 2d 238 (Tenn. Ct. App. 1958).
57. *Detwiler* v. *Detwiler*, 162 Pa. Super. 383, 57 A.2d 426 (1948).
58. See generally, McCurdy, *supra* note 54.
59. See M. Paulser, W. Wadlington and J. Goebel Jr., *Cases and Materials on Domestic Relations* 220–224 (1970).
60. See H. Clark, *Domestic Relations* (1968).
61. *Id.*
62. Particularly good language is found in *Beaudette* v. *Frana*, 285 Minn. 366, 173 N.W.2d 416 (1969), abrogating interspousal tort immunity in Minnesota.
63. An enlightening judicial discussion of the collusion-insurance issue is in *Gibson* v. *Gibson*, 3 Cal.3d 914, 479 P.2d 648, 92 Cal. Rptr. 288 (1971). Although it is an intra-family rather than interspousal immunity case, its reasoning is equally applicable in both situations.
64. *Detwiler* v. *Detwiler*, 161 Pa. Super. 383, 385, 57 A.2d 426, 427 (1948).
65. See I *Children and Youth in America* 104 (R. Bremner ed. 1970).
66. 84 N.H. 352, 150 A.905 (1930).
67. *Id.* at 363, 150 A. at 910.
68. *Id.* at 367–368, 150 A. at 913.
69. 45 Cal.2d 244, 288 P.2d 868 (1955).
70. *Emery* v. *Emery*, 45 Cal.2d 421, 289 P.2d 218 (1955).
71. *Id.* at 430, 289 P.2d at 223–224.
72. *Gibson* v. *Gibson*, 3 Cal.3d 914, 479 P.2d 648, 92 Cal. Rptr. 288 (1971).
73. *Id.* at 915–16, 479 P.2d at 648, 92 Cal. Rptr. at 288.
74. 313 S.W.2d 161 (Mo. Ct. App. 1958).
75. *Id.* at 165.
76. *Wurth* v. *Wurth*, 322 S.W.2d 745 (Mo. 1959).
77. See *Wadoz* v. *United National Indemnity Co.*, 274 Wis. 383, 80 N.W.2d 262 (1957).
78. See, e.g., *Parker* v. *Parker*, 230 S.C. 28, 94 S.E.2d 12 (1956).
79. 263 N.C. 317, 139 S.E.2d 753 (1965).
80. Compare the Gillikin case with *Detwiler* v. *Detwiler*, 162 Pa. Super. 383, 67, A.2d 426 (1948).
81. See, e.g., *Carricato* v. *Carricato*, 384 S.W.2d 85 (Ky. Ct. App. 1964).
82. *Gibson* v. *Gibson*, 3 Cal.3d 914, 479 P.2d 648, 92 Cal. Rptr. 288 (1971); *France* v. *A.P.A. Transport Co.*, 56 N.J. 500, 267 A.2d 490 (1970); *Streenz* v. *Streenz*, 106 Ariz. 86, 471 P.2d 282 (1970); *Rigdon* v. *Rigdon*, 463 S.W.2d 631 (1970); *Gellman* v. *Gellman*, 23 N.Y.2d 434, 245 N.E.2d 192, 297 N.Y.S.2d 529 (1969); *Tamashiro* v. *De Gama*, 51 Haw. 74, 450 P.2d 998 (1969); *Schenk* v. *Schenk*, 100 Ill. App. 2d 199, 241 N.E.2d 12 (1968); *Sileski* v. *Kelman*, 281 Minn. 431, 161 N.W.2d 631 (1968); *Hebel* v. *Hebel*, 435 P.2d 8 (Alaska 1967); *Nuelle* v. *Welis*, 154 N.W.2d 364

(N.D. 1967); *Briere* v. *Briere,* 107 N.H. 432, 224 A.2d 188 (1966).

83. See note 1 *supra.*

84. See, e.g., *McCarthy* v. *Boston & L. R. Corp.,* 148 Mass. 550, 20 N.E. 182 (1899).

85. *Id.*

86. 133 Ky. 669, 118 S.W. 956 (1909).

87. *Id.* at 677, 118 S.W. at 958.

88. See *Perkins* v. *Robinson,* 140 Cal. App. 2d 536, 295 P.2d 972 (1956).

89. See *Allen* v. *Arthur,* 139 Ind. App. 460, 220 N.E.2d 658 (1966).

90. See e.g., *Schirtzinger* v. *Schirtzinger,* 95 Ohio App. 31, 117 N.E.2d 42 (1952).

91. *Id.*

92. *Id.* at 32, 117 N.E.2d at 43–44.

93. 441 S.W.2d 105 (Ky. Ct. App. 1969).

94. In a similar situation where another court has also held that the duty of support may attach once again, the child had enlisted in the armed forces. See *Corbridge* v. *Corbridge,* 230 Ind. 201, 102 N.E.2d 764 (1952).

95. 441 S.W.2d at 107–108.

96. 62 Misc.2d 498, 410 N.Y.S.2d 26 (1970).

97. *Id.* at 503–504, 310 N.Y.S.2d at 32.

98. *Turner* v. *Turner,* 441 S.W.2d at 108.

99. It will be interesting to see if the results in cases in this area differ in those states which have adopted "nofault" divorce, where the notions of blame and guilt have been dropped, at least theoretically.

100. *Dunlap* v. *Dunlap,* 84 N.H. 352, 365, 150 A.905, 911 (1930). See also *Gillikin* v. *Burbage,* 263 N.C. 317, 322, 139 S.E.2d 753, 757 (1965).

101. See, e.g., *Wurth* v. *Wurth,* 322 S.W.2d 745 (Mo. 1959).

102. See, e.g., Cal. Civ. Code, §§ 224, 224m, 224n (1971 Supp.); D.C.C.E., 32–786 (1972 Supp.); Code of Ca., §§ 63.1–56, 631–204 (1950). The effect of these statutes is to terminate the parent-child relationship, thus obviating the need for obtaining parental consent to the adoption.

103. See *In re* Sonnenberg, 256 Minn. 571, 99 N.W.2d 444 (1959).

104. *Id.*

105. *Inhabitants of Camden* v. *Inhabitants of Warren,* 160 Me. 158, 200 A.2d (1964).

106. *Id.* at 162, 200 A.2d at 422.

107. *Town of Tunbridge* v. *Town of Eden,* 39 Vt. 17, 21 (1866).

108. *In re* Sonnenberg, 256 Minn. 571, 576, 99 N.W.2d 444, 448 (1959).

109. 261 Iowa 376, 154 N.W.2d 149 (1967).

110. *Schoenung* v. *Gallet,* 206 Wis. 52, 238 N.W. 852, 853 (1931). See also *Shellabarger* v. *Jacobs,* 316 Ill. App. 191, 45 N.E.2d 184 (1942).

111. *Id.*

112. 35 Wis. 2d 20, 158 N.W.2d 288 (1968).

113. 337 S.W.2d 713 (Mo. Ct. App. 1960).

114. *Id.* at 719.

115. *Id.* at 720.

116. *Jolicoeur* v. *Mihaly,* 5 Cal.3d 565, 488 P.2d 1, 96 Cal. Rptr. 697 (1971).

117. *Id.* at 579, 488 P.2d at 10, 96 Cal. Rptr. at 706.

118. *Id.*

119. *Rounds Bros.* v. *McDaniel,* 133 Ky. 669, 676, 118 S.W. 956, 958 (1909).

120. *Ala. Code Ann.,* tit. 27, §§ 13–20 (1958): *Ark. Stat. Ann.,* §§ 34–2001, 34–2002 (Supp. 1971); *Kan. Rev. Stat.,* §§ 38–108 through 38–110 (Supp. 1971); *La. Civ. Code,* art. 385, §§ 3991–3994 (1961); *Miss. Code Ann.,* tit. 10, §§ 1264–1268 (1942); *Okla. Stat. Ann.,* c.10, §§ 91–94 (1966); *Tenn. Code Ann.,* §§ 23–1201 through 23–1204 (Supp. 1971); *Tex. Civ. Stat. Ann.,* tit. 96, art. 5921–5923a (Supp. 1971).

121. See *Emancipation of Dupuy,* 196 La. 439, 199 So. 384 (1940).

122. Alabama, Arkansas, Texas and Tennessee.

123. *Ark. Stat. Ann.,* §§ 34–2001 (Supp. 1971).

124. *Tenn. Code Ann.,* §§ 23–1204 (Supp. 1971).

125. This is the feeling expressed in the

compiler's note to the Tennessee statute. On the other hand, it is difficult to understand why the Tennessee legislature did not repeal the emancipation statutes if that was really the intended effect of lowering the age of majority.

126. See *Crabtree v. Bonner*, 192 Ark. 377, 93 S.W.2d 134 (1936).

127. 212 Ala. 64, 101 So. 676 (1924).

128. *McLeiter v. Rackley*, 148 Miss. 75, 114 So. 128 (1927).

129. *Ala. Code Ann.*, tit. 27, S.14 (1958).

130. *Kan. Rev. Stat.*, § 38–109 (Supp. 1971); *Okla. Stat. Ann.*, c.10, § 92 (1966).

131. *Ark. Stat. Ann.*, § 34–2002 (Supp. 1971); *Miss. Code Ann.*, tit. 10, § 1264 (1942); *Tenn. Code Ann.*, § 23–1201 (Supp. 1971); *Tex. Civ. Stat. Ann.*, tit. 96, art. 5921b, 5922a, 5923a (Supp. 1971).

132. The confusion surrounding this issue in Arkansas is heightened by the procedural posture of a recent case. In *May v. Spivey Chevrolet*, 241 Ark. 1098, 411 S.W.2d 528 (1967), the mother, as next friend of her son, moved to set aside a decree of emancipation granted to her son. If the disabilities of minority had been removed by the decree, it is unclear why the son did not bring this action himself. If the decree only partially emancipated the son, what does this say about parental participation in initially petitioning the court for a decree relieving the child of the disabilities of minority?

133. See, e.g., *La. Civ. Code*, art. 3992 (1961).

134. *Miss. Code Ann.*, tit. 10, § 1265 (1942); *Tenn. Code Ann.*, § 23–1202 (1955).

135. *La. Civ. Code*, art. 3992 (1961).

136. *Ala. Code Ann.*, tit. 27, § 13 (1958).

137. See, e.g., *Okla. Stat. Ann.*, c.10, § 93 (1966).

138. The decisions in *Stanley v. Illinois*, 405 U.S. 645 (1972), and *Rothstein v. Lutheran Social Services*, 405 U.S. 1051 (1972), seem to indicate that the consent of a putative father to the adoption of his illegitimate child is constitutionally necessary. For a discussion of this issue see Schafrick, *The Emerging Constitutional Protection of the Putative Father's Parental Rights*, 70 *Mich. L. Rev.* 1581 (1972) reprinted in 7 *Fam. L. Q.* 75 (1973).

See also H. Krause, *Illegitimacy: Law and Social Policy* 32 (1971); Katz, *Judicial and Statutory Trends in the Law of Adoption*, 51 *Geo. L. J.* 64, 77–85 (1962).

139. *Gaston v. Rainach*, 141 La. 162, 74 So. 890 (1917).

140. 196 La. 439, 199 So. 384 (1940).

141. *Emancipation of Dupuy*, 196 La. 439, 443–444, 199 So. 384, 386 (1940).

142. See, e.g., *Ala. Code Ann.*, tit. 27, § 13 (1958).

143. See note 135 *supra*.

144. *Id. La. Civ. Code*, art. 3993 (1961).

145. See, e.g., *Miss. Code Ann.*, tit. 10, S.1268 (1931).

146. 175 Miss. 328, 166 So. 917 (1936).

147. *Id.* at 336, 166 So. at 919.

148. 129 Kan. 196, 281 P. 908 (1929).

149. For the latest developments in this field and a complication of statutory materials, see Pilpel, *Minors' Rights to Medical Care*, 36 *Albany L. Rev.* 462 (1972).

150. The states not yet providing for such care are Idaho, Tennessee, Vermont, West Virginia, and Wyoming.

151. See, e.g., *Va. Code Ann.*, § 32–137 (Supp. 1971).

152. *Cal. Civ. Code*, § 34.7 (1968).

153. *Mass. Gen. Laws Ann.*, c.111, § 117 (1967).

154. *Fla. Stat. Ann.*, § 384.061 (Supp. 1971).

155. *Compare Hawaii Rev. Stat.*, tit. 31, § 577A (Supp. 1970), with *Ill. Stat. Ann.*, c.91, § 18.4 (Smith-Hurd 1969).

156. See, e.g., *Ga. Code Ann.*, §§ 74–104.1 through 74–104.3 (Supp. 1971).

157. See, e.g., *Conn. Stat. Ann.*, § 19–139K (Supp. 1972).

158. See, e.g., Fla. Reg. Sess., c.72–131
     (1972).
159. *Cal. Civ. Code,* § 34.6 (1968).
160. *Conn. Stat. Ann.,* § 19–142a (Supp.
     1972).

161. See, e.g., *Va. Code Ann.,* § 8–135.1
     (Supp. 1971).
162. *Ky. Rev. Stat.,* § 304.14–70 (1969).
163. *Cal. Civ. Code,* § 35 (Supp. 1971).
164. *Mass. Gen. Laws Ann.,* c.90, § 2c
     (1971 Supp.).

Families do not end when children attain their majority and a corresponding inner emancipation. But one finds in our time no agreement on the requirements of family life after that stage. On the one hand, there are grown children who devote their lives to caring for needy parents; on the other, children equally able who neglect their equally needy parents. Some assume that grown children who cope with parents' needs are only doing their duty; others that they are doing far more than duty requires, and that neglectful grown children of needy parents do nothing wrong.

In "What Do Grown Children Owe Their Parents?" Jane English considers whether grown children are morally bound to help and care for their parents. She argues that emancipated adult children do not owe help to parents as a "debt" of gratitude, but that when there is a close bond between parent and child, then they ought to help one another as other friends do. In friendship, the abler should help the needier; but where friendship is gone, nothing is owed.

WHAT DO GROWN CHILDREN OWE THEIR PARENTS?

JANE ENGLISH

What do grown children owe their parents? I will contend that the answer is "nothing." Although I agree that there are many things that children *ought* to do for their parents, I will argue that it is inappropriate and misleading to describe them as things "owed." I will maintain that parents' voluntary sacrifices, rather than creating "debts" to be "repaid," tend to create love or "friendship." The duties of grown children are those of friends and result from love between them and their parents, rather than being things owed in repayment for the parents' earlier sacrifices. Thus, I will oppose those philosophers who use the word "owe" whenever a duty or obligation exists. Although the "debt" metaphor is appropriate in some moral circumstances, my argument is that a love relationship is not such a case.

Misunderstandings about the proper relationship between parents and their grown children have resulted from reliance on the "owing" terminology. For instance, we hear parents complain, "You owe it to us to write home (keep up your piano playing, not adopt a hippie lifestyle), because of all we sacrificed for you (paying for piano lessons, sending you to college)." The child is sometimes even heard to reply, "I didn't ask to be born (to be given piano lessons, to be sent to college)." This inappropriate idiom of ordinary language tends to obscure, or even to undermine, the love that is the correct ground of filial obligation.

1. Favors Create Debts

There are some cases, other than literal debts, in which talk of "owing," though metaphorical, is apt. New to the neighborhood, Max barely knows his neighbor, Nina, but he asks her if she will take in his mail while he is gone for a month's vacation. She agrees. If, subsequently, Nina asks Max to do the same for her, it seems that Max has a moral obligation to agree (greater than the one he would have had if Nina had not done the same for him), unless for some reason it would be a burden far out of proportion to the one Nina bore for him. I will call this a *favor:* when A, at B's request, bears some burden for B, then B incurs an obligation to reciprocate. Here the metaphor of Max's "owing" Nina is appropriate. It is not literally a debt, of course, nor can Nina pass this IOU on to heirs, demand payment in the form of Max's taking out her garbage, or sue Max. Nonetheless, since Max ought to perform one act of similar nature and amount of sacrifice in return, the term is suggestive. Once he reciprocates, the debt is "discharged"—that is, their obligations revert to the condition they were in before Max's initial request.

Contrast a situation in which Max simply goes on vacation and, to his surprise, finds upon his return that his neighbor has mowed his grass twice weekly in his absence. This is a voluntary sacrifice rather than a favor, and

Max has no duty to reciprocate. It would be nice for him to volunteer to do so, but this would be supererogatory on his part. Rather than a favor, Nina's action is a friendly gesture. As a result, she might expect Max to chat over the back fence, help her catch her straying dog, or something similar—she might expect the development of a friendship. But Max would be chatting (or whatever) out of friendship, rather than in repayment for mown grass. If he did not return her gesture, she might feel rebuffed or miffed, but not unjustly treated or indignant, since Max has not failed to perform a duty. Talk of "owing" would be out of place in this case.

It is sometimes difficult to distinguish between favors and non-favors, because friends tend to do favors for each other, and those who exchange favors tend to become friends. But one test is to ask how Max is motivated. Is it "to be nice to Nina" or "because she did x for me"? Favors are frequently performed by total strangers without any friendship developing. Nevertheless, a temporary obligation is created, even if the chance for repayment never arises. For instance, suppose that Oscar and Matilda, total strangers, are waiting in a long checkout line at the supermarket. Oscar, having forgotten the oregano, asks Matilda to watch his cart for a second. She does. If Matilda now asks Oscar to return the favor while she picks up some tomato sauce, he is obliged to agree. Even if she had not watched his cart, it would be inconsiderate of him to refuse, claiming he was too busy reading the magazines. He may have a duty to help others, but he would not "owe" it to her. But if she has done the same for him, he incurs an additional obligation to help, and talk of "owing" is apt. It suggests an agreement to perform equal, reciprocal, canceling sacrifices.

2. The Duties of Friendship

The terms "owe" and "repay" are helpful in the case of favors, because the sameness of the amount of sacrifice on the two sides is important; the monetary metaphor suggests equal quantities of sacrifice. But friendship ought to be characterized by *mutuality* rather than reciprocity: friends offer what they can give and accept what they need, without regard for the total amounts of benefits exchanged. And friends are motivated by love rather than by the prospect of repayment. Hence, talk of "owing" is singularly out of place in friendship.

For example, suppose Alfred takes Beatrice out for an expensive dinner and a movie. Beatrice incurs no obligation to "repay" him with a goodnight kiss or a return engagement. If Alfred complains that she "owes" him something, he is operating under the assumption that she should repay a favor, but on the contrary his was a generous gesture done in the hopes of developing a friendship. We hope that he would not want her repayment in the form of sex or attention if this was done to discharge a debt rather than from friendship. Since, if Alfred is prone to reasoning in this way, Beatrice may well decline the invitation or request to pay for her own dinner, his attitude of expecting a "return" on his "investment" could hinder the development of a friendship. Beatrice should return the gesture only if she is motivated by friendship.

Another common misuse of the "owing" idiom occurs when the Smiths

have dined at the Joneses' four times, but the Joneses at the Smiths' only once. People often say, "We owe them three dinners." This line of thinking may be appropriate between business acquaintances, but not between friends. After all, the Joneses invited the Smiths not in order to feed them or to be fed in turn, but because of the friendly contact presumably enjoyed by all on such occasions. If the Smiths do not feel friendship toward the Joneses, they can decline future invitations and not invite the Joneses; they owe them nothing. Of course, between friends of equal resources and needs, roughly equal sacrifices (though not necessarily roughly equal dinners) will typically occur. If the sacrifices are highly out of proportion to the resources, the relationship is closer to servility than to friendship.[1]

Another difference between favors and friendship is that after a friendship ends, the duties of friendship end. The party that has sacrificed less owes the other nothing. For instance, suppose Elmer donated a pint of blood that his wife Doris needed during an operation. Years after their divorce, Elmer is in an accident and needs one pint of blood. His new wife, Cora, is also of the same blood type. It seems that Doris not only does not "owe" Elmer blood, but that she should actually refrain from coming forward if Cora has volunteered to donate. To insist on donating not only interferes with the newlyweds' friendship, but it belittles Doris and Elmer's former relationship by suggesting that Elmer gave blood in hopes of favors returned instead of simply out of love for Doris. It is one of the heart-rending features of divorce that it attends to quantity in a relationship previously characterized by mutuality. If Cora could not donate, Doris's obligation is the same as that for any former spouse in need of blood; it is not increased by the fact that Elmer similarly aided her. It *is* affected by the degree to which they are still friends, which in turn may (or may not) have been influenced by Elmer's donation.

In short, unlike the debts created by favors, the duties of friendship do not require equal quantities of sacrifice. Performing equal sacrifices does not cancel the duties of friendship, as it does the debts of favors. Unrequested sacrifices do not themselves create debts, but friends have duties regardless of whether they requested or initiated the friendship. Those who perform favors may be motivated by mutual gain, whereas friends should be motivated by affection. These characteristics of the friendship relation are distorted by talk of "owing."

3. Parents and Children

The relationship between children and their parents should be one of friendship characterized by mutuality rather than one of reciprocal favors. The quantity of parental sacrifice is not relevant in determining what duties the grown child has. The medical assistance grown children ought to offer their ill mothers in old age depends upon the mothers' need, not upon whether they endured a difficult pregnancy, for example. Nor do one's duties to one's parents cease once an equal quantity of sacrifice has been performed, as the phrase "discharging a debt" may lead us to think.

Rather, what children ought to do for their parents (and parents for chil-

dren) depends upon (1) their respective needs, abilities, and resources and (2) the extent to which there is an ongoing friendship between them. Thus, regardless of the quantity of childhood sacrifices, an able, wealthy child has an obligation to help his needy parents more than does a needy child. To illustrate, suppose sisters Cecile and Dana are equally loved by their parents, even though Cecile was an easy child to care for, seldom ill, while Dana was often sick and caused some trouble as a juvenile delinquent. As adults, Dana is a struggling artist living far away, while Cecile is a wealthy lawyer living nearby. When the parents need visits and financial aid, Cecile has an obligation to bear a higher proportion of these burdens than her sister. This results from her abilities, rather than from the quantities of sacrifice made by the parents earlier.

Sacrifices have an important causal role in creating an ongoing friendship, which may lead us to assume incorrectly that it is the sacrifices that are the source of the obligation. That the source is the friendship instead can be seen by examining cases in which the sacrifices occurred but the friendship, for some reason, did not develop or persist. For example, if a woman gives up her newborn child for adoption, and if no feelings of love ever develop on either side, it seems that the grown child does not have an obligation to "repay" her for her sacrifices in pregnancy. For that matter, if the adopted child has an unimpaired love relationship with the adoptive parents, he or she has the same obligations to help them as a natural child would have.

The filial obligations of grown children are a result of friendship, rather than owed for services rendered. Suppose that Vance married Lola despite his parents' strong wish that he marry within their religion, and that as a result, the parents refuse to speak to him again. As the years pass, the parents are unaware of Vance's problems, his accomplishments, the birth of his children. The love that once existed between them, let us suppose, has been completely destroyed by this event and thirty years of desuetude. At this point, it seems, Vance is under no obligation to pay his parents' medical bills in their old age, beyond his general duty to help those in need. An additional, filial obligation would only arise from whatever love he may still feel for them. It would be irrelevant for his parents to argue, "But look how much we sacrificed for you when you were young," for that sacrifice was not a favor but occurred as part of a friendship which existed at that time but is now, we have supposed, defunct. A more appropriate message would be, "We still love you, and we would like to renew our friendship."

I hope this helps to set the question of what children ought to do for their parents in a new light. The parental argument, "You ought to do x because we did y for you," should be replaced by, "We love you and you will be happier if you do x," or "We believe you love us, and anyone who loved us would do x." If the parents' sacrifice had been a favor, the child's reply, "I never asked you to do y for me," would have been relevant; to the revised parental remarks, this reply is clearly irrelevant. The child can either do x or dispute one of the parents' claims: by showing that a love relationship does not exist, or that love for someone does not motivate doing x, or that he or she will not be happier doing x.

Seen in this light, parental requests for children to write home, visit, and offer them a reasonable amount of emotional and financial support in life's crises are well founded, so long as a friendship still exists. Love for others does call for caring about and caring for them. Some other parental requests, such as for more sweeping changes in the child's lifestyle or life goals, can be seen to be insupportable, once we shift the justification from debts owed to love. The terminology of favors suggests the reasoning, "Since we paid for your college education, you owe it to us to make a career of engineering, rather than becoming a rock musician." This tends to alienate affection even further, since the tuition payments are depicted as investments for a return rather than done from love, as though the child's life goals could be "bought." Basing the argument on love leads to different reasoning patterns. The suppressed premise, "If A loves B, then A follows B's wishes as to A's lifelong career" is simply false. Love does not even dictate that the child adopt the parents' values as to the desirability of alternative life goals. So the parents' strongest available argument here is, "We love you, we are deeply concerned about your happiness, and in the long run you will be happier as an engineer." This makes it clear that an empirical claim is really the subject of the debate.

The function of these examples is to draw out our considered judgments as to the proper relation between parents and their grown children, and to show how poorly they fit the model of favors. What is relevant is the ongoing friendship that exists between parents and children. Although that relationship developed partly as a result of parental sacrifices for the child, the duties that grown children have to their parents result from the friendship rather than from the sacrifices. The idiom of owing favors to one's parents can actually be destructive if it undermines the role of mutuality and leads us to think in terms of quantitative reciprocal favors.

Note

1. Cf. Thomas E. Hill, Jr., "Servility and Self-Respect," *Monist* 57 (1973). Thus, during childhood, most of the sacrifices will come from the parents, since they have most of the resources and the child has most of the needs. When children are grown, the situation is usually reversed.

COURT DECISIONS AFFECTING PARENTS AND CHILDREN

DAVID A. J. RICHARDS

Family Rights (Seen as a Unit) against State

Prince v. *Massachusetts*, 321 U.S. 158 (1944). State law prohibiting child labor was upheld against a challenge by the child and her guardian that their religious freedom was being restricted by this prohibition. The Court held that even the primary right of parents to care for and educate the child, and the child's right to freely exercise religious beliefs, were subject to restriction where the state's interest in protecting children's welfare led to a prohibition of potentially harmful conduct.

Wisconsin v. *Yoder*, 406 U.S. 205 (1972). Compulsory education laws were held inapplicable to the parents of Amish children who had completed eight years of public school education. Secondary education created influences at odds with the Amish religious beliefs and hampered integration of the children into the religious community. The alternative style of education offered by the Amish community would adequately serve the state's interest in protecting the children from ignorance, according to the Court.

Tinker v. *Des Moines School District*, 393 U.S. 503 (1969). Students are entitled to the constitutional protection of the First Amendment absent a valid reason to regulate their speech. The wearing of black armbands to protest the Vietnam War is symbolic speech, protected against arbitrary interference by school personnel.

West Virginia Board of Education v. *Barnette*, 319 U.S. 624 (1943). A board resolution required all students and teachers to salute the flag or suffer expulsion. The Supreme Court enjoined enforcement of the resolution as a violation of the First Amendment rights of the parents and their children.

San Antonio Independent School District v. *Rodriguez*, 411 U.S. 1 (1973). The Supreme Court upheld the state scheme for school financing against a charge that it discriminated against children in poor school districts and denied some children their fundamental right to education. The Court found the state scheme to be rational and, further, stated that no constitutionally protected interest and no "suspect class" were involved.

Due Process— Parental Rights (against State)

Roe v. *Conn*, 417 F. Supp. 769 (M.D. Ala. 1976). Summary seizure of an infant by the state is unconstitutional absent exigent circumstances. Before a child may be removed from an allegedly neglectful parent, there must be notice and a hearing with counsel for both parents and child. Since the state must have a compelling reason to intrude, an overly broad or vague definition of neglect renders the statute unconstitutional. Furthermore, both mother and child have rights requiring procedural protection when a declaration of paternity is sought.

Alsager v. *District Court of Polk County, Iowa,* 545 F. 2d 1137 (8th Cir. 1976). Before a state may permanently terminate parental rights, it must show harm to the child sufficient to support a compelling interest of the state in termination. Parents must be afforded procedural protections as well.

Smith v. *Organization of Foster Families For Equality and Reform (O.F.F.E.R.),* 431 U.S. 936 (1977). When the state seeks to remove a child from a foster home, the procedure is adequate to protect the interest of both the natural parents and the foster parents. Since the state created the relationship into which it seeks to intervene, there is no right to family integrity and no expectation of privacy implicated by the state's acts. The child has no right to be protected, other than as provided by state law.

Juvenile Right to Privacy versus Parental Right to Control (State Support)

Planned Parenthood of Central Missouri v. *Danforth,* 428 U.S. 52 (1976). The state may not impose a blanket provision on unmarried minors seeking abortions that requires them to obtain parental consent. Constitutional rights do not mature magically at a state-defined age or majority, and the state may not give a third party a veto power over the exercise of such rights.

Bellotti v. *Baird,* 428 U.S. 132 (1976). The court remanded for statutory construction, stating that a possible interpretation of the Massachusetts abortion statute would avoid or substantially modify the federal constitutional challenge. If, as appellants asserted, the statute would allow parental veto over a minor's decision to obtain an abortion

1. only when the child's best interest is the basis, and
2. subject to exceptions where prior or subsequent court approval of the abortion decision is obtained,

the Court indicated that the statute might be constitutional.

Doe v. *Irwin,* 441 F. Supp. 1247 (W.D. Mich. 1977). Focusing on the rights of parents to control and educate their children, the district court held that state-operated clinics dispensing contraceptives to minors without notifying and consulting the parents were infringing on the parents' constitutional rights. The Court held that, absent a compelling state interest, the state may not totally exclude parents from a minor's decision respecting sex and contraceptives.

Ginsberg v. *New York,* 390 U.S. 629 (1968). The state has the power to proscribe the sale to minors of material defined as obscene, but which would not be obscene for adults. The power of the state to control the conduct of minors, and to support the role of parents and teachers, reaches beyond the state's power over adults.

Juvenile Rights (against Parents)

In re Snyder, 532 P. 2d 278, 85 Wash. 2d 182 (1975). In a proceeding initiated by a minor, the court upheld a finding that she was incorrigible and that the parent-child relationship was completely broken down. The minor's expressed refusal to return to her parents, as well as testimony of family members and psychiatrists as to the difficulty of the situation, supported the finding that a breakdown had occurred and the decision to remove her from her parents' custody.

Due Process—
Juvenile Rights (against State)

In re Gault, 387 U.S. 1 (1967). Juveniles accused of delinquency and faced with the possibility of severe state action must be accorded certain basic constitutional protections, including: notice to the child and the parents of the charges; the opportunity to confront and cross-examine witnesses; the right to counsel; the privilege against self-incrimination.

In re Winship, 397 U.S. 358 (1970). Due process requires that an adjudication of juvenile delinquency be based on a finding of proof beyond a reasonable doubt.

McKliver v. *Pennsylvania,* 403 U.S. 528 (1971). A jury trial is not essential to the accuracy of the fact-finding process, and is, therefore, not required by due process and fundamental fairness in a juvenile delinquency adjudication.

Goss v. *Lopez,* 419 U.S. 565 (1975). Before a student may be suspended from public school, his or her liberty and property interests must be protected by some form of notice of a hearing on the charges. In emergency cases, the notice and hearing may follow the suspension.

Ingraham v. *Wright,* 430 U.S. 651 (1977). Neither the Eighth Amendment prohibition against cruel and unusual punishments nor the Fourteenth Amendment right to due process is violated by school disciplinary procedures permitting "paddling." A student has no right to any form of notice and hearing, even informal, prior to being subjected to physical punishment.

J. L. v. *Parnham,* 412 F. Supp. 112 (M.D. Ga. 1976), U.S. App. pen'g, argued 12/6/77 431 U.S. 936. Dkt. 75–1690. The lower court held that the state procedure whereby minors could be voluntarily committed to mental hospitals by their parents denied the minors due process of law.

CONTRIBUTORS

Natalie Abrams, Philosophy and Medicine Program, New York University Medical Center, New York City

Russell Baker, *The New York Times*

Michael D. Bayles, Department of Philosophy, University of Kentucky, Lexington

Jeffrey Blustein, Department of Philosophy, Barnard College, New York City

Martha Brandt Bolton, Department of Philosophy, Livingstone College, Rutgers University, New Brunswick, New Jersey

Lawrence Crocker, Department of Philosophy, University of Washington, Seattle

Jane English, Department of Philosophy, University of North Carolina, Chapel Hill

Virginia Held, Department of Philosophy, Hunter College, The City University of New York

Kenneth Henley, Department of Philosophy and Religion, Florida International University, Miami

Laurence D. Houlgate, Department of Philosophy, George Mason University, Fairfax, Virginia

Raymond M. Herbenick, Department of Philosophy, University of Dayton, Ohio

Sanford N. Katz, Boston College Law School, Newton, Massachusetts

Seymour Lederberg, Division of Biological and Medical Sciences, Brown University, Providence, Rhode Island

Edmund Leites, Department of Philosophy, Queens College, The City University of New York

Ruth Macklin, Department of Philosophy, Institute of Society, Ethics and the Life Sciences, The Hastings Center, Hastings-on-Hudson, New York and Albert Einstein College of Medicine, Bronx, New York

Robert H. Mnookin, University of California School of Law, Berkeley

Onora O'Neill, Department of Philosophy, University of Essex, Colchester

David A. J. Richards, New York University School of Law, New York City

William Ruddick, Department of Philosophy, New York University, New York City

William A. Schroeder, Monroe County Legal Services Corporation, Rochester, New York

Lawrence R. Sidman, Fried, Frank, Shriver & Kempelman, Washington, D.C.

Michael A. Slote, Department of Philosophy, Trinity College, Dublin

Rena K. Uviller, American Civil Liberties Union, New York City